The Real Story
of the
USS
JOHNSTON
DD-821

As told by the officers and sailors who served aboard her

Editor & Contributing Author: George A. Sites

Special Thanks

This book would not be complete without a special thanks to USS Johnston sailor James Martin (MM-3, 1952-1954) whose wisdom and foresight started the formation of the USS Johnston DD-821 Association in 1991. As a result, the association membership continues to grow each year.

We also owe many thanks to the Johnston officers and sailors who provided their stories for inclusion in this book.

Thanks to all!

Dedication and In Memory Of

This book is dedicated to all the officers and sailors who served aboard the USS Johnston DD-821 during her 35 years of service to the greatest Navy in the world and to the United States of America.

Your service and sacrifices are appreciated by all of America.

Not to be forgotten, our beloved fallen shipmates. May you rest in peace.

NOTES

Editor and contributing author:
George A. Sites, RD2
USS Johnston 1969-1971

Assistant Editor: Alida L. Breen

Cover designed by: Roy A. Sites

CONTRIBUTING AUTHORS

(Names are in alphabetical order and the rates shown are during the sailor's Johnston service)

Acord, Price Darrell
(PNCM) 1971-1972

Adams, Gordon
(LTJG) 1962-1964

Argonti, John
(FTG2) 1966-1968

Ball, Paul
(EMFN) 1947-1950

Batsche, David
(FTG2) 1960-1963

Berridge, Charles A.
(FT3) 1947-1949

Beyerle, Dana
(QMSN) 1971-1972

Boltik, John
(FTG3) 1964-1966

Burke, Edward M.
(QM2) 1946-1951 (Plank-Owner)

Buesing, David
(FT3) 1955-1956

Camerano, Carl A.
(BT3) 1950-1953

Chavez, Mark
(RD2) 1966-1969

Cobb III, W. Frank
(LT) 1966-1969

Cook, Billy
(FTG3) 1965-1968

Copeland, Charles
(MM3) 1964-1968

Crum, Brion W.
(BTFN) 1971-1974

Damm, Art
(F1/c) 1946-1947 (Plank-Owner)

Dencer, Larry
(ETC) 1971-1975

Ferraiola, Tony
(GMSN) 1962

Frost, Bob "Frosty"
(RM3) 1952-1955

Gadell, Pat
(SM3) 1969-1971

Garrison, Morrow Brown
(BT1) 1949-1952

Georgen, William "Bill" M.
(LTJG) 1950-1951

Gilbert, John
(LTJG) 1965-1968

Gilmartin, Mike
(EM3) 1975-1976

Goicoechea, Pascual "Cubes"
(SH3) 1970-1973

Goodrich, Richard A.
(PCSN) 1960-1964

Grantham, Jesse E. "Gene"
(SK3) 1964-1966

Graziano, Michael L.
(LT.) 1979-1980

Guere, Leonard "Lenny"
(SA) 1952-1955

Guilfoil, Ken
USS Torsk SS-423

Hagen, Robert C.
(LT. USNR DD-557) 1944

Hanson, William V.
(Ensign) 1945-1948 (Plank-Owner)

Harris, Daun "Harry"
(RD3) 1968-1970

Heitzman, Dwayne
(BTC) 1949-1956

Hocking, Ralph
(DC2) 1951-1955

Hughes, Jack
(LTJG) 1962-1965

Ismer, Bill
(BM3) 1961-1965

Jones, John H. "Johnny or Jonesy"
(PC3) 1968-1969

Joy II, Ernest "Ernie"
(LT.) 1970-1972

Licht, Daniel W.
(ET1) 1948-1951

Love, Bobby
(RD2) Mid 1960's

Ludtke, Robert O.
(GM) 1955-1957

Mack, Jonathan "Toby"
(LTJG) 1966-1968

Maggio, Michael "Magg"
(OS3) 1974-1976

Mallast, Duane
(RD3) 1962-1964

Martin, James
(MM3) 1952-1954

McCaffree, Burnham C. "Mike"
(Commander) 1970-1972

McGunagle, Fred "McGoo"
(PSN3) 1956-1957

Myers, Albert C.
(LTJG) 1970-1973

Mingo, John J.
(Commander) 1965-1967

Misslin, Pete
(Ensign) 1969-1970

Morris, Wayne L.
(SFP3) 1961-1965

Murray, Thomas
(LTJG) 1945-1949 (Plank-Owner)

Nava, Robert "Bob"
(SM3) 1957-1959

Nebelle, Richard "Dick"
(S1/c) 1947-1949 (Plank-Owner)

Nelson, Terry
(SOGSN) 1962-1963

Norton, Oliver W.
(F1/c) 1946-1947 (Plank-Owner)

Nugent, George
(Ensign) 1950-1951

O'Brien, Tim
(MM2) 1970-1971

Odom, Harry W.
(DK3) 1949-1951

Oliver, Joseph E.
(MM3) 1952-1953

Olsen, Harold
(MM3) 1946-1948 (Plank-Owner)

Otto, Ronald E.
(QM3) 1954-1958

Paquette, Ray
(HM1) 1947-1950)

Pierce, Rick
(CS3) 1964-1967

Ponsell, Raymond "Harold"
(SM3) 1967-1968

Prezioso, Aldo
(SO3) 1952-1955

Ramirez, Sam
(YN3) 1973-1976

Rausch, John
(LTJG) 1969-1970

Rey, William
(SN) 1960-1962

Ricketts, Benny
(BM3) 1963-1965

Rosenthal, Harold
(YN2) 1957-1958

Rozinak, George K.
(Ensign) 1974-1977

Sauerwine, Bruce
(QM2) 1971-1975

Sheda, Mike
(SN) 1975-1977

Sites, George A.
(RD2) 1968-1971

Smith, William "Bill"
(RD-QM) 1947-1950

Smith, Robert E. "Bob"
(QM3) 1947-1950

Snyder, Ernest B. "Buck"
(RD2) 1964-1967

Stepien, Robert
(SN) 1969-1971

Stokes, Robert J.
(CS3) 1970-1974

Street, Richard
(SK2) 1967-1969

Sudholz, Herman O.
(LT) 1959-1963

Takesian, Eli
(Chaplain) 1964-1967

Tomasin, Tony
(EM2) 1968-1971

Turner, Ralph A.
(LCDR) 1967-1968

Walsh, John
(MR3) 1955-1956

Zaikowski, Ed
(Historian)

Zenes, Steve
(RM1) 1975-1977

Zieba, Terry
(STG2) 1973-1976

LIST OF NEWSPAPER/MAGAZINE ARTICLES

(In order of publishing date)

"Destroyer Rams Submarine in R.I. Maneuvers"
May 1947
Newport, R.I. Newspaper

"Big Mo" Heads Task Force Here On Visit – Halifax Host To United States Task Force
Summer 1951

"2 Destroyers Collide, But No One Hurt"
December 1960
St. Paul Dispatch & Pioneer Press, St. Paul, MN.

"Charleston-Based Destroyer, USS Johnston is Polaris Aid"
Date late 1963
Newspaper unknown

"Destroyers are now getting in on Polaris act, Johnston leads"
Date late 1963
Navy Times Magazine

"U.S.NAVY HELPS KEEP FLAMES FROM SPREADING"
Monday, February 28, 1966
The Daily Cleaner
Kingston, Jamaica

"Yanks Chase Russian Ships in Frenzied Operation Tattle-Tale, NAVIES PLAY HIDE-AND-SEEK GAMES IN MEDITERRANEAN"
Sunday, July 25, 1971
Hugh A. Mulligan
Columbus Dispatch

Columbus, Ohio

"VISITING SHIP TREATS NCO CLUB MEMBERS; PRESENTS PLAQUE, 'SMOKE'"
September, 1971
Giovanni Argentina
The Apulia Scene
Brindisi, Italy

"LIQUID COAL"
March, 1974
John A. Oudine, Editor
All Hands Magazine

"U.S. Gobs Declare Halifax 'Friendly'"
Saturday, June 19, 1976
Hattie Densmore, Staff Reporter
THE MAIL-STAR"
Halifax, Canada

"TRANSFER AT SEA"
March 1988
By: William V. Hanson USNR (Ret.)
SHIPMATE

"WHAT DID YOU DO DURING THE WAR? Part Thirty-Seven: Nebelle vs. the Carrier"
Wednesday, May 6, 2009
Jeff Hunt, News Editor
Mt. Pleasant News
Mt. Pleasant, N.C.

TABLE OF CONTENTS

Chapter 1 – History of the USS Johnston

Chapter 2 – Technical details

Chapter 3 – From Commissioning to 1949

Chapter 4 – Years 1950 through 1959

Chapter 5 – Years 1960 through 1969

Chapter 6 – The Vietnam War

Chapter 7 – Years 1970 through 1979

Chapter 8 – The Final Five Days

Chapter 9 – Old Sailors and Veterans

Chapter 10 – On the Lighter Side

Appendix A – Commanding Officers

Appendix B – USN Ships we operated with

Autographs

FOREWORD

The purpose of this book is to memorialize the stories and experiences of the officers and sailors who served aboard the USS Johnston DD-821.

It is not intended to be a "History Book" in the true sense of the words. It is simply a collection of Johnston stories as told by those who served aboard her in their **own words**! Some of the stories are similar but the details may be slightly different - keep in mind each story is how the author remembers it.

Like it, love it or hate it, without question this is the most complete story of the USS Johnston DD-821 available anywhere.

We hope you enjoy it!

Chapter 1

HISTORY OF THE USS JOHNSTON DD-557 & DD-821

(Much of this chapter is from NAVSOURCE.ORG/ARCHIVES/02/231.HTM)

Our story would not be complete without knowing a little history on the USS Johnston's namesake – John Vincent Johnston of Cincinnati, Ohio. He entered the Navy in September 1861 as First Master on the gunboat ST. LOUIS. He assisted in the Union gunboat attacks that captured strategic Fort Henry on the Tennessee River February 6, 1862. The night of April 1, 1862 he was the Navy commander of a combined Army-Navy boat expedition from ST. LOUIS which landed and spiked the guns of Fort No. 1 above the Confederate stronghold, Island No. 10. He was promoted to Acting Volunteer Lieutenant for gallantry in this expedition. After joining in the bombardments of Vicksburg, he took command of the gunboat FORREST ROSE to patrol the Mississippi and its tributaries. On February 15, 1864 his gunboat repelled the attack of confederate raiders, saving the town of

Waterproof, Louisiana and its federal garrison. Lt. Johnston resigned from the naval service June 23, 1864 and died April 23, 1912 at St. Louis, Missouri.

DD-821 was not the first US Navy ship to carry the Johnston name. It was actually the USS Johnston DD-557. Here is a little history and a short story on DD-557.

USS JOHNSTON DD-557

The USS Johnston DD-557 a FLETCHER-class destroyer was built by the Seattle-Tacoma Shipbuilding Company of Seattle, Washington. She was sponsored by Mrs. Marie S. Klinger, great-niece of LT John Johnston. She was commissioned on October 27, 1943, Commander Ernest E. Evans commanding. The day the DD-557 was commissioned, CDR Evans made a speech to the crew, "This is going to be a fighting ship. I intend to go in harm's way, and anyone who doesn't want to go along had better get off right now." Wow, if he had only known the Johnston's future.

The main battery consisted of five 5-inch 38 caliber guns and ten 21-inch torpedo tubes. General Electric geared turbines and twin screws gave her a speed in excess of 30 knots. Full load displacement was 2,700 tons; length was 377 feet; beam, 39 feet, and draft, 14 feet.

On 1 February 1944, the new destroyer bombarded Namur Island. A huge structure believed to be a shore magazine that remained standing after bombardment from American heavy caliber shells was destroyed by the JOHNSTON's 5-inch projectiles when the ship entered the lagoon and laid a stream of fire upon the structure's inshore walls. The seaward walls which had taken the punishment from heavier ships were constructed of reinforced concrete, but the bulkheads facing the lagoon were not reinforced.

During the day prior to the Namur bombardment the vessel raked the shores of Mellu Island of the Kwajalein group. Light opposition was encountered in both engagements and no casualties occurred.

A five-day bombardment of Eniwetok Atoll, lasting from February 17-22, came next. Fire support was furnished to invasion forces and several pillboxes and revetments along the beach were taken under fire.

On 28 March JOHNSTON with a primary mission of searching for enemy shipping took time to bombard the Kaping Maranga Atoll in the Carolinas. An observation tower, several blockhouses, pillboxes, and dugouts along the beach were shelled.

Working with the aid of a spotting plane the destroyer steamed into the mouth of the Maririci River, southeast of Empress Augusta Bay, Bougainville, on 31 March and laid a heavy barrage of fire into the area.

Between bombardments, the busy destroyer took a regular turn on anti-submarine patrol stations. As a result of action May 16, the JOHNSTON was awarded a "B" assessment for the probable sinking of a submarine.

The month of June was spent preparing for a long bombardment at Guam, 21-29 July. Firing was conducted throughout the days and submarine patrols were run at night. The ship was straddled repeatedly but escaped un-hit. It was definitely known that the destroyer's fire shattered two enemy 4-inch battery installations as well as numerous pillboxes and buildings.

JOHNSTON's final engagement before the Battle for Leyte was the bombardment of the Western Carolines from 6 September to 14 October.

Now read the exciting story that follows as DD-557 was sunk during WWII and as told by Lt. Robert C. Hagen, USNR. If it wasn't for this terrible event, our DD-821 would never have been built.

WE ASKED FOR THE JAPANESE FLEET AND GOT IT

By: Lt. Robert C. Hagen, USNR USS Johnston DD-557

On the night of October 24, 1944, while we were cruising about fifteen miles off Samar Island, listening to radio snatches of the naval battle down in Surigao Strait, Comdr. Ernest E. Evans, skipper of the destroyer USS JOHNSTON DD-557, said to me, "Well Hagen, we're within three days of being one year old. It's been an uneventful year." The skipper is a fighting man from the soles of his broad feet to the ends of his straight black hair. He was an Oklahoman and proud of the Indian blood he had in him. We called him - though not to his face -

4

the Chief. The Johnston was a fighting ship, but he was the heart and soul of her. "Yes, sir," I answered, trying to sound gruff. "I wouldn't mind seeing a little action." Of course, we'd only been through four invasions, but, since we hadn't even had a flake of paint knocked off us or a man killed by an enemy shell, it was "uneventful."

We saw little action, all right. Less than eight hours later, we were involved in what seemed to us a practically single-handed surface fight with four Japanese battleships, seven cruisers and nine destroyers, and, a couple of hours after that, those of us who were alive were in the ocean, desperately swimming away from the foaming whirlpool of our sinking ship. The Johnston never did make that first birthday.

Somewhere toward the middle of our fifty hours in the Philippine Sea, while I was clinging to a floater net and puffing on an imaginary cigarette through swollen lips, I thought about that conversation with the skipper. I thought about the stupendous pre-commissioning party we'd pitched in Seattle, and about the ice cream and cake the skipper had promised us for our first birthday at sea.

Despite the loss of a good ship and the 183 men who lost their lives or are missing in action, I think the Johnston paid her way. In that last fight alone, our torpedoes delivered the death blow to a Jap cruiser five times our weight damaged two others plus a couple of destroyers, and annoyed hell out of at least one battleship with our peashooters. If ever a vessel earned the right to be called a "one-ship task force," it was the Johnston.

I am telling this story because I am the Johnston's senior surviving officer. The Captain and the executive

5

officer are listed as missing in action. I think I can tell the story without undue immodesty because I was only a small part of it. As gunnery officer, I kept the guns going to the last, trying to get the best possible results. That was my duty. But it was Commander Evans who fought the ship, far over and beyond the call of duty.

The Johnston was commissioned on October 27, 1943. I remember a prophetic line from the skipper's speech. "This is going to be a fighting ship," he told us. "I intend to go in harm's way, and anyone' who doesn't want to go along had better get off right now."

I previously had been assistant communications officer on the Aaron Ward, but was wounded in the Battle of Guadalcanal. I didn't consider myself lucky at the time the doctors were cutting a useless artery from my arm and removing shell fragments from my leg, but those wounds kept me off the Aaron Ward when she went down later off Tulagi.

The "GQ Johnny" -- the crew called her that because, in her 363-day career, she seemed to be at general quarters most of the time, she was a sweet ship. She was one of our newest destroyers, next in size to the latest 2200 ton class. Her principal weapons were five 5-inch, 38-caliber guns, ten torpedo tubes and a sizable assortment of 40-mm and 20-mm for antiaircraft purposes. Compared with the old Aaron Ward, also a new but smaller tin can, the Johnston seemed almost like a cruiser.

Eighty-five per cent Of her crew of approximately 300 were green hands. Only one third of her officers ever had been to sea, and the skipper and, plus a few of the crew, were the only ones who ever had seen action. After my first experience with the men I was supposed to whip into shape as expert gun crews, I sourly wrote a friend on another ship: "Stay out of our gun range - anything can happen." A few months' later I wrote the same guy: "You now may bring on the Jap fleet."

Three months after the Johnston was commissioned, she was bombarding the beaches at Kwajalein. I knew, after that show, we had a good ship and a captain who could strike fighting spirit from his men the way steel strikes spark from a flint. Commander Evans was magnificent. I can see him now: short, barrel-chested, standing on the bridge with his hands on his hips, giving out with a running fire of orders in a bull voice. And once he gave us an order, he didn't ride us, but trusted us to carry it out the way, he wanted it done; it was that quality of leadership which made us all willing to follow him to hell.

We plastered Eniwetok next and then joined the anti-submarine patrol, at Bougainville. Three months of this was sheer boredom for us, except for the time we scored a highly probable "kill" against a Jap sub the first 2100-ton destroyer to do so.

On August twenty-first, GQ Johnny teamed with that ghost from Pearl Harbor, the battleship Pennsylvania, to bombard Quam. We outdid ourselves. In four days the Johnston poured more than 4000 rounds ashore. Next, we protected baby flat-tops off Peleliu, Angaur and Ulithi, and being young, brash and not at all meek, felt ourselves much misused, since we knew by this time we were the finest bombardment ship in the fleet.

That was our fourth campaign. Our battle casualties thus far had consisted of one boy who got the Purple Heart for getting nicked mysteriously by a piece of metal--probably ours--at Eniwetok. But Fate had a bill for us which was about due.

On October twelfth, we sailed for Leyte as part of a task unit of Vice Admiral Kinkaid's 7th Fleet assigned to screen an escort carrier group from submarine or air attack. Now we were sore-saddled with those pestiferous flat-tops again. How were we ever going to keep our shooting hand in, playing nursemaid to plane-toting tubs? What was the matter with the admiral anyhow? Didn't he know what we'd done at Guam?

So from October eighteenth on, we mother-henned the floating airfields for the fly boys who plastered Leyte, and things were so quiet that the Chief even had time to think about promoting us some ice cream for our first birthday party.

On October twenty-third, we forgot about ice cream. Early that morning, American submarines discovered the Japanese fleet coming from the South China Sea toward our precarious Leyte bridgehead. The submarines attacked, inflicting some damage, but the Japanese came on, splitting into two forces. One went through Surigao Strait into Leyte Gulf, where it was neatly and thoroughly taken care of by Vice Admiral Oldendorf's forces. The other, and larger, force was attacked on October twenty-fourth by Admiral Halsey's carrier planes, and presumably turned back. Then Admiral Halsey hurried north to meet the large Japanese carrier-and-battleship force that was steaming toward the Philippines.

That left us sitting east of Samar off San Bernardino Strait on the night of the twenty-fourth. You'd hardly have called us "formidable." There were the destroyers Johnston, Hoel and Heerman, and the destroyer escorts, Roberts, Raymond, Dennis and Butler, protecting the six escort carriers, Fanshaw Bay, St. Lo, White Plains, Kalamin Bay, Gambier Bay and Kitkum Bay. It never even was contemplated that we would come up against any surface units.

8

The sea was calm, the wind was gentle, and any poet would have admired the rather picturesque cumulus clouds drifting lazily through the sky. We had just gone through another dawn alert. I was standing watch aid, feeling hungry, had asked the mess boy to bring me a fried-egg sandwich and some coffee. At 06:50, hell broke loose. I never did get that fried egg.

One of the pilots flying patrol reported-and not calmly, either! That what looked to him like the whole dam Jap fleet was steaming through San Bernardino Strait, headed straight for our unit. Aboard the Fanshaw Bay, Rear Admiral C. A. F. Sprague, in command of our unit, hardly could believe the report. "Get verification," he ordered. It was true, all right coming at us were four battleships, the Yamoto, Nagato, Kongo and Haruna; seven cruisers and at least nine destroyers. They were the surviving elements of the central force which Admiral Halsey's fliers had attacked the day before. Only, after starting to retreat, they had reversed their course, maneuvered the extremely hazardous passage through San Bernardino Strait, and were corning in to attack.

We felt like little David without a slingshot. Admiral Sprague began calling for help. South of us were two other support units, respectively thirty and eighty miles away. We were hoping their destroyer screen would come to our aid, but they didn't appear. The big Jap task force was all ours.

These matters, of course, did not concern us aboard the Johnston. We had only one job --to fight -- and we did it. Commander Evans was out of his sea cabin in ten seconds. I could see the man from my station in the gun director above the bridge, and I can swear his heart was grinning as he went into battle. There was not a moment's hesitation or delay on his part; even as he came out, he gave the order.

"All hands to general quarters. Prepare to attack major portion of Japanese fleet. All engines ahead flank. Commence making smoke and stand by for a torpedo attack. Left full rudder."

In less than sixty seconds we were zigzagging between our carriers and the Japanese fleet, putting out a smoke screen over a 2500-yard front. We were the first destroyer to make smoke, the first to start firing, the first to launch a torpedo attack. Even as we began laying smoke, the Japanese started lobbing shells at us and the Johnston had to zigzag between the splashes.

The Japs were using dye in their shells, so they could tell by the colored splashes where each shell was hitting. The red, green, purple and yellow colors might have been pretty under different circumstances, but at this moment I didn't like the color scheme.

For the first twenty minutes, we were completely helpless, because the cruisers and battleships had us within range and our 5-inch guns couldn't reach them. The part of the Jap force coming at us was composed of three columns: first, a line of seven destroyers; next, one light and three heavy cruisers; then the four battleships. Off somewhere to the east, to appear later, were three other cruisers and two or three destroyers. Luckily, up to this point the Jap's marksmanship was not good.

By 07:00, our six baby flat-tops had launched all available planes for the attack. They scored some hits, but still the Japs pursued us. The carrier formation turned to a southwesterly course away from the Japs. GQ

10

Johnny was way out in front-she was all there was between our ships and the Japs.

All this time, I had been completely, sickeningly impotent. I had checked my gun stations, seen that everything was in order, but after that there' was nothing I could do but wait. Meanwhile, the skipper had given me an over-all order to commence firing at any Jap target as soon as range was closed, so when it did close, I did not have to wait for permission. At 07:15 we closed range and I opened fire on the nearest cruiser. We scored a number of hits.

I presume our first hit made the Japs angry. Maybe they were insulted by our colossal nerve. At that time, remember, we were within range of even the enemy destroyers. They were to our starboard, while the cruisers and battleships were in echelon to our port in a position where they could fire all their forward guns at us without shooting over one another. The Yamoto, a 40,000-tonner, had nine 16-inch guns, which throw a one-ton shell; the other battleships had both 16-inch and 14-inch guns; the cruisers had 8-inch and 6-inch guns, and, between the cruisers and destroyers, they must have had at least 120 5-inch guns to our five 5-inchers. Later, when I was convalescing, I took a pencil and paper just for fun and figured what those Jap ships could throw at us. They could put out at least 80,000 pounds of shells; our five batteries could answer with 275 pounds.

The Japanese fire was decidedly unimpressive. They should have sunk us immediately. Even so, their shells finally started straddling us, and the captain realized we couldn't live long at that rate. He made one of his lightning decisions to attack with torpedoes. At 07:15 we started bearing in straight for the nearest cruiser, a 12,000-tonner of the Tone class.

Looking through my telescope, I could see the cruisers vengefully shooting at us, splash, splash, splash, zing'. One 8-inch shell landed in the water right off our bow and splashed red dye in my face. I mopped the stuff out of my eyes and said to the five men in the director with me, "Looks like somebody's mad at us." During the five minutes in which we bore in for the torpedo attack, no less than four of the big ships were shooting at us simultaneously at any given moment. Still they didn't hit us. In those five minutes, we fired more than 200 rounds and scored at least forty hits, inflicting serious damage.

At 07:20, Commander Evans ordered: "Five torpedoes." We let go with all ten fish, then whipped around immediately and began retiring behind a heavy smoke screen. The torpedoes ran "hot, straight and normal" a torpedo man's dream. Two heavy underwater explosions were heard; seconds later, a third and fainter explosion. We believed -- and I later stated this in my official report -- that two hits on the cruiser were scored, and that the third explosion possibly was a hit on one of the battleships in the farthest column. When we came out of our smoke sixty seconds later, the leading cruiser was burning furiously astern. She later sank.

At 07:30 we got it. Three 14-inch shells from a battleship, followed closely by three 6-inch shells from a light cruiser, hit us. It was like a puppy being smacked by a truck. The hits resulted in the loss of all power to the steering engine, all power to the three 5-inch guns in the after part of the ship, and rendered our gyro compass useless.

I was looking out of the director at the time. Everything happened at once. A portion of our equipment which we in the Navy family call the "whirling bedspring" came tumbling down past my head -- snapped cleanly from the mast by the mere shock of the hits. At the same time, in almost low-comedy fashion, my helmet, telephone and binoculars blew off, and the cotter pin which locked my stool in an elevated position, so I could look through the telescope, snapped, causing me to drop, downward and sustain a somewhat inglorious wound - a quarter-inch gash in my knee cap.

I came up yelling with pain from that silly knee blow, scrambled for my equipment, took a look out the hatch-and swore. The Johnston was a mess. There were dead men on the deck and gaping; holes from the 14-inch shell through which a fat man could have plummeted. In some sections below deck -- as I learned later -- almost every man had been killed. The bridge looked like a kid's B-B target. LTJG Jack Bechdel, my assistant gunnery officer, whom we called "Junior", was lying on the bridge fatally wounded; so was the machine-gun officer, Ens. Gordon Fox. LTJG Joe Piska, standing near to the skipper, had been killed outright.

The skipper was standing bareheaded and bare-chested. His helmet and all but the shoulders of his shirt had been blown away; the hair on his chest was singed, and blood was gushing from his left hand where two fingers had been shot away. Shell fragments had ripped his neck and face. The doctor rushed to his aid, but the skipper waved him back, saying "Don't bother me now. Help some of those guys who are hurt." The skipper then wrapped a handkerchief around the stumps of his fingers and carried on.

I had to take this in quickly, for I had work to do. "All stations--control testing!" I yelled, waiting anxiously to learn the damage.

They came back, "Gun One, aye!... Gun Two, aye!... Gun Three, aye!… Gun Five, aye!... Plot, aye!…" All answered but No. 4. In a few seconds, I heard from it. The gun captain, a smart lad named Bob Hollenbough, from Goshen, Illinois, sent a messenger to another station to notify me his communications were out. Gun 1 and 2 still had power; Guns 3, 4 and 5 were without power and had to fire manually. Hollenbough was in the worst fix of all; being cut off from the director and plot, which direct the fire against the target, he had to fire by eye. Sharp shooting was O.K. for Dan'l Boone, but it doesn't lead to much accuracy on a destroyer.

In three minutes, we were prepared to carry on the best we could on one engine and half power. The ship had to be steered by hand-a terribly difficult thing when your heavy rudder is bucking the sea. Our strongest - backed men sweated like slaves over the rudder, but they had to change shifts every fifteen minutes.

The Johnston had her share of heroes - men who lost their lives trying to save shipmates from compartments filled with scalding steam; others who passed ammunition until water rose to their necks. One I never shall forget was Warrant Machinist Marley Polk, of Bremerton, Washington, father of a new baby he'd seen only briefly before going to sea. Polk took a heavy wrench and swam under a grating in a dark, flooded compartment below deck, trying to shut off a leak. Just then the ship took additional hits, dislodging machinery that fell on him and trapped him. With the water rising Polk ordered shipmates, who were attempting to extricate him, to leave him. Then the water slowly rose over his head.

Just after the first hit, a rainstorm came up. It was sheer providence. We ducked into it. I remember that it got my cigarettes wet; it was the first time in my life I didn't mind having a package of cigarettes ruined. While we were hiding in the rain, we got off 100 rounds at the nearest Japanese cruiser and at the destroyer leader.

At 07:50, Admiral Sprague ordered the "small boys" - destroyers- to make a torpedo attack. That obviously couldn't mean us, for we had no more torpedoes and, with one engine, couldn't keep up with the others. I never believed we would go in for another attack. The Johnston certainly could have retired with honor after that episode. The Hoel, Heerman and the destroyer escort Roberts swished by us at full speed. I thought we would go back to the carriers. But that wasn't Commander Evans' way of fighting.

"We'll go in with the destroyers and provide fire support," he boomed. I answered, "Aye, aye, sir?" and added to myself: Oh, dear lord, I'm in for a swim.

We went in, dodging salvos and blasting back. The other ships got off their torpedoes. As we turned to retire after them, we closed our range to within 6000 yards of the leading Japanese cruiser. We shifted fire and managed to pump at least ten shells into her. I began to feel pretty good about my gunners.

By now we had taken the worst that the Japs had to offer and still were alive, but I wasn't optimistic about our chances of surviving. Then at 08:10, we had another paralyzing experience - and it was one of our destroyers that supplied it?

We were coming out of a heavy smoke screen. Suddenly we saw the Heerman, only 200 yards away, headed straight at us on a collision course. The skipper bellowed, "All engines back full?" - That meant one engine for us. With one engine, we could do hardly more than slow down. I felt a curious, hopeless, detached sort of wrung - out unconcern as I looked over our bow and couldn't see water

15

- only the Heerman. Hope we don't batter her up too much, I dreamily thought, for our bow was pointed straight at her bridge. Finally, the Heerman's two engines backed her barely out of the collision course - we missed her by less than ten feet. As soon as we got out of this mess, we assumed all possible speed. There was so much smoke that the skipper ordered not to fire at anything unless I could see the ship--it might be one of ours. At 08:20, there suddenly appeared out of the smoke a 30,000-ton Kongo-class battleship, only 7000 yards off our port beam; I took one look at the unmistakable pagoda mast, muttered, "I sure as hell can see that!" and opened fire. In forty seconds. We got off thirty rounds, at least fifteen of which hit the pagoda upper-structure. As far as accomplishing anything decisive, it was like bouncing paper wads off a steel helmet, but we did kill some Japs and knock out a few small guns. Then we ran back into our smoke. The BB belched a few 14-inchers at us, but, thank God, registered only clean misses.

The Johnston now was headed southwest, several miles behind our main force. On our port quarter was the Jap cruiser and battleship force, and on our starboard were the Jap destroyers, pouring steel our way. At all times, the leading enemy ships were within 12,000 yards' of us. At 08:30, we observed that the Gambier Bay was under heavy fire from a big Jap cruiser. Commander Evans then gave me the most courageous order I've ever heard. Commence firing on that cruiser, "Hagen," he said. "Draw her fire on us and away from the Gambier Bay."

Again I said, "Aye, aye, sir," and under my breath again I said, Surely you jest. A crippled tin can engaging in a deliberate slugging match with a heavy cruiser. We closed to 6000 yards and scored five hits. Reacting with monumental stupidity, the Jap commander ignored us completely and concentrated on sinking the Gambier Bay. He could have sunk us both. By permitting us to escape, he made it possible for us to interfere a few minutes later with a destroyer torpedo attack that might have annihilated our little carrier force.

At 08:40 the captain broke off the futile battle with the cruiser when he saw seven Jap destroyers closing in rapidly on the carriers. By this time, the Hoel had been severely damaged and was sinking; the Roberts was burning furiously and the Heerman was off with the main carrier force, so the Johnston took them on alone. Hopeless' as it was, Commander Evans outfought them as long as he could.

First we pounded away at the destroyers; they were sleek, streamlined Terutsuki-class vessels, our match in tonnage and weight of guns, but not current match in marksmanship, crippled as we were. We should have been duck soup for them, but, though we were taking hits, we were giving back better than we received.

First, we scored twelve devastating hits on the destroyer leader. She quit cold and retired from the fight. Next we concentrated on the second destroyer and got in five hits. Then a most amazing thing happened. Instead of coming in for the kill, all six remaining destroyers broke off the battle and began following their vanishing leaders away from the scene. They waited until they were well out of our effective gun range before launching their torpedo attacks - this was about 09:20 - and all their fish went wild.

We can only guess what happened, but apparently the Nip admiral got his wind up and decided he must retreat through San Bernardino Strait quickly or face annihilation. If the Nip had possessed one tenth the courage of our skipper, he would have fought his destroyers five minutes longer and scored some real victories. Commander Evans, feeling like the skipper of a battleship, was so elated he could hardly talk.

He strutted across his bridge and chortled; "Now I've seen everything!" But we had more fighting to do, and GQ Johnny's number was about up. At 0900, the Gambier Bay was lost, but we still were battling desperately to keep the destroyers and cruisers, which also were closing in, from reaching the five surviving carriers. At 9:10 we had taken a hit which knocked out one forward gun and damaged the other. Fires had broken out. One of our 40-mm ready lockers was hit, and the exploding shells were causing as much damage as the Japs. The bridge was rendered untenable by the fires and explosions, and Commander Evans had been forced at 09:20 to shift his command to the fantail, where he yelled his steering orders through an open hatch at the men who were turning the rudder by hand.

In the gun director we were having our own troubles. The place was full of smoke, our eyes were streaming and we were coughing and choking as we carried out our duties. We now were in a position where all the gallantry and guts in the world couldn't save us. There, were two cruisers on our port; another two cruisers ahead of us, and several destroyers on our starboard side; the battleships, well astern of us, fortunately had turned coy. We knew we could not survive, but we figured that help for the carriers must be on the way and every minute's delay might count.

Down at one of my batteries, the gun captain, a Texan, kept exhorting, "More shells! More shells!" and one of his gang, even while breaking his back at the task, grumbled, I'm sure glad there ain't no Japs from Texas!"

By 09:30 we were going dead in the water; even the Japs couldn't miss us. They made a sort of running semicircle around our ship, shooting at us like a bunch of Indians attacking a prairie schooner. Our lone engine and fire room was knocked out; we lost all power, and even the indomitable skipper knew we were finished. At 09:45 he gave the saddest order a captain can give: "Abandon ship." Up in the gun director, what with the smoke and lack of communications, in there we were a little slow in getting the word. The five stalwart men in there with me - Hemelright, Buzbee, Powell, Gringeri and Thompson - were standing by quietly. There was nothing more we could do. I peered out and couldn't see a living soul on the foc'sle. "What the hell are we doing here?" I said. "Let's abandon ship."

The last word hardly was out of my mouth when the five men as one were out of the director and racing for the rail. I was so surprised that I stood stock-still a moment, then lit out myself. I made my way to the foc'sle - I couldn't get aft without walking over piles of bodies - and, like a man in a dream, very carefully and leisurely took off my shoes and dived in. Taking off my shoes, incidentally, was the worst mistake I could make. My feet got so sunburned in the water that I limped for days after.

When I got into the water, one of those utterly mad things that you wouldn't believe if it hadn't happened to you, occurred. My torpedo man, Jim O'Gorek swam over to me and, as brightly as if he were meeting me on the street corner, said, "Mr. Hagen, we got off all ten of them torpedoes, and they ran hot, straight and normal!"

At 10:10 the USS Johnston rolled over and began to sink. A Jap destroyer came up to 1000 yards and pumped a final shot into her to make sure she went down. A survivor saw the Japanese captain salute her as she went down. That was the end of the Johnston.

There is more to the story. The details are grim, but they seem anticlimactic after the battle story of the Johnston. Of our approximately 325 officers and men, sixty had been killed in the battle, and more than 120 others died in the water or are missing. Commander Evans last was seen with other officers and men in a small boat, if the Japanese picked him up, we do not know it.

One hundred and forty-one were saved by clinging for fifty hours to three life rafts and two floater nets, and two seamen, William Shaw and Orin Vadnais were saved after four days in the water in their life jackets. I saw thirty-five of my own group die before my eyes or drift away. One man was killed by a shark. Another, Chief Gunners Mate Harry Henson, who boasted he had been in the Navy so long he'd become salty, apparently was salty enough to prove distasteful to a shark; one bit him, turned loose, took another bite, turned loose again and swam away - and Henson has two sets of shark's teeth imprints in his right thigh to prove it. If any armchair ichthyologist ever tells you there is no such thing as a man-eating shark, you can refer him to me! I fell asleep and drifted away once myself, but woke before it was too late to swim back to the raft.

Maybe we were a little bitter about being in the water so long, especially after three separate friendly planes had zoomed us within two hours after the ship sank. We were very weary, a little sick and maybe even a little crazy from fighting, bleeding, vomiting and seeing our friends die. We were only fifty miles east of Samar and we had figured we'd be picked up in a few hours, with so many ships around. A lot of men would be alive today if rescue had come sooner.

At noon on the twenty-seventh, the same day and almost the same hour of the Johnston's commissioning a year ago, while I was dreaming of a glass of ice water, an LCI gunboat picked us up. They say that three Jap betties attacked us a few minutes after our rescue. I wouldn't know about that. I was below deck, sleeping peacefully.

JOHNSTON went down only two days short of celebrating her first year of being in commission. The commission pennant was hoisted on 27 October 1943, and by the first of the next year, the JOHNSTON was on her way to war.

Lieutenant Commander Ernest E. Evans, USN placed JOHNSTON in commission and remained in command until he went down with his ship. All officers and men who survived unanimously recommended him for the Congressional Medal of Honor for his outstanding work in the final battle. He was awarded this citation posthumously on 26 August, 1945.

USS JOHNSTON DD-821
(From NAVSOURCE.ORG/ARCHIVES/02/231.HTM)

USS Johnston (DD-821) was laid down 26 March 1945 by Consolidated Steel Corp., Orange, Tex.; launched 10 October 1945, sponsored by Mrs. Marie S. Klinger; grandniece of Lt. J.V. Johnston, and commissioned 23 August 1946, Commander E. C. Long in command.

After shakedown in the Caribbean, Johnston reported to Newport, R.I., 16 May 1947 for duty with the Atlantic Fleet. Operating out of Newport, her home port, she sailed 9 February 1948 for Northern Europe where she visited ports in Great Britain, France, and Scandinavia before returning to Newport 26 June. For 14 months she operated along the Atlantic coast, then sailed 23 August 1949 for the Mediterranean. From then until 4 October 1961 she deployed with the mighty 6th Fleet on eight occasions and supported peace-keeping efforts in the Middle East.

While on her first Mediterranean deployment, she helped to stabilize the Adriatic Sea during the Trieste crisis; and she patrolled the coast of Greece to bolster her freedom and national security against threatened Communist domination. Johnston returned to Newport 26 January 1950.

She operated out of Newport from Canada to the Caribbean until 4 June 1951 when she departed with Midshipman at sea training off Northern Europe. Following her return to Newport 28 July, she cleared the East Coast for the Mediterranean 3 September and joined the 6th Fleet in operations that carried her from French Morocco to Turkey; she then returned to home port 4 February 1952.

Johnston departed Newport 7 January 1953 for NATO operations in the North Atlantic. Before sailing for duty in the Mediterranean 16 March Johnston aided the Dutch after storms in the North Sea had caused extensive flooding in the Netherlands; her crew donated bundles of warm clothing and more than $1,200 for the storm victims. She operated in the Mediterranean until 8 May when she steamed for Newport, arriving 18 May.

After a 4-month deployment in the Mediterranean during early 1954, Johnston operated for more than 17 months along the Atlantic coast from New England to Cuba. On 5 November 1955 she steamed for maneuvers off Northern Europe, followed by another tour of duty in the Mediterranean While operating in the eastern Mediterranean during February 1956, she patrolled off

Israel and Egypt as the Middle East rumbled over the developing Suez Canal crisis. Returning to Newport 5 March, she embarked midshipmen 5 June for 2 months of at-sea training off Northern Europe, after which she resumed operations out of Newport.

Johnston sailed once again 6 May 1957 for peace-keeping operations with the 6th Fleet. Before returning to the United States 1 August she ranged the Mediterranean from Spain to Sicily on ASW barrier patrols. While at Marseilles, France, 3 July, she helped fight a destructive blaze on board Lake Champlain (CVS-39). Steaming from Newport 3 September, she joined the mighty Atlantic Fleet for the NATO Exercise "Strike Back" in the North Atlantic. She returned to Newport 22 October and then resumed operations that sent her into the Caribbean and the Gulf of Mexico.

Returning to the North Atlantic 6 June 1959 for further NATO maneuvers, Johnston steamed to Charleston, S.C., 25 July and joined DESRON 4 for deployment to the Mediterranean. Departing Charleston 21 September, she conducted Fleet operations in the western Mediterranean; on 18 December she joined naval units from France, Italy and Spain along the French coast for a review in honor of President Eisenhower. Following patrols along the Greek coast, she departed Athens for the United States 24 March 1960, arriving Charleston 10 April.

Before deploying again to the Mediterranean, Johnston joined in NATO Exercise "Sword Thrust" during the fall of 1960; then she departed Charleston 8 March 1961 to bolster the 6th Fleet's continuing efforts to maintain peace in the Middle East. After returning to the United States 4 October, she steamed 19 November for patrol duty off the Dominican Republic. During this brief but important duty her presence did much to stabilize a situation "which had threatened to plunge the country into bitter fighting and a return of the Trujillo dictatorship."

Johnston returned to Charleston 26 November; and following coastal operations, she steamed to Boston where she underwent FRAM I overhaul from 4 January to 31 October 1962. During this time she received the latest equipment, including ASROC system and DASH facilities, to prepare her for new assignment in the modern Navy. Departing Boston 2 November, she arrived Guantanamo Bay, Cuba, via Charleston, 10 December for Caribbean operations. While steaming near Mona Island 1 February 1963, she rescued sinking Honduran freighter Kirco and towed her to Mayaguez, P.R. Continuing her Atlantic operations, she supported Polaris missile firing tests. As Thomas Jefferson (SSBN-618) fired two underwater missiles off the Florida coast 14 March, Johnston became the first destroyer to serve as "primary support ship for an underwater firing of a Polaris missile."

After more than 4 months of ASW tactical operations, Johnston departed Charleston 6 August for her ninth deployment to the Mediterranean. While operating with the ever-vigilant 6th Fleet, she steamed the length and breadth of the Mediterranean and entered the Black Sea 27 September. During the cruise to Turkish Black Sea ports she served as a symbol of America's determination to safeguard peace on land through strength on the sea. Following 2 months of ASW operations, Johnston departed Cannes, France, for the United States 7 December and arrived in Charleston 23 December for coastal operations through 1964.

The veteran destroyer departed Charleston 6 January 1965 for the Mediterranean to resume peace-keeping operations with forces of other NATO countries. She returned to Charleston 7 June, and devoted the rest of the year to operations with Polaris submarines, amphibious exercises, and overhaul to prepare for future service.

Johnston began New Year 1966 as sonar school training ship at Key West, Fla. During this period of training she visited Guantanamo Bay, Cuba, for refresher training; and in February while Johnston's crew was spending weekend liberty at Kingston, Jamaica, her sailors swiftly answered a call for help on the 27th. The famous Myrtle Bank Hotel had caught fire and threatened the whole water front. Johnston sailors rushed to the fire and averted disaster.

Johnston operated off the East Coast until departing Charleston 29 September for Mediterranean and Middle East deployment. After operating on the far side of the Suez Canal, she again transited the Suez Canal to rejoin the 6th Fleet in the Mediterranean. There her exercises with this powerful deterrent force helped to stabilize the area while bringing her to peak readiness for any emergency which might threaten the peace. She returned to Charleston 9 February 1967 and operated on the East Coast through mid- year.

After returning to her home port, Johnston entered the Philadelphia Naval Shipyard in 1973. She left the Philadelphia Naval Shipyard on 15 November 1973 and continued to operate on the East Coast until she was decommissioned in October 1980 and transferred to Taiwan on February 27, 1981.

There is a gap in the history from 1967 to 1973, then from the end of 1973 to 1980. Hopefully the following stories will help fill in these gaps of the important history of DD-821. Here is what you have been waiting for: **The Real Story of the USS Johnston DD-821**.

DD-821 ASSOCIATION HISTORY

By: Dwayne Heitzman, BTC

Years on board the Johnston – 1949 to 1956

In 1991 James Martin contacted the "Tin Can Sailors" organization, requesting names of those who served on the Johnston DD-821 from their database. With this list he contacted "Military Locator and Reunion Services" (MLRS).

They contacted the people on the list, and the first reunion was in 1992. MLRS did all of the planning and looked for additional crewmembers. They also sent out a newsletter now and then.

The first reunion attendees elected James Martin, President. A.F. Brown, Treasurer. I am unsure of the V.P. and Secretary.

My 1st reunion was in 1996 in Baltimore, '97 in Virginia Beach, '98 in Las Vegas. At that reunion I volunteered to serve as President. The '99 reunion was in Branson.

A set of By-Laws was presented to the reunion attendees and after floor discussion was adopted by a majority vote. Thus "The Association" was born.

The reunion for 2000 was held in Charleston and 2001 in San Antonio.

We do have Association dues and the association works hard to keep the dues low. However they are not a requirement to be listed on the official roster. Dues-paying members receive all correspondence generated by the elected officers. Non-dues paying personnel will be contacted by the elected officers with pertinent information.

The annual reunions are held in late April. At this time we have the country divided into time zones; Eastern, Central and everything that is left. We alternate zones.

Business meeting are held annually at the reunion. All other official business through out the year is conducted by USPS (snail mail) or email.

The USS Johnston DD-821 Association officially becomes a "not-for-profit" association in 2010.

Chapter 2

TECHNICAL DETAILS

International call sign "November Alpha Yankee Kilo"
Radio call "Tampico"
Thanks to "Buck" Snyder
Prior Radio Call "TEABALL"
Thanks to Fred McGunagle "McGoo"

A Gearing Class Destroyer as Originally Constructed

Displacement: 2,616 tons (3,460 tons full load)
Length: 390 feet 6 inches
Beam: 41 feet 6 inches
Draught: 14 feet 4 inches (mean)
Machinery: four Babcock & Wilcox boilers;
2-shaft G.E.C. geared turbines
Performance: 60,000 shp for 36.8 knots
Bunkerage: 740 tons
Range: 4,500 nautical miles at 20 knots

Guns: six 5 inch DP; twelve 40 mm; eleven 20 mm
Torpedoes: ten 21 inch in two mounts

FRAM 1 completed October 1962

Displacement: approx. 3,500 tons full load
Length: 390 feet 6 inches
Beam: 41 feet 6 inches
Draught: 19 feet (mean)
Propulsion: Steam turbines, 4 boilers,
2 shafts, 60,000 shp, @ 35+ knots
Crew: approx. 225
Aviation: aft helicopter deck and hangar; 1 Dash
Radar: SPA 29 air search, SPS 10 surface search
Sonar: SQS-23 hull
1   8-cell ASROC
2   5"/38 mounts fore and aft
2   triple 12.75 inch torpedo tubes.

The pre-eminent destroyer to emerge from World War II - the Gearing class with the help of the Fleet Rehabilitation And Modernization program (FRAM I) Survived for three and one- half decades as a useful arm of the fleet.

Laid down by Consolidated Steel, Orange Texas June 5 1945

Launched October 19, 1945

Commissioned August 23, 1946.

Decommissioned in Philadelphia, PA
Stricken October 1, 1980

Transferred to Taiwan February 27, 1981
Renamed Chen Yang DD928

Reclassified Guided Missile Destroyer DDG-928

Decommissioned on December 16, 2003

Target - Sunk - July 20, 2006

Total service - 58 years

Here are the technical details after conversion to the DDG-928 by the Taiwanese Navy and provided by the Chen Yang DDG-928 Association.

Displacement: approx. 3,500 tons full load

Dimensions: 119.03 x 12.52 x 5.8 meters (390.5 x 41 x 19 feet)

Propulsion: Steam turbines, 4 boilers, 2 shafts, 60,000 shp, 27 knots

Crew: approx. 275

Aviation: aft helicopter deck and hangar; 1 MD-500 helo
Radar: DA-08 air search

Sonar: DE-1191 (SQS-23H) hull

Fire Control: STIR-18 missile control, HW-160 gun control
EW: Chang Feng III active/passive suite, 4 Kung Fen decoy
Armament: 4 Hsiung Feng II SSM, 10 SM-1MR SAM,

1 8-cell ASROC, (1) 76 mm OTO DP, (2) 40mm/70 AA, (1) 20 mm Phalanx CIWS, (2) triple 12.75 inch torpedo tubes.

USS Johnston DD-821 Firing ASROC Rockets

Service Ribbons (shown on back cover) earned by USS Johnston DD-821 (listed as they would be worn top to bottom, left to right)

Enlisted Surface Warfare Specialist (ESWS) (1979 and after) Pin worn on your breast above your ribbons/medals. It is silver for enlisted and gold for officers. Design is slightly different.

Combat Action Ribbon (Feb-9/12-1968)

Navy "E" Ribbon (Oct-1-1976 to Sept-30-1977 & Oct-1-1977 to Sept-30-1978)

World War II Victory Ribbon (1946)

Navy Occupation Service Ribbon (Europe) (1948-1950)

National Defense Service Ribbon (Korean emergency; 1 bronze star for second award (Vietnam emergency))

Armed Forces Expeditionary Ribbon (Cuba) (1962)

Vietnam Service Ribbon (1968) (3 bronze stars: Vietnam Counteroffensive Phase III, Tet Counteroffensive, Vietnam Counteroffensive Phase IV)

Sea Service Deployment (1974 and after)

Navy and Marine Corps Overseas Service (1974 and after)

Vietnam Gallantry Cross Unit Citation with Palm (Feb-8 to Feb-12-1968, Feb-15-1968, Feb-19 to Feb-28-1968, Mar-1 to Mar-9-1968, Mar-28 to Apr-2-1968)

Vietnam Civil Action Unit Citation with Palm (Jan-7 to Jan-28-1968, Feb-8 to Mar-10-1968, Mar-22 to April-11-1968, Apr-21 to May-6-1968)

Ships' honors are expressed in terms of ribbons, rather than medals. Stars on the **Vietnam Service Ribbon** are expressed simply as "stars" not "engagement stars." They do not refer to any combat operation, but simply indicate that a ship was in the area defined for Vietnam during a particular time period.

Any award won by a ship is automatically conferred on any sailor attached to the ship during the period the award applied too.

Typical Statistics for a 6-month MED cruise
(Based upon the 1969/1970 MED Cruise)

Length of Cruise	202 days
Number of miles steamed	Over 40,000
Number of ports visited	Twelve
Average Speed	16 knots
Amount of fuel used	3,072,236 gallons
Fresh Water used	1,631,883 gallons
Movies Shown	606
Food Served	150,000 meals
Beef	28 tons
Loaves of bread	20,000
Milk	10,000
Cokes sold	75,000
Candy sold	$21,000
Clothes washed	108 Tons
Personnel Visiting Ship	9,950
Refuelings	58
Disbursing of Crew Pay	$328,844.95

Chapter 3

COMMISSIONING TO 1949

The Johnston and Me

By: Thomas J. Murray, LTJG (Plank-Owner)

Years on board the Johnston: 1945 to 1949

This is a story about the US Navy Destroyer USS Johnston DD-821 and me from its commissioning through my detachment in 1949.

World War II was over, and I had finished my duty as a 20-year-old Ensign out of the NROTC unit at Brown University in the antiaircraft battery of USS Nevada (BB-36). We had been at Iwo Jima and Okinawa and now there was a great exit from the Navy by the people who were on duty to win the war and whose time was up. When my time was up, I was ordered to Naval headquarters Boston for discharge. I was brought up on an island in Narragansett Bay, watching the beautiful gray ships come in to port every summer, so the question was put to me. Do you want to be discharged? I opted to go regular Navy.

To set the stage: World War II had just been won and some combat ships were utilized to bring servicemen home from overseas battlefields (Operation Magic Carpet). Men with sufficient service points were being discharged in large numbers so they could get home to pick up their civilian life again. Many Navy ships were losing personnel so fast there was a shortage of men left to man them and ships were scrounging men from other ships to get underway.

The war production machine was being shut down. In the ship construction effort, depending on an assortment of things, some hulls were finished and others closed down and were scrapped. The construction for the Johnston was allowed to go ahead to completion and acceptance by the Navy.

In the big international policy picture, the allies won WWII but clouds were forming regarding Russia and its effort to spread communism throughout the world and to expand its area of influence. The United States could not afford to let our influence in world affairs diminish and the need to maintain an effective naval force was recognized. This then set the stage for bringing the USS Johnston into the Navy to play its role in international affairs in keeping the peace.

I was ordered home for 30 days leave, while they figured out what to do with me. Orders came to proceed to Orange Texas for new construction and assignment to

the ship upon commissioning of the USS Johnston DD 821.
Keep in mind that I had been commissioned for the two-
years and stood watch only on the aircraft battery; I
think I was in the conning tower of the Nevada only once
and that was while she was on a magic carpet run from
Hawaii to the United States.

The point here is that I was at that time completely
unqualified to properly discharge any duty in a
destroyer. But that was characteristic of many of the
men assigned to the ship, because the fashionable thing
to do at that time was to leave the Navy and get back to
civilian life, but the Navy needed its ships manned and

ready! So it was up to
all of us to learn and
do our job in order to
be the force ready to
fight the cold war.
Looking back on the
Johnston experience, we
did that and with
colors proudly flying!
And all are to be
commended.

I reported to the
office of the
Consolidated Steel
Corp. at Orange Texas
and met the prospective
commanding officer,
Commander Elmer C.
Long. His nickname was
Spike and he was a
member of the Academy
class of 1933, I
believe. His class was

U.S.S. JOHNSTON
LAUNCHING - OCTOBER 19, 1945
COMMISSIONING - AUGUST 23, 1946
ORANGE, TEXAS

noted for having been sent back to civilian life after

Commissioning, during the Depression as the Navy had no budget for additional officers. Spike (of course, we didn't call him that) was a thorough going, crusty destroyer man and a strong leader. He had been a boxer at the Naval Academy. Lieutenant Commander Deibler Jr. was the Executive Officer. In addition to the Captain and the Executive Officer, Lieutenant Aldrich, Lieutenant Junior grade Webster and Ensign Hansen were the only Academy officers assigned. I was given the assignment to be the Communications Officer and the Register Publications Officer until it was realized that I didn't know top-secret from restricted and wasn't very good at paperwork. So, considering my gunnery experience, they assigned me to be the First Lieutenant and first division officer in the gunnery department.

**USS Johnston DD-821 Commissioning Ceremony –
Manning the Rails**

When all the advanced planning was completed, the ship was commissioned on August 23, 1946. The vice president of Consolidated Steel Corp. delivered the ship to the Navy. Commander Haney, representative of Commander Eighth Naval District and supervisor of ship building Orange Texas, accepted the ship for the U.S. Navy. Here is a picture of the commissioning.

We were to go to Galveston and because the Houston Ship Canal had a limited depth, the sonar dome was not installed at Orange. The ship then proceeded down the Houston Ship Canal to Galveston where it went into a shipyard, high and dry in a graving dock to install the sonar dome. As luck would have it, shortly after becoming high and dry the Merchant Marine went on strike and formed a picket line on the other side of the water way, which we and the shipboard workers had to cross to get to and from the yard, and so the shipyard was closed down. Johnston, therefore, stood high and dry for the entire period of the strike, a period during which much of the housekeeping at the yard had to be carried out by the ship's company. This time allowed ships company to enjoy Galveston. If you wanted a drink in Galveston you had to belong to the Texas Athletic club. Most of us became members.

When the strike was over and the sonar dome attached, the ship became water borne again and sailed for Algiers, the naval ammunition depot across the Mississippi River from New Orleans. We arrived there, and liberty was granted. Lieutenant Aldrich and I went ashore and spent the whole night going from place to place listening to music and not getting into any trouble, arriving back at the ship as the sun was coming up. Think about having to count bullets and powder as they came aboard having spent the night awake!

Upon completion of the arming of the ship, we shoved

off from New Orleans and Algiers going down the Mississippi River into the gulf with our destination Guantánamo Bay Cuba. I found myself, now, qualified officer of the deck, standing regular watches at the con. Despite my inexperience, the ship was in good hands because Captain Long was always on deck or in his sea cabin available for instructions or correction.

Shipboard routine when underway included watches on the various stations aboard. For a watch in three, the watch stander would stand one watch, then the third thereafter working around the clock. As for instance, suppose I had the 8-12 watch. I would get up early enough to go to breakfast, be on the bridge at 8:00 and stand the watch until 12:00 when my relief would appear and take over the watch. I would go down to the wardroom for lunch then do my days work until the evening meal, after which I would take the 6-8 watch. I would turn in for sleep, then take the 4-8 watch. I'd be off the next day doing routine work until 4-6. Followed the mid-watch the 12-4, then the afternoon watch, the 12 noon – 4 and so forth. We then spent either 6 or 8 hours on watch every day.

We ran into some very heavy weather as we approached the Western end of Cuba and upon reporting the weather situation to the authorities and asking for an advisory, we found we got our own information back. We had run into a major hurricane, which no one had reported. This was in the days before aircraft hurricane hunters. So we were on our own in a new ship with an inexperienced crew facing a major hurricane! All went well until we were required to make a turn to the east, which put us in the trough. Ensign Hansen who had the mid watch told me later on that the captain was quite concerned that the new and inexperienced crew in the engine spaces might lose the load. Consider a ship without power in the midst of a terrifying hurricane. The engineers were put to

39

their first test, and performed admirably.

Shakedown training in Guantánamo was intense and tough. We were given a break from the training with a stop for liberty at St. Thomas in the Virgin Islands. Shore fire training at Vasquez was enlightened with participation in a major Army airdrop exercise. We watched hundreds of troops parachuting out of Army aircraft over the island.

Returning to the States, we entered the shipyard at Charleston, South Carolina for a post-shakedown availability. The crew had an opportunity to see and enjoy southern hospitality. While in Charleston, LCDR William H. Deibler Jr., the Executive Officer was relieved by LCDR Bernie Fold, whose leadership and personality enlivened the spirit of the ship.

On 16 May 1947, the Johnston reported for duty assignment to the United States Atlantic Fleet at our homeport, Newport, Rhode Island. The ship participated in training and other duties out of Newport. One event occurred while we were assigned on a routine basis to serve as target ship for the submarine training school out of New London Connecticut. Our job was to steam on a zigzag course and to allow the students in submerged submarines to fire dummy torpedoes at us. One day when I was officer of the deck, the training submarine came up under us and surfaced in our wake. The only damage to the ship was a small leak in the forward fire room. The submarine damaged her periscope shears and went back to New London. We set sail at Boston but were directed to return to Newport to go alongside the tender to provide a temporary repair of the damage. We subsequently went to Boston to have a permanent repair done.

Here is a copy of my entry in the log:

1216 steaming as before. 1219 commenced run #3. Base course 320, speed 15 knots. Zigzag plan #15. 1241, while steaming on course 260T and pgc speed fifteen knots (137 rpm) at problem time 22, felt shock in the ship somewhere below the bridge. Called repair parties to investigate cause and possible damage. USS Torsk (SS-423) surfaced off the stern 150 yards at a steep angle. Periscope housing and radar masts bent to the side and aft. Went to collision quarters. Forward fire room, reported hull holed at frame 76 port, 2 feet below the turn of the bilge. Exact position 41 12 54 N. -71 28 17 W. 1244 standing by submarine ready to render assistance. 1304 submarine reported no personnel casualties, no assistance needed and was ordered to return to New London. 1310 set course 070T and pgc 086 psc, speed 10 knots, proceeding to Boston, Mass. 1330 changed speed to 15 knots (137 rpm). 1335 changed course to 125T and pgc, 136 psc. 1350 changed course to 090T and pgc 105 psc. 1403 passed Block Island light abeam to starboard, distance 3000 yards. 1405 changed course to 053T and pgc 171 psc. 1427 changed speed to 20 knot 188 rpm. Hole plugged and flooding is being controlled by a portable submersible pump. 1434 changed course to 045T and pgc 1449 changed course to 055 true. Signed, Thomas J. Murray LTJG OOD

Let your mind run on this, suppose the submarine came up with additional force and made a major breach in the hull; or suppose on the way aft the submarine fouled the propellers. What turned out to be a relatively minor accident could have been a significant tragedy!

Subsequent to that the ship participated in training

and other duties out of Newport. Johnston joined the rest of the Atlantic Fleet in New York for fleet day during which we watched the premier of a movie called "Paul Jones".

A scheduled pre-deployment availability at the Brooklyn Naval Shipyard took place. During this time, I accompanied Ensign Bill Hansen on a trip to Washington, DC, where he introduced me to the woman who would become my wife. This brings up a story about discipline. I had the Christmas duty during which time one of the largest snowstorms to hit New York occurred. I was the Command Duty Officer. I did not write up the members of the crew who came in late because of the storm. Captain Long had been in Washington, DC during the storm and came back and walked with his wife to his quarters nearby. My plans were to go to Washington to meet with my friend for New Years celebration. When he returned to the ship, he wanted to know where the reports on the late members of the crew were. He insisted that I find out those who arrived late, write them up and stand for Captain's Mast. It caused me to be delayed in my departure for New Year's in Washington. It was his way to let me know that the discipline provided that he alone had the authority to forgive the lateness on the part of the crew. I was furious but learned a lesson.

Upon completion of the navy yard availability, the ship departed for Guantánamo again for refresher training prior to our departure for Europe. She came back to Newport for a 30 day period and departed Newport in company with all eight ships of DesRon 8 in column formation. Steaming in column required the officer of the deck to maintain station 1000 yards from the ship ahead. He measures that distance by use of a stadimeter with a split mirror system, bringing the masthead of the ship ahead down to the water line and reading the distance on a dial on the instrument. The proper distance was maintained by adjusting turns of the propellers, for example, add 4 rpm or take off 3 rpm. The men at the throttle in the engine spaces must have loved this process. The ship ahead had to make adjustments also, so there was a constant changing of speed all the way across the ocean.

Johnston and William R. Rush were detached as we approached the continent to arrive at our first port. While we were proceeding together I spotted a floating mine close aboard, a relic of the fighting in WWII. The assumption is that over time, marine growth would cause the mine to sink harmlessly to the bottom.

It needs to be explained regarding our North European duty that in peacetime, Sea Power exists as an instrument of international diplomacy, intended to further peace in the world. The visits to our ports while personally memorable to us, like the memoirs of passengers on cruise ships, had that very serious and important objective. The Port visits let the people of the ports know that our naval power existed and that behind the power were people much the same as themselves representing as ambassadors of our country. President Eisenhower's "People to People" program applies here and that too was part of our mission. So, while we personally benefited by seeing and learning about foreign ports and the people there, we were working toward accomplishing a national objective. Well done Johnston!

Our first stop was Bergen, Norway, where the American aircraft carrier, USS Valley Forge CV-45, having stopped in Bergen on her way home from the Pacific, needed to make a turn to depart, did it by using operation pinwheel. Aircraft were positioned in all four corners of the flight deck and the propellers revved up as needed to swing the ship. Bergen harbor is in a bowl-like geographical formation and all the noise echoed throughout Bergen. What a racket!

Another incident had to do with our Executive Officer, Bernie Fold, saving a cable car from disaster by his quick thinking. Bill Hansen's story about the Johnston going out to pick up an appendicitis case from submarine discusses Bernie's heroism.

Our next destination was Copenhagen, Denmark. Enroute there while transiting the Skagerrak, USS Fresno in the lead and standing communications guard, followed by Johnston and William R. Rush in column. The captain and the executive officer were on the bridge, because we were on sounding. Fresno started to send a flashing light message to Johnston, and I was officer of the deck. The captain was looking over the shoulder of the signalman recording the message. He called, "Murray, come over here." I came over thinking the message would call for a change in course or change in speed or some other maneuver. The message was from my intended, having sent the telegram to Western Union addressed to me and Western Union sent the telegram to Navy communications. Navy communications put the message on the Fox schedule. The Fox schedule is a broadcast system intended to provide messages to ships of the fleet no matter where they might be and so they wouldn't have to answer. Each ship guarded the frequency and listened to the service to take down messages addressed to that ship. The message was addressed to me at USS Johnston; it started out with "Darling, what is the date of our wedding?" Imagine, the entire fleet knew! On departure we talked about July 3, and of course that's the day before a holiday so we had to compromise and move the wedding date back to July 2. That was the objective of the message.

The ships visited Copenhagen and moored to the pier where the statue of the mermaid stands. A welcoming dinner was given by the officials of the city and country to us. In return, the King of Denmark paid an official visit to Admiral Conley in the Fresno. All officers from Johnston and William R. Rush went aboard for his review. They were thrilled at the opportunity to shake the hand of the King and here is the picture.

L-R, Admiral Conley, CDR Elmer C. Long (Captain, USS JOHNSTON), King of Denmark shaking hands of the officers of the USS Johnston, USS William R. Rush and the USS Fresno

The next leg of the Johnston's trip was through the Kiel Canal in Germany, what an exciting experience that was!

We visited Brest, France. It was a city quite close to where the Allied forces entered France. The entire city was leveled and a scene of past battles. Two things stand out in our memories of the Brest visit. A Catholic boy's school was attempting to return to normal, and the brothers asked several of the officers to come to lunch. The lunch was sumptuous and extremely well done. When you realize it was not too long ago that the ground was fought over, putting it on was quite an accomplishment.

The other item had to do with the three of us officers deciding to go to Paris. I took High School French, so when we got off the station at Paris, I went up to a policeman asking in my best high school French, where is a good hotel? He sent us to the hotel Prince de Gaules getting a suite costing $17 a night. We saw the Follies Bergere, the Notre Dame Cathedral and Versailles.

Our next stop was Cardiff, Wales, where their ships go in through gate locks which are then closed to preserve the water depth when the tide goes out. Other than their pier system, I have no significant memories of Cardiff.

The next leg of the trip ended in Dublin, Ireland where we found that we were the first US naval ships to call in Ireland since before World War I. I believe that to be true, but I do know that Ireland declared itself neutral in World War II. Our Admiral was Richard L. Conolly of Irish descent. We were welcomed royally, including a dinner in our honor by the chief of Staff and officers of the Army Headquarters, Dublin. We reciprocated by a reception aboard the Fresno. When high ranking people from Ireland came aboard, it was my honor to escort the President of Ireland, otherwise called the Taoiseach, to Fresno's bridge. Johnston and William R. Rush were nested together, alongside the south wall, a pier directly across for the Guinness brewery. Great numbers of visitors came aboard the two destroyers. While the ship was in Dublin, I was able to take a short leave and visit relatives in Glasgow and County Down in North Ireland.

Our next stop was in Plymouth, England, a major United Kingdom naval base. My only memory about Plymouth, in addition to being impressed because of its Navy connection, was a ferry boat propelled across its waterway to the use of an endless rope. After leaving port, we anchored for some reason off Plymouth. Upon weighing anchor we found it was fouled on a communications cable. With some ingenuity, the anchor was cleared. The captain noted that he was pleased because the event was a learning experience.

We bid goodbye to northern Europe with a short visit to a place called Torque, located on the most western part of the British Isles. It was time for the Johnston to join up with the remainder of the squadron, getting ready to cross the Atlantic for home. We stopped for a short visit at Gibraltar. We went to Algiers for another visit, where we saw the sights of another culture.

Johnston, along with the ships of Destroyer Squadron 8 got underway and joined up for the trip across the Atlantic, arriving in Newport 20 June 1949. Ensign Bill Hanson and I were the first to leave the ship as I had a date to marry Jean Shaw in Washington, DC on 2 July and then to enjoy a honeymoon leave.

The ship conducted routine operations out of Newport where Johnston experienced the second hurricane in its short life. A hurricane was looming and expected to hit

Narragansett Bay, so all ships deployed to avoid the storm. As the fates allowed the storm did not get Newport, but we steamed right into it. Some of the ships suffered significant damage.

A new captain reported aboard, and my time was up. I had orders to report to new construction in Massachusetts in the commissioning crew of the new 8inch heave cruiser named Des Moines CA-134.

I have not said much about the individual names of the wonderful people in the crew. Memory fails me here, be mindful this is 63 years since. I do remember faithful members of the gunnery Department, the deck force, CIC, the bridge team and the torpedo team to name just a few. I do want to cite an incident which happened when I was obliged to paint the ward room at night by myself. One of the crew volunteered to help me accomplish the job so I am indebted to him. It broke my heart when I felt I had to discipline him at a later date regarding his participation in an incident near a mosque in Algiers.

I am thinking about Chiefs Lewandowski, Farmer and Ciuti. I am thinking of the Fire control-man who with his crew doing the impossible when we had a casualty in a large electric motor in the Mark 37 director, which was vital for the operation of the director. He and his crew were able to take that huge weight from the director to the tender for repair and return. I remember Boatswain Mate 3rd Calhoun, Torpedo-man Koch . . . and didn't Riley become our yeoman? I know I'm missing the names of men close to me who did so much to make the Johnston function, but considering that my memory has to stretch back 63 years I didn't do so badly.

I departed Johnston with the feeling that I really wasn't a destroyer man. Included in that feeling was the thought I really didn't have the right stuff. However, after my time in the cruiser Des Moines, I was ordered to the re-commissioning detail of USS Blue DD-744 out of the San Diego Reserve Fleet, serving as gunnery officer during the Korean War. Later, after schools in Monterrey, duty as communications officer on staff of Commander Amphibious Transport Squadron 24, a tour as officer in charge of the Communications School, Officers Short Course. At Newport I was ordered to USS Hale DD-642, Executive Officer. After three tours in Destroyers, I guess finally I can call myself a Destroyer-man.

My last assignment was in the Pentagon attached to the CNO's staff and in the Future Plans and Policy section of the Director of Naval Communications. I retired as a Lieutenant Commander in 1964. My civilian career has been in Financial Planning, I still go in to the office daily at the age of 85.

Destroyer Rams Submarine in R.I. Maneuvers -
Both Vessels Make Port, Saving Scores, After Sea Accident
Appeared in a Newport, R.I. Newspaper May 1947
Submitted by Thomas J. Murray LTJG

The lives of scores of men hung in the balance yesterday when the Destroyer Johnston plowed into the Submarine Torsk, submerged to periscope depth, during maneuvers off Block Island.

The submarine captained by Comdr. Richard Holden, suffered considerable damage to her periscope, topside and radar equipment, but surfaced immediately before she took in enough water for danger.

Her pumps kept the craft at an even keel and she was able to make her way back to her base at new London under her own power.

The Johnston, skippered by Comdr. E.C. Long, reached Newport at 3:40 p.m. with a hole several feet long punched in her bow.

According to the public relations office at new London, the Torsk was engaged in routine torpedo practice and simulating an attack on the Johnston when the collision occurred.

The Block Island correspondent of the Providence journal reported that the weather had been rough and foggy off the island for the past five days.

Neither the First Naval District at Boston nor the Third naval district at New York had received a report of the collision last night.

The public relations officer at the submarine base said an investigation will be conducted to determine the exact cause of the mishap.

TRANSFER AT SEA

by: William V. Hanson (CDR USNR, retired Plank-Owner)

Years on board the Johnston: 1945 to 1948

Editor's Note: Commander William V. Hanson served as the Johnston's Engineering Officer. This story originally appeared in the March 1988 Edition of "Shipmate" magazine provided by Thomas J. Murray.

The story by Captains Greenbacker and Gex in the January – February 1987 issue of *Shipmate* brings to mind a memorable experience aboard JOHNSTON (DD-821) commanded

by the late Cdr. Elmer C. "Spike" Long, '33 in the Spring of 1948. "Spike" Long was one of the finest seamen I ever had the privilege of serving. He was a consummate ship handler. "Spike" had complete faith in his officers and fully delegated responsibility to his department heads, backing them completely. At the same time, he always remained in full command of his ship.

JOHNSTON along with RUSH (DD-714) had been detached from the Mediterranean Forces (this was before the days of the Sixth Fleet) and DesDiv 102 to proceed to the English Channel. We were to be based in Plymouth. RUSH was sent on a good will tour of Scandinavia in general and the Baltic Sea in particular. She was well equipped with intercept gear.

USS Johnston entering Cardiff, Wales

We on JOHNSTON made good will visits to Brest, France; Torquay (the English Riviera); Cardiff, Wales; Liverpool and Dublin. RUSH and JUNEAU (CL-19) joined us in Dublin. We were the first United States warships ever to visit the Irish Free State. Needless to say, we received a tremendous reception and were royally entertained. One of the highlights of our visit was a baseball game between a team from the DD's and one from JUNEAU. It was held in a large stadium usually used, I assume, for soccer or rugby. There was standing room only! Naturally, the "cans" won.

From Dublin the three of us rendezvoused with VALLEY FORGE (CV-45) off the Shetlands and proceeded to Bergen, Norway to "Show the Flag" on May Day. The passage through the fjords was beautiful. We had a wonderful visit although we found the Norwegian people very reserved. There were no "red" riots – the real reason for our visit – but we did have a harrowing experience on a tourist excursion. A group of civilians and members of our crew were riding in a sightseeing train through the mountains when it went out of control. The train engineer panicked and froze. Our exec. LCDR. "Bernie" Fold (size 54+ chest) started pulling levers, turned down the speed control and we all held our breath – the train stopped.

From Bergen the cruiser and the two DD's proceeded to Copenhagen. Wonderful, wonderful Copenhagen. What a delightful place! How regally we were entertained. One highlight was a luncheon given by the Crown Prince for all the officers, local American businessmen and Danish dignitaries. On our tables were small shot glasses and after we finished eating, the waiters filled these glasses with an innocuous looking liquid. Following brief introductions and talks, the Crown Prince proposed a toast to our Navy and said, "Skoel." At which time LTJG Murray (who never drank) gulped his drink and almost fell flat on his duff. Our introduction to Aquavit.

After Copenhagen we began our passage back to England through the Kiel Canal and out into marked channels in the North Sea. It was very foggy and we were happy to have JUNEAU leading the way. Fortunately we never made contact with any of the unswept, drifting mines which were still in the area.

Along the way VALLEY FORGE rejoined us. She had been on a separate goodwill tour. The skipper of JUNEAU, being senior, led the column and VALLEY FORGE fell in astern of the "small boys." It was night and the carrier seemed to be steering a small sine curve – that poor OD trying to keep on station astern of two destroyers and an AA cruiser.

The carrier left us and headed for Southampton and we three went to Portland for a little R&R. Portland is a submarine base with a school – the British New London. It is best noted for a peninsula jutting out into the Channel known as Portland Bill. There wasn't much activity, social or otherwise, so it was a good place to recover from our partying and an opportunity to get the ship in shape. As Engineering Officer I had the "black gang" do some much needed maintenance. Among other things we had #1 boiler taken off the line for cleaning firesides and watersides.

On our first Sunday there our Captain asked JUNEAU to conduct an administrative inspection on JOHNSTON to fulfill part of our training requirements. About half way through the inspection the 21 MC blared forth, "Make all preparations for getting underway."

"What's going on?" I asked the inspecting officer. He had no idea.

I rushed up to the Captain's quarters. "What's happened?" I asked.

"We're taking two doctors from the cruiser and proceeding at all possible speed to meet a submarine located south of Ireland." The Captain replied. "They have a hot appendix aboard."

"For God's sake, Captain, we only have about 50,000 gallons of fuel and #1 boiler is all over the deck plates. Can't RUSH go?" I should have known better.

Number 3 boiler was already steaming for auxiliary power. We lit off #2 and #4, getting underway cross-connected. Unusual to say the least.

We had about 350 miles to go so I figured that at 28 knots we should make it in about 12.5 hours. Estimating on the high side at 3500 gallons of fuel per hour, we would require about 45,000 gallons. I instructed the "oil king" to check consumption every hour.

We settled down at 29 knots. Normally we got 27.5 knots out of two boilers either split-plant or cross-connected – we had added about 1 ½ knots to our usual speed.

I decided we should take steady-run-data which, I am sure, was the first and perhaps the only time that ever happened at 29 knots on three boilers cross-connected. The steady-run-data proved that we could control an unbalanced system but that we had to pay particular attention to our de-aerating feed tanks and pumps and to the water level in our boilers.

We had things pretty well under control when I took the deck at 1200. (We "snipes" had to stand deck watches – not enough officers on board to allow us to hide below deck.) When I left for the bridge I told my Assistant Engineer, "Buzz" Carder, to stay in #1 engine room and keep a close watch on how things were going.

The run down the Channel was beautiful. The wind about Force 4 and it was sunny and warm. Most unusual weather for the English Channel.

After taking steady-run-data, Buzz called me and asked me, "Is it OK to try for more speed?"

I relayed the question to the Captain.

"Go ahead, "he replied.

JOHNSTON reached 30 knots! – and – the safety valves started to lift on #3 and #4 boilers. I called "Buzz" and he assured me not to worry.

"Everything's under control," he said.

When I was relieved of the watch I hastened down to #2 fire room to find out what was going on. I found out! The fireroom crew had tied off the relief valves on the fuel oil service pumps and the firemen were controlling the burner pressure by hand. The pressure would periodically shoot over 400 PSI before they could cut off the oil. No wonder the safeties were lifting.

The "oil king" had been giving me fuel readings every hour and his reports were not exactly encouraging. She was consuming over 3,500 gallons every hour. Our three boilers were consuming fuel at the standard rate for four boilers at full power with a tight plant. We couldn't maintain this speed.

After I finished checking the fireroom I returned to the wardroom. The two doctors were suffering from *mal de mer*.

"We can't stand the vibration and the violent motion," one explained.

I assured them that we weren't going to fall apart. They should have tried the fantail!

Early evening I suggested to the Captain that we cut back our speed and soon after recommended securing #2 and slowing down more – we would have to slow down soon anyway and this would conserve fuel.

We met with the submarine, TRUMPETFISH, close to the time I'd predicted. It was a "guppie" with a streamlined sail – the first one any of us had ever seen. There were no cleats, shackles or anything else to which to make a high line fast. After a bit of discussion with our Deck Department Head and the Chief Boatswain's Mate, we ran a mooring line over from our starboard 400 mm gun tub and the "deck gang" on the sub ran the line around the sail. It was the damndest looking rig I'd ever seen, but it worked.

The patient came over in a stokes basket and was taken immediately to the wardroom where the doctors were waiting. We took off for Plymouth at 27 knots but the doctors called and asked us to slow down, the vibration was just too great to operate. We slowed to standard speed (15 knots). It sure helped with the fuel consumption. I checked with the "oil king" and told him our ETA. We both agreed that we could make it back to Plymouth.

The operation was a success. The patient was moved to one of the officers' bunks where he rested comfortably until the early morning. We call British Headquarters in Plymouth as we passed Eddy Stone Light and they had a launch waiting for us at the harbor entrance. The doctors, with the patient, were taken aboard the launch and on to shore. The doctors were especially happy to be off our ship. They had never ridden a "can" at full power and much preferred the comfort of a light cruiser.

After we had off loaded, the "oil king" reported 5,000 gallons of oil left. I told the Captain.

"Can we make it back to Portland?" he asked.

We had about 150 miles to go.

I replied that our tanks had always been free of water and besides – "We've made it this far, so why not."

We made it.

GOING BACK OVER 59 YEARS

by: Art Damm, Fireman (F1/C) (Plank-Owner)

Years on board the Johnston: 1946 to 1947

I entered the service on November 23, 1945 in Philadelphia at age 17. The next day I reported to Boot Camp at Camp Perry, Williamsburg, Virginia. I was assigned to Company 869 which had 120 boots. The picture is from Boot Camp. I spent my 18th birthday in Boot Camp. I got transferred to the Fire Department at Newport, Rhode Island on March 12, 1946. I served five months in the Fire Department and then was transferred to the USS Johnston DD-821 on August 13, 1946. I then made F1/C and was assigned to the Machine Shop because I had four years of vocational school in Machine Shop.

When I boarded the Johnston, my work station was the Machine Shop compartment C-205-L - next to the clineometer. My job was to re-work small valves, replace gaskets, broken studs and lap seats to eliminate leaks. Even though the valves were all new, it was no time at all before many of them needed service. Chief Turner (with 16 years in the service) was my boss. He spent many hours with me in the shop and we got along great.

One day he came into the shop, turned around and set all the dog latches on the lock. He then turned around and said to me "Teach me to run this lathe." I was shocked. With four hash marks under his belt, he never ran a lathe?? He caught on very fast and in no time he was getting the basic hang of it. I never mentioned this to anyone. I guess this was between the Chief and me. His main job was to oversee the lighting off of the main engines and getting the ship under way.

This picture is John Cadnick and me. John was my best buddy. We spent all our time together in the Newport Fire Department. Unfortunately, he lost part of his left leg and that's why he is unable to make it to any of the Johnston reunions. We talk often on the phone.

Commissioning plus two years!
By: Oliver W. Norton, Fireman (F1/C) (Plank-Owner)

Years on board the Johnston: 1946 to 1947

I went to Boot-Camp at Great Lakes, ILL. in May 1946. After finishing boot-camp I was immediately assigned to new construction and sent to Orange Texas to board the USS Johnston. We commissioned the ship on August 23, 1946 and after a few weeks we sailed to Galveston and went in to dry dock. After a few weeks we sailed over to New Orleans to take on ammunition. From there we set sail to Guantanamo, Cuba for a shake-down cruise. On this voyage I experienced one of my memorable experiences.

We had been at sea on our way to Gitmo and we headed straight into a tropical hurricane like I hope to never

experience again. The next most frightening thing I experienced was the time we were training anti-submarine warfare off the coast of New London, Connecticut and a United States submarine surfaced underneath our ship.

I enjoyed my time on the "Mighty J" and I am proud to be a PLANK. In the fall of 1947 the J was going on a one-year goodwill tour of the Mediterranean and I didn't have enough time left on my enlistment so I was transferred to a DE in Norfolk, Virginia.

I married my high school sweetheart while serving aboard the J and we have just celebrated our 63rd anniversary. We have three children and nine grand kids and one great grandson. After I was discharged I returned to my hometown at Albertville, Alabama. I enrolled in college in the fall of 1948 and I graduated from the University of Alabama in 1952. After graduation I went to work for Southern Bell Telephone Company. I worked there for 37 years and retired in 1989. I have had 20 good years in retirement.

AS I RECALL IT

by: Edward M. Burke, Quartermaster (QM2) (Plank-Owner)

Years on board the Johnston: 1946 to 1951

AUGUST 23, 1946 - Orange, Texas Commissioning Day. We were loading stores all week and this day was no different. The crew would just walk off the ship, go down the pier, grab a box and carry it back on board. With no ceremony attached, came the commissioning, then they posted the gangway watch and the loading continued. Another sailor and I started to walk off the ship and the Petty Officer of the Watch said, "Hold it, you have to ask permission to leave the ship."

"Why?" said my shipmate.

"Because you're in the Navy now." Said the P.O.

"Big deal, where the hell was it this morning?" said my shipmate.

SPRING 1948 - We were in the Brooklyn Naval yard from late 1947 till early 1948. We took off the 20mm Anti-Aircraft guns, added new radar gear and painted the entire ship. When we left the yard, we proceeded to Earl, New Jersey to load ammunition. The ammo was at the end of the pier and we had to carry the stuff down the pier to the ship. It was late and the civilian crew was

61

going to knock off at 1630. The Captain did not want to stay in Earl over night so we just stacked the ammo on deck. We finished loading before the civilians quit, got underway and anchored in Gravesend Bay.

After chow that night, the stowing of the ammo continued until it was all finished. It was the night that Joe Louis fought Billy Conk for the championship. The Captain had it broadcast over the loud speakers so everyone could hear it. Louis won!

On the way to Europe in the spring of 1948, we went down to the Caribbean Sea and took part in fleet exercises. When that ended, the Johnston and other ships headed east towards the Mediterranean Sea to relieve the 6th fleet. Just before we were to separate from the rest of the ships to head north to England, we pulled along side a Cruiser for what was supposed to be a brief replenishment exercise and refueling. As it turned out I was on the telephone hooked up to the Cruiser. The phone talker on the Cruiser was named Kelly, QM-2. All was going well and then the Admiral on the Cruiser decided to top us off. As it happened, the hose connection began to come apart and it was located right between the two ships and kept dripping in to the ocean. Captain Long said to tell them to stop pumping. So I told Kelly to halt pumping! Too late. The connection came apart and the hose flipped into the air spraying diesel fuel all down the port side. So much for our nice clean paint job! Chief Stark had his crew scrubbing the paint for days.

VICTORY AT SEA – Shortly after the "Repo" incident and a few days out of Plymouth, England, we were signaled by a British freighter on her way to Canada. It seems they had two stowaways on board. Where the Germans lost the North African Campaign, the prisoners were sent to Canada and North America where they worked on the farms. After the war, they were sent back to England where they were temporarily held in repatriation camps pretty much unguarded waiting to be sent home to Germany. These two guys decided Germany had nothing to offer so they decided to head west. Unfortunately they were found. We took them aboard and the Captain had them locked up in the Seabag locker. When we reached Plymouth, England, we turned them over to the British Navy. Thus, the USS Johnston DD-821 captured the last two German prisoners of the war. The war was officially declared over December 31, 1946.

BASEBALL — The Johnston had a pretty good baseball team. We played any other tin can that had a team. We even took on the Air Base at Quonset Naval Air Station. The only team that gave us trouble was the semi-pro team in the Sunset League. We were never able to beat them. DESLANT was stationed on board the Vulcan which had a team as well.

When we returned from Europe in '48, we went to Kittery, Maine to help them celebrate their 300th anniversary. Margaret Chase Smith who was Maine's US Senator wanted a Carrier and a squadron of tin cans to go up for the anniversary. She got us and another tin can. The bay there could not hold any more than us anyway. Getting to Kittery we had to pass the Naval Brig at Portsmouth. As we passed, those of us on the bridge were silent as we watched the prisoners making little stones out of big rocks. The Marines at the brig had a good baseball team and so the challenge was on. It turned out to be the best game of the season. However, after nine innings the score was tied (two to two, I think) and we played two more innings. The Captain was at the game and was one of the team's best rooters. As a matter of fact, he was so happy for our team's effort against the Marines that he even gave the P.A.C.'s liberty. After the extra innings we finally lost to the Marines. When the summer ended, the baseball season moved to the Navy Championship series in Norfolk, Virginia. All of the destroyer Commanders told DESLANT to send the Johnston to represent the destroyers in Newport, Rhode Island. They were told that our schedule would not permit us to play so they sent their own team from the Vulcan. Guess who they played? The Marines from the Navy brig and they cleaned the Vulcan's clock! So much for the best man wins theory.

RESCUE AT SEA, 1948 - Halfway through the cruise we were at anchor in the British Naval Base at Portsmouth, England. We were there for the annual Navy Preparedness to be carried out by a US Navy Cruiser also stationed at Portsmouth. After the personnel inspection we went to our stations for the ship to be inspected. While I was stationed in the pilot house, the Executive Officer (LTCDR Berney Foal) told me to pass the word "Make all preparations for getting underway." I said that means we have to break out the charts and then it's no part of the inspection. He then went on to say, "This is no drill, inspection team to muster at the quarterdeck, stand by to receive a medical team!" So one team left the ship and the medical team came on board. That ended the operational readiness inspection. It turned out that there was a US submarine 300 miles off the southwest coast of Ireland with a bad case of appendectomy on board. It seems that the poor guy couldn't take anymore morphine so an operation was necessary. We left Portsmouth so damned fast there was a sign on the sea wall that said "NO WAKE!" We managed to cover it with ours. About 0200 in the morning, we met up with the submarine. The high lines were transferred and the patient was on his way between ships. All the crew had their night vision connected when all of a sudden there was a bright flash. It seems Ensign Simmons was an amateur photographer and wanted a shot. You should have heard the Captain. The patient was rushed down to the Ward Room where the medical team was waiting. There were two doctors in the team, one on each side of the table. To stabilize the doctors, the crew formed a wedge between them and the bulkheads. A chief held a bottle lantern over his head and shined in on the patient so the doctors had enough light. That light must have weighed a food forty pounds. We headed back to Plymouth and arrived early in the afternoon and transferred the patient and medical team to a British hospital. Then we got underway for Torquay which was the Captain's favorite anchorage. I reminded the XO that Saturday was payday so we all got paid on Sunday.

HURRICANES – After commissioning, we went down the Sabine Riser to Galveston, Texas. We arrived at night and the next morning the shipyard workers went on strike for thirty days leaving us high and dry in the dry dock. Once the strike was over, we went to New Orleans for ammunition. We were there three or four days and left for Gitmo. About two days out we ran into our first hurricane. Most of the crew were right out of boot camp like I was and this was our first shot at being sea sick. My battle station was telephone talker in repair one and the ship was buttoned up tight as a drum. I sat on a hatch with my feet hanging down the opening most of the night. All told, we went through four hurricanes during my time on board the Johnston. I recall one as we left Newport, R.I. and ran south down the Jersey coast. One minute we were in the trouth, the next we were on the crest of a wave. Off to port was an Aircraft Carrier. When we got back to Newport and then on liberty, I asked a bartender if they had any damage from the storm and he said, "What Storm?" As you know whenever a storm threatens the Naval Base, all the ships go to sea.

DUBLIN, IRELAND – There was a Carrier and a few tin cans making an "Around the World" good will tour in 1948. We joined up with them and sailed into Dublin about April 20th or so. I turned 20 on the 23rd. We moored in the

Lilly River at Sir John Rogerson Qucy right in the heart of town, a few hundred feet from the O'Connel Street Bridge. What a spot!

The citizens of Dublin were down on the Qucy and gave us a real Irish welcome. They lined the Qucy side all night long and when we showed the movie that night, we had to hang the movie screen on the Jack staff so the people on the Qucy could see it also. The Irish pubs keep the same hours as the British. Open at 11:00 and close at 3:00 then reopen at 5:00 and close at 11:00. The Irish pub owners didn't throw any one out while we were there. If you were in at closing time, you were locked in. If you were out you were locked out. Our money was no good and we couldn't buy a drink. All the Irish kept buying the beer and almost everyone had a relative in the States. Ireland did not have a rationing system during the war so food was plentiful. They thought we were nuts when we ordered steak and eggs for lunch.

BERGEN, NORWAY – We left Ireland the end of April and headed for Bergen, Norway. It seems May 1st is a big day in Europe and we were part of the parade. As we headed up the Fjord, it was like driving through the Alps. Mountains were on both sides. Halfway up to Bergen a snow squall came right out of the Mountain and the bridge was covered in snow. One of the signalmen made a snowball and threw it forward toward the Con. The timing was perfect as the Norwegian pilot stepped out of the pilot house and turned forward. The snowball hit him square in the behind. He turned and looked aft with a quizzical look on his face. The guy who threw it just waved and said "Hi."

During the war the Germans used Bergen as a Sub base. While we were there, there was still a German U-

Boat in the bombed out Sub Pen. Bergen was not such a hot liberty town.

BREST AND PARIS - We pulled into Brest on the Channel Coast around Easter time. It was an old French Naval base that the Germans used as a Sub base. The British couldn't bomb it because the pens were too thick so the French underground assassinated the German Commander. As retaliation the Germans rounded up the men in the town and shot them down in the village square. The rubble from all the bombing was still there. Those of us who went to Paris caught the train. It was quite a ride. Every time the train stopped at a station, the guys would hang out the window and buy a bottle of wine. I don't know how many stops we made but a lot of wine was consumed. We arrived in Paris in late afternoon. We checked into the hotel and hit the town. Paris was Paris and on the way back to Brest, not much wine was bought.

And that is how I remember it.

OLSEN RECOLLECTIONS

by: Harold Olsen, Machinist Mate (MM3) (Plank-Owner)

Years on board the Johnston: 1946 to 1948

I was aboard the USS Johnston DD-821 from August 1946 until January 1948 and am a plank-owner because I was on the ship when it was commissioned. We went on a shakedown cruise out of Orange, Texas toward Cuba. About one day after we sailed into Cuban waters, we found we were in the midst of a hurricane. Because of the storm, our radar was knocked out of commission and we were unable to know our exact location. The Captain ordered us to sail straight ahead for about 30 minutes and then issued an order to prepare to come about and we would turn 180 degrees and go back in the direction we had just come from. This was repeated several times until the storm subsided. As far as I can recall, the storm lasted about eight hours. Everyone was very relieved to go back on an even keel. As a Fireman second Class, I stood watch in the after engine room as the throttleman. To the left of me was the ship's listometer and I could see the needle swinging back and forth. I was later told that we were within two degrees of capsizing.

About a year later, while on maneuvers, we had the unfortunate experience of having a collision with one of our submarines which was surfacing as we crossed in front of it. The submarine hit us causing a hole in the forward fireroom. Fortunately, no one aboard the sub or the Johnston was injured.

I have many fond memories of my time on the Johnston and my shipmates and have enjoyed reliving our memories at our annual Johnston reunions.

USS TORSK - COLLISION

By: Art Damm, Bill Smith, Ed Burke, Roland Genett, Bill McCann as told to Tony Tomasin

Years on board the Johnston: 1940's

Each of these Johnston sailors was on board the Johnston when it collided with the submarine USS Torsk SS-423. They contacted Tony Tomasin and here is their story. The Johnston was homeported in Newport, Rhode Island at the time and was off the coast of New London on May 26, 1947 acting as a decoy for submarine exercises with the submarine USS Torsk. After a practice torpedo run, the Captain of the Torsk turned the conn over to PCO Student, LTCDR T.H.Williams of the US Navy. Shortly afterwards, at 1240/30, the Torsk collided with the USS Johnston DD-821 at Latitude 41-13'-50" North, Longitude 71-48"-09" West, keel depth 58-1/2 feet, with ships heading of 312T. The Captain of the Torsk then assumed the conn, ordered an emergency surface. The Torsk had suffered extensive damage to it's periscopes, periscope shears, radar masts and antennae, hydraulic hoisting gear for the periscopes, radar and radio antennae. The Johnston suffered a hole in her bottom resulting in flooding of the forward fire room. The Torsk stayed surfaced and proceeded to US Naval Submarine Base, New London, CT for repairs. The Johnston crew managed to make emergency repairs and the crew was excited thinking that they would proceed to the Boston Navy Yards for repairs and some liberty. The joy was short lived as they proceeded back to Newport, Rhode Island for dockside repairs. Once tied up to the pier, divers went over the side and welded patches on the bottom of the ship. The water was so cold that the pharmacists mate was told to supply the divers with medicinal brandy. The ship was made sea worthy and was able to continue its mission as before – much to the disappointment of the crew. In addition to this accounting, Phil Demmel has provided us with this very informative website about the USS Torsk and this incident.

http://usstorsk.net/photoalbum/47guilfoil/tpic471.htm

The event as KEN GUILFOIL, a sailor aboard the Torsk during the event remembers it.

"We were at periscope depth when the tin can hit us and I was in the control room (as part of my qualification process) standing just about under the lower conning tower hatch. Water started coming into the conning tower and the collision alarm sounded. The diving officer ordered the lower hatch closed, as I stepped up to the ladder to dog it down, I heard someone in the conn say "Oh my poor wife". That's when I thought I should have listened to my Mother; the last thing she said to me the day I left home for the Navy was "remember Kenneth, no submarines". I said OK Mom, knowing full well that was where I was going. I was only aboard a short time when this happened and I was scared out of my wits. Who ever the voice in the conning tower was, he was not alone in his fear, he had a lot of company. But that did not stop anyone from doing his job. I learned a very important lesson that day that stayed with me for the 20 years I was on the boats. When you have a well trained crew and

70

every one does their job as they have been trained to do, you can handle the situation. As was done that day by all hands aboard USS Torsk SS-423.

We flooded negative and the trim tanks, dropped down far enough to let the tin can pass over the top of us and when we were clear of it did a blow and surfaced with a bunch of very wet sailors in the conn, but with no one hurt.

Take care and keep a zero bubble" KEN GUILFOIL, May 25, 1999.

Boxing Champ

By: Ray Paquette, HM1 (USN RET)

Years on board the Johnston: 1947 to 1950

As for the Johnston I came aboard sometime in September 1947. I had dropped out of the Hospital Corps and came aboard as an Seaman Apprentice and was assigned to mess-cooking duties for three months. I was a brash young guy off the streets of Providence, R.I.

My first year on the Johnston was nothing to brag about so I won't go into those details. I remember after reporting aboard we left on a shake down cruise to GITMO, Puerto Rico and Panama. The first few days of that trip were miserable sailing just off the coast of North Carolina in the worst weather I had ever experienced (Cape Hatteras)??

Having worked on deck for most of my 3 years on the Johnston and not being able to advance to BM3, I transferred into the Fire Control gang. The Johnston had

71

been in the naval shipyard where 3"58 guns were installed. After that, we spent most of the next few months correcting errors the shipyard had made.

I recall the time we had the accident with the aircraft carrier and the Johnston being escorted back to the Boston shipyard by the USS Kennedy to make repairs. After three years aboard the Johnston I was offered shore duty at the Philadelphia Naval Base. My whole Navy Career changed after that transfer. I ended up going back to the Hospital Corps School and later on to Medical Photography School and eventually advancing to HM1.

After I left the Johnston, I continued my boxing career winning several championships and the DESLANT title in Newport, Rhode Island while representing the destroyer tender Everglade.

The one thing I remember most of my Naval career is the several times we went through Cape Hatteras. I was on the bridge one trip and we set a new record on the listing device. I thought we were going all the way over!!!!!!

WHAT DID YOU DO DURING THE WAR? Part Thirty-seven: Nebelle vs the carrier

By: Jeff Hunt, News Editor, Mt. Pleasant News, Wednesday, May 6, 2009

Dick Nebelle, Seaman First-Class (S1/C) (Plank-Owner)

Years on board the Johnston: 1947 to 1949

It was 1945. Dick Nebelle, a Chicago native, had joined the Navy, gone through boot camp, and was now off to win the war. He had joined at the age of 17, and even his mother said the war wouldn't be over until Dick had a chance to end it. Two months after Dick entered the military, the Japanese surrendered, but that's another story.

Nebelle was in the process of crossing the Atlantic Ocean. He was a tin can sailor, serving on the destroyer U.S.S. Johnston. The Johnston and her sister ship were accompanying an aircraft carrier overseas. As was the case so often, the sailing was far from smooth. Nebelle said it was at this time that an accident occurred.

"Our skipper got too close on a swell," Nebelle said. "We rolled into the carrier, taking out all of our radio communications, our smoke stacks, our radar, just everything on our ship that was there."

Nebelle said he was one deck below the one that had been damaged. "If it had gone down one deck farther, there would have been significant casualties due to that accident," Nebelle said.

Nebelle said there was a rip in the seam at the waterline and was taking on water. Repairs were made at sea and the Johnston returned to port in Boston where it was in drydock for several months while repairs were being made.

Nebelle said there were a few injuries on the Johnston, and three men on the aircraft carrier were killed. Millions of dollars in damage was done to the destroyer.

"It was all due to negligence by our skipper," Nebelle said. "At the time of the accident our executive officer put him under arrest and took over the ship. The last I saw of him was when he was taken off the ship by shore patrol in Boston. I understand he was charged with dereliction of duty and spent some time in jail."

After the war Nebelle had the opportunity to tour Europe where he was treated as a goodwill ambassador. When he returned to the United States he was stationed in Memphis, Tenn., and then in Ottumwa. While in Ottumwa, Nebelle met his future wife, Helen. The two were married and celebrated their 60th wedding anniversary in June 2009.

Dick served aboard the Johnston as a S1/c from 1947 to 1949. Unfortunately, Dick passed away shortly after this story was printed. Dick's wife Helen sent this for inclusion in the book shortly after Dick's passing. This is a postcard Dick sent to his mother on August 4, 1945 from United States Training Command "bootcamp", Great Lakes, Illinois. On the back it reads:

Hi Mom,

Well here's my prayer and believe me it's all the truth. I'm going to a show tonight so I don't have much time.

Love Dick

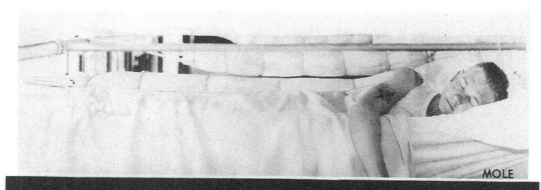

A SAILOR'S PRAYER

NOW I LAY ME DOWN TO SLEEP
I PRAY THE LORD MY SOUL TO KEEP;
GRANT NO OTHER SAILOR TAKE
MY SHOES AND SOCKS BEFORE I WAKE;
LORD, GUARD ME IN MY SLUMBER
AND KEEP MY HAMMOCK ON ITS NUMBER;
MAY NO CLUES NOR LASHINGS BREAK
AND LET ME DOWN BEFORE I WAKE.
KEEP ME SAFELY IN THY SIGHT
AND GRANT NO FIRE DRILL TONIGHT;
AND IN THE MORNING LET ME WAKE
BREATHING SCENTS OF SIRLOIN STEAK.
GOD PROTECT ME IN MY DREAMS
AND MAKE THIS BETTER THAN IT SEEMS.

GRANT THE TIME MAY SWIFTLY FLY
WHEN MYSELF SHALL REST ON HIGH
IN A SNOWY FEATHER BED
WHERE I LONG TO REST MY HEAD
FAR AWAY FROM ALL THESE SCENES
AND THE SMELL OF HALF DONE BEANS.
TAKE ME BACK INTO THE LAND
WHERE THEY DON'T SCRUB DOWN WITH SAND;
WHERE NO DEMON TYPHOON BLOWS
WHERE THE WOMEN WASH THE CLOTHES;
GOD THOU KNOWEST ALL MY WOES —
FEED ME IN MY DYING THROES;
TAKE ME BACK I'LL PROMISE THEN
NEVER TO LEAVE HOME AGAIN...

★ FOUR YEARS LATER ★

OUR FATHER WHO ART IN WASHINGTON
PLEASE, DEAR FATHER, LET ME STAY
DO NOT DRIVE ME NOW AWAY
AND LET ME STAY FOR THIRTY YEARS
PLEASE FORGIVE ME ALL MY PAST
AND THINGS THAT HAPPENED
    AT THE MAST
DO NOT MY REQUEST REFUSE
AND LET ME STAY ANOTHER CRUISE.

- -

YOUNG MAN FROM OHIO

By: Charles A. Berridge, Fire Control Technician (FT3)

Years on board the Johnston: 1947 to 1949

A Partial History of Service on the "Jolly John", as one classmate at the Advanced Firecontrol Technician School in Anacostia referred to U.S.S. Johnston months before I had the slightest idea I would end up on that ship.

I reported on board at the Brooklyn Navy Yard where she was nested under the Brooklyn Bridge with two or three other destroyers, all undergoing some kind of repairs and/or modifications. This was the Christmas season and the massive U.S.S. Missouri was in dry-dock nicely decked out stem to mast to stern in the lights of the season, a very impressive sight to this small-town boy from the farm country of northwestern Ohio.

The Bow of the USS Johnston looking up the fjord toward Bergen, Norway.
(Photo courtesy of Mark Kaufmann and "Life" magazine)

Later, my first time on any vessel larger than a 12 ft. motorboat, we put to sea through N.Y. harbor on a cold sunny day, passing the Statue of Liberty on the way, headed to Guantanamo for exercises. As I remember it , we must have hit a big storm some time in the wee hours because the next morning walking to chow some were complaining of being tossed out of their racks but I hadn't noticed. With the passing of much time the memory of sequence of trips is not clear but we were in and out of Newport, R.I. and in the spring in a task force that included the Constellation. We went to England (Plymouth, Torquay, Cardiff, Liverpool), Ireland (Dublin), Denmark (Copenhagen), Norway (Bergen and made the cover photo of "Life Magazine"; the photographer was standing beside me in the Mark 37 director) (one memorable event of that trip was being able to read a sun-lit newspaper on the bow at midnight), then France (Brest, with liberty in Paris), Gibraltar and Tangier. We returned to Newport in June 1948.

Johnston made subsequent visits to Cuba with one involving a 2 to 3 day stop in Santiago. One other failed adventure was a task force to study the performance of equipment in cold weather conditions. I believe this was in the Nov.-Dec. of 1948 where we left Newport, after acquiring those nice foul weather jackets, had an overnight stop in Halifax in rough weather, then headed up into the Davis Straits where we were to conduct exercises and make detailed observations. The only problem was the weather turned as mild as any October in Newport.

We once were ordered out of Newport harbor to go to sea to avoid a hurricane coming up the coast. We ended up meeting the hurricane out to sea where, according to one of the quartermasters we came perilously close to the 45^0 mark on the inclinometer during the night. We endured heavy seas but good weather for several days thereafter. One other memorable event was after we switched captains, we were conducting maneuvers with the fleet that included the battleship Missouri. Again according to one of the quartermasters we crossed her bow in the night at what might be best described as being unusually risky. It was on that same trip where we were alongside the aircraft carrier (probably delivering mail) and rose up under one of the structures below the flight deck (like a gun tub) and squashed the top part of a stack. (I can still recall the noise that it made down in the fire-control and ships-gyro compartment. Thus quickly up the ladder to the main deck to see the port side of the carrier just yards away.

We spent many cold days at a dock in Boston harbor, where we had to walk by the U.S.S. Constitution coming and going. I left the ship in March 1949 to go to Chelsea Naval Hospital, and missed the scheduled trip down to Trinidad, which I regret. When I left the hospital, going through the Receiving Station I was given the opportunity for early discharge, and that was the end of my naval career.

This report is as accurate as 60 years of memory can make it.

SAILING THE HIGH SEAS

By: William "Bill" Smith, Jr. (RD-QM)

Years on board the Johnston: 1947 to 1950

USS Johnston DD-821, Brooklyn Shipyard, December 1947 – record snow fall, everything is shut down and I had to walk across the Brooklyn Bridge.

The Johnston left in January 1948 and landed in the gulf in Guantanamo Bay, Cuba. We exercised in the area with other ships and then left for England in February.

After many days at sea and only a few days from England, we were signaled from a freighter to take two stowaways whom happed to be two escaped German prisoners. Naturally we took them aboard and when we landed in Plymouth, England, we handed them over to the government.

German prisoners being taken aboard the USS Johnston

We then sailed to Brest, France where the port city had been completely destroyed during World War II. I found out later that my uncle was in three bombing raids over France looking for German U-Boats that had sunk many U.S. ships in the Atlantic Ocean. During our stay in Brest, many of us took a ten-hour train ride to Paris in March of '48 for three days.

Train Ride to Paris
L-R, LT Cdr Fold (XO), LT Deets, LTjg Carter

We later sailed for several ports such as Cardiff, Wales, Liverpool and Dublin, Ireland. The Johnston, Rush and Fresno were the first U.S. Naval ships there in 23 years. From there we sailed over the North Sea to Bergen, Norway on May 1, 1948 in a snow storm.

From Norway we sailed to Copenhagen, Denmark, then through the Kiel Canal in Germany and then back to England. We then left England in June for Gibraltar and North Africa. We arrived back in Newport, Rhode Island in June of 1948.

After a short stay in our homeport, we made several short trips to different ports including Rockland, Maine for the Lobster Festival and then six different trips to Cuba including Santiago, Cuba before Castro took over.

We left Newport for our next major cruise on August 23, 1949. We arrived in Gibraltar on 1 September; Corfu, Greece on September 6 to 12; Venice, Italy on September 14 to 19; Trieste, Italy near the Yugoslavian border on September 19 to 30; Golfe Juan, France (French Riviera) from October 4 to 10; Argostoli, Greece on October 15 to 24. We did a lot of operating with U.S. submarines for a few days then on to Mersin, Turkey October 28 to 31. We spent Thanksgiving Day in Greece then on to Augusta, Sicily December 15 to 19; Naples, Italy on December 20 to January 1950. During Christmas and New Years holiday, I took a three-day bus trip to Rome. We then left for Oran, North Africa and stayed Jan 7 to 13. Finally we set sail for home and arrived in Boston late January 1950.

I was discharged in March, 1950.

BOB'S LATE NIGHT DATE

By: Robert "Bob" E. Smith, Quartermaster (QM3)

Years on board the Johnston: 1947 to 1950

It was quite an exciting day in mid-1948 when the "Jolly J" tied up to the dock along Sir John Rogerson's quay in Dublin, Ireland. Also, tying up alongside us was the USS Rush, DD-714. We were to be there for a couple days' visit.

It wasn't long before curiosity seekers began gathering on the dock to get a good look at a couple of American warships. And the crowd continued to grow as the day wore on. But the real excitement evolved the next day when we opened up the quarterdeck to tours for the general public.

It was then that I met a beautiful . . . and I mean Beautiful . . . girl when she came to my workstation on the bridge to look around. One thing led to another and I convinced her to meet me on the dock that evening in front of what was called Smyth's Bar.

A couple things should be noted . . . at least 1500 people showed up on the dock that night, and technically, I didn't even have liberty. But anyway, I jumped off the ship onto the dock (unseen from the quarterdeck) and quickly got lost in the crowd. I met the girl in front of the bar and away we went.

My biggest mistake was returning to the ship about 3 in the morning. I said goodbye to the girl under one of those monstrous dockside cranes and began walking along the edge of the quay toward the ship. It's bad enough that when I jumped off the ship there were about 1500 people there . . . but when I returned there were only about 3. And worst yet . . . the tide came in while I was gone and the "Jolly J" was sitting way . . way up.

My first thought was "How in the hell am I going to get back on board?" I couldn't go over the quarterdeck or I would have been apprehended immediately. I was standing alongside, forward of the quarterdeck and just aft of the second 5″ gunmount, when the forward sentry cam alongside, saw me, and asked what I was doing. I told him I jumped ship and I gotta get back on board.

I happened to spot two hooks on the edge of the deck and I told the sentry I was going to jump and grab them. I said if I miss them call for help because I couldn't swim. "(I only learned to swim after I got out of the Navy) I grabbed one of the hooks, missed the other, and the sentry got hold of me and helped me back on board. He quickly ran toward the bow, and as he was running he said "I didn't see anything!"

As it turned out, I also ran toward the other side of the ship, down the hatch, into my compartment, climbed up to my third high bunk and pulled the covers up over me. That quick, someone came down into the compartment and began looking around with a flashlight, but he never saw me.

I would hope that all who read this historical episode . . . keep it quiet . . . don't tell anyone, because in June 2010 I'll turn 80 years old, and I'd hate to have the Navy come after me and put me in the brig. I'm an old man, and besides, I didn't get caught. So it's my word against theirs. If you're wondering what happened on my date, I really don't remember, but then again, I may have Alzheimer's, Old age does have its benefits.

BALL RECOLLECTIONS

by: Paul Ball, Electricians Mate (EMFN)

Years on board the Johnston: 1947 to 1950

On our first trip over seas, the Johnston along with the USS William R. Rush DD-714 (tin can) and the USS Fresno CL-121 (Light Cruiser) was privileged to visit Dublin. It was said that we were the first American men of war to visit there in 28 years, which I can believe. The first night ashore we went to a bar at the end of the dock. At Midnight the bar closed but the owner suggested we just step out side and wait. Soon after, he came out passing out free drinks to all that stayed; Irish and American sailors alike.

On 5/13/48 all ships were tied up in Portland, England. The skipper gave orders to ready for sea, though we were scheduled to stay there a week. Two men came aboard the Johnny. As soon as we cleared the harbor it was flank speed for 6 hours, where we met the sub Trumpet Fish. We took a sailor off the sub and the two men operated on him at 0100 in the officer's mess. As soon as that was over with, flank speed back to port. It seems that the two men were from the Fresno. We were just faster than the other two ships. Never knew the sailors name, but it was said that he had appendicitis.

NOTABLE EVENTS ON-BOARD THE USS JOHNSTON - COLLISION!

By: Daniel W. Licht, Electronics Technician (ET1)

Years on board the Johnston: 1948 to 1951

My life aboard the Johnston started on June 30th 1948 when I graduated from Radar School in Boston. My first assignment was compartment cleaner as soon as we got underway. Being seasick I created more messes than cleaning up others. When I took my watch at the SR Radar, one additional piece of equipment I had to operate was emptying the bucket between my legs. This experience took about two weeks to resolve itself.

In 1948 I became an ET. While we were preparing to join a task force to sail the North Atlantic, our QGA Sonar equipment failed. We traced the problem to the transducers in the sea chest under the hull. This normally would require a navy yard dry dock. It was Easter weekend and I was looking forward to going to the Sunrise service at the Newport Naval Station. However we discussed a plan to repair the unit while at anchor. Our plan involved various talents of the crew. First we sent divers over the side to swim under the ship to plug up the holes in the sea chest that allowed water to flood the transducer. Next we needed the damage control party to rig a hoist in the living compartment to access the overall assembly. This was followed by the machinist mates to remove all the bolts that anchored the top plate of the housing. Now we could lift the transducer from the sea chest very carefully. We had no idea what to expect, because we never knew of any other ship that performed this operation. The next task was to remove the plate that is activated by the signal from the many individual electro-magnet coils that make up the overall transducer. Obviously the salt water corroded the bolts and made removal more difficult. The machinist had their work cut out for them. They were successful in removing the bolts and where necessary they had to make new blots while we made other repairs. Once the unit was on the hoist we had to circuit check the unit to find and repair the malfunctioning units. With repairs complete, we had to reassemble the housing in the reverse order, making sure all watertight seals worked. Once we lowered the unit and bolted it down, the divers had to go over the side to remove the plugs they put in the sea chest. When all was cleared we fired up the Sonar and we were back in operation and prepared for sea. This operation took over 24 hours, but it demonstrated how much talent and team work the Johnston crew was capable of.

Later on this same cruise, we were sailing as part of a screen/plane guard flotilla with the aircraft carrier USS Kearsarge CV-33. Part of our duty was to retrieve the mail that was flown in for the flotilla and distribute it to the other ships. Seas were a bit rough. We were to come along side and receive the mail bag by high line. As we came along side the carrier, we got caught in a wave trough and we went down. As we came up on the next crest we listed toward the carrier and our mast speared the gun galley on the carrier. I understood it killed a marine in the accident. Damage to the Johnston included the starboard yard arm, main battery gun director and parts of the bridge deck. A photographer aboard the carrier caught the scene just before the main event. One critical event for me was to crawl out on the damage yardarm to restring our long wire antenna for the TBL long range transmitter. Fortunately, I had a lifebelt wrapped around me. Doing this while the ship is tossing gave me an insight to what sailors had to do in sailing ships.

Then there was the time, on another cruise in the North Atlantic, we learned some mess cook at the last supply delivery, lined the entire floor of the refrigerator with tins of canned hams. This was not caught until we were on our way back to Fall River, Mass. For about four days at sea, we ate ham slices for every other meal. When we got to Fall River all we wanted was a steak dinner ashore.

Engineer on the Johnston

By: Morrow Garrison, Boiler Technician (BT1)

Years on board the Johnston: 1949 to 1952

I was born in Danville, Alabama on March 21, 1930 to Leldon D. and Grace Lorraine Garrison. I'm known as Gary by most of my friends. I attended the Winton Alabama Grammar School and Cotaco High School.

In 1948, I volunteered and served my country in the Navy with active duty until 1952 which included a tour of duty in Korea and two in the European Theater as an engineer on the destroyer USS Johnston DD-821. I earned the rank of first class petty officer and received my honorable discharge with a good conduct medal and a captain's commendation. While the ship was refitting for six months in our home port of Newport, Rhode Island, I met a charming young woman from the Boston area and began to commute there with increasing frequency. After my return to civilian life, I married my sweetheart, Gertrude Bouzan on June 13th, 1953.

Trudy's family and my desire to complete my education brought me back to New England to Northeastern University where I received my degree of Bachelor of Science with a major in accounting in 1957. I took jobs as a painter and as an apprentice building superintendent to make ends meet while I went to college.

After college, I went on to hold numerous positions in the manufacturing industry.

WHERE SPEED COUNTS

By: Dwayne J. Heitzman, Boiler Technician (BTC)

Years on board the Johnston: 1949 to 1956

During the Mediterranean deployment in 1951 we were operating with the U.S.S. Roosevelt. (Actually it was the Kennedy, Roosevelt and either Ware or Fiske). On plane guard duty naturally, and we were bringing up the rear. Maybe two weeks prior to this our Engineering Officer LCDR Andrewson had been reassigned to the Roosevelt as the Engineering Officer and our M.PA.G.P. Hevenor moved up to Engineering Officer. I'm not positive of the separation between ships while plane guarding, but it went something like this: Johnston DD-821 [1500yds], Ware DD-865, Fiske DD-842 [1500yds], Roosevelt CV-42 [1500yds], Kennedy Jr. DD-850 - - - That put us two and a half miles to the rear of Kennedy. Our next port of destination after Flight Ops was Piraeus, Greece. The Admiral on the Carrier, upon the completion of Flight Operations, put out something to the effect of,

"Whoever gets there first goes in first." Of course, at the moment in time all the ships were at flank speed and had been for some time, and headed in the direction of Piraeus.

I know I was on watch in the Forward Fireroom.

To shorten the story, we were tying up and just seeing smoke on the horizon......

Needless to say, LCDR Andrewson came aboard when the Roosevelt got in and accused us of all kinds of nefarious black deeds. I don't think he was ever convinced that we were just "GOOD!"

It happened again in 1964, and I have the movies to prove it. So that does mean the crews of the Johnston knew what they were doing. Of course I always knew that, we were the "BEST." Duane

----

"Big Mo" Heads Task Force Here On Visit – Halifax Host to United States Task Force

From: Unknown Newspaper, Summer, 1951

Submitted by: Harry W. Odom, DK3

Years on board the Johnston: 1949 to 1951

The city of Halifax, steeped in Navy tradition, is host this week to approximately 5000 officers and ratings of the United States Navy who are paying a four-day

formal visit to the port as part of their six-week' training cruise with Task Force 86.

Led by the famous 45,000-ton battleship Missouri, the task force, which includes two destroyer divisions, steamed into Halifax Harbor out of fog banks Saturday afternoon.

Thousands of Halifax citizens lined the seawall, the breakwater at the Royal Nova Scotia Yacht Squadron, and other vantage points, to greet the warships and their personnel. Many small pleasure craft ventured into choppy waters to extend a first-hand welcome.

The Task Force under Rear Admiral John H. Carson, U.S.N., was scheduled to arrive at the port Saturday morning but heavy fog off the coast delayed arrival until 3 p.m. "Big Mo" steamed around Georges Island and with the aid of several tugs, was nosed into Piers 20 and 21, her stern pointed to sea.

The destroyers, consisting of the Brownson, McCard, S.B. Roberts, C.H. Roan, J.P. Kennedy, Jr., W.R. Rush, Johnston and Fiske, were berthed at H.M.C. Dockyard.

By late afternoon, Halifax again took on a wartime appearance. Streets, restaurants, theatres and other places of amusement were thronged with the visiting officers, midshipmen and normal complement.

This is the first port of call for the Task Force. The warships will remain here until Wednesday and then head for New York. After a brief visit there, they will head for southern waters and call at Guantanamo, Cuba. Halifax was chosen as the first port of call because of close naval associations between this city and the United States navy in two World Wars and in peace years.

The U.S.S. Missouri, largest United States Navy ship afloat, with a brief but action-packed war record, was launched in the New York Naval Shipyard in January of 1944 and was commissioned in June of the same year. During her period of service in the Pacific, she participated in actions supporting the seizure of Iwo Jima and Okinawa and carrier raids on Tokyo, Okinawa, Kyushu, Inland Sea area and various bombardments and anti-aircraft actions.

The Missouri figured prominently in the news on two occasions. As the Flagship of Admiral W.F. Halsey, U.S.N., the battleship was the scene of the signing of formal Instrument of Surrender of Japan in Tokyo Bay, September 2, 1945.

This brief but historic ceremony is commemorated by a brass plaque set in the Surrender Deck. Early this year, "Big Mo" ran aground on a mud bank in Norfolk but escaped without damage.

Her present commander, Captain L.T. Duke, U.S.N., has been commanding officer since April of this year, while Rear Admiral Carson assumed command of Task Force 86 earlier this month.

Trainees with the Task Force include 639 midshipmen from the United States naval Academy, 690 from 19 universities and 50 cadets from the United States Military Academy, at West Point. The Missouri has a normal complement of 1,300 officers and enlisted men.

There are many interesting facts about the 45,000-ton battlewagon. For instance:

91

She can make 80,000 gallons of water daily, more than 35,000 meals are served each week, 430,000 man days went into the plan design and 3,300,000 man days went into her construction. She has a complete hospital and dental facilities, a uniform shop, tailor shop, barber shops, cobbler shop, bakery, laundry, soda fountain, post office, library, print shop, machine shop, electrical shop, welding shop, carpenter shop and a plumbing shop.

Chapter 4

Years 1950 through 1959

MY TWO MEMORABLE MOMENTS

by: George R. Nugent, Ensign

Years on board the Johnston: 1950 to 1951

Job: Assistant O Division Officer, assistant CIC officer at first. Later, O Div. officer, CIC officer, ASW officer

There are two episodes that stick in my mind.

The first: Thanksgiving, 1950. My wife and I had an apartment in Newport, Rhode Island and it was our first

93

Thanksgiving as a married couple. We had just sat down to eat when the XO's wife called and said everyone is to report to the ship ASAP! The XO was LCDR Noel Burkey. With no further information, I had no choice but to get to the Fleet Landing immediately. As soon as those who got the word were on board, we headed out to sea. No one told us what we were doing. We stood extra watches because we were shorthanded. Mine were in CIC. After a couple of days of steaming back and forth along the southern coast of New England, we went back to the buoy. Rumor had it that we were searching for a Soviet submarine, supposedly engaged in landing spies in the United States. Does anyone really know what happened? I never found out for sure.

The second incident: In June of 1951 we had Midshipmen aboard for a summer cruise, which included stops at Edinburgh, Scotland and Rotterdam, Netherlands. While crossing the Atlantic, we hit some rather heavy weather. One day, during this rocking and rolling, I was to lecture a Middie group on the organization and duties of the Operations Department. We gathered topside in a gun tub and I began my little spiel. Many of those Midshipmen looked rather green, and I doubt that much of my carefully prepared lecture was absorbed. During this weather, by the way, another DD lost a propeller, and Johnston was chosen to escort her to a shipyard in England. Because of this, we no longer had to maintain station with the rest of the fleet and headed off on a new course altogether with the stricken ship. After leaving the other ship at Plymouth, England, we sailed alone up the English Channel to Scotland.

I must say that as a brand new Ensign - the bottom of the food chain, so to speak - I felt almost completely ignorant in those first few days and weeks. But as time went on, I did learn a lot, and if there are any O Division men from the period I was aboard who read this,

I say to you, "Thanks, guys. You helped a kid through the tough times until he was ready to do the job assigned."

When I qualified as Officer of the Deck underway in 1951, I knew I was ready for whatever came next.

About 10 years ago I met another Johnston crewman in Rochester, New Hampshire. He reported to the ship a couple of years after I had left. I wish I could remember his name, but alas, at the age of 80, the mind only remembers what it wants to.

Recollections of Duty aboard USS JOHNSTON (DD-821)

By: William "Bill" M. Georgen, LTJG

Years on board the Johnston: 1950 to 1951

I reported as a LTJG to JOHNSTON at Boston Naval Shipyard on 9 May 1950 after completing the Anti-Submarine Warfare Officers Course at the Fleet Sonar School, Key West, Florida. Soon after, the ship departed for Refresher Training at the Naval Base at Guantanamo Bay, Cuba.

Within weeks the North Koreans invaded South Korea on 25 June 1950. Five days later, President Truman ordered U.S. ground and naval forces into action, setting off major changes in the Navy. Older destroyers were taken out of mothballs, experienced crew members were ordered to the reactivated ships and reserve officers were ordered to active duty. At one time, the nine regular officers aboard the JOHNSTON when I reported ballooned up to a maximum of 19 regular and reserve officers.

Eight of the nine destroyers in our Atlantic squadron were ordered to the Korean theater. Our skipper, Commander William C. Howes, was the senior commanding officer in the squadron, and elected to remain in the Atlantic when given first choice.

In the summer of 1950, after Refresher Training, JOHNSTON participated in an abbreviated Midshipman Training Cruise to Halifax, Nova Scotia, and spent the fall and winter in Underway Training and various Fleet Exercises. In August 1950 I was sent to DESLANT Afloat Gunnery School in WILLIAM C. LAWE (DD-763), and became Gunnery Officer of JOHNSTON in October.

More Atlantic Fleet Exercises were conducted in the spring of 1951, and in March I led a platoon of JOHNSTON sailors in a St. Patrick's Day parade through the streets of Savannah, Georgia. In June we took aboard 65 midshipmen for the annual midshipman cruise, this time to Edinburgh, Scotland, and Rotterdam, Netherlands. Enroute to Edinburgh, I alternated OOD watches around the clock with LTJG Raymond G. O'Kane, USNR, because of the lack of qualified OODs underway.

In August 1951, CDR John B. Dudley, Jr., a submariner, relieved CDR Howes as Commanding Officer, and I was moved to Operations Officer to fill a temporary void until a more senior officer was installed. LTJG O'Kane took over as Gunnery Officer.

One payday about this time, our Supply and Disbursing Officer, LTJG Burton R. Bley, arrived in the wardroom with moneybag in hand and a .45 caliber semi-automatic handgun strapped to his waist. He took the Captain's seat at the head of the table and placed the gun with ammunition clip removed on the table to his right. LTJG O'Kane took the seat on the right while questioning the paymaster's need for a gun in the officer's wardroom of a U.S. Navy ship. He playfully picked up the gun and pulled the trigger.

Bill Georgen on the bridge of JOHNSTON taken on June 14, 1951, enroute to Edinburgh, Scotland

I was talking to LCDR Edward S. "Ted" Eunson, the Executive Officer, just forward of the wardroom when the loud report of a .45 handgun reverberated throughout forward officers quarters. We rushed to the wardroom expecting to find a body.

As luck would have it, however, O'Kane had pointed the gun between his knees before pulling the trigger, not realizing that there was a bullet in the chamber. The bullet passed downward between his feet, and ricocheted off a deck plate into the table pedestal. The new Gunnery Officer had fired his first salvo.

Shortly after, in September 1951, JOHNSTON departed Newport, R.I., for a five-month deployment to the Mediterranean. After being at sea for several weeks, the crew was rewarded with a two-day visit to Argostoli, Greece, a small town on the island of Cephalonia in the Ionian Sea. Since the island's principal attraction was scenery, a group of officers elected to embark on a healthful hike into the countryside. Dressed in suitable hiking clothes and outfitted with canteens of lemonade, courtesy of our Supply Officer, LTJG Bley, we sailed forth in the motor whaleboat for the beach.

The island had suffered major destruction during World War II and there wasn't much to see when we arrived. We discovered a good road leading out of town in the direction of some rolling hills. Running parallel to the road on the left was a canal. On the right were signs warning passersby of land mines in the fields left over from World War II.

We hiked several miles before the road abruptly ended at a pile of trash and garbage. We had arrived at the town dump.

Discouraged but unbowed, we reversed course and headed back to town hoping to do some shopping and to get something to eat, only to find that nothing opened for business until afternoon. With a stroke of luck, however, we found an open bar and settled in to sample the specialty of the house – ouzo and cherry brandy.

Three hours later, the liberty party from JOHNSTON discovered the bar in which their officers were "hiking," and joined the party. When LTJG Bley fell off his chair and required assistance to stand up, the officer group retired from the bar, staggered through town to the quay, and sent for the ship's whaleboat. I was the only one to make it up the accommodation ladder without assistance.

So began our Mediterranean cruise of 1951-1952. The next stop was Piraeus and a visit to Athens, Greece. I leave the stories of our voyage to my shipmates. On a personal note, in Piraeus I received word that my father had died in Ohio and that my wife was pregnant with our third son. A life at sea is not all ouzo and cherry brandy.

JOHNSTON returned to Newport, R.I., at the end of January 1952 and entered the Naval Shipyard, Philadelphia, in April. I was detached on 5 May 1952 for duty at the U.S. Naval Academy, and our skipper, John B. Dudley, followed in August. He retired as a Captain in June 1963 and died in North Port, Florida, in August 1982. My first skipper, William C. Howes, retired as a Captain in August 1960 and died in Fort Myers, Florida, in July 1994.

"From Ship to Shining Ship" via "High-Wire"

By: Carl A. Camerano, Boiler Technician (BT3)

Years on board the Johnston: 1950 to 1953

It was two weeks after my seventeenth birthday when my Dad, finally agreed to let me join and came with me so I could sign up and join the US Navy. I reported to the Great Lakes Naval Training Center in Chicago on March 22, 1950 for Boot Camp training and graduated 6/17/1950. After graduation, I went home to Massachusetts on a 12 day leave, after which on June 30, 1950, I reported aboard the USS Johnston DD 821 stationed in Newport, Rhode Island.

In May 1951, my shipmate Ray Capriotti and I were sent to Fireman's Operational School at the Naval Boiler & Turbine School in Philadelphia, PA for three weeks of BT training. Upon completing the BT course, June 1951, we were supposed to return to Newport to board the Johnston but we were told the ship had left port and was now in the Mediterranean Sea. Well, now we had to report to the PVT Elden H. Johnson, a type of troop transport ship which was leaving the Philly Naval Yard for Portsmouth, England. When we arrived in Portsmouth, we now had to report aboard the cruiser USS Columbus, CA 74,

stationed in Portsmouth and heading out to the Mediterranean for naval fleet maneuvers which also involved the USS Johnston. So, now we're on the USS Columbus, on maneuvers in the MED, when the Columbus contacts the Johnston to report they had two of Johnston's men on board. When BT Chief William Rice got word, he requested the Columbus to transfer Capriotti and me....via "High-Wire" from their cruiser (CA 74) to our destroyer (DD 821). You probably know that a "High-Wire" is a cable with a small, hanging, "bucket-type seat" that gets suspended from ship to ship over open waters. Can you imagine the experience, in the middle of the Mediterranean Sea, sitting on a small seat, dangling from a cable, suspended over open waters, one hand holding on to the seat, the other hand tightly holding on to your duffle bag, slowly sliding down from a towering cruiser ship down to a destroyer. One wrong move and you were in the drink! It probably took only minutes, but sure seemed longer. Fortunately

for us, the sea was semi-calm that day. As a fearless seventeen year old, no problem… it was an exciting experience for me… today, as an old Navy vet, I'd surely have second thoughts and be a lot less fearless. It isn't everyday a sailor gets to experience that maneuver. It truly was a great experience and we were very happy to be back aboard the Jolly J with the rest of our shipmates.

As a young teenager, my admiration for my Uncle Johnny, a WWII Navy man was enough to convince me to join the US Navy. After discharge, I worked building construction and became a professional Dry-Wall finisher. Later, I attended night school, took courses and became a machinist.

As a retiree, I've enjoyed the past few years working as a currier for a local used car dealership, going to Motor Vehicle Registries and insurance companies and meeting lots of various people. I also get to drive a different vehicle almost every day.

As an Old Navy Tar, I truly enjoy the Jolly J reunions and reminiscing about the good ole' days with my fellow shipmates.

ACCORDING TO RALPH

By: Ralph Hocking, Damage Controlman (DC2)

Years on board the Johnston: 1951 to 1955

Two of my all-time favorite squelches/rejoinders are:

1 – George Bernard Shaw was introduced to a theatre audience to provide a lecture. The audience applauded enthusiastically with the exception of one woman in the balcony. Shaw, displaying his well-known ego, responded, "I quite agree with you, madam, but who are we two against so many."

2 – Several men were discussing a mutual acquaintance not present. One of the men referred to the absent fellow, saying "He is his own worst enemy."

Another in the group proclaimed "Not while I'm alive!" I offer these two examples to share the anecdote I mentioned about experiences and memories of life aboard the Johnston. This is certainly trivial when memories are brought from the recesses of the mind but the picture remains quite vivid.

We were refueling at sea from a carrier sometime in the early '50s. The carrier's band was playing on the flight deck, refueling procedure going smoothly. John Brooks, a metalsmith-striker stepped out on the deck, a cigarette (unlit) dangling from his mouth. Chapman, a raspy-voiced Boatswain's Mate in the Second Division roared, "Brooks! The smoking lamp is OUT! Get rid of that cigarette."

Startled, Brooks replied "But Chappie, it ain't lit."

"I don't care", shouted Chapman, "get rid of it!"

"But, but Chappie", stammered John, "I got an ass in my britches but I ain't shittin'."

Chapman shook his head and turned away.

L to R – Gerry Wilson, Carl Camerano, Ralph Hocking and Dick Wolf (Trieste, Italy 1951)

OLIVER'S TALES

by: Joseph E. Oliver, Machinist Mate (MM3)

Years on board the Johnston: 1952 to 1953

I got out of boot camp the middle of January 1952 and picked up the USS Johnston at the Philly Navy Yard. The ship was in dry dock being overhauled. I came aboard as a Fireman Apprentice and was assigned to the after engine room. The Master of Arms of the Engineering Department was a boiler tender named Havner. He told me that he had to put me in "skid row" which was in the deck force compartment, (a dark little corner) until some of the Division guys got off the ship. There weren't any lockers in that area, so I had to live out of my sea bag. He told me to hang in there for about a week. He was right on. A week later he told me to get my gear and to meet him in the E. Div. compartment. It was a top bunk right next to the ladder and on the bulkhead was this big loud speaker. I was just about to ask the M.A.A. a question when it started. First it blasted the Boatswain's pipe, then the "now hear this" and the message. This went on every few minutes. The M.A.A. gave me a look and said it was the best he could do for the time being but there were more guys leaving in a few weeks and he would make sure I would have my pick of bunks! As I was reaching over the bunk to fix my blanket, I felt a drop of water hit me on the back of my head. Up above, running right over my bunk was the salt water fire and flushing water line!!!! - A big five-inch pipe with this big gate valve at the other end of the bunk. It was leaking at the bonnet, a very long DRIP - DRIP - DRIP. This was the reason the mattress was folded in half against the speaker. I went up on deck and found a quart pineapple can, cleaned it out and attached a piece of wire to the can and hung it under the valve. Now I can't put my pillow on that end because there wasn't room for my shoulders. I would have to lie on my back! Anyway, the lesser of the two evils, I slept with my head right under that loud speaker. I must say that Havner did keep his word. A few weeks later, he gave me first choice of bunks. I picked one right on the starboard side, middle bunk near the machine shop and that was my home for two years.

One of my jobs at the shipyard was to walk around with a fire extinguisher following a yard bird welder. I don't know what he was welding but we walked all over that ship----Engine rooms, Fire rooms, compartments. On this particular day the welder was tacking something on the bulkhead up forward before the bridge. Little did I know the compartment on the other side of the bulkhead belonged to Captain Dudley. The next day when we had 8 o'clock muster, Chief Bender made this little speech about the people doing fire watch with yard birds. It seems Captain Dudley's new foul weather jacket had this big hole burnt in the jacket and he wasn't too happy. The rule is and will always be, whenever the yard bird welds on a bulkhead, deck and overheard, the fire watch goes on the opposite side because the welding rod makes this bright red ring and will burn anything that's flammable on the other side. I thought the Captain was going to follow-up on who was responsible but that was the end of it. The crew showed a lot of respect for the skipper and would bend over backwards for him.

JOHNSTON'S HURRICANE WATCH - NORTHERN EUROPE CRUISE (1953) - The worst disaster over the past two centuries was to hit northern Europe. A winter storm with hurricane winds was steering right in the North Sea and heading smack into Holland. The destroyers Johnston DD-821 and Bristol DD-857 would be right in its path!

January 7th, 1953, a drizzly dark morning, the Johnston and the Bristol cast off from the fueling dock at Melville, Rhode Island and headed out Narraganset Bay and turned north toward Argentia, Newfoundland. The Bristol, being a Sumner class destroyer didn't have the fuel capacity as the Gearing class Johnston with an extra fuel tank. The first stop was the Naval Air Station, Argentina on the 9th of January. The Bristol with the Commodore on board led the way into Placentia Bay, Newfoundland with the Johnston following behind. There was a Navy tug that came out and stayed alongside the Johnston. I'm not sure if he dropped the pilot off on the Bristol. The ships took on fuel and water and gave the crew liberty. The crew was divided into Port and Starboard. This way half the crew had liberty and the other half stayed on board in case the ship had to get underway in a hurry. The weather started to get ugly and it started to snow. If anyone went on liberty the nearest city was St. John's and it was quite a few miles away from the base.

Amsterdam 28 Jan. - 5 Febr. 1953

The ships left Argentia and the next stop was Londonderry, Northern Ireland. The North Atlantic is cold and rough that time of year. The ship was about one day out of Londonderry. There was an incident aboard ship. There never were enough coffee mugs, spoons and forks at noon or evening chow. So what you had to do, when the food tray was full of food you would wait until someone finished eating and grab what you needed from his tray and the only way to clean the dirty mug, fork or spoon was at the drinking fountain or whatever was handy. I guess everyone had just about had it and started banging the trays and yelling to get the supply officer's attention. The crew's mess being in the forward part of the ship, the racket traveled right up the hatch into officer's country. Somehow, the Captain heard the noise and sent the Officer of the Deck to check it out! The O.D. gave the Captain the report on what the commotion was all about. The next day on the 17th of January, the ship pulled into Londonderry and took on supplies and that included cups and utensils. The Captain had the O.D. eat at evening chow in the crew's mess for a few days to make sure every thing was up to Navy standards. Problem solved!

After a few days stay in Londonderry, the ships left Northern Ireland headed north to the Outer Hebrides around the Northern tip of Scotland into the North Sea on the 21st of January. After a rough ride the ships visited the city of Dundee, Scotland. Liberty was given to the crew. There was a bus tour to Edinburgh Castle and tours of Dundee. The Black Watch Bagpipers came on the pier and put on a show for the crew. It as raining on and off at this port of call and I ended up with a bad cold and a fever. It was still raining when we left Dundee and the next stop was Amsterdam, Holland. My cold wasn't getting any better, so I went to sickbay and Hospital Corpsman Griffin gave me a shot of penicillin in my butt. That needle was so big, just like they gave to horses back on the farm. I should have known.

January 28th, the Johnston and Bristol entered the locks and were lowered in to Zuider Zee which is the entrance from the North Sea into Amsterdam. The ships tied up to the pier and took on fuel and water. Cote and I had the water detail - hooking up the water lines from the water barge to the ship.

I guess I was allergic to the penicillin shot. When I noticed my skin turn red as a beet (like bad sunburn) and my skin started to peel off my body in sheets, I headed back to sickbay and Corpsman Griffin told me that I was allergic to the Penicillin shot. He told me there wasn't much he could do and that I should go back to my rack, lie down, and let it wear off.

Port or starboard liberty was given to the crew and because I was as "sick as a dog", I stayed on board the ship. The weather was low clouds and it looked like rain. It wasn't until the 30th when Kramer, the 2nd class of the watch came down to the compartment and got me out of my rack to help light off the pumps. This was about 2000 hours and we stayed there all night until the early morning because as luck would have it, the ship had port and starboard liberty and most of the starboard group was ashore and the port group ran the ship.

The storm started on the 29th of January as a low pressure, southeast of Iceland. For the next 30 hrs the storm headed east. By 6pm on the 30th of January, the storm entered the North Sea and the surge swept southwards. With a combination of a moon tide and hurricane force winds it hit the coast of the United Kingdom. The storm came barreling right through Belgium and Holland. The dikes in Rotterdam gave way in some places flooding that area. In Amsterdam, the sea level crested 12 to 15 feet above Amsterdam's water level. The dams held!

As the storm was howling all around us, the ships; Johnston and Bristol had their plants on line and the special sea detail was set. Krammer the 2nd Class P.O. of the aft engine room rounded up everyone he could find to light off the plant. We stayed on that special sea detail watch from 2000 hours until late morning the next day. Howie Krefft who had the job of roving security (he used to patrol the ship with a 45 hanging on his side) came down to the engine room for a mug of coffee. He said the wind was so strong topside, he was afraid the wind would blow him off the deck plus all the debris blowing around was troubling.

Over 1800 people lost their lives in this storm, most of them in Holland. The dikes held in Amsterdam. Most of the damage was in the city of Rotterdam. The United Kingdom and Belgium also suffered damage from the hurricane.

In the middle of all this, around midnight, the radio room sent a messenger with a Navy-gram informing me that my wife Annie gave birth to a baby boy on the 30th of January. I was a first-time father and would have to wait until May to see my wife and son.

Wow!!! What a night! A terrible hurricane hitting the area, my skin peeling off like a bad sunburn from the penicillin shot and a Navy-Gram giving me the good news that I was now a proud Papa! The sun came out the next day and a couple of days later the ships left Amsterdam. The hurricane was world-wide news with extensive television coverage.

Note: A couple of years ago, I was at an antique car show in Temecula, California wearing my USS Johnston cap. This young fella stopped and told me his father had served on the Johnston and maybe I knew him? I asked his name and he told me Howie Krefft. Who would have believed it; we had served on the Johnston at the same time and were buddies. I think I blew him away and he was so thrilled to hear my stories about his recently deceased Dad.

One of the little games that was played in the engine room to break the boredom was to dump a bucket of water down the speaking tube to the lower level onto a new boot coming aboard… When I came aboard as a Fireman Apprentice, I got my shower while the ship was operating in the Caribbean in August of 1952. That particular bucket was refreshing in that hot engine room.

Let me give you a picture of the engine room layout. On the main level you have the throttle board, turbines, reduction gears and the main generator. The lower level you have all the pumps (lube oil, feed pumps, etc. two of each). In order to communicate from one level to another, there was an "S" shaped pipe about 4 to 5 inches in diameter. On the top level the tube had a brass cone attached to speak through. On the right side of the speaking tube was a bell button which when pressed sounded like a cow bell. The lower level had the same setup except the brass cone was much larger. Due to the noise factor in the engine room, the person calling or answering had to stick his whole face in the tube to listen and talk.

On this particular day, the new victim was Fireman Apprentice McGrath, who was down below checking pump temperatures. Now out comes the bucket of water and the cow bell is rung! Fireman McGrath sticks his face inside the tube and gives a "What's up?" Down comes the water! Now, everyone on the upper level is laughing and waiting for him to come up to the main level. But the person coming up from below isn't McGrath but the Assistant Engineering Officer with one side of his khaki trousers all wet and behind him looking over his shoulder with a big smiling grin is McGrath. What we didn't know at the time was the Engineering Officer had come down the inboard ladder and spotted McGrath at the pump level and continued down to that level to check what was going on. Well!!!!! When the cowbell rang, he happened to be standing right next to McGrath when the deluge hit. WOW,

Engine Room — Speaking Tube behind friend drinking coffee. "Vincy" at the throttles with Joe Oliver in the background.

did it get quiet in that engine room! We couldn't believe what had just happened! Anyway, the Engineering Officer asked, "Are you all done playing firemen?" and with that said, he climbed the outboard ladder. We sweated that out for a few days. The officer didn't make it an issue. He still made his usual rounds checking the engineering spaces to see if we had any problems with the equipment or other issues.

This is what made the Johnston a great ship considering all the people crammed in a small area day in and day out (not withstanding the boredom).

DD-821's FIRST REUNION

By: James Martin, Machinist Mate (MM3)

Years on board the Johnston: 1952 to 1954

Years after I was out of the service, I was working at the Police Harbor in the city of Philadelphia. An officer that I worked with that knew I had served in the US Navy mentioned the "Tin Can Sailors" organization. It sounded interesting so I joined. Eventually I started receiving the "Tin Can Sailors" magazine and I noticed that other ships were having reunions but not mine, DD-821.

A little while later my wife, Sandy and I were at the VFW and we started talking about how nice it would be to start a reunion for the USS Johnston. Someone else at the VFW mentioned that Larry and Brenda Eckard at "Military Locators" in Hickory, North Carolina could help with the planning. Larry and Brenda's business was working with other people to help to help start military reunions.

I later called them and they explained that you just need to find out who served on the ship and then let them know you're thinking about starting a reunion. With that information, I contacted the "Tin Can Sailors" who provided me with a list of all that had registered with them as having served on the Johnston. Larry and Brenda then took my list, combined it with other lists they had acquired and sent out invitations to the first reunion.

We held the first reunion in 1992 in Myrtle Beach, South Carolina. We had about 80 guests which included wives. A great start to a great organization – the USS Johnston DD-821 Association. The reunions change location each year and we have between 40 and 100 guests each time. My wife and I look forward to the reunion each year.

USS JOHNSTON TIME: While on the Johnston, I served in the After-Engine room. In my opinion, we had the cleanest engine room in the fleet. I really enjoyed my time on the Johnston because we were always traveling. Most of the time, we didn't spend more than 3 or 4 days in any one port. It was a great way to see the world.

Another memory that comes to mind isn't quite as pleasant. One time while in port while doing cold iron watches, the forward-engine room flooded. The check-valve on the bilge pump hadn't closed properly. By the time someone found the leak, the leaking water had already gone above the auxiliary pumps. We had to disassemble the pumps and then take the motors to the nearby Destroyer Tender. They reworked the motors and then we reinstalled them. It was a good thing someone found the leak before it was too late, otherwise the whole engine room could have been flooded and it would have been much worse.

Here is a story my Grandson Cole wrote in sixth grade about me serving in the Navy.

My Grandfather was in the service from 1952 to 1954. During that time he served in the Navy. He was a Machinist Mate aboard the USS Johnston. He said he really enjoyed what he did on the ship so that it would keep running. He told me that one of his favorite things he used to do when he needed a break from the work was sneak ice cream into the engine room and would eat it with his best friend in the Navy. He and his friend, Felix Bernabella were good friends with the Cook on the ship and so the Cook used to give them food to eat when no one was looking. They used to stay up all night working and just laugh while they enjoyed their ice cream, cake or even hamburgers and fries.

My Grandfather and Felix, who was a Machinist Mate just like my Grandfather still talk and see each other when they go to the reunions. They both belong to the "Tin Can Sailors". "Tin Can Sailors" is for people that used to be in the Navy and retired. Each year they all get together and talk about everything they did to serve their country and also about the fun and sad times. They always talk about how proud they are of all the past and present soldiers that fight for our Freedom.

Jim Martin, his wife Sandy and Grandson Cole

My Grandfather always makes sure he visits the walls put up for fallen soldiers with my Grandmother and they talk about all of the men and women that helped us stay free for all of these years. They also talk about my Uncle Jackie, who served in the Army for over twenty years. He was a Staff Sergeant and was in Communications out in the field. He fought in Dessert Storm and also spent a year somewhere called the Demilitarized Zone. When he was there, he used to have to make and keep a lot of the food he ate in the ground because there was nowhere else to keep it. One time he was

116

on a mission and his radio went out so he was lost and no one could find him. They had to call my Aunt and tell her that my Uncle was missing. He finally was able to find him way back to the camp a couple of days later. He used to say that the Army trained him in what he needed to do to stay alive when he was lost in the field.

After September 11th, 2001 the United States Government sent a letter to my Uncle Jackie to ask him to come back and serve the country in a different way. He worked for Colin Powell, who was the US Secretary of State and went to work at the US Embassy in Ethiopia.

And that's just the beginning of the many stories they've told me about serving our Country.

GROWING UP ON THE JOHNSTON

By: Leonard "Lenny" Guere, Seaman Apprentice (SA)

Years on board the Johnston: 1952 to 1955

Ahoy Mates! I have many stories about my 3 1/2 years Aboard the Jolly J. I will tell you the very first thing that happened to me when I reported aboard. As I reached the top of the gangway the O.O.D asked for my orders and when he looked at them he looked at me and said,

"Oh no, not another punk from Brooklyn!"

Needless to say he and I never hit it off during his stay on board. But my remaining years got even worse. You see I was only 17 years old and straight from an orphan home in B'klyn for all of my first 17 years. This was my first taste of life, other then Boot Camp in the outside world. I had a lot to learn and it wasn't going to be easy.

My first trip across the big pond (as we called it) included our first port in Europe in Londonderry Ireland. After a few more ports and a lot of fun we pulled into Wilumshaven, Germany. We were the very first American warship to visit this port since World War II. The locals were hostile. We could not leave the ship at first. They were throwing garbage and yelling insults at us. We even had a tough time tying up to the dock. After a while (a couple of hours) the Town Mayor came down to the dock and restored order. Many of us were very reluctant to go ashore. However things worked out, we had a good time and there was no more trouble. Since we were the first Americans since World War II, we were awarded the Navy Occupation Medal, European Clasp.

I was in the galley waiting for the coffee to be done. In comes another sailor (I don't remember his name). He pulls the handle to get a cup of coffee and the pot tips over on me. I was sent to the hospital in Newport with bad burns on my face and head. The burns were so bad I didn't have to wear my white hat for about 2 weeks.

While on the Johnston I broke my arm and believe it or not, I don't remember how! Later on, when I went to get my cast removed at the hospital, the nurse dropped the scalpel and it stuck in my shoe. When I got back to the ship with my foot bandaged and my shoe in one hand and the cast from my arm in the other the O.D. said Seaman are you Lollygagging or something like that......

I'll tell you the truth' I wasn't a very good sailor at first because of my initial meeting when I first boarded The Jolly J. I've had a few Captain's Masts and a Court Martials. I weathered them and got an Honorable Discharge. Life aboard the "J" was a lot of fun. Oh yeah once I was hanging in a boatswains chair over the side and a mess cook threw garbage over the side and it hit me squarely on the head. All of "my friends" on deck had a great laugh. Since we were moored I took a plunge into the drink. I was given a Captains Mast for that. Why I don't know. I was on report more than any other sailor on board - shirt out, hat on the back of my head, a lot of silly little dumb things. Even though I got in trouble a lot, I loved the Jolly J.

FROSTY HERE!
By: Bob "Frosty" Frost, Radioman (RM3)

Years on board the Johnston: 1952 to 1955

Hellos fellow shipmates, Bob "Frosty" Frost here! I was an RM3 and served aboard the "Jolly J" from January 1952 thru September 1955.

In 1952 we spent a long time in dry dock at the Philadelphia shipyard. When the overhaul was complete, we went to GITMO, Cuba.

I left the Johnston for Class "A" Radio School from July 1952 until January 1953.

I was temporarily assigned to the USS Cascade AD-16, a tender. I sailed with her to Naples, Italy and then took other forms of transportation thru Paris and Nice, France, London and Belfast before I finally caught up with the Johnston in Londonderry, Ireland. From there we hit the following ports: Athens, Greece; Pireaus, Greece; Argostoli, Greece (which sunk into the ocean from a volcano eruption sometime after we left), Rhodes, Greece; Rock of Gibraltar; Oran, Africa; Izmir, Turkey; Halifax, Nova Scotia; San Juan, Puerto Rico; St. Thomas, Virgin Islands. That was all in 1953.

In 1954 we hit the following ports: St. George, Bermuda; Trieste, Italy; Venice, Italy; August Bay, Sicily; Athens, Greece: Rock of Gibraltar; Londonderry, Ireland; Wilhelmshaven, Germany (we were the first American ship to dock there since 1939. It was a place where German U-Boats were built. The people there were fabulous and treated us great. We were not allowed to pay for anything and many of them took us into their homes for food and drinks. It was a great liberty

port.); Bremerhaven, Germany; Lorient, France (This port was a disaster. It was a Communist city and they did not want us there and no one wanted to go on liberty so they had two or three from each division to go and there were fights all over the city. The Captain made everyone come back to the ship and we sailed out of there around midnight to go to our next port.); Cardiff, Whales; Newcastle, England; Dundee, Scotland; Amsterdam, Holland; Portsmouth, England and Argentia, New Foundland.

In 1955 we hit the following ports before I was sent to an outgoing unit in Newport, Rhode Island: GITMO, Cuba; Kingston, Jamaica; Santago De, Cuba and San Juan, Puerto Rico.

I was the duty Radioman during the Memorial Day weekend (I believe it was in 1955). I was watching a movie in the Mess hall when I was called to the Gunnery Storeroom. When I got there the FBI and CIA were there already. The First Class Gunnersmate had shot his brains out with a 45 caliber pistol through his right eye. I believe his name was Johnson and was from Philadelphia. I found out that he had received a "dear john" letter from his girlfriend. I was up all night sending messages to Washington and other places about the accident.

On my first cruise out to sea, we were going through some rough seas so I thought it would be great if I got a picture of the water breaking over the Bow. I took my camera and stepped out of the hatchway to snap a good shot. Not too smart of me. The water came over the Bow and hit me as I was about to snap the picture. The next thing I knew, I was tangled up around the life line. Thank God for that life line or I would have been in the ocean and gone. This particular picture was taken at approximately the same time and is the Johnston refueling from the USS Midway CV-41.

During one of our visits to GITMO, a group of us went to the "White Hat Club". I think we were expecting trouble because we wrapped marine belts around our waists under our jumpers. We had trouble! We met a group from the USS Black DD-666 and before you knew it, we were in an all out brawl. Remember we all had on white uniforms. The fight lasted until the Shore Patrol got there and sent us all back to our ships. There was a long line at sick bay that night. I ended up with five stitches in my lip. We were all drinking Rum Cokes, they were cheap and you really only paid for the coke in it because the Rum costs next to nothing. By the way, you should have seen our white uniforms. Most of them were red with blood.

I really enjoyed my time on board the Johnston. It was a great ship and a great group of guys.

Ensign Mudd saves my Life!
By: Aldo Prezioso, Sonarman (SO3)

Years on board the Johnston: 1952 to 1955

I walked aboard the Johnston in late 1952 as a Deck Hand. My second day on board, I was summoned to the Quarter Masters shack by Ensign Mudd. The man saved my life.

You are probably wondering, "How did Ensign Mudd save Aldo's life?" I was 17 years old, a high school dropout from the Bronx and had just entered the U.S. Navy. I did very well on all the tests I took in boot-camp and was even told at a boot-camp interview that I would probably go aboard a carrier as an air-dale and learn a good trade there. So when I graduated from boot-camp I was primed and ready to go. Then I received my orders - a deck hand on a tin can. As I said earlier,

Mr. Mudd just happened to be in the QM shack the next morning looking for a sonar striker. He picked up my jacket and liked what he saw. He called me in, we spoke and instead of moping decks as a deck hand that morning I was moving my gear to the sonar shack. I picked up the job easily, so much so that they put me on the range recorder during general quarters. Later came Class "A" school for 6 months in Key West, Florida. It was smooth sailing from then on. Without Ensign Mudd, I would not have gotten the opportunities I received on the Johnston.

The Johnston had special electronic gear on board so in '53 and '54 when we went on MED cruises, the Johnston and another DD would break away from the fleet and head for Northern Europe. We were in Northern Europe (I believe) in '54 when they had some bad storms and we lost power to our forward 5 inch guns. The country of Holland had breeches in some dikes and we were sent in to be of any help we could offer. Holland did not need us but we collected money, food and blankets and donated them to their government.

I had a great three plus years on board the Johnston. I got to go to a Class "A" school in Key West and met my future wife through a sonar man named George Prescott. He along with Bob Dunn and Mark Bonjorno and I have a relationship that has lasted since then and we still see each other on occasion. Our wives who knew each other then, still keep in touch.

DAVID BUESING'S U.S. NAVY TALE
by: David Buesing, Fire Control Technician (FT3)

Years on board the
Johnston: 1955 to 1956

*Editor's note: Putting the
USS Johnston story together
has been a real pleasure.
One of the down-sides to
being editor is learning of
another Johnston sailor's
death. However, this one is
a little different. Not
long after David Buesing's
death I received the
following letter from his
wife. The letter is
touching and I thought it
would be appropriate to
share her story with you prior to David's.*

To George A. Sites

    *I am David Buesing's wife and I am writing
to you to let you know that David passed away
on June 6, 2009. Dave suffered with ALS (Lou
Gehrig's disease) for almost 10 years.*

    *He always read your newsletters of the USS
Johnston reunions. The one that he would have
loved to have attended was the reunion at Great
Lakes naval Training Center where Dave got his
training. Unfortunately he was unable to
travel. The disease took away his ability to
talk and walk but it didn't take away his mind.
He was able to communicate with a communication
device that had a printer attached to it. He
would print out his messages. He printed out a
Navy tale of the years he served in the U.S.*

Navy - 1954 to 1958. I am sending you a copy of what Dave printed out.

He loved his years in the U.S. Navy. After his time in the Navy, he attended the University of Wisconsin in Madison, Wisconsin for 5 years and got a Bachelors Degree in Electrical Engineering (Thanks to the G.I. Bill). He worked at IBM Corporation for 28 ½ years. He had to take early retirement when IBM was downsizing in 1991.

He was an avid fisherman and during his retirement before he got his disease, we spent 9 great years at an RV Park outside of Hayward, Wisconsin on the Chippewa Flowage.

If it wasn't for those 3 months of the U.S.S. Johnston being in dry dock at Brooklyn Naval Shipyard, I would never have met Dave. So I have to thank the U.S.S. Johnston for bringing my husband to me.

Thank you so much for sending the U.S.S. Johnston newsletters to David.

We were married for 52 years when Dave passed away.

Sincerely,
Frieda Buesing

NOTE: The following story was originally prepared for use in a DynaVox, speech synthesizer. In that environment, periods are used to indicate vocalizing the previously entered data. A comma is then used normally where a period would normally be used. Some upper case symbols have restricted usage. To get the correct pronunciation of words, I phonetically spell the word. Another idiosyncrasy is with USS. For example, the DynaVox in speak mode will try to "say" USS as a valid word. To get USS properly vocalized, you must write as U S S.

I wanted to see the world, so I joined the Navy. Really! I also wanted a university education. The best way for me to achieve that, was through the G.I. Bill. The bill offered assistance for education to those in the military during the Korean conflict. The conflict was going to officially end soon, so I enlisted to get the benefits.

Racine, Wisconsin was my home town and boot camp would be at Great Lakes, Illinois, only thirty miles away from Racine. I enlisted on Mother's Day, 1954 - another thoughtless action on my part.

The 15 weeks of boot camp went by quickly. I played a baritone bugle in the Recruit Training Drum and Bugle Corps (RTDBC). One of my fellow recruits used to march with the Scouts. He was a member of the RTDBC too.

Service school selection was easy for me. I only looked at the duration of the schools. I found a school that was 44 weeks long for Fire Control Technician. An FT maintains and repairs the equipment that aims and points the guns.

Upon graduation, I was assigned to the USS Boston CAG1 - Cruiser Attack Guided Missile. The main armament was two gun turrets forward. Each turret had three eight-inch guns. The primary anti-aircraft defense was two missile launchers aft.   Each launcher held two Terrier missiles.

I reported for pre-commissioning training at the Philadelphia Naval Ship Yard. I enjoyed the city of Philadelphia. I took dance lessons while attending FT school. I found a dance hall and a favorite gal to dance with. While in Philadelphia, I also saw an Army Navy football game. I made too many trips to a friendly VFW club in Paulsboro, New Jersey with a bunch of sailors.

After less than a year on the Boston, I transferred to the USS Johnston DD-821, home port Newport, Rhode Island. But when I transferred, she had just gone into dry dock for an extensive overhaul of three months in the Brooklyn naval Shipyards. I was very busy during those three months. I was assigned Shore Patrol duties at Penn Station and Grand Central Station. I also managed to find a great USO club in the basement of a Synagogue. It was there that I first eyed Frieda. I married her within the year. A man approached me one evening at the club and struck up a conversation. After fifteen minutes or so, he asked me if I would like to be on the game show called "Name that Tune". I was on the show and could not name a single tune.

I sailed on the Johnston for about a year. For armament she had a gun turret forward that had two five-inch guns. There was a mount port and starboard for twin three-inch anti-aircraft mounts. Amidship, port and starboard, were three torpedo tubes for anti-submarine warfare. We sported two racks of depth charges aft and hedge hog weapons.

After about five months on the Johnston, I was transferred to the USS Hawkins, a sister ship of the Johnston and part of Destroyer Squadron 8.

I mad port in the following places: Guantanamo Bay, Cuba; Port of Prince, Haiti; Toronto, Italy; Naples, Italy; Scotland; Spain; France and Monaco.

One event I still vividly remember and you may find it interesting so I will tell you the story.

We were tied up to a pier in Naples, Italy. I was ordered to report to an Italian Police station for shore Patrol duty. They would buddy us up with an Italian cop and we patrolled together. We were assigned to the "Red Light" district. We must have stopped by ten or so brothels. Some wee small operations like six beds. Others were large like sixteen beds like I now describe.

We went up steps to the second floor of the building. Opened the door and went in. It was like a hotel lobby. Maybe it was a hotel in a different life. Sofas and chairs neatly arranged for optimum seating. About a third of the seating is taken. Many different military uniforms from different countries were present along with the obvious tourists and locals. Sitting next to an arched entry way was a stout middle aged woman with a huge purse on her lap. In the purse is folding money, lots and lots of folding money. All colors of the rainbow can be seen. The stout lady must be a genius to know the exchange rate of the money she has. I went over to the arched entry way and walked through it peering up and down the long hallway. I see a few topless women with their sheer slacks on and mulling around. I would estimate there were sixteen bedrooms off the hallway.

It was tough duty, but someone had to do it.

I thought for sure we would capsize!
By: Ronald E. Otto, Quartermaster (QM3)

Years on board the Johnston: 1954 to 1958

After Boot Camp, I was assigned to the USS Johnston DD-821 at the Philadelphia ship yards. Shortly before we departed for Guantanamo Bay, Cuba I became a quartermaster. Not long after setting sail we ran into a extremely bad storm near Cape Hatteras. It was really rough, I thought for sure we would capsize.

We received "Notice to Mariners" -- a book that notified any changes in navigation and any needed changes on our navigation charts. Once we made the changes were completed, the books were thrown away. In the back of these books were sightings of strange things that rose up out of the sea. They were really interesting. I wish I had kept them from being thrown out.

A Gunner's Mate

By: Robert O. Ludtke, Gunners Mate (GM)

Years on board the Johnston:
1955 to 1957

It was 1955 and I was
working on my uncle's farm near
Glenwood City, WI when I got the
call to report to duty. We were
bused to St. Paul, MN to complete
the paper work. My intentions
were to go into the navy, but it
was going to be a four year sign
up so I decided on the Army for
two years instead. Then we found
out there were a few openings for
two years in the Navy so I got
what I wanted anyway.

We were taken by train to Great Lakes Naval Center
for six weeks of basic training and then sent to New
Port, R.I. I was assigned for duty on the USS Johnston
DD821, but had to spend a month on the USS Yosemite (a
Navy tender) while waiting for the Johnston to return
from Europe. Because they wanted someone who had
experience with fire arms I became a Gunners Mate
Captain. I knew how to take care of guns and keep them
firing. New Port, R.I. was our home port. My places of
duty were winter training cruises in Guantanamo Bay,
Cuba; Mediterranean Sea; Naples, Italy; Lebanon; Suez
Canal; Marseilles, France; Baltic Sea; Stockholm, Sweden;
Norfolk, VA; Charleston, NC; and back to Cuba.

While in Europe we were part of the 6th Fleet. We had
just finished two weeks of "Carrier Ops," (following the
aircraft carriers and fishing out any pilots who go into
the drink) when we got a radio call that the Lake
Champlain Carrier was on fire. Our destroyer helped fight
the fire in which three of their crew members lost their
lives.

When I was discharged at New Port, three other shipmates and I pooled our money and bought a blue 1951 Plymouth for $200 to drive home in. I lived the furthest distance and ended up with the car. To their surprise I sent them each $50. We still keep in touch with each other, and I regret not keeping that blue car!

MY NAVY YEARS

By: John Walsh, Machinery Repairman (MR3)

Years on board the Johnston: 1955 to 1956

While attending Bloomfield High School, the Korean War was being reported on a daily basis in the News Media. My Dad, brothers Bob and Bill before me had served in the armed forces. I would be doing the same and my choice would be the U.S. Navy. Assisting me to make this decision was the knowledge that I would be served a daily meal and would be sleeping on clean white sheets. I joined the United States Naval Reserve in my junior year of High School in 1953. I attended monthly meetings at the Naval Reserve Center in Hartford, CT.

During the monthly meetings we learned all the different naval terms such as the deck (floor), bulkhead (wall), overhead (ceiling), head (toilets) and many others. If we mispronounced any of these terms we were quickly corrected or given an additional task in reading the Naval Booklet. I learned these terms quickly. The wearing of our Navy uniform to and from our weekly meeting was a strict requirement and we must be ready for our units Roll Call and inspection.

During the summer of 1953 I was required to complete two weeks of naval recruit training. On August 1st I received orders requiring two weeks of recruit training at the Naval Training center located in Bainbridge, Maryland. I departed by train at 0400 hours from Union Station, Hartford, traveling to New York City Penn Station. Arriving in New York I boarded a bus, which took me to Jersey City, then by train to Baltimore, Maryland. Arriving in Baltimore, a bus transported me to the training station arriving at 2330 hours in Bainbridge. I was now a member of a larger group of Naval Reserve Recruits. A drill instructor (DI) welcomed us while offering instructions and directions. He immediately began shouting orders for all of us to double-time to our assigned barracks. He explained, in no uncertain terms, he would not be expected to train us to be real sailors during the following two-week period, however, he would do his very best to educate us in the proper terms, customs and methods of the real Navy. We were given a bunk and received instruction on the proper method of making up our bunks. Monday morning at 0400 hours we were awakened by a loud police whistle blowing. Our DI was shouting for us to wake up, take showers and assemble in front of the barracks in twenty minutes, ready to march to the chow hall for breakfast. This morning was a very damp, dark and raining day. It would be a day I would never

forget. We formed outside and marched to the chow hall,
waiting in the downpour for our breakfast. We marched
into the mess hall and was served a very delicious
breakfast.

Once we finished breakfast, again we assembled into
formation and marched back to our barracks. As we
approached our barracks we could see a large number of
mattresses and pillows outside the barracks laying every
which way, some in puddles of water and mud. When the DI
ordered us to halt, he then began to rent and rave how
some of us did not follow his instructions on the proper
method to make our beds. We were dismissed and we ran
over to see if our mattresses or pillows were among those
lying on the wet and muddy ground. Both my mattress and
pillow was lying in a puddle and water-soaked with mud.
I carried them into the barracks, replacing the soiled
sheets and pillowcase with clean ones. We quickly
realized that we had to tuck the ends of the sheet covers
back inside so they were not exposed when the inspection
was in progress. Whenever we were not in class during
the week or marching around the training center, we each
took our turns standing four-hour watches. We learned to
stand watch over the cloth lines, dumpsters, fire watch
over empty barracks, the mock navy ship and anything and
everything the DI felt should be guarded. We learned the
Military Code of Justice as any officer could request us
to recite any part of this manual. When Saturday arrived
we were allowed to go on liberty. Blues would be
available to take us to either Perryville or Baltimore.
We needed to sign up before breakfast, as the bus would
leave by 0830 hours. I choose Baltimore, Maryland.
During this two-week period I made a few friends from
Hartford. We visited a roller-skating rink and enjoyed
most of the afternoon.

The two weeks passed very quickly and before I knew
I was on a train taking me to Hartford. In September

1954 I entered my Senior Year in High School. On March 10th I turned eighteen and volunteered to be drafted into the Active Naval Reserve. In June, I graduated from High School and received my official selective service notice to enter the Army. The Officer in Charge at the Naval Training Center completed the required paper work and on Monday morning October 1st, I climbed the stairs for the train at the Union Station to travel to the Naval Fleet Operation Center in New York City. Upon arriving at the Naval Fleet Operations Center, I successfully completed a medical examination. The Officer in Charge congratulated me after a quick interview. I was now officially on active duty with the United States Naval Reserve for two-year duration. He presented me with a ticket for the B&O Railroad. He informed me that I needed to be on the train at 1300 hours. He told me I would not make it if I took a taxi. He gave me the directions and suggested I run as fast as possible. Within a few minutes I quickly departed and was off to catch the ferryboat which would take me to Jersey City. I accomplished this task and boarded the train, arriving in Baltimore, Maryland at 2130 hours, carrying my orders. As I walked into the receiving unit a drill instructor is teaching a class. He stops and very loudly states "Who in the Hell are you and why are you two days late? You were supposed to be here on October 1st." He then very loudly states to everyone "Well this new recruit is a Yankee and those Yankees can never do a damn thing right!" He tells me to sit down and he will assist me when he is finished with this class. He enrolled me into the class, which was a good thing for I would have had to wait two weeks before another class would start.

I passed all of the required testing both physical and academics. Our class graduated on December 19, 1954 and we received the normal recruit training which lasted 12 weeks and we were then allowed to leave for Christmas.

One of the important classes for all of the Naval Personnel was the class on firefighting. The reason this class was so important was whenever a fire was reported on any naval vessel, it had to be extinguished swiftly. If a fire or the water overtakes the ship, all the sailors and officers will go down with the ship unless they have the opportunity to jump into the ocean.

Upon the completion of our leave we were required to report to our training center in Bainbridge on December 29th. Once back at the center, we were now part of the OGU (Out Going Unit) while awaiting our next naval assignment. I spent New Years Eve attending Mass on base and was assigned guard duty from Midnight until 0400 hours on January 1, 1955. I received my orders January 6, 1955 to report on January 7th for duty aboard the USS Johnston DD 821, homeport Newport, Rhode Island. At 0530 hours January 7th I was on board the B&O train heading from Maryland to Providence, Rhode Island. I arrived in Providence at approximately 1600 hours. In Providence I was required to board a local bus to Portsmouth, Rhode Island. After arriving at this destination, I would sail on a small motor craft, (liberty boat) out to my new ship the USS Johnston. It was now 2030 hours (8:30pm). I climbed a rope ladder from the small craft to my new living quarters of the next 23 months. My new ship seemed very large and I could not understand why it was called a Tin Can.

Once onboard the ship, I reported to the OD (Officer on Deck). He called another sailor which escorted me to my new sleeping bunk and a small locker. I was told to just place my sea bag on the deck and crawl into the bunk for the rest of the night. Once I was in the rack, I quickly fell sound asleep.

I received additional information the next day. I was awakened at 0630 hours Tuesday morning. I was dressed in the dungarees and the blue navy issued shirt. I was given a tour of the ship and completed all paperwork including the payroll information. My new assignment was a deckhand. I joined the work party and was introduced to my fellow shipmates. They were busy chipping the lead paint off of the deck and I quickly joined them. I became part of the deck hands because I was lacking any special skills which the Navy could use on this ship. Being part of this group was not to my liking. I decided I could accomplish a better assignment for the next two years. We were the first group awakened in the morning at 0430 hours whenever the ship was making preparation to get underway. Whenever the ship docked, we were the last to leave on liberty. We were the sailors that were required to attach all the ropes tied to the ship at dockside. Over the next few days I was busy chipping and painting any metal surfaces chosen by First Class Dick Lewis. He was in charge of all the seamen. Often while in port we were required to sit on a small chair placed over the side of the ship and paint the exterior sides of the ship. I was happy to learn that I was able to go on a 72 hour pass from Friday, 1200 Noon until 0800 hours on Monday. My first leave while in Newport, Rhode Island would be leaving the Johnston and heading for my home in Bloomfield, Connecticut.

Friday arrived and I boarded a local bus that traveled to Providence. At the train station I attempted to purchase a ticket to Hartford. I quickly learned that the train does not travel from Providence to Hartford. I was required to travel from either Providence to Boston or New Haven. I choose to go to New Haven. This was the wrong choice. As I arrived in New haven at 1700 hours, I found out the next train to Hartford was two hours later. I arrived home at about 2200 hours. In the future I either hitchhiked or rode a bus from Providence to Hartford (during the 1950"s, the military personnel would be offered a ride when they hitchhiked). I enjoyed my weekend home and reported back on board the ship Sunday at 2300 hours. All of the deckhands were wakened the next morning at 0430 hours to make preparation for our departure on January 10th to Guantanamo Bay, Cuba.

While sailing out of Newport, I thought to myself this is not too difficult. After all, I was leaving the cold New England for a nice warm trip to the Caribbean Islands. Additional deckhand duties were to complete the topside four-hour sea duty watches. Those deckhands not assigned to the watch details began their daily work assignments at 0700 hours until 1600 hours, Monday through Friday. After 1600 hours you were required to report for a four-hour sea duty watch. If you did not have the watch it was your free time. We were soon sailing off of the Rhode island shores causing the ship to begin rolling from side to side with about a 20-30 degree lisp. The weather was cold around 20 degrees F with the winds at about 25 M.P.H. This was January 10th and I was feeling the cold. I was topside so when the waves became larger we were compelled to travel inside the ship. I reported for my watch at 2400 hours outside the wheelhouse where the OD would be guiding the ship throughout the night. Our Captain, Paul T. Roy (CDR) checked our progress throughout the night while underway. It was raining and bitter cold and the cold sea splashed my face. As the ship rolled to the port side the water would slide off of the wheelhouse roof giving me a good soaking. When it rolled to the starboard side, the spray from the waves would give me another soaking from the opposite direction. This soaking began with the start of my watch at Midnight. I was very happy when 0400 hours arrived and I would gracefully welcome my relief. The Officer of the Deck (LCDR John Hart) came outside his wheelhouse and inquired how I was handling everything. I really respected him and we seemed to appreciate our friendship which was new. I said I would be very happy when my relief arrives. He informed me his visit was to assess how I was handling my duties. During his time, most of the officers and sailors were stricken with severe seasickness. He informed me that I must stand the watch for another four hours. I informed him I have only one request. "Sir, may I have permission to go below and change into some dry clothes?" He quickly assures me that permission was granted. "Of course you may and I will cover your station while you are gone. You may also stop at the galley and obtain a sandwich and hot coffee. While you are going back aft, mop up the vomit that is in the starboard passage."

Aye, Aye Sir!" with a hand salute I left and returned back to my watch within 30 minutes. The next day the sun appears and the ship returns to normal after taking a beating from the ocean and storm. I learned that during the night while I was on watch the ship rolled on its port side to 47 degrees. They say if any ship take a roll of 56 degrees, the ship will roll completely over. We would have gone down with the ship if it had rolled much more. What a night, a night this sailor will never forget. We had been sailing outside the Carolina's close to Cape Hatteras when this storm occurred. This area is always receiving heavy rains with strong winds during these winter months.

Two days later, we arrived in Cuba with the sun shining and the temperature in the 80's. Within a few days the ship docked and we replenished our supplies of food and ammunition. Half of the ship is offered liberty and we can visit the base entertainment shops and beer halls. This is a very important Naval Port for the Navy during the Cold War period. It is homeport to a large submarine base and a Naval Air Station. Gitmo has a large area for destroyers to dock. The submarines and destroyers would leave early every morning and do the cat and mouse war games to increase the officers and sailors skills. We also went to sea and practiced our General

Quarters in addition to the artillery gunnery abilities using a drone being pulled by an airplane. We also practiced shooting at sea targets being pulled by a ship. All the new sailors quickly learned that we needed a great deal of training which was very improved before leaving for Kingston, Jamaica two weeks later.

Whenever I was not working with the deck hands or standing a 4-hour watch, I would travel around the ship making new friends. I soon learned that our ship possessed a small machine shop. This was a very lucky find for this sailor. Before I entered the Naval Reserve for active duty I worked par-time at the Johnson Gauge Manufacturing Company in Bloomfield, Connecticut. I began this job as a truck driver and was offered a position working inside on a bench lathe. I soon learned many of the machinist skills: I resigned when I joined the active reserve.

During our off-duty hours either in port or at sea, many of the skilled navy technicians would gather in this small machine shop. There always was hot fresh coffee available, electricians, machinery repairmen, damage control men (firefighters) and others. There were three machinery repairmen under the direct leadership of a 3rd Class David Cote and an assistant Charles Essex. I still remember Charlie Essex being a large sailor standing approximately 6 feet tall and when he finished his time of his draft, he was going to become a state policeman in Virginia. I do not remember the third member of this crew but he was the first that would be completing his draft assignment. Mr. Cote and I became friends. He informed me one of those assigned to his division was completing his draft assignment and would be discharged within the next month. This would create a vacancy within his division. I knew immediately that I would gain entry into this R Division in any manner that I requested.

The following evening I was assigned the quarterdeck watch with the OD being Mr. Hart. I began a friendly conversation with him asking much about his naval career. Before long, I mentioned that I worked part-time in a gauge factory and would be interested in joining his engineering crew. He asked me many questions concerning what types of machines this gauge company used and various questions concerning the tools I used while employed there. I guess I answered most of the questions correctly. He informed me that he would be requesting a meeting with First Class Lewis tomorrow to enable him to accompany me to the machine shop for a test of my skills. Once our watch duty was completed we both departed and I said I looked forward to meeting him the next day.

While on the deck chipping paint, Mr. Hart appeared as promised and requested Mr. Lewis to excuse me for about on-half hour. We both then started down the passageway and down the ladder to the lower deck to the machine shop. We entered the shop and 3rd Class Repairman Cote was introduced to me. Neither he nor I informed Mr. Hart that we already knew each other. Mr. Hart picked up a small drill and requested that I sharpen the drill. I took the drill over to the grinding machine and sharpened it. He inspected it without any comments. Next he handed me a micrometer and a piece of steel and requested that I measure it and tell him what the reading was. I informed him of the reading and again no comments. He then requested me to cut the steel rod to an 8 inch length making a thread using the lathe. I asked him what thread and pitch he desired. I started making it and a few minutes into the process he stopped me. Turning to 3rd Class Cote, he said "Seaman Walsh will be reassigned to your M-Division starting the first Sunday in February." This was the best news I had received since joining the Naval Reserve.

I was assigned duty the Sunday when I reported to the R-Division and was given a new bunk and locker. I was offered my own cup to use for coffee or whatever I desired to drink. I was given a tour of the entire ship, entering spaces I never knew existed. I was shown all of the machinery which our repair division would be responsible for repairing and maintaining. This included all of the refrigeration equipment from the electric water fountains and the refrigerators, all of the machinery in the ship's gallery and the smoke generator located in the after steering room. I would respond to after steering whenever general quarters were sounded. This sure beat manning the 5″ guns on the main deck. Our Division had the responsibility for all the high and low-pressure air systems. I was quickly overwhelmed with all of the responsibility for such a small division. I realized I would be getting an interesting education on a large number of different machines. I also worked in the two boiler-rooms which tended to be very hot.

During one hot afternoon I was again excused from work and escorted down to the boiler-room to be introduced to Chief Andy Anderson who was in charge of all of the engine room personnel. He was standing in front of a very large aluminum wheel and instructed me to look up at the steam gauge above my head. As he turned the wheel to the left the gauge needle would raise and when he turned it to the right the gauge would decrease. He handed me a set of earphones and told me to take the wheel and listen to the orders being sent to the engine room. I was now receiving orders from the ship's bridge requesting new speed increases or decreases. Once I was transferred into the R Division, I stood in front of these gauges many times operating the aluminum wheel. If I turned the wheel to fast and lost steam, the whole ship would go dark and the emergency generator would start. If this happened, you received a good ass chewing from Chief Anderson. He took extra time to teach you everything concerning the engine room. If you made a mistake, it was not because h didn't teach you, you simply screwed up.

I never lost steam while serving many hours in the engine room. However, I will admit to letting the evaporators drop in pressure which allowed the freshwater to be spoiled with salt water and I will never forget that experience.

The following Monday with the entire machine shop crew back onboard, I was introduced. Our shop leader Mr. Cote distrusted his verbal orders for each of his crew. On my first day, I followed him while he performed the work. I was assigned a different shipmate each day during the following two weeks. I was quickly learning the location of all of our machinery and the spare parts lockers. They gave me my own set of keys to all the areas we had responsibility for.

During the course of the next several months the USS Johnston made visits to 12 ports outside the United States. All of them were exciting for this young sailor.

During my spare time while underway, I studied for my promotion to Machinery Repairman. I passed the entire test. Soon after that, I received my promotion and when Mr. Cote and Mr. Essex were discharged, I was put in charge of the R Division. I was very proud to hold this position at the young age of 19.

My last port of call was the Brooklyn Naval Yard - the very same port that my Dad was assigned during World War II.

In September of 1956 the ship was undergoing some major repairs while at the Navy Yard. I was off duty lying on my bunk reading. I was not a member o the assigned duty shift. Many of my shipmates were engaged in a baseball game on the dock. Suddenly the ship's loud speaker began to announce, "All damage control members report to the lower aft deck passageway for a reported fire!" I knew that many of the assigned damage control party would not be within listening range of the announcement. I immediately jumped down from my bunk and was running toward the aft passageway to the after steering compartment. Located about 20 feet forward of this compartment was the damage control equipment locker. I open the compartment as the dense black smoke began to impair our focus. I lowered myself to a squatting position and pulled out the OBA (oxygen breathing apparatus) and placed it over my face and began the process to activate the breathing mass. The smoke was now very dense and we needed to stay low and using the hand lights I knew that I had another member next to me and he was also using the OBA. I informed him that he should follow me to obtain the closest hose line. I reached for the hose and immediately opened the nozzle while advancing toward the fire. Shortly before our vision became completely impaired, I did see flames coming from a locker toward the rear on the port side of the passageway. Lucky for us we had a fire axe within our area and we broke the padlock and opened the locker door. We immediately sprayed the area with water and then we could see what was on fire. We extinguished the fire. The locker was stocked with the winter foul weather jackets to the top. Someone had removed the glass light bulb cover. The jackets were in contact with the bulb and caught fire. During the following week I completed my paperwork at the naval shipyard and was once again just plain John Walsh.

Waves of Fish Tales Aboard the "Jolly J"

By: Harold Rosenthal, Yeoman (YN2)

Years on board the Johnston: 1957 to 1958

Saluting the Quarter deck, I said "Harold Rosenthal, Yeoman 3rd, permission to come aboard, sir?" After reviewing my orders the OOD, the ship's Exec, asked "We are billeted for four YNs and PNs. We have seven now. Why are you here?"

Now that was an interesting question. I was a Selectee. The Navy's term for one who was drafted into the Service. In my case it occurred December, 1955 during a 10 day period the Navy was drafting shortly after I was graduated from law school.

After Bainbridge Boot Camp I had spent a year at USNAS Brunswick, Maine. As the only attorney on base the skipper had tried to keep me there. But sea duty beckoned. Now, with sea bag on my shoulder, in answer to the Exec's question, I stood dumb until with a wave to the Boats standing by I was directed to the aft crews' quarters of USS Johnston (DD821) which I learned to warmly call the Jolly J.

My rack was third high. By holding the blanket in my mouth with the end tucked under my toes I would do a skin the cat to get up. Years later well after my discharge I was aboard her a bit before she was decommissioned. These Fish Tales will flip in no special order. But I will tell of that last visit on the Jolly J at the end.

I was Captain's Talker. All information and requests for orders came to me through the static and noise of sound powered phones which I then relayed to the Captain for his response. This was 1957. We were in between Korea and Vietnam. I honor those of my fellow shipmates who served during war. How during an engagement vital information could be passed via sound powered phones is a mystery I cannot fathom.

We hit a North Atlantic Storm. Actually it hit us with 50 foot waves burying the forward part of the ship and smashing against the Wheel House. For 29 hours our Captain stayed OOD watch, with me as Captain's Talker. He kept our prow facing into the wind and against the ocean stream. In an amazing piece of seamanship he battled both forces which were trying to turn us sideways and finish us off.

Someone said if we roll 47 degrees we would get water down the stacks which would crack the boilers making us dead in the water. All eyes were drawn to the inclinator on the bulkhead. An inclinator is a simple instrument. It has a clock like handle pin-held at its top. It always points straight down without moving while the ship, like a pendulum, swings very slowly back and forth under it. Below it is a protractor shaped device with gradations running from 0, dead center, up to 60 degrees, port and starboard.

We all know it is normal for a ship to roll. That is why we develop sea legs aboard and are made fun of ashore as we wallow-walk with our legs far spread.

Watching that damn pointer handle as the gradation device under it indicates the ship is slowly creeping between port and starboard, yet never going past 39 degrees, may have made all in the Wheel House comfortable. But pity the swabbies below whose stomachs were emptied by these swings and were now in "dry heave" mode.

Seas can be angry. They can also be friendly. We all remember lying around bullshitting on the fantail, the days the ocean was so flat it looked like we were gliding on a mirror and the beauty of sunsets and rises. Then there were the night ASW conditions. During moonless nights and without the ability to see a horizon or the ocean you sometimes felt the ship was flying above the sea.

"Captain, there is smoke coming from the rear deck of the Lake Champlain." "Where?" said the Captain as he grabbed my phones and raised his binoculars? That started the strangest repartee between us and the carrier as it sat just outside Marseille's harbor. "Shall we come to your aid?" "Why?" from the Champlain. "You're on fire." "Where?" "About frame ???" responded the Captain.

Two unrelated events on the carrier had joined to cause the fire which resulted in the death of three sailors, five civilians, the loss of at least two planes I saw pushed over the side and other equipment in the water I could not identify.

The Champlain was anchored out doing off loading operations onto civilian barges of its vehicles, fuel and other supplies. These were to serve our 17 ship flotilla during its liberty time to be spent in Marseille.

Though the smoking lamp was out, a Marine on 05 deck was caught smoking. On orders he tossed the lit cigarette over the side. A fuel hose which had slipped free from its connection to a fuel tank on a barge began swinging wildly splashing gasoline on several of the barges waiting their turn to load or were already loaded. Down came the lit cigarette starting a catastrophe to the barges and sending flames shooting up the carrier's side and onto her flight deck.

We were ordered to foam the burning barges and keep a section of the carrier's haul cooled by continuous water hosing. That section housed her nuclear weapons which we were told could take us and Marseille to a spectacular conclusion. True or not we were brought bow in to about 20 feet from her as our fire detail worked to keep those plates cool.

The scene on the Champlain's flight deck was surreal. One group of sailors were fighting the fire, foaming planes, getting others out of the way and pushing two burning planes over the side. A second group dressed in liberty whites surrounded the fire detail watching them work and taking pictures.

In the water were floating bodies and burning barges. The air was filled with the smell of smoke and roasting potatoes. Go figure the potatoes.

By the time we cleaned up the Jolly J, changed into liberty whites, birthed and went ashore, well after the other 16 ships including the Champlain's party, I was told the beer was warm and the girls were cold.

You want to chance starting a war with Russia? -Not the weakened Russia of today, the nasty, mean, powerful in your face Russia of the 50's. Claim exclusive jurisdiction over the big bathtub. No submarine is permitted in the Med without identifying itself to us. We are the United States Navy.

Some eight to ten destroyers, including the Jolly J, were each assigned a segment between the toe of Italy and coast of Africa. For two days we steamed back and forth over our segment while Sonar listened for contacts. Hearing one which was not a rock or a cold water stream, we transmitted a Morse code message by turning Sonar on and off demanding the sub surface and identify itself.

Four times we found a sub or rather it found us. It could pick up our Sonar signal well before it was strong enough to bounce back to us. As we faced the sub doing 16 knots, she would come directly toward our bow and then suddenly make a left or right turn. Since we could not make the sub's tight turn, this caused us to circle way around. Again would begin the game of find the sub which led to a repeat of her frustrating maneuver. Only one sub broke periscope and then disappeared without identifying itself.

Here was the scary part. We dropped hand grenades at 30 second intervals. I was told it is an international signal to rise and identify. Did the sub know that? Would she think we were firing at her? These were diesels, not nuclear subs, with a limited time they could stay submerged. Our depth charge racks were unchained and primers activated. Any idiot could shove the handle and a charge would roll off the fantail to explode below and cause what?

One moonless night during ASW conditions we steamed through blobs of fluorescent micro creatures. They were green and red and blue all separated by holes of inky blackness. Some were a yard wide and some more than a thousand yards as our darkened prow knifed them apart. Because the darkness hid a horizon, there was no point of reference. Sometimes we saw the fluorescent spectacle below us. Sometimes we seemed to sink into the surrounding blackness as if the fluorescence was above. Unless a ship steams through total darkness, no moon and no running lights, I doubt many have been awed by the show we saw that night.

Let's talk about the incident of our almost getting stepped on by a cruiser. First understand our Captain was only a Lieutenant Commander. All other DD skippers were full commanders. That meant we got the worst duty. You know. I am talking about the end of the stick stuff.

We were ordered to pick up every Navy captain in the bathtub, the Mediterranean, where we were steaming as part of DESDIV 8. Admiral Arleigh Burke was aboard the cruiser and had invited all the captains to lunch. During high line operations transferring all these captains to the cruiser, our Captain stayed on the quarter deck. He had begged off going to the lunch claiming he felt his duty was to guard the cruiser. He weighed over 300 pounds and could not fit into the boson's chair. Could that have been his reason?

We were on the cruiser's starboard side when I, as Captain's Talker, received and communicated the command from SOPA on the cruiser to our OOD, "Q-ball [that was us] away. Make turns for 16 knots." We were doing 11 during high line operations.

The OOD rang up the turns and ordered "Left standard rudder." The helmsman, as required, answered smartly "left standard rudder?" causing the OOD to repeat the command. Saying "Left standard rudder, aye," the helmsman executed the command. From my station on the port side I watched what I thought was our swinging away. Ships turn from the rear I learned as, luckily because of our increasing turns, we moved in front of this hulk. Its foredeck was even with the height of our Wheel House. We were a 2,200 ton long bow; she displaced 22,000 tons.

All three hundred pounds of our Captain was suddenly there as he pushed the helmsman away, breaking his arm. He then ran the helm to its starboard chucks. I also learned ships on water do not respond as quickly as automobiles on blacktop. We looked back. I could see no water between us and the cruiser. "If she steps on us" I heard, "we will go down in seconds." Suddenly she fired at us – I thought. The blasting sound was her safeties as she reversed engines and had to get rid of the pressured steam in her forward turning turbines.

As we pulled away, SOPA was at me again. "Q-ball. You are back under my command. Take your position 500 yards behind our starboard rear quarter." We followed like a puppy who knew it was wrong to have peed on the floor and standing there was its owner. After a long silence, I heard the command the Captain dreaded but knew was coming. "Have the person in charge of your Captain's log on the fantail to receive a letter from a helicopter for his file." Years later I met the Captain. His naval career had finished as security officer at the Panama Canal and ended as captain of a tanker.

I mentioned I was an attorney. I was the Jolly J's legal yeoman. My duties included determining charges and punishments which could be meted out for infractions. My knowledge of the UCMJ indicated the officer who had given the command which had endangered the crew and the ship was eligible for a General Court Marshal. If found guilty, he could serve 20 years hard labor and receive a dishonorable discharge.

After typing up my report I brought it to the Captain. He ordered me to tear it up and bring the officer to his state room, with me also in attendance. This was one frightened to death officer. The Captain told him there were officers on board who were making their last Med cruise. Because in port we would be port and starboard details, if someone would volunteer to be OOD in every port more of the officers could enjoy their last times in port. This would mean that volunteer would not go ashore. You never saw someone so anxious and quick to volunteer. The Captain dismissed him after which I asked a question out of rank, "Why?" The Captain replied

"My career is ruined. I would get no pleasure in ruining another man's career."

Our Captain was a full blooded Chippewa Indian and a mustang officer. To me he met that other word few officers I met equaled. He was a gentleman.

Because of his heritage and his becoming an officer starting from an enlisted man, I believe those were the reasons he was the only Lieutenant Commander captaining a destroyer.

As two Navy ships approach each other the ship captained by the junior officer dips her ensign, the flag, to the senior. When another destroyer approached us we would wait until she asked for our Captain's date of rank. Since it was assumed he was also a Commander, if the other captain's date of rank was junior, she would dip to us and our crew would go nuts laughing.

As a career line officer, the goal is to command what is referred to as a ship of war or a ship o' the line. Captaining a ship like a tanker or a supply ship is a put down. The letter placed in our Captain's file after the incident with the cruiser permanently degraded him only to these types of ships.

The Captain had been up as OOD (officer of the deck) without sleep for two solid days as we clambered all over the med to pick up and greet all these other captains. The OOD duty would normally rotate with other officers on four hour shifts. What he had done, the fact he was not OOD at the time of the cruiser incident, or even on the bridge, were not factors to be considered in ruining his career. "A captain on board is always on duty." There are no mitigating circumstances considered. Truman said a weaker parallel; "The buck stops here."

151

We had a chess match on the ship in which several officers including the Captain participated. Eventually all were eliminated except for the both of us. We were to play each other. Before the day of the game he told me in confidence if I beat him he would take away my "open gangway." That term, meant when I went on liberty I could stay ashore until 0600 the next day if I wished. Only senior officers and no other enlisted man had that privilege. I was given open gangway because I wrote or edited, in confidence, many of the reports to be signed by the Captain and some other officers which were required to leave the ship. Also at 25 I was the same age as many of the officers.

By this time I was directly under the command of the Executive Officer who is second in command. He was also a Lieutenant Commander with date of rank a few months junior to the Captain. There was a bit of friction between them. The Exec told me, again in confidence; if I did not beat the Captain he would take away my open gangway. I know you won't believe it. No one on the ship did. But it's true. We played to a draw.

There was Ensign Ruff Ruff, the name I gave him, and my almost being court marshaled. On coming aboard he was put in charge of the laundry, made legal officer and therefore believed he owned me. Since few sailors go AWOL while at sea and there was room for only four of us assigned to the Ship's Office, I was often on the fantail during duty hours. This seemed to bother My Lord whose command to me was "Rosenthal, get busy!" He was annoyed with my asking, "Busy doing what?"

I was married and I had bad handwriting. Still am and still do. So every night about 0200 I went into the empty Ship's Office to type a letter to my wife. One night in walks My Liege. He charged me with using Navy issued paper on a Navy provided typewriter for personal, not military, use. There had already been a mean history between us. This was that straw and that camel's back thing.

I got up, squeezed past him and dogged the hatch. Turning I reminded him I produce all the official mandatory reports he had to sign which go to Boston and various commands. Unless he got off my back I would produce them with errors he would not be able to find. This would cause him to remain an Ensign during his entire military career. I was shaking. I knew what I had done would get me a Special Court Marshal. He was shaking also. He tried to undog the hatch. But shaking so hard he could not. In the Office's narrow space I pushed passed to stand beside him. Both of us together undogged the hatch so he could leave.

Did you ever get a pencil point break off under your finger nail? I did. -In my right hand middle finger. There I sat in sick bay with the corpsman standing in front and between me and the open Dutch half hatch as he was trying to tweezer out the pencil point. Along comes Ensign Ruff Ruff and demands I tell him why I was there. Before I could explain but after I held up just my middle finger so he could see my injury, he took off. He reported to the Captain I had been discourteous or some other phrase.

I was ordered to appear in officers' country where the Captain, sitting around a table with other officers and my accuser, asked me what had happened. I explained in order to offer full response to the Ensign's command, I had held up my injured middle finger for him to see. Before I could explain the cause of the injury, my accuser left. The Captain and every officer, except my tormentor, broke up laughing. I was dismissed after being told the Exec would become the legal officer which would leave the laundry as the Ensign's sole responsibility.

"Why is that line floating in the water?" I asked the two sailors working the air pump for our hard hat diver. He was below checking our rudder prior to crossing the Atlantic on our way home. Seeing the line's bitter end they immediately dove in. It was the diver's lift line which was floating free. In 20 feet of water they took off his weight belt and weighted shoes so he could float to the surface. Several of us helped to pull him aboard. A fully equipped diver cannot be lifted by his air hose.

After taking off his hard hat and smoking a cigarette, he asked to be readied to dive again. By then the Captain was there. He ordered "No more dives today." "By your leave sir, if I do not dive now just to touch bottom and come up at once," he convinced the Captain, "I will never be able to dive again."

-A little humor. The hard hat dive incident happened while we were ported at Gibraltar to be fueled for our return. No liberty except for the Captain and some senior officers. By claiming I needed to buy a special film to take photos of the officers for the cruise book I was editing, I wheedled permission to go ashore. There I was trying to purchase a gorgeous cashmere jacket when the Captain appeared and ordered me to leave. To hurry the sale two salesmen placed jackets of different sizes one on each arm as the Captain approached. He grabbed the two collars and ripped the jackets off leaving me with a sleeve of each jacket still on my arms as we rushed out. It was more than 60 years ago. Yet I know there are two mad salesmen on Gibraltar waiting for me to return. I did get the film; it was standard stuff.

For the few who have read this far it is time for the promised ending. In the late 80's I met a friend who was a Reserve Lieutenant Commander in charge of Reserves at the Philadelphia Navy Yard. Learning I had been in the Navy he invited me as his guest on a family one day cruise aboard a ship under his command.

And there she was. My Jolly J. I had not mentioned to my friend she had been my ship nor had he told me the name of his ship. Aboard her, the USS Johnston (DD821), it was strange. I may have been the last regular United State sailor to steam aboard her. Eventually she was sold to the Taiwanese Navy. When her boilers went she was sent down to live with Davy Jones and the creatures of the sea.

I visited all her spaces including my duty stations in the Wheel House and Ship's Office. All seemed familiar yet a lot smaller than I recalled. I found my rack, remember, third high, and tried to get up onto it. There was no way I could.

Life for all of us has changed since our time as ship's company no matter when we served aboard our tin can. But the memories, perhaps softened a bit by time, are still with us. I am proud as I know you are to have served her. I hope I served her well.

MY JOHNSTON STORY

by: Robert "Bob" Nava, Signalman (SM3)

Years on board the Johnston: 1957 to 1959

My story started when I finished Boot Camp. I was given liberty and then told to report to the Receiving

Station at the old Brooklyn Navy Yard. I was 18 years old and born and raised in Brooklyn New York. However, except for Boot Camp, I had never been out of New York. I was nervous and excited all at the same time. At the receiving Station we were told to scan the sheets of paper on the wall and look for our name to see where we would be assigned. I found my name and next to it was the USS Johnston DD-821. I asked someone what "DD" meant and they said it was a Destroyer. I was told to report the next day (Sunday) with my seabag to Grand Central Station where I would be meeting up with three other sailors. We were all taking a train to Providence, Rhode Island and then a bus to Newport, Rhoad Island. We were all Seaman Apprentices except for one sailor who was a Seaman First Class and was put in charge of our detail. I noticed he was older than us and he had two Hash Marks on his sleeve. I remembered from Boot Camp they told us each Hash Mark stood for four years of service, so I started thinking either he was very stupid or he screwed up because after eight years in the Navy, he ought to be more than a Seaman First Class. Later on, I found out he was an excellent Seaman but couldn't take orders and was always fighting.

When we finally arrived in Newport, we were told to go to the Fleet Landing and wait for the motor whaleboat that would take us out to where the Johnston was anchored. We had been traveling all day and it was around 11pm. You can imagine being just an 18 year old kid who didn't have a clue and thinking what have I got myself in to. I was nervous and tired and this was a lot of information to digest in a short period of time. When we got out to the ship, we had to climb up a latter while the ship was rocking back and forth. I thought to myself, if I can survive the first day, I might make it. Once we finally were on the Quarterdeck, it was almost midnight and we were told to hit the rack since reveille was at 0600 in the morning. I was assigned to the First Division as a Seaman Apprentice and at muster we were told the ship was going on a Mediterranean Cruise and join the 6th Fleet. So here I was, an 18 year old kid about to undertake the adventure of a life time and nervous as hell!

Our trip over to the MED was exciting. We left Newport on May 6, 1957. On May 13 during our cruise across the Atlantic, we found a small plane that had gone down. We were ordered to sink it since it was a navigational hazard. We were then engaged in Anti-Submarine Warfare operations as we entered the Straits of Gibraltar. However, the most exciting and saddest event happened on July 3rd off the coast of Marseille, France. We were just dropping anchor when we heard the Boatswain Whistle saying for all Hands to man their fire stations. The Aircraft Carrier USS Lake Champlain had just caught fire while refueling. They needed our assistance in fighting the fire. The Johnston charged toward the carrier Bow first. I was in the 1st Division and would be handling the fire hoses. As we got closer, we could see sailors floating in the water as well as some vehicles and airplanes that had been pushed overboard to help prevent the fire from spreading. Everyone on the Johnston was involved in fighting the fire. After a while, the adrenalin wore off and we could see the damage and lives that had been lost.

As a young scarred kid, I had to grow up fast. I will never forget that sight.

I will never forget all of the exciting ports we visited including: Lisbon, Portugal; Valencia, Spain; Barcelona, Spain; Cartagena, Spain; Palma Majorca, Spain; Marseilles, France; Cannes, France; Gibraltar and the Suez Canal.

THE LAKE CHAMPLAIN FIRE

by: Fred McGunagle, PSN3

Years on board the Johnston: 1956 to 1957

It was the morning of 3 July 1957, and we had just finished two weeks of Carrier Ops in the Mediterranean.

"Carrier Ops" meant following the carrier and fishing out any pilots who went in the drink.

DESRON 8 was scheduled for nine days in Marseilles, France. The USS LAKE CHAMPLAIN (CVA 39) had already entered the harbor and berthed. We were at Special Sea Detail, so I was on the bridge as the captain's talker.

I don't remember the CHAMPLAIN's radio call, but suddenly over the radio in the pilot house, where people always spoke calmly, came an excited shout: "Teaball, the [LAKE CHAMPLAIN's call name] is on fire!"

I turned, and a few hundred yards across the harbor thick black smoke was boiling up out of the carrier's stern and rising hundreds of feet into the air in a plume that kept going higher. I don't know if we asked if they needed assistance or they radioed us first, but we were asked to go over and hose down their port side to cool the magazine. We put our bow a few feet away and played hoses on the hull — somewhat nervously at first, because only a few feet and the thickness of the LAKE CHAMPLAIN's hull separated us from the ordnance that threatened to provide Fourth of July fireworks a day early.

We were secured after 20 or 30 minutes and proceeded to dock. The citizens, by the way, were less than thrilled. Marseilles had elected a Communist mayor and the Frenchmen on the "Can o' beer" (Rue Canobiere) showed what they thought of Americans by spitting in our direction when we walked by.

Two weeks later, when we got into Valencia, I received a dozen or more back issues of the Cleveland Press, for which I had worked before I was drafted in 1955. The banner head in the July 3 city edition was to the effect that "CARRIER EXPLOSION IN FRANCE KILLS U.S. SAILORS." I hadn't known the casualty count. The story said three sailors and a French dock worker died when a launch into which they were offloading vehicles caught fire, presumably from spilled gasoline. We got a mention: "Firefighters from the U.S. destroyers aided the French fireboats.

I made a printout of the front page, but the only edition on microfilm was the home edition, and in that the fire had yielded to a Kremlin shakeup as the play story. It was still on Page One, albeit under a one-column head, and I reproduced it. I had forgotten the part about arriving at 3 a.m., but I'm pretty sure we stood outside the harbor until daylight.

It also seems that somebody on the LAKE CHAMPLAIN - I assume a JO (journalist) -- got a picture from the carrier deck of us squirting water and just about the whole crew except the snipes standing on deck watching. We used it as the title page of our Med cruise book.

For the benefit of crew members from other eras, the other ships in the squadron at this time were the USS JOSEPH P. KENNEDY JR. DD 850 (named after the brother of the future president), USS PERRY DD 844 and USS WARE DD865. Our radio call was "Teaball," and COMDESRON 8, who had his flag on the KENNEDY, was "Chariot GOLF. The WARE was "Wireworm" -- "Teaball, Teaball, this is Wireworm." (I'm sure you remember that GOLF was, as of 1956, the seventh letter of the International Pronouncing Alphabet we learned in boot camp. I can still signal ALFA-BRAVO-CHARLEY-DELTA-ECHO-FOXTROT-GOLF, but when I get to HOTEL-INDIA-JULIET-KILO you have to use both arms and I've forgotten.)

I was the co-editor, with Hal Rosenthal, of our cruise book, and with the indulgence of the webmaster I'd like to quote what I wrote on the last page, because it holds up pretty well:

With time, the details of the cruise will fade, leaving only memories, different with every person, because everybody chooses among thousands of impressions, good and bad, the ones he wants to remember.

But most people, being optimists in spite of themselves, will with the years forget the disagreeable part: reveille, and stew, and water hours, and chow lines, and all the irritations that people cause other people because they want to show their authority, or because somebody else gave them a hard time, or maybe simply because it's been a long cruise for them too.

And the things that remain will be: the black shadow of the mast slowly rocking across a sky of stars; and the sun setting gold and purple on the sea while the IC men wait to start the movie; and coming back to the ship, pleasantly shot down after an evening of wandering around town with the boys; and mail call, and rack time, and coming home, of course; but most of all just the guys, 279 of them counting officers (officers are guys too, deep down), who worked and loafed and ate and slept and wrote letters and sweated inspections and lived with you on the same 400-foot hunk of tin that was home.

And so, this book is dedicated to those 279 guys, in the hope that, in five or ten years, when life aboard the Johnston seems as hard to remember as life anywhere else seems now, they may look through it and say, "Oh, yeah, remember that bar in Palma?" or "I wonder whatever happened to old So-and-so," or even "We didn't have such a bad time then after all," which, when you come right down to it, is about as much as you can say about life.

It wasn't what I wanted to be doing at the time, but, more than 50 years later, I've got to say it: We didn't have such a bad time then after all.

THE JOLLY "J" AND I

HERMAN O. SUDHOLZ, LT (CDR USN RET)

Years on board the Johnston: 1959 to 1963

PROLOGUE - I guess my story starts at Princeton Univ. in New Jersey, which I was visiting during my senior year at nearby Lehigh University as a Civil Engineering student. Everyone was talking about what we were going to do concerning the military draft, as our college student exemptions would expire upon graduation. There were those who had 4 years of ROTC completed and whose future was pretty well spelled out. Then there were the rest of us who had had maybe 2 years of ROTC at most and not a clue as to what to do. I had done some crewing on sailboats on Long Island Sound and my family had a long history of Merchant Marine service, so a foxhole wasn't something I was looking forward to. One of the guys at Princeton said that he had applied for

162

the Navy Officer Candidate School (OCS) at Newport, RI where after 4 months you would graduate and serve 3 years as a commissioned officer in the Navy Reserves. Hey, that was a lot better than a cold, wet, foxhole, so I applied.

Not having heard anything from the Navy I took a job after graduation at the New Jersey Highway Department. In about October I was ordered to report to the infamous U. S. Army Induction Center on Canal St., New York City. The day I was to report, which I did, I received my acceptance to the Navy OCS with a start date of 3 January 1959.

So on what I thought was the coldest, wettest and windiest day in my life I reported for duty. I figured that I could take on almost anything for 4 months so I rolled with the punches when they came and kept my barracks, uniform, and nose neat and clean. Near the end of the 4 months we were all interviewed as to what type of following duty we would prefer. With a Civil Engineering degree I of course said I wanted to be a Seabee. "Sorry we aren't graduating any Seabees from this class". OK lesson number one from the assignment branch. Never ask for what you really want. So I pointed in the direction of the Destroyer piers in nearby Middleton, RI and said, "I'll take one of those."

Before graduation I received my orders to report to the USS Johnston (DD-821) as Damage Control Assistant (DCA) via 2 months at the Navy Damage Control, NBC Warfare and Firefighting School in Philadelphia. Little did I know that my OCS graduation date of May 1st would make me senior to all the Naval Academy and ROTC graduates who would not be graduating until 2 - 4 weeks later in 1959. Hey, seniority has its perks. - Like choice of upper or lower bunk, etc. up forward in "Boy's Town" where the Ensigns stowed their gear. We certainly didn't live there.

By the time I had finished with the DC School, etc. it was August and the ship's homeport had been changed to Charleston, SC. After graduation and with the prospect of a steady income I bought my MG and looked forward to tooling south to meet the ship. I arrived at about 8 PM on a Sunday evening and reported to the OOD who assigned me a bunk for the night and informed me that we were getting underway the next morning at 0800.

NEOPHYTE - I think I slept in as I was tired from the long drive south, but when I did get up I put on my new Service Dress Khaki and wandered up to the foc'sle to watch the getting underway evolution. I knew from my OCS training that I was supposed to visit the Executive Officer (XO) immediately upon reporting aboard. However, he wasn't aboard the previous evening and I thought that he must be pretty busy that morning getting the ship underway. The Commanding Officer of course spotted this unidentified officer on the foc'sle and asked the XO who he was. When the XO couldn't answer I was summoned to report to the bridge IMMEDIATELY where LCDR (later to become RADM) Stanley Fine let it be known that my conduct on board to date, all of about

10 hours, was totally unacceptable.

I don't remember where we went or what we did on that underway period but there were many and they all ran together as we were working up for a Mediterranean Sea deployment. I became acquainted with my division CPO and the other officer's on board. There was CDR Smith the CO; LCDR Stanley Fine XO; LT Dave Denton, Ops; LTJG Bill Brewer ASW: LTJG Gus Laskaris, Guns; LTJG Ray Burchell, CIC; LTJG Vito Giordano, First Lt.; LTJG Jim Muller, COMM; ENS Dave Asher, EMO; ENS Pat McCall, NAV; ENS Jim Person, MPA; ENS Tom Dewitt, Assist COMM- bachelors all, except for CO, XO, & Ops.

One of the thrills of becoming a "Destroyer Man" was to be able to time your step off into space at the top or bottom of a ladder and end up on the deck above or below without going up or down as the ship pitched. The other was to be able to sleep next to the outer skin of the ship, all 3/16" thick, and hear the waves pound the dents into the sides of the "Tin Can" we called home. I learned to eat standing up, drink mid-watch coffee, eat sandwiches days on end and at times never dry out. I also learned life lessons such as you cleaned up after yourself ("Snipes" topside if they spilled oil, etc), and you showed up early for your watch, and assumed responsibility for your own actions and decisions. I will confess here that I also had the most total, utmost respect and admiration for the engineers on the ship. I quite frankly I was terrified when in the engineering spaces. I always had visions of a high-pressure steam leak cutting someone in two. I was much more cut out to be the old-fashioned mariner and seaman on deck. Maybe that's why I ended by Navy career as I did 25 plus years later.

On 21 September 1959 we finally got underway for the Med. I was finally becoming mariner and a world traveler. Our first stop was in Rota, Spain for fuel – what else. I remember hearing the dockside locomotive with its high-pitched whistle like all European trains not the woo-woo of American trains. I said to myself, "I'm really in Europe". A group of us went to the Officer's Club for lunch. It was in the middle of an olive grove.

The standard routine in the Med at that time was to spend about 10 days at sea in exercises, chasing carriers, underway replenishment, ASW, refueling, and then spending 5 - 7 days in port somewhere in Spain, Greece, Italy, France, or Turkey. Ships seldom visited any northern African ports or Lebanon or Israel. Christmas and New Year's Eve would be spent in Naples, Italy.

LTJG Ray Burchell, ever the ladies man, somehow found out the names of four American young ladies who were dependents of US military officers stationed in Naples at the NATO headquarters. Prior to our arrival, and the in the logistics requirement's message the presence of the 4 ladies was requested on board for lunch on the day of our arrival. We picked the ladies up in the motor whaleboat and brought them across about 6 other identical tin cans in the nest for lunch. I don't remember too much about the lunch. Remember, I was still next to the bottom of the seniority pecking order and am not even sure I got a chance to talk to any of them. But I do remember going on the tour of the ship with them and suitably impressing them with our sophisticated weapons (Hedgehogs), Air and Surface Radar, Fire Control Directors, etc. Little did we know that LTJG Burchell had gotten their names from other ships who had all entertained these same 4 ladies and given them "the tour" so that they knew all there was to be passed out about the standard American Gearing Class destroyer. They were good sports though and didn't let on just how bored they were.

Speaking of being in a nest of identical DD's - it was always good fun to find out the morning after that you had spent the night on the wrong ship because your counting skills had been severely hampered the night before.

Standard routine in the Med was port and starboard watches so that as a minimum one half of the crew was always onboard. And that of course meant limited time available to spend with any new acquaintances. I was fortunate enough, however, to get to go to the New Year's Eve party at the NATO Officer's Club with one of the aforementioned ladies. I don't recall her name. One of the things I will always remember was that when it came to the obligatory Midnight kiss I was completely blown away by Cynthia. Cynthia also suitably impressed others although not necessarily kiss wise. LTJG Gus Laskaris even painted a picture of her after we left Naples. To my knowledge no one onboard ever communicated with any of the 4 ladies again. Love them and leave them. The wardroom theme song on liberty was the then popular song, "Your eyes are the eyes of a woman in love". Were we suitably impressed by ourselves or what?

We visited Piraeus and Athens and were there during the filming of the movie "Never on Sunday". I watched the fireworks scene from the foc'sle on one of my duty nights.

Two of my leading petty officers, SF1 Powell and DC1 Kuhrt were true married men and the best of friends. They never went ashore choosing to stay clear of the temptations. One night they did go ashore together but I don't remember what port it was. We were starboard side to and the brow was aft on the fantail and fairly level. I had the OOD watch on the quarterdeck at the expiration of liberty. Just before liberty expiration Powell and Kuhrt came weaving up the pier supporting each other just as good friends do. At the foot of the brow, first one then the other offered to let the other go first. The politeness continued and finally developed into a major altercation with punches being thrown on both sides. It took a full handful of duty personnel to separate them and get them put to bed. I don't remember which one was brought aboard first. They remained good friends but never went ashore again until Charleston.

Sometime that winter we ran into one hell of a storm that kept us from going where we were supposed to be headed. I don't remember where that was but we were on the windward side of the island of Sardinia, I think. Green water was coming over the bridge and all anyone could do was to hang on and minimize movement about the ship. At one point after we caught a huge wave on the port quarter there was a constant thumping back there and someone had to find out what it was before it tore up the ship. As DCA I was "nominated". I started out aft on the O1 deck on the starboard side. Someone was watching me from the bridge level – I don't remember who it was. I was about half way back to the Motor Whale Boat (MWB) when I heard the wave coming. I looked up just in time to see it coming over the bridge and I ducked behind the secondary con shield. After the wave passed who ever was on the bridge stood up and couldn't see me and started to sound the "man overboard alarm". I stood up just in time to prevent that. We laughed about that later, but if I had been washed overboard there is absolutely nothing the ship could have done to pick me up. There was only one safe heading for the ship at that time. It turned out that one of the MWB lashings had broken and was causing the boat to bang against its bilge shoe.

Sometime in mid-December President Eisenhower was making a trip across the Med from somewhere in North Africa to somewhere in Southern Europe. The Sixth Fleet ships were to be presented to him in a naval review with little advance notice. The entire Sixth Fleet hove to for a day in order to "paint half- a- ship" of only the side of the ship that was to be visible from the President's cruiser depending on the ship's assigned position in the review. We even rigged lights over the side that night so we could continue to paint the sides. The next morning the ships all lined up to pass by the Commodore for inspection. All passed inspection except one. I believe it was the USS Rush (My apologies if I have the wrong ship), which had painted the wrong side. There was no way it could be corrected because all the other ships were painted correctly. They spent all day of the review painting the "other" side to their ship. In today's world some commander would have stepped up and said, " No, the Fleet is too busy waste its resources on some stupid naval review. However, it was a different world then and priorities were different.

We had a hell of a good crew that I think enjoyed serving together. I know we in the wardroom liked each other and enjoyed working and hanging out together. One day while standing a bridge watch on a beautiful spring day, the sky was blue, the Med even bluer. There on the horizon was the American Export Lines, SS Constitution with a whole lot of people on board paying thousands of dollars for what Uncle Sam was paying me to do. Not a bad life. By now I had become a seasoned European traveler. These were the days when officers had to a wear a coat and tie ashore but in return the American military ID card was as good as any passport and gave you pretty much the right to roam anywhere and at times it got you out of trouble. By now I had been to Naples, Pisa, Genoa, and La Spezia, Italy; Thessalonica, Piraeus, Athens, Greece; Barcelona and Rota, Spain and Istanbul, Turkey. Places that I would never had had the opportunity to visit. I even met an American college girl who was a student at Chico State College, in CA. I took the famous Blue Train along the French Riviera from

Nice, in order to meet her in Marseilles, France. Cary Grant and Grace Kelly never had it so good driving along the magnificent Côte d'Azur and stopping for lunch in a little café overlooking the Med.

GOLD BRAID IS STARTING TO TURN GREEN - After our return from the Med and a 30-day stand-down, people got transferred and new people arrived. I guess we probably had at least a 30% crew and officer turnover. As part of the process, I was moved from DCA to First Lieutenant. In those days Ensigns got promoted, unless you really fowled up, to LTJG after 18 months of service. I of course got my promotion 1 month prior to the other Ensigns on board due to my earlier OCS graduation date. I enjoyed the extra half stripe for about a month.

Somewhere in here we participated in a North Atlantic NATO exercise off of the coast of Iceland. I remember that the new CO, CDR Bill Morgan, was eying the closeness of the Artic Circle and was looking for an opportunity to duck across so that we could all claim to be "Bluenoses". We were on our way one day when the radio crackled directing us to pick up some arresting gear from a USN Carrier and take it to HMS Ark Royal. No Bluenose certificate for the Johnston sailors. I had always heard terrible stories of how rough the North Atlantic was, but on this voyage we had absolutely beautiful weather.

At the end of the exercise we were given a 5-day port call in Portsmouth, UK. I took the opportunity to take the train to London, hop a plane to Bremen, Germany by way of Amsterdam, Netherlands. I got to meet my grandmother, aunts and uncle for the first and unfortunately last time. Never have I seen so many absolutely gorgeous girls than in the Amsterdam airport.

There was another exercise we participated in which involved finding infiltrating '"enemy" ships and involved merchant ships. Full darken ship was authorized which meant no night running lights. The different ships were all assigned a patrol area and we were to check out all ships in our respective patrol areas. One night I and the rest of the ship awoke to the sound of the Collision Alarm – a frightening sound at night. It seems that one of Johnston's OOD's got a little too zealous in checking out all contacts and we ended up bumping the destroyer in the adjacent patrol area. We lost some portside deck stanchions and got a few more dents in our side but the most significant damage was to the very front of the bow, which was bent about 5 degrees to starboard. That caused us to spend about a week in the Norfolk Naval Shipyard.

Once back in Charleston we started on our workup for the next Med deployment. One individual who reported aboard before our deployment was one whom I will always remember and admire. It was Boatswain's Mate First Class Anspach. He had come from the Presidential Yacht "Potomac" where he had been the leading boatswain. He was now my and the Johnston's leading boatswain. As a Division Officer I immediately backed off with my directions and left more and more to BM1 whom seemed to be everywhere and had a handle on everything. He also taught me a lot about basic deck seamanship. Those were lessons I carried with me during my entire Naval career. He was a spit and shine sailor who could be elbow deep in paint and brass polish all day and still look like he was ready for inspection. In my mind he was the individual most responsible for Johnston's reputation for the sharpest tin can in the fleet.

Once we deployed and arrived in the Med, we reported for duty to the Squadron Commodore. He commented. That's the sharpest looking destroyer I have ever seen". We could do no wrong after that.

SETTLING DOWN - In March or April of 1961 NATO celebrated its twenty-fifth birthday and Johnston participated in the Naval Review in the Bay of Naples. I remember it as a very long day on the bridge as all the US and foreign ships attempted to line up in a single column as ordered. Later that afternoon, after the review, we were scheduled for refueling. I don't remember the oiler's name but I do remember that we got in a little too close and we kissed her side and left our port anchor on her deck as we separated. I think it was the next day when we returned to visit Naples again for a week in port. For those who remember visiting the Med, smaller ships such as destroyers entered the inner port and did what is called a Med-moor. That is you back in to a breakwater or sea wall and the ship is held in place by mooring lines aft and an anchor or two forward. Mooring was made a bit more difficult that day as we had one less anchor.

HRH Queen Elizabeth had arrived in Naples onboard the British cruiser HMS Lion that was also in port. On the evening of our arrival, HMS Lion's commanding officer held a reception on board for senior officers in the area. Our CO, CDR Morgan attended. Also attending the reception was Cynthia and her mother. (Her father was away in Germany on NATO business). When she learned that the Johnston was back in Naples she left the reception early knowing that someone from the wardroom would phone. And as I had the good fortune to have the first night in port off, I did.

The following day I was assigned as the Beach Guard Officer at the Fleet Landing. A duty that I had for the entire time we were in port. That meant that I didn't have to stand any duty on board but had the 12 hour 7 AM - 7 PM duty at the landing every day. That gave me plenty of time to spend with Cynthia. Her parents were gracious enough to drive me to the Fleet Landing at about

6 AM where I'd catch a boat to the Johnston, shower, shave, and change uniforms for the next 12- hour shift at the Landing.   On some days Cynthia would come by and bring me sandwiches, etc.

During the day excursion ships to and from Capri, Ischia and Palermo would come and go from alongside the fleet landing.   Since they all used the Med-moor, stern in to the pier that meant that they had to spin the ship around and back in.   There was an old Italian in a small row boat who would row out to some point and the ship would come in heading right for him.   At the last moment he would row like hell as the ship dropped its anchor right where he had been, spin on the anchor and make a perfect landing. Fascinating to watch. He did that all day long.

After dating for about 56 hours Cynthia and I decided to get married. Now comes the hard part. As in all countries where the US has armed forces stationed there is an agreement between the counties called the Status of Forces Agreement.   In our case the defining agreement was between the US and Italy.   The agreement had all kinds of statements covering marriage between Italian citizens (girls) and US soldiers and sailors (men).   There was nothing that covered US Citizen Dependents of US Forces (Cynthia) and US Armed Forces officers (me).   We investigated all kinds of possible ways to get married, i.e. at sea by the captain of either the SS Constitution or SS Independence, US flag liners (nixed by Cynthia as those marriages are ruled by the laws of the ship's homeport, in this case New York and NY considers marriages at sea to be common law marriages and at best questionable): marriage by a chaplain on board Johnston during the forthcoming short trip from Naples to Gaeta (nixed by the US Consulate – Navy Regs say a marriage on board has to be witnessed by a Consular Officer and take place at least 3 miles off shore.   The

Consular Officer said his jurisdiction ended 3 miles off shore.) To add to the urgency, Cynthia's father was being transferred back to the States and retirement at the end of June.

Two problems to overcome were becoming clear; one was that I needed to get permission to marry from the chain of command. Our CO was all in favor and he forwarded my request up the chain of command. My request eventually reached ADM "Cat" Brown, CINCSouth (NATO) and ADM Anderson, COMSIXTHFLT. They forwarded my request to ADM Arleigh Burke, the CNO who referred it to the Chief of Chaplains and the Navy JAG. All these messages were sent with a copy to Johnston. I still have copies of all of them. The second problem was that we needed our "original" birth certificates. These would then be sent to the USA for the local Italian Consular official's verification, a process that could take 6 months or more. In the mean time Johnston's stay in Naples ended with no marriage resolution and we left for our next 10 days or so at sea.

While we were at sea an Italian lawyer who worked for the Naval Support Activities in Naples learned of our attempt to get married. He contacted Cynthia's father and told him that he could arrange for us to get married according to Italian law but that I of course would have to be present. Cynthia's father sent a message to Johnston stating the need for me to return to Naples. Our next port visit was Cannes, France. I called Cynthia's father by phone when we got in and he informed me that there would be a Navy COD (Carrier Onboard Delivery or mail plane) arriving in Nice the next day and that it would take me to Naples.

So I requested 3 days leave and sat on the mailbags to Naples. It wasn't until years later that I realized that I had left France and entered Italy illegally. When

I arrived in Naples I was informed that I would be getting married the next day in an Italian civil ceremony. It seems that the Italian lawyer found out that in lieu the original birth certificate, and for a slight fee, a judge would grant the permission to marry if 5 persons could swear before him that they were present at Cynthia's birth. And, for an addition fee, he would do likewise for me. Now it happens that Cynthia and I were born 6 weeks apart, one in Texas and one in New York. Cynthia's father went through his office and designated 5 "witnesses", and requisitioned a van to transport us all to the courthouse where the 5 witnesses swore to the judge that they were present at both Cynthia's and my birth. The judge issued a very official document, complete with stamps, signatures, etc. giving us permission to marry.

There was one other small issue remaining, I needed to be assigned for duty to a US military post in Italy. Fortunately after the morning session at the courthouse we went to the O-Club where I just happened to run into our squadron commodore. I told him of the problem and he promptly issued me verbal orders to report for temporary duty to NATO headquarters in Bagnoli (a suburb of Naples).

That afternoon, on the 6th of June, with the CO Naval Support Activities Naples, and the US Consul General of Naples present as witnesses, Cynthia and I were married in a civil ceremony by the Mayor of Bagnoli. Italy being a good Catholic country now considered us officially married. However, Cynthia still wanted a church wedding. That would have to wait. Fortunately, Johnston was scheduled back in Naples on the 26th of June. Schedules, however, were known to change. The next afternoon I again sat on the mailbags and flew back to Nice and Johnston.

Fortunately Johnston arrived back in Naples as scheduled. The Senior Watch Officer, Ops, hadn't made out an officers watch bill at the time of arrival and since we were still in a port and starboard rotation, I didn't know what duty section would provide my best man and attend the wedding. I didn't even know when or where the wedding ceremony would take place. Then there was the problem of swords. Could we muster up eight swords, enough for the wedding honor guard? Fortunately Cynthia anticipated that problem and had an American teenage boy, the son of another officer stationed at NATO, with instructions pinned to his jacket lapel and an armload of swords waiting on the pier when we moored.

With the problems of what duty section had off and which had the duty and with enough swords solved half of the wardroom officers went to the chapel (actually a Quonset hut with a steeple) at the Naval Air Station Naples for the wedding ceremony.

When we arrived about 10 minutes before the appointed hour there was no one there. Nada. Was I stood up? Naw, we already had the civil ceremony. About a half hour after the scheduled wedding time the chaplain's wife arrived with many apologies. It seems that Naples was experiencing one of its periodic traffic gridlocks and everyone was struck somewhere in traffic. She had come to be the organist for the wedding so she entertained us with songs like "She'll be Coming Around the Mountain When She Comes". Not funny. Of course I caught a lot of ribbing from my fellow officers for being technically stood up.

The wedding finally did take place and all present made our way to the NATO officer's club for the obligatory reception. As it turns out this was the day that Cynthia's parents were due to board the Military Sea Transportation Service (MSTS) ship for the return trip back to the states. When it came time for them to head for the pier, her father gave me a wad of Italian Lire in order to pay the club bill. After the reception Cynthia and I went to the pier to wave her parents off. A friend of her parents who were off on an R&R trip to Germany let Cynthia and I use their apartment in Naples for our honeymoon.

The Johnston left Naples and made the short trip up the coast to Gaeta, the new homeport for the Sixth Fleet flagship, where I rejoined the ship. Cynthia was left to fend for herself and find a way home. I still hadn't learned that a wife is a fiscal responsibility and I was to provide for her food and shelter. With her knowledge of Italian and the family friends still in Naples she did OK. She even traveled to Genoa, our next port of call. It was there that because of the weather that the carrier had a large number of crew stranded ashore when boating was cancelled. Our CO, ever the gracious host and while ashore, invited a number of aviators to spend the night on board Johnston. I had the mid-watch on the Quarterdeck when these flyboys came aboard with the CO. The CO gave one of them my bunk and told me that he would take my place in the duty section when I got off watch and I that I could go and spend the night, what was left of it, with my new wife in her hotel.

Well it seemed like a good plan, but when I got off watch and to her hotel I found that the hotel, as with most hotels in Europe, had a locked metal gate. To get in I had to wake the watchman who was sleeping in the lobby. That took about 30 minutes. Then I had to convince him in my best Italian that my wife was registered there. Another 15 minutes. Then I had to convince Cynthia that it was really I knocking on her door at 5 AM. I had to be back onboard at 7 AM so we had some breakfast in the hotel lobby café which opened at 6 and I went back to the ship not having had any sleep since 11 PM the night before. The "flyboy" in my bunk got to sleep late, as he couldn't get back to the carrier anyway. Thanks for nothing Captain.

Cynthia finally convinced the MSTS representative to let her work as a baby sitter on board a ship in exchange for transportation back the USA since as a dependent of an afloat person she was not entitled to MSTS transport. She lost that perk when she married me.

EXOTIC LANDS - After our next 10 or so days at sea Johnston visited Piraeus, the port city of Athens, Greece. From there we headed for an exciting time — two cool months, July and August in the Red Sea and the Arabian Sea gathering intelligence.

We transited the Suez Canal leading the southbound convoy. What was interesting was that while waiting for the canal pilot in Port Said, the canal authority hung this huge box from our bow. It turned out that this was a big lantern of sorts, which was controlled by an Egyptian sitting all cramped up inside the box. Since the transit would take the greater part of a full day and night he was in there during the heat of the day and at night. At the southern end they cut the box loose and dropped it with the man still inside into the water where it was retrieved to be used again.

Our first patrol area was in the southern Red Sea, an area about 20 miles long North to South which we were to traverse every 2 hours or so. This made our speed about 10 knots, the same speed as the prevailing wind. During the day the ambient temperature was just about 100 degrees and at night it cooled to about 85 degrees. The decks got so hot that one couldn't stand in one spot too long least the heat penetrate the soles of your shoes. There was a very fine dust that penetrated everything including the A/C filters, the electronic gear filters, etc. It was too hot to sleep below decks so many chose to move their mattresses topside on top of the hot deck. Note the wind speed was about 10 knots, that meant that when the ship was heading in the same direction as the wind there was no relative wind over the deck and the stack gasses settled over the ship. Once the ship turned and we had a relative wind over the deck one could usually sleep for those 2 hours. Of course you had to be careful where you placed your mattress to be sure that you weren't going to be shielded from the hot breeze every two hours. As I remember tempers got a little testy when the men who normally slept aft wanted to sleep up forward. Officers got to sleep on the 01 or 02 deck but space was really limited.

We got to visit Djibouti, French Somalia, and a dusty, port city in a much contested area of West Africa. The CO had requested the use of a car for the wardroom. Sure enough when we pulled in there it was, a bright red, 1961 Chevy Impala convertible with driver. Wow! We couldn't wait to arrive downtown sitting in the back of that set of hot wheels. Well there really wasn't any downtown and as it turns out all the taxis in town were red 1961 Chevy Impala convertibles. What a bummer.

After some more patrolling in the heat, our next stop was in Aden for fuel. Aden was a small city-state much like Singapore, back then it was a British Protectorate as there was no country of Yemen yet. One day the American Consul requested that Johnston take on board a couple of cases of hand grenades that were in the Consulate because as he put it "the natives were getting restless and there was a very real potential for an overthrow of the British Government". He was afraid that the grenades would fall into the wrong hands.

I was detailed to take the MWB to the landing with an armed boat crew plus a landing party of 6 Gunner's

Mates, go to the Consulate and fetch the grenades. I strapped on my trusty .45 Colt and we headed off to the landing. Although we were armed, the 5 - 6 block walk to the Consulate was uneventful. However, the walk back to the boat with 4 men carrying the two cases of grenades with an armed Petty Officer leading the way and me bringing up the rear, crowds started to gather. The hair on the back of my crew cut head stood straight up for the entire trip back. We made it back to the Johnston without incident, but I do remember that this is the same port in which the USS Cole got bombed 39 years later.

After some more patrolling we were sent to Bahrain, an island British Protectorate in the Arabian Sea. The ambient water temperature was 85 degrees and we had great concerns that the condensers wouldn't make sufficient water for the ship. But they worked just fine. When we arrived off of the British base of HMS Jufare we sent the MWB in to make arrangements for fuel, provisions, etc. The MWB didn't fair as well as the condensers. The engine overheated due to insufficient cooling from the hot water. The Royal Marines had to come and give us a tow to shore. There were a lot of red faces in the USN that day. We did get some liberty there and the sightseeing was interesting. The one thing I remember most is that unlike in the US where all motels, etc advertise, "heated pool", the pool at the Officers' Club was refrigerated down to about 70 degrees.

At the end of our 2-month tour in what is now known as South Asia we again transited the Suez Canal and headed home. Our westward trip across the Med, however, was interrupted by the discovery of a group of Soviet submarines also transiting westward. We were assigned to keep a close watch on them and gleam whatever intelligence we could from them. They kept us busy by their individual, random surfacing and diving trying to keep us from getting an exact count of how many there actually were. We also had to be sure that one or two of them didn't slip away. We didn't have any camera with a high-powered lens on board so I used the signalman's "big eyes" and made drawings of the subs that were then submitted to Naval Intelligence. The ship got a nice letter of appreciation for ingenuity. It turned out that the Russian's were moving a group of relatively obsolete subs from their Black Sea Fleet to their Northern Fleet and chose to keep the Sixth Fleet busy in the meantime.

At this time I also applied to augment to a regular, USN, commission instead of the USNR commission I had been granted at the end of OCS. This was approved later in the fall.

AN OLD SALT - Finally, one more sea detail and home. For the fist time I experienced the homecoming to loved ones waiting on the pier. An event I was to experience too many times again. As was usual we went into a 30-day stand-down with liberal leave and liberty. I of course took full advantage of this policy as Cynthia and I tried to make our little 3rd Floor walkup apartment into a home.

On Halloween night Cynthia and I, being newly weds, and have just returned from the Med had forgotten to buy Halloween candy. Since we lived in a 3rd floor walkup we figured that we probably wouldn't get any trick or treaters anyway. Never-the-less we turned off most of our lights and tried to make as little noise a possible. Suddenly there was this loud knock on our door. We didn't say or do a thing hoping that they would go away. Well they did. A short time later the phone rang. It was Bob my old high school buddy who was in town on his way North from Fla., having just finished his hitch in the Air Force. It was he who had knocked on the door earlier. Remember, no cell phones yet so he had to find a pay phone before calling us. He returned and we were having a good time when there came the sound of heavy footsteps on the stairs. Bob and I both figured it had to be teenagers up to no good. So he and I decided that I would fling the door open and he would rush out, grab the first one and fling him down the stairs. Well the plan worked, however, the guy Bob had by the scruff of the neck and was ready to throw down the stairs was the CO, CDR Morgan. The other "teenagers" were 2 to 3 other officers from the wardroom who had decided to harass the newly weds on Halloween. Thank goodness I stopped Bob in time.

On a November Sunday night at about 3:45 AM the phone rang and it was the duty officer telling me that the ship had bee ordered to get underway at 8 AM for the Dominican Republic and that there would be a car (one of the other officer's) to pick me and a few other officers up within 45 minutes. So for the first, but not the last time, I left my bride on short notice, for distant lands.

Since we were in a post deployment stand-down the most we could gather was about half of the officer's and crew. There would be no three-section watch standing. In addition we were missing some key personnel. We were asked to identify those that were critical rates and they were flown down to us via COD to the aircraft carrier and then by highline to us. They had an exciting trip. It turns out that there had either been a coup or an attempted coup and the Navy was ordered to make a show of force off shore in order to show our backing for one party or the other. A week later we were back home in Charleston without a shot being fired or troops ashore.

We knew that the ship was scheduled for a Fleet Rehabilitation and Modernization (FRAM) overhaul but we didn't know where or when. Orders finally arrived for the overhaul in Boston to commence on January 5th 1962 almost 3 years exactly to when I first reported for duty at OCS in New England.

Now plans had to be made on how to make the move to Boston. Most of the crew including the Captain had orders to detach for new assignments upon arrival in Boston. A core group of us the XO, now LCDR Howard Kay, and all the Department Heads would stay with the ship along with about 25 -30 senior enlisted personnel. As I had recently been promoted to Gunnery Officer I would get to stay too.

Cynthia and I decided that we would drive as far north as New York where I would leave her and the car with my folks and I would fly back to Charleston and return to pick her up once the ship got to Boston. We shipped everything we couldn't fit into the MG on Dec. 24th and the now pregnant Cynthia and I spent Christmas Eve sleeping on the floor. Christmas morning we started out hoping to get as far north as Norfolk were a group of Cynthia's old friends were to have a party to meet and hopefully approve of me. We found long distance traveling on Christmas Day very taxing. Nothing was open. Gas stations were few and too far between. The restaurants were all closed. We ate out of vending machines that hadn't been filled in a while at the few gas stations we were able to find. Now I know why there was no room at the inn. Everything was closed because it was Christmas. Well we rolled in at the party later than expected but intact and none the worse for wear. The rest of the move went as planned and I returned to Johnston for the trip to Boston.

Upon our arrival in Boston after a rough voyage the ship took on board a whole group of shipyard personnel and then headed back to sea for a day of sea trials and equipment checkout. I never understood the need for that as most of the equipment was to be either removed and replaced with new and better gear or completely overhauled during the FRAM conversion. For those of you familiar with Boston - it requires a very long Sea

183

Detail. Since the First Lieutenant had been transferred and I had until just recently been First Lt. I was stationed on the foc'sle. First for the trip in then for the trip out and then for the trip back in. It was and will always be remembered as the coldest, wettest day in my life. Due to the high-speed runs and rapid maneuvering required by the sea trials the foc'sle and a good part of the rest of the ship was covered with ice. We tried to take shelter behind mount 51 but the wind and water found us and froze us to the bone. There would be no medicinal brandy for us – it had been off loaded in Charleston.

The very next morning, those staying with the ship moved into our new offices on the top floor of a WWII wooded barracks building. We all got rooms in the BOQ as we were required to have a duty officer in the yard at all hours. Duty officers had to spend the full working day on board. All of us except the XO, who was now CO, stood watches.

Cynthia and I found an apartment in Cambridge and I took the subway, known as "The T" in Boston, to the shipyard everyday including weekends if I had the duty. Cynthia would take "The T" to her periodic pre-natal visits at the Chelsea Naval Hospital and after-wards stop by the shipyard were we would have lunch together. Our daughter Kristin was born there on July 17, 1962.

Sometime during this time I was sent to Weapons Officer and Nuclear Weapons School in Dam Neck, VA. They changed the title Gunnery Officer to Weapons Officer when the primary weapons on board were no longer guns but torpedoes, ASROC, DASH, etc.

During our period in Boston, the CNO put out the word that he wanted all ships to have some sort of quarterdeck display when in port. This should include a picture of the CO, something of its history, etc. The CO selected me for the task. Up until that time I never gave the history of Johnston a thought. I knew it was named for a WWII ship that had been sunk but that is all. Wow, was I off base. USS Johnston DD-557 was our namesake was probably the most famous and notorious destroyer in WWII. CDR Evans her CO was awarded the Medal of Honor for taking on a Japanese fleet of at least 4 battleships, cruisers, and destroyers and in the process end up sinking one of them before getting blown out of the water during the Battle of Leyte Gulf. For those who want to read more about the fabulous actions of the first Johnston I've added a list of books at the end of this story. The first Johnston was named after a Union Navy Lieutenant in the Civil War.

Our new CO, CDR Fay reported aboard in about September. Other officers and crewmembers had been reporting almost daily since mid-summer to fill out the ship's manning.

One day in October with about 3 months remaining in the overhaul we received orders to put to sea as soon as possible. President Kennedy and Russia's Nikita Kruschev had reached an impasse over the placement of missiles in Cuba. The shipyard went to work around the clock. The Supply Center sent all kinds of outfitting equipment and parts. Engines and electronic equipment were tested. We moved from the barracks building and BOQ back on board. There was only one-way military traffic through the shipyard gates – in. No one got to leave once on board. Cynthia got a neighbor, a Canadian naval officer, to deliver me my uniforms using my MG, which had a base decal on the window, and wearing my hat. They waved him right through. He got back out by putting on his Canadian hat - so much for shipyard security. I did get enough time off in order to take Cynthia and our 3-month old Kristin to the airport for a flight to California and her parents.

Our orders were to make the best possible time to Yorktown, VA to load ammo and then on to Charleston for fuel. Since we were going to stop for fuel in Charleston the CO allowed us to load a number of cars into the new hanger and on the new flight deck. My MG as it was the smallest and lightest car got to go. Three days after getting the word to sail, I as the new Sea Detail OOD got the ship underway for Cuba by way of the Cape Cod Canal.

The trip down was smooth and uneventful. The cars were unloaded in Charleston; we took on fuel and proceeded to Guantanamo Bay (GITMO) for Refresher Training (REFTRA). All civilian personnel and dependents had been evacuated and additional Marines brought in. Although still technically unqualified we took our place in the rotation of destroyers in the northern end of the bay for Naval Gunfire Support for the Marines should Fidel Castro decide to take them on.

REFTRA went well and a number of officers event got a chance to go ashore – armed. We got a tour of the base by a Marine and were suitably impressed by the preparations the Marines had made. There were bunkers, gun emplacements, barbed wire and tank traps all along the border with Cuba and even the downtown part of the base had machine gun nests covering each intersection. Nothing like a day sitting poolside at the Officer's Club with a cold Cubalibre (rum and coke) in hand and your carbine within easy reach along side your chair. War is hell. Cuban nationals were still running The Club having chosen to stay on the base when the gates to the town were closed. They had chosen very sparse quarters and US Marine protection on the base to Communist Cuba.

Later on when the threat of Cuban invasion had diminished some enlisted were allowed to go ashore. One night when I had the duty I was called to the quarterdeck by the OOD. Seems there was a completely nude person walking up the pier towards the ship. As it turned out he was a Johnston sailor who had gone ashore on liberty in a proper white uniform earlier in the day but lost it sometime, somewhere on the base. He of course has no memory of this and can't account for the loss of his uniform. I don't recall his name and even if I did I wouldn't relate it here. His uniform was never found or returned to the ship. Now remember there were no bars on the base except the Enlisted Club, no women, and took it place in the days before drug use became common place. It's puzzlement.

We did a hell of a good job at surface and shore gunnery completely destroying the target sled with plaster-loaded shells. The REFTRA gunnery observers gave me a picture of the destroyed sled to keep. That is a picture of it. The F-4 jets gave us fits though. The 5"/38 guns were designed in WWII for use against Japanese Zeros not 600 + knot jets. They were great against ships and for shore bombardment and continued to be so up through the end of the Vietnam War. I don't know why the Navy continued to make us train with them in the anti-air mode. Old ideas change slowly, especially in the Navy.

A couple of times our training was interrupted by the need to replace another destroyer, which had suffered a casualty on the barricade line of the island. One night while on patrol our radar picked up a high-speed target heading our way from the land. We knew the Cubans had PT boats. Was this one of more of them? We went to full speed and General Quarters (GQ). It was a fuzzy radar return and so we tried to get a Fire Control Radar lock, which we did but then lost it again. Fire Control acquired and lost lock on and off. Were we being jammed?

187

Sonar didn't pick up any noise from the unknown's direction. After about 2 hours of boring holes in the ocean we decided that it wasn't a PT boat and slowed down to a crawl back to our patrol station. It was a flock of birds that when flying close together gave a radar return but when further apart the return was lost.

Midway through REFTRA we were given a two-day R & R port call in Christensted, Virgin Islands. Half of the crew got off on each day. On my day off a group of us went into town early for breakfast. We found this neat rooftop restaurant overlooking the harbor. By the time we finished our breakfast it was getting hot so we thought that a couple of scoops of ice cream would sit nicely. We got our ice cream and the waiter inquired if we would like some topping. Sure some chocolate syrup, nuts, etc. would go well. He brought us a multi-tiered turn-about full of Virgin Island toppings - Crème de Menthe, Drambuie, Crème de Cacao, Kha'lua, Contreau, etc.

To tell the truth I don't remember anything of the rest of the day.

Christmas was to be a special time. Bob Hope and his troupe were coming to GITMO and we were scheduled to be in port. Unfortunately, another tin can conveniently broke down and we were sent back out to the barricade. Needless to say we all missed Bob Hope's show. Every so often I see old movies or pictures of Bob Hope in GITMO entertaining the troops. There, right behind the stage, is the starboard side view of the destroyer we had to relieve instead of Johnston. What a bummer.

REFTRA, which is normally 6 weeks long, had now gone on for about 10 weeks and we are only about half way through mainly due to the many requirements to serve as part of the fleet. We, therefore, were given another R & R port call in Kingston, Jamaica. On the way to Jamaica and while in the Mona Passage, between Puerto Rico and the Dominican Republic we were sent to the aid of a fishing boat that was taking on water. At about 8 or 9 PM the ship was sighted and a repair and salvage crew consisting of the DCA with a damage control party and I with a towing party, were sent over to secure and prevent the ship from sinking. We took a P-250, some hose, patching material, etc. The Captain of the ship, of course didn't speak any English so we more or less ignored him. That wasn't to be nautically incorrect or disrespectful, after all it was his ship, but to save him from himself as his ship was about to sink. All too often the USA gets a bad reputation for just rushing in and taking charge of a situation and ignoring the locals. That may be so in many cases such as this, but what the h___ we saved this guy's ship and maybe his life. What was keeping the ship afloat was the air in the cargo hold. The damage control team rigged the P-250 pump and started pumping. The deck force rigged a towline to Johnston and the MWB was towed astern of the fishing boat so as to be available as a lifeboat should that become necessary. After everything was stabilized and the ship was being towed to the nearest port, I went aft on the fishing boat to be the towline safety observer. I promptly fell asleep wrapped in my kapok life jacket.

When we got to port the next morning we wanted to drop the fishing boat's anchor. The captain would have none of this. According to him once the anchor was down he didn't have the capability to lift it up again as his winch was inoperative. Our take on this was, "He shouldn't be at sea at all". His ship was full of holes, and he had an inoperative anchor. He would be safer staying in port, so we let the anchor go and left him the P-250 pump. I hope he got enough gasoline for the P-250 to keep his ship afloat.

Because of all the time we spent actually patrolling and away from REFTRA, and thanks to the efforts of our XO LCDR Kay, Johnston crewmen got to wear the Armed Forces Expeditionary Medal for our time and efforts during the now famous Cuban Crisis.

Our return to Charleston was to be short lived. Do to all destroyers being needed again, this time to assist the submarine force in qualifying there new SSBNs to fire the new Polaris missiles. We deployed from Cape Canaveral where we loaded a tracking van onto the flight deck and monitored the underwater firing of the first of the "boat of the month club" submarines, the USS Thomas Jefferson (SSBN-618). I actually got to take a day trip on board the Jefferson. I can't say I was impressed. I never knew when we left the pier, submerged, surfaced and returned to port. No thanks I'll take a destroyer any day.

OLDER AND WISER - My time on board was getting short, I hadn't seen my daughter since October and I felt that I had learned as much as I could from my time onboard. I was ready to move on with my new Navy career and a shot at shore duty. In April of 1963 I packed my duffle bag, loaded the MG and saluted the quarterdeck for the last time.

CHARLESTON-BASED DESTROYER
USS JOHNSTON IS POLARIS AID

Unknown Newspaper, date late 1963
{Provided by: Herman Sudholz

Polaris problems at Cape Canaveral put a Charleston based destroyer in the spotlight in a test of an "instant tracking station" plan early in March.

The USS Johnston, commanded by Cmdr. Robert J. Fay of North Charleston, acted as a link between the Nuclear Submarine Thomas Jefferson and range operation and safety officials at Cape Canaveral.

In all 51 previous test firings from new Polaris submarines the specially-designed floating laboratory USS Observation Island did the work. But these tests were of 10 submarines within 32 months and the observation island does other Polaris research between submarine firings.

Starting in July or August, 18 new submarines within as many months are scheduled for testing. To take some of the workload off Observation Island but to avoid the expense of another such vessel, special instrument vans designed to fit on any helicopter deck were constructed. The Observation Island will be working on the advanced A3 Polaris model, and the new system will be sorely needed.

"The Johnston was selected as the initial test ship for the experiment because it was available." Cmdr. Fay said.

"The crew was briefed on the job before the Johnston left Destroyer Squadron Four here, but no physical preps was made until arrival at the Cape." Cmdr Fay said.

The vans were installed in 36 hours. The Johnston crew had nothing to do with operating them. A nine-man team of officers and enlisted men from the Navy's Fleet Ballistic Missile and Instrument Group at Cape Canaveral, experienced in work aboard Observation Island handled the actual work.

The test was a success as the missiles were fired. One, the second test missile to do so went haywire on surfacing and fell back into the ocean. The Johnston team was able to record the failure, helping to pinpoint the cause, where the shore-trace teams were useless.

The second was a success, zipping flawlessly to a target down-range. Submarine crews have no way of knowing what the missile does after it is fired.

DESTROYERS ARE NOW GETTING IN ON POLARIS ACT, JOHNSTON LEADS

Navy Times, date late 1963
Article provide by: Herman Sudholz

Charleston, S.C. - The destroyer Johnston has chalked up a first in the Navy's missile program. Skippered by Comdr. Robert J. Fay, she has successfully served as primary support ship during Polaris missile firing by the A-Sub Thomas Jefferson.

Previously only the specially-modified USS Observation Island was used in this role. The primary support ship acts as a communications link with the various Atlantic Missile Range Facilities and receives and records telemetry data on the missile before and during the firing.

The Johnston was modified for her "missile age" role through the use of relatively inexpensive portable instrumentation vans placed on the ship's helicopter deck.

With the Johnston successfully covering the Thomas Jefferson's missile launches the way is cleared for widespread us of "cans" in support of the Polaris project, freeing the Observation Island for other phases of missile development work.

Chapter 5

YEARS 1960 THROUGH 1969

TID-BITS by BATSCHE

By: David Batsche, Fire Control Technician (FTG2)

Years on board the Johnston: 1960 to 1963

I reported aboard as a SOGSN fresh out of sonar school in Key West Fla. Later on my hearing went bad and I was turned into an FT after going to FT school in Bainbridge Md.

In 1961 before the ship went back to the Mediterranean three of us (I don't remember who the others were) were sent to a Marine museum somewhere around Boston, the "Old Man" had a friend (retired Marine) who was in charge. We were told not to get into any trouble as no one on the ship would know anything about our mission. Well we picked up a 50 cal. Machine gun which ended up mounted on a tripod on the main deck forward by the bosuns locker in a very visible position.

My guess is someone knew we were going to go through the Suez Canal and end up in the Gulf in 1961 when there were hostilities. Way back then we had to forego our scheduled liberty in Karachi Pakistan. We were the only Tin Can over there with an impressive machine gun mounted for all to see.

On that same cruise somewhere around Sicily we picked up a Russian Sub tender and 5 or 6 subs. They were easy to follow as the tender was pretty slow, but the subs would dive and surface all day and all night. We would track them with sonar and on occasion run right over the top of them or how about cranking it up to about 25 knots and steaming right through their little formation! I suppose it could have been considered harassment?

My last little tid-bit is an add-on to Dwayne Mallast's Enemy Target story. On the way to Cuba in '62 I was an FT in the main battery director above the bridge operating the FT radar on condition 3 watch. The main ships radar picked up the "target" then the MBD swings around and acquires the same "target". I kept loosing it and had to keep telling the bridge "lost target" then "locked on and tracking" then "lost", etc. As it turned out in the scuttlebutt it was a SA or SN signalman who had the guts to remove the lens cover off the signal light and reveal the true "target as a flock of gulls". Also at the same time, the bridge still unaware of the ID of the target was trying to get permission from Washington to load the guns. This was taking some time and in the meantime they couldn't find the keys to the fwd magazine so they couldn't get to the ammo. Turns out a GMSN took a fire ax and broke the lock. Kind of like the old Chinese fire drill!

David reports that during the collision covered in the following newspaper article he was in

Fox division and their berthing department area was beneath the mess decks close to the impact. He says they had broken glass on the deck from all the shaving kits that had fallen and the collision alarm was a rude awakening that early in the morning. He also says the Chief's quarters were foreward of them almost to the boswains locker. He was told that several of the Chiefs were ejected from their bunks.

He says the sad part of the whole deal was the fact that the Captain's career was over. The Captain was asleep at the time but it seems he was still responsible.

2 Destroyers Collide, But No One Hurt

Appeared in the St. Paul Dispatch & Pioneer Press, St. Paul, MN. December, 1960
(provided by: David Batsche)

NORFOLK – Two Atlantic Fleet destroyers collided today while engaged in exercises off the North Carolina coast, but no one was hurt, Atlantic Fleet headquarters reported.

The destroyers, USS Johnston and USS Keppler, were participating in Lantex I-61, a large Atlantic Fleet training exercise when the accident occurred at 4:29 a.m.

The Keppler suffered only superficial damage, a spokesman said and is expected to continue with the training operation. The Johnston sustained some damage to her bow area.

He said, and has been ordered to proceed to her home port of Charleston, S.C.

There a determination will be made on the full extent of the damages, the spokesman said.

The Johnston, a 2,400-ton destroyer, is commanded by Cmdr. E.P. Smith, USN. The Keppler, commanded by Cmdr. E.L.Vitci, USN is home ported in Newport, R.I.

THE RACE

By: Richard A. Goodrich, Postal Clerk (PCSN)

Years on board the Johnston: 1960 to 1964

I reported aboard in 1960 as a Seaman Apprentice and started working with the deck gang. When we went to sea, I was transferred to the operations department as a quartermaster striker and stood watches on the bridge. At some point during that year, I was asked to take over the Post Office, which I did. I still stood QM watches while underway.

If my memory serves me right, I believe our captain was E.P. Smith, CDR.

While cruising in the Atlantic under EMCON conditions, we were hit by another Navy destroyer, the USS Keppler. Our bow was heavily damaged. We were boarded by the fleet damage control officer to access the damage. We were ordered by fleet commander to proceed to Norfolk for emergency repairs. This happened at 04:22 on Friday the 13th in January 1961.

Our captain was relieved of command and replaced by LTCDR William Morgan. He was promoted to full commander a few months later. He was the crew's captain. What I mean is that he laid out to the crew what he wanted and expected: exactly how the ship would run and operate. If all went according to this, we would all get along fine.

He was as proud of us as we were of him. He won a lot of divisional awards that year.

After returning from the Mediterranean, we were ordered to report to Boston Naval Shipyard. We needed permanent repairs of the bow damage and complete overhaul.

We were hurried out of Boston in October, 1962 due to the Cuban missile crisis. The ship arrived in Cuba mid-October and remained there until after Christmas.

We then proceeded to Charleston, our home port. The orders were to prepare for another seven-month Mediterranean cruise, including stops in Spain, France, Italy and Greece.

During our deployment, we also docked in Eregli, Turkey. While there, a friend and I stopped into an American school. The teacher was Miss Fay Destro. She expressed the desire to have an American flag for the school. We returned and discussed this with the Captain. He gave us a flag to present to the school on behalf of the crew of the USS Johnston. This photo is from the "Navy Times" magazine.

Upon our return to Charleston, a new captain took command. His name was CDR Robert J. Fay. In March, 1963, my daughter was born. The Chaplain and Captain asked if I would like to have her baptized aboard the ship in the ship's bell. I was elated and proud and accepted immediately. Photos of the event were published in "Navy Time" magazine.

BAPTISMAL BELL
PCSN and Mrs. Richard A. Goodrich watch proudly as Chaplain Robert E. Gordan baptizes their daughter, Paula Jean, from the ship's bell on board the destroyer USS Johnston, at the U.S. Naval Base. Cmdr. Robert J. Fay, skipper of the Johnston, looks on at the ceremony rarely held onboard a Navy man-o-war.

We made several more Mediterranean trips with many happy memories.

In one particular instance, a couple of days out of Charleston, the various squadrons fueled-up for the last time. One of our division ships called over and wanted to race home. The engineering officer told the Captain, who agreed to race. WOW! What bets we made!! Our engineering officer was LT Robert L. Daughenbaugh.

Unknown to the Captain, LT Daughenbaugh had called the oiler and asked how much fuel the ship we were racing

had taken on. He then calculated how much fuel we would need just to make it into port. We took on that very minimal amount. The next day, at sunrise, the race was on. The Johnston took a lead due to our lighter weight. At the entrance to the harbor, we were ahead. Proceeding up the Cooper River, past the Cooper River Bridge, we ran out of fuel. You can imagine the commotion that this incident caused.

This picture was taken right after the race. Left to right is myself, LT Daughenbaugh and on the right, Yeoman 3rd Class Steve Linehan.

APPENDICITIS!

By: William Rey, Seaman (SN)

Years on the Johnston: 1960 to 1962

I joined the Navy in June of 1959. After Boot Camp, I was stationed at Great Lakes for a year at which time I earned my Navy drivers license. After shore duty, I was ordered to report to the USS Johnston DD 821 in 1960.

We were on maneuvers off the Carolina coast when we collided with the USS Keppler. I believe it was January 13, 1961 around 0430 hours.

Later and after entering dry dock, I was ordered to the Quarter Deck in my dress blues. Man was I scared. They had discovered that I had a Navy driver's license. The rest of my time in dry dock, I was the sole driver used to transport the Captain and others to and from their different destinations. Here all my shipmates were standing fire watches while I sat in a nice warm car.

We were on a Mediterranean cruise about the middle of 1961. We were leaving Naples, Italy going toward Cannes, France when I came down with appendicitis. They had to take me back to Naples where I was transported to a United States Naval Hospital.

I was discharged in 1962 when the Johnston was in dry dock undergoing structural modifications.

The following picture is of the "Get Well" canvas that my fellow shipmates made for me.

I RECALL THE TIME.....

By: Wayne L. Morris, Shipfitter (SFP3)

Years on board the Johnston: 1961 to 1965

I recall the time about 1963, when I was sent to the Chief's quarters to remove some wall lockers (the rest of us had lockers on the deck, under our racks).   The lockers were welded to the bulkhead using angle iron. I was new at this, so I took the cutting torch and not knowing YOU CANNOT CUT A WELD I tried to cut as close to the bulkhead as possible. Soon after starting the cut, I saw daylight outside. I had cut a hole in the ship (ABOVE THE WATER LINE THANK GOD). I can't remember the Captain's name at the time, but during his change of command he said, "Morris, as I leave this ship, please don't cut anymore holes in it!" Ohhhhh yes, I remember it well, as I had to weld the hole shut, then grind it all down, so they could x-ray and pressure test my welding.

The moral of the story is cut in front of the weld and grind the weld flush with the bulkhead. My boss at the time was SF1 Harold Taylor and he was tough.

MAN OVERBOARD!

By: Bill Ismer, Boatswain Mate (BM3)

Years on board the Johnston: 1961 to 1965

I was born and raised in Pittsburgh, PA., educated in catholic schools and joined the Navy at age 17. After attending a cold great lakes boot camp in the winter of 1961, I was assigned to the USS Johnston DD-821. While in boot camp after an aptitude examination I was interviewed by a salty Chief who said: "Looks like you should go to electronics technical school."

I said, "Sir, what would Errol Flynn want to be in the Navy?"

He responded with passion "A boatswain mate, the last of the right arm ratings like me."

I told him, "Sign me up for that, I want to be a real sailor." Next thing I knew I'm driving a security vehicle in Bayonne, New Jersey. The Johnston, my assigned ship was on a cruise and I had to wait for its return. My strongest memories of that time are of seeing the Statue of Liberty each morning from my bunk and the large rats that roamed the old piers at night.

It was now 1962 and I was learning my trade on our ship as a boatswain mate learned to chip, grind, wire brush, prime and paint everything that did not move. The ship was undergoing a complete overhaul. The Navy called it a Fram 1 conversion and it was amazing to witness and be a part of it firsthand.

The entire ship's main deck upward was removed and once exposed the steam turbines, boilers and reduction gears were rebuilt. The main deck upward was replaced with aluminum and welded to the steel main deck. Since that time I have been told by professional welders that you can't weld these two metals together. However, I witnessed the process many times and the weld would later prove to be strong enough to hold together in the North Atlantic during a horrific (walk on the bulkheads) storm. During our stay in Boston I met a girl in the Boston common park, downtown Boston. The night before the ship was to leave Boston on our shake-down cruise in Cuba; I was with this girl and woke up late. I knew that missing ship's movement was a court marshal MCMJ violation.

Stumbling out of the hotel in downtown Boston I found a cab and immediately gave him whatever cash I had and pleaded with him to get me to the ship ASAP! He was an excellent high speed driver; we slowed only slightly at the main gate where a compassionate marine allowed the cabbie to drive me directly to the pier. The gangplank was up and the lines were being pulled unto the ship when I made a lunge onto the ship. Errol Flynn would have been proud because that was a close one.

The Johnston was now very fast, the removal of the weight of the original steel superstructure and rebuilding its power plant produced at flank speed a rooster tail almost as high as the superstructure. During the shake-down cruise after correcting a vibration in one of the propulsion shafts, we were able (as I recall) to run 36 knots and that's faster than many modern ships that are in the Navy today. This I learned during the Johnston navy reunions where old Johnston sailors were allowed to visit current Navy ships and ask questions.

Upon arrival in Cuba we found ourselves in the middle of a showdown between the USA and Russia. The Cuban Missile Crisis according to some experts would bring the world closer to World War III than at any other time during our history. The Johnston would be the recipient of a Presidential commendation and the crew a special metal for our involvement in repelling the Russian ships during this world crisis.

After Cuba we spent some time in the Caribbean and after that in 1963 we headed for the Mediterranean and Black sea. I was assigned to lead the forward refueling/replenishment station. I enjoyed it because the waves would sometimes crash over us and we were always working on a wet deck and it was very challenging. During one of our replenishing details the cargo net snagged on a stanchion and boxes of meat started falling into the Atlantic Ocean. I jumped into the net and started throwing boxes to my deck crew. One of the hooks became lose and I handed it to Seaman Rensell at that exact time the ships separated slightly and the hook snagged his lifejacket tossing him into the air toward me. I was able to grab a stanchion with one hand and the back of his life jacket with the other. However, he weighed about 200 pounds and his life jacket was wet. It seemed like slow motion as he slowly slipped out of my grip and started falling two decks toward the fast moving ocean. He entered the water directly below and emerged at mid ship with a lot of splashing and hen he was gone. I pulled myself onto the deck and requested that the emergency breakaway signal be given to the supply ship. The bridge denied the request citing that a following ship would pick him up. I remember thinking that our screws would probably suck him in or the cold water would be equally fatal. However, we received a message a short time later that he had survived and had been picked up by the following ship. We had fun high-lining him back. I remember him saying he could feel the pull of the screws and swam as hard as he could to get away from them.

The Johnston was the first US Navy ship to enter the black sea with nuclear weapons onboard and the Russians were not happy about that. We had the new ASROC system (Anti Submarine Rocket) and a modern version of that system is still in use by our Navy today. The Russians assigned two of their warships to shadow us and they were always within our view. We would enter a port and those Russian ships would remain waiting for us when we went back out to sea. I guess Captain Fay had finally had enough because at one point he ordered the Johnston to turn around and head directly toward them. The Russian ships maneuvered close to each other and our rooster tail was on full display as we closed the distance very quickly toward them. We passed between them close enough to see the face's of the Russian sailors as we threw rotten potatoes in their direction. Their ships were older and the Russian sailors were frantically covering their WWII weaponry. I don't think they followed us anymore after that incident.

First Division, first class petty officer Curtis created a competition between myself, a mere BMSN with an excellent crew to be responsible port side of the ship and Larimore BM3 an his deck apes on the starboard side. This competition involved our crews maintaining one half of the appearance of the ship and all that it entailed. Curtis enjoyed this highly spirited competition that on more than one occasion resulted in physical altercations while on liberty.

During this time of my life I was very agile and strong, I volunteered for every challenging assignment. Being able to ascend a rope climbing like a monkey with my hands only was a valuable asset. One of my favorite jobs necessitated the climbing of the wet motor whale boat divots to launch the boat in heavy sea conditions. Another was diving from the bow of the ship and swimming to a sea buoy, climbing the razor sharp barnacle clad buoy and engaging our mooring system to the sea buoy.

The Johnston also engaged in some racing. I recall being ordered to remove the wind resistance canvas from between stanchions during one such race that we eventually won.

After a kitty cruise of almost four years, my enlistment was over and my Errol Flynn adventure would come to an end.

Shortly after my discharge, I would see a Hollywood movie titled the "Bedford Incident" and in that movie they showed the actual activation, duel key protocol and firing of the ASROC. I was aware of these things because of being one of a handful of security cleared armed guards for that weapon system.

Many years later I would see the Johnston again one more time. She was visiting Port Everglades in Fort Lauderdale. It was quite a thrill for me to walk her decks again. Of course, the port side of the ship still looked the best.

I am writing this account 45 years later and recalling this time of my life is still exciting to me. It was an amazing time. I would go on to have a 30 year career in law enforcement achieving the rank of Captain and retiring in 1995. In 1998 I was living in my condo on the beach in Juipiter, Florida. I was jogging, swimming and riding my bike daily when suddenly awakened in the middle of the night with a massive heart attack. My heart was severely damaged and I spend most of 1999 in the cardiac care unit of Tampa General Hospital awaiting a life saving heart transplant. When the gift of life arrived, my heart, I gave it away when my favorite nurse agreed to marry me.

Nurse Debbie and I have now been married almost 10 years and have been blessed in every aspect of our lives.

A CUBAN EXCURSION

By: Duane Mallast, Radarman (RD3)

Years on board the Johnston: 1962 to 1964

The night was warm and we had been on station for a couple of days. Our station was on the Southern coast of Cuba approximately 25 miles off the coast. The radar picked up a contact coming at us from the coast of Cuba. It seemed the contact was extremely small and at first was thought to be a glitch in the radar. The contact continued to close on the Johnston though.

General Quarters was called to have all stations manned and ready at approximately 22:30. A dispatch was sent to the Guantanamo Bay Base, stating our situation. With the contact continuing to close, with a speed of 15 knots, the Captain turned the Johnston towards the contact. As the contact came within 200 yards of the ship, radar lost contact. The lookouts were trying very hard to pick up movement in the water. Flashes of light were thought to have been seen, but nothing confirmed. Being it was night and having an overcast sky, it was very hard to see any movement on the water.

General Quarters was not secured but relaxed for the moment. Our previous heading was resumed. Then radar reacquired the contact at our stern; the contact was turning and setting a course to follow us. Tension was very high through out the ship. The Captain turned away from the coast and tried to acquire the contact visually with the lookouts and other personnel on the bridge. But this time the contact was doing a much better job of staying out of our way, turning before we could get close enough to try for identification.

This continued on for approximately three hours as we played cat and mouse with this contact, never really getting real close to the contact. When we were approximately 50 miles off of the coast of Cuba and again closing on the contact from its stern, all of the ship spotlights were put at the ready, when we again closed to within 200 yards and lost contact on the radar. All of the spot lights were turned on to get an identification of the unknown contact.

To the amazement of the Captain, and all of the crew, the Johnston had been at GQ for the past three hours chasing a very large flock of birds that appeared to be seagulls. A dispatch was sent to Guantanamo telling them what had been identified and that we had secured GQ and were returning to our station.

MY JOHNSTON STORY

By: Gordon Adams, LTJG

Years on board the Johnston: 1962 to 1964

I arrived at Charlestown Naval Shipyard, Boston (the former NSYBSN) in July of 1962. The Johnston was completing her FRAM II process and the ship was a mess. The engineering officer, whose name I can not recall, was probably working harder than any other person, officer or enlisted. He was putting in 14 hour days routinely, mostly in the form of paperwork. One Monday we arrived at the ship offices and his desk was bare. We were all tremendously impressed with all the work he had to have done to finish all those forms. When in fact, he had actually deep-sixed them, thus freeing him up to actually spend time on the ship to make sure the work was been done properly. Sadly and not really surprisingly, I think he said he received one reminder from Buships that he had neglected to file a certain report. His seven page letter of resignation was a scathing denunciation of how the Navy worked, or did not work. Sad for the Navy, he was such a good officer.

I was OC division officer which meant our men bunked down in a compartment near the stern. One morning, RMCS George Bogle, whose naval experience placed him far beyond salty, came to me saying that the deck hatch normally in the compartment was ready to be reinstalled. Problem was it was a hatch which was not flush with the deck. Rather it stuck up probably four or five inches. It was a nasty thing to be in a man's way coming off watch at 0400 in some kind of sea.

Chief Bogle did happen to mention that there was a flush deck hatch in plain sight in a storage area next to ours, probably belonging, as I remember to another ship in our division. Of course I expressed hot outrage that OUR hatch had found its way into another ship's storage area, so the chief and I put on our dress whites and both of us had clipboards which made us look official. We gave the seaman guarding the area an official looking chit, expressing our embarrassment that their hatch had found its way onto our ship. The exchange was made and the guys in OC division had one fewer distractions to life below the fantail.

Later on as we steamed from the shipyard enroute to our homeport of Charleston, SC, the ship transited the Cape Cod Canal. Impressively the student body of the Mass. Maritime Academy had been lined up to salute one of their graduates our captain, Commander Robert Fay. We rendered honors to the school and they responded. It was impressive to a young JOOD on the bridge.

It was not at all impressive the noise we heard all over the ship as all sorts of gear went flying as we steamed through some weather while approaching Norfolk. The noise from the mess decks was impressive, since a large part of the crew had come aboard during the yard period. It sounded like everything except the smoke shifter had gone adrift.

After leaving our homeport, we arrived at Gitmo at the beginning of October, 1962, at the height of the Cuban Missile Crisis. As Comm Officer I was reading the AP wire and the news was disturbing. When I asked the Captain about it he told me to relax that everything was under control. Turns out he was very wrong. I read a book recently and it said that the Russians had a nuclear-tipped guided missile targeted on Guantanamo Bay. The author of the book states that in his estimation the world was about 45 minutes away from WW III. WE were that close to being vaporized and did not know it.

We had an electronics officer aboard whom the navy had put through college, where he majored in physics and Russian. Gary Burdick was an interesting person and most intelligent. His idea of fun was tuning our radars. Accordingly, we were assigned to sail to a certain location off Cuba, where we sailed a five mile or so square for a period of a couple of weeks, keeping an eye on the U-2 planes flying over Cuba.

During that period some stewards and bosuns mates got bored, so they got a grappling hook which happened to be bated with some steak probably pilfered from the Officers Mess, and went trolling. They hooked what looked to be a twelve foot long shark which thrashed about for quite some time before it gave up the ghost. I am assuming that the chiefs got the best cuts from that unlucky shark. The officers if I remember correctly got the fins for soup or something.

We were steaming at flank speed back to Gitmo and all over the ship the officers and crew were watching movies, when the GQ alarm went off. We secured the movie watch and went to general quarters. There was a sizable contact matching our course and speed about five hundred yards to port. Mr. Burdick's well-tuned ANSP-29 radar was working to perfection. After a while, the captain secured us from GQ and the movie watch proceeded once more. A few minutes later the alarm went off again. Same story same plot. I suggested to the Captain that we put a signal light off to port to see what was there. The suggestion was rejected out of hand. What would some green Ensign know? So I suggested the same idea to the OOD, Lt Sam Knox and he suggested it to the Exec and he suggested it to the Captain. Following the chain of command, the Captain agreed that it was a good idea. SM1 Wall, put a light off to port and we all could see a large flock of sea birds having fun with us.

I had the deck in port on New Year's Eve, 1963, when we were the fourth ship in a nest of destroyers, when some very tipsy deck people came on board with their whites bulging with bottles allegedly filled with milk so they would have good teeth. Young Ensign that I was I could not believe the story so I sent them packing with instructions to get rid of the bottles.

Some time later, the messenger of the watch noted some activity on the pier. I strolled to the bow staying in the shadows. The sight was most impressive. There were about a half-dozen enlisted deck men, so far gone they could hardly stand up. Drunk as they were they managed to get over a messenger line to an accomplice they had placed or located on the ship. Then a heavier line followed and they managed to set up a land to ship high line. I sent the messenger to the bow where he swears he collected all the bottles and gave them to me in a bag. I placed the bottles in a safe which was not intended for such use and the next day I happened to mention to Chief Bogle that some bottles of whiskey had come into my possession during the previous mid watch. I told Bogle that it was too dark for me to recognize any of the perps, noting that their training had enabled them to do the transfer while fall-down drunk. Such training, I opined, should not be overly punished and the chief agreed. Who knew, maybe at some point in the future I myself might have to be high-lined to another ship. The members of the chief's quarters were happy to receive the loot when we tied up in Charleston. I assume they gave away the whiskey as Christmas presents since there was not a drinker in the bunch.

Another story from Gitmo illustrates how our enlisted sailors handle a less than adequate officer. Our Engineering Officer, a ring knocker was not at all respected by his men. As JOOD I did not look forward to standing watch when he was OOD underway. He seemed to get by on his BS rather than any solid knowledge and understanding of how to react in a fully professional way to any kind of out of the ordinary event. His men must have seen the same thing. So when we were going to go into the fueling pier which had a dead end, that officer convinced the Captain that he could take the ship in at full speed and then back down thus impressing the brass which was apparently waiting on the pier.

We did go in at twenty knots, and when we gave the emergency back full bells, any informed observer could tell that the snipes manning the ahead and astern throttle wheels were kind of sleeping. We hit the end of the pier probably moving at about five knots and the Jolly J forever after wore the noticeable dent in the bow from that event. And the event was observed by a couple of four stripers and a Rear Admiral. I am now wondering if that officer himself went on to become an Admiral?

After our 1963 Med tour was complete and our DesDiv Four was steaming back to Charleston, the Commodore decided we should have a full-power race for one hour. Of course all ships came up with significant amounts of money and bet on the event. The evening before the race all ships refueled as required. The evening and early morning were really exciting. There was a rumor that one of the ships was sporting a couple of fuel injectors (I don't recall the correct term.) sized for a heavy cruiser's boilers. On the Johnston, we put the electrical load onto the emergency diesel generators and removed the limit controls on the forced draft blowers. At the appropriate hour, the four ships were steaming at standard speed, a thousand yards apart in line ahead. As the signal flags came down we turned ninety degrees to starboard and went to flank speed.

An interested observer could indeed see tremendous amounts of black smoke coming out of the stacks on one of the ships. The Johnston of course was emitting a regulation light brown haze. Our surface search radar picked up a large contact directly ahead and it turned out to be a commercial ocean liner. And for the first and only time in my bridge experience on the Johnston, that commercial ship acted as if there were actually a person standing watch on the bridge. It started making a lot of smoke and made a one hundred eighty degree turn. Boy was that fun for a young ensign to see.

The Johnston won the race of course and we lead the parade up the rivers into Charleston. As we tied up at the pier, everyone noticed something strange. The Johnston was about four or five feet higher in the water than the other ships. Rumor going around the ship had it that the Captain or someone else had figured out just how much oil we would need to get back to Charleston at the speed we would be making and that was how much oil we took on. Cheating? Or just a captain who thought like a war-time commander?

Sadly, Capt Fay was transferred to Viet Nam where he was killed in action shortly after arriving there. He did know how to handle that ship. On our way to Norfolk one time, it was so foggy that we could not locate the harbor pilot even though we were in contact on the harbor net. Capt Fay just sighed and said he would take us in on his own steam. And he did it by memory getting sightings from the navigator. He put us into the correct nest and secured us for evening mess and liberty. Just as cool as could be!

God rest his soul.

SHORT BUT MEMORABLE

By: Tony Ferraiola, Gunnersmate (GMSN)

the 2nd Div. gunnery.

Year on board the Johnston: 1962

I was on the Johnston crew for a very short time. She was just about done with the FRAM modifications and we were living in the barracks. I never got the chance to go to sea on her. I was close to being discharged and my ship The USS Boston was about to depart for a Med cruise so they transferred me to the Johnston for a few months until my discharge. I was assigned to

MY FIRST UNDERWAY WATCH AS A REAL OOD

By: Jack Hughes, LTjg (LCDR, USN Retired)

Years on board the Johnston: 1962 to 1965

In late May of 1964, the USS Johnston departed the destroyer piers in Charleston, SC loaded with a couple of dozen midshipmen from the Naval Academy and various college NROTC programs for a three-month deployment in the sunny Mediterranean Sea. Unfortunately for both me as MPA and our very freshly relieved skipper, Cdr. Robert Pringle, we go underway four hours late and on only one shaft. We had been unable to raise vacuum in the after plant and the skipper was not happy. Neither was our newly minted chief engineer, Lt. Bill Griffis. Last on the unhappy list was me because I was at the end of the line for all the stuff that was coming downhill.

Finally we discovered that the after fire and bilge pump was still running on compressed air as it typically did in port and shore power. That pump exhausts into the condenser which was why we could not pull a vacuum. Once all was set right, we cranked her up and went flying after the rest of DesRon 4.

That is not the story but instead sets the tone for the story: the skipper was new, the engineering officer was new and, still an ensign, it was only in the past week had I been qualified as a Fleet Operations Officer of the Deck. I had yet to stand my first underway bridge watch as the OOC.

Our squadron Operations officer enjoyed exercising the troops with weird maneuvers and formations and usually got really weird on the mid-watches. As I worked and fretted my way through the first few underway watches, I noted that the new skipper seemed to spend a lot of time on the bridge during my watches.

About the third night out, my turn for the mid rolled around. I duly relieved and started mentally preparing for a night of thrashing around in the ocean. When I relieved, we were in a bent screen about a mile ahead of the flagship, DD-940, the USS Manley. We were directed into various formations as the watch proceeded and at about 0230, after successfully executing several course and position changes, I thought I was holding up my end pretty well. I secretly wished the skipper would come out and observe what a fine job his newest OOD was doing.

About the time we received the next maneuvering order from the Manley, I was experienced enough to do maneuvering board problems in my head using the center line pelorus as my board in case we got a quick "Execute" order and wanted to be ready with a rough course to be fine turned by the wizards in CIC. I could not believe what we had been ordered to do and called CIC: "Combat, bridge. Confirm stationing course 165 degrees."

"Bridge, combat. Combat recommends stationing course 168 degrees."

As I was moving toward the voice tube into the Captain's cabin to advise him of the position change, I simultaneously heard the rear hatch of the bridge open. The quartermaster then announced the Captain's presence on the bridge and the "Execute" order from the Manley. If there was ever a time to ignore a maneuvering order, this had to be it, skipper on the bridge or not. What the Squadron Ops Officer had unwittingly done was order each ship to the position 180 degrees from its existing position and ordered the maneuver "Expedited". IN THE UNDERSTANDING OF AT LEAST SOME OF THE OTHER OODS, THAT MEANT DIRECTLY THROUGH THE FORMATION, THE MANLEY AND EACH OTHER!

The skipper, of course did not know this. "Officer of the Deck."

"Yes, Sir."

"Did I not hear a maneuvering order executed as I came on the bridge?"

"Yes, Sir. You did."

"Can you tell me why you have done nothing?"

"Yes, Sir, but you will understand the situation more clearly by a look into the radar repeater."

Captain Pringle was a very large man given neither to temper tantrums or swearing unless circumstances required. Evidently his was one of the times. He was moving toward the overhead R/T handset when the OPS officer's voice came over the speaker inquiring as to our intentions and (sarcastically) whether the skipper was on the bridge. The Captain grabbed the handset and shouted: "This is TAMPICO'S Charlie Oscar. Our intentions are to standby and rescue survivors. TAMPICO out!"

After a very short delay, the order came to cancel the maneuver and return to our previous stations, which, of course, we had never left. The Captain climbed into his chair, still fuming. The bridge crew returned to the usual night-time fog. We were then advised that practice was over for the night. After the discussion between the

Captain and the Commodore the next day, we had no more practice until the return trip three months later.

In a little while, Captain Pringle called me over close to him and said quietly, "You're fairly new to this aren't you?"

"Yes, sir. This is my first mid-watch as an OOD, but I've had a lot of recent conning time under the other OODs."

"Well, for an experienced officer, you did very well. For a first timer, you did remarkably. I guess we are in good hands."

A few days later we were scheduled for a routine refueling, mail drop and maybe exchange with the INDEPENDENCE (CVA-62). Captain Pringle called me up to the bridge as we went into the standby position. I reported and he said to me very matter of fact. 'You're taking us in."

"Me Sir?"

"Yes, you. This is what you need to know. At 600 yards, you want the carrier's stern light at 3 degrees relative to course. At 300 yards, you want it 6 degrees. When our bow passes his stern, cut power to replenishing speed. You'll coast into perfect position."

That is what I did and that is exactly what we did. Once we were hooked up and transferring, he said, "If you need me, I'll be in the sea cabin. Let me know when we cut loose." And he walked off the bridge.

I was two weeks away from the promotion to LTjg.

PRESIDENT KENNEDY SHOT!

By: Terry Nelson, Sonarman (SOGSN)

Years on board the Johnston: 1962 to 1963

I was on board from August of 1962 until Dec 23rd of 1963. I was an SOGSN when I was separated on Dec 23rd 1963. I can only think of one event that stands out as "unforgettable".

The MED cruise was quite interesting. We sailed from port to port and did our sea duties. We were sailing just outside of Cannes, France and I was on watch with another Sonarman. As I recall, it was about 2100 hours when we got the word; "President Kennedy – Shot and Killed!" Obviously we were stunned. We could not believe what we were hearing.

In those days we didn't have ready access to the news while at sea. After a few days of not hearing any more about the event, our lives went back to normal.

SOCCER IS ROUGH!

By: Benny Ricketts, Boatswain Mate (BM3)

Years on board the Johnston: 1963 to 1965

Prior to joining the Johnston, I served aboard the USS Forrest B. Royal (DD-872) stationed in Mayport, Florida.

The biggest story while I served aboard the Johnston happened during a Med cruise in which we sailed the Black Sea and visited Turkey. The Johnston had a soccer team

and we played the Turks at several different locations. The biggest event at one of the games involved me playing. While I was playing, I broke a Turk's leg when I went to kick the ball and kicked the Turk in the leg by accident. I broke his leg! I felt really bad about it.

We also kept eye on one of the Soviet ships that was DIW "dead in the water". While watching them, we kept doing crazy things to aggravate them.

WHEN THE DRAFT BOARD COMES CALLING!

By: Charles Copeland, Machinist Mate (MM3)

Years on board the Johnston: 1964 to 1968

I enlisted into the Navy in July 1964 at age 17. After bootcamp, I went aboard the USS Johnston DD-821 in October 1964. The Johnston was on a Mediterranean cruise from January '65 to June 65. One day sometime in April or May as I recall, we had mail call and I received a letter from the United States draft board to register for the draft. I though it was kind of funny. I guess this happened to a lot 17 year old sailors. When we returned to Charleston and I went on leave, I went directly to the draft board and had things squared away.

ABOARD THE "JOLLY J"

By: John Boltik, Fire Control Technician (FTG3)

Years on board the Johnston: 1964 to 1966

Fresh out of "A" school as an FTGSA, I reported aboard in April, 1964. Like all new 'boots' I spent the first months aboard compartment cleaning and mess cooking.

I remember my very first trip out the Cooper River – it was hot and I was compartment cleaning, and yes, I got seasick and hurled on the compartment deck! We had not even been under the Cooper River Bridge yet! But that was the one and only time I ever got sick on the ship!

Some of the memorable cruises included the Med and of course the Caribbean.

I remember going to the Dominican Republic to remove American citizens sometime in 1965 or thereabouts. We also did rescue off Cuba when we were in Gitmo - we picked up some refugees in a small boat one night. We also went to Cyprus to evacuate folks when the Turks and Cypriots had a big disagreement.

I remember one plane guard incident in the Med when a sailor walked off the flight deck of a carrier – Intrepid or Shangri-La (don't remember which one). Anyway, it was a calm night and the sea was flat as glass. We got the call late at night and as we searched the area, we picked up the sailor shouting – you guessed it, he was using the mother of all words to get our attention. I best remember him kissing the deck after we got him aboard and saying he would never say a bad thing about destroyer sailors again!

We were lucky enough to get to do some Gemini capsule recovery work as we had a capsule mock up on board and a small crane welded to the deck near after steering. We would kick the capsule overboard and then go get it. The closest we got to the real thing was when the Lake Champlain picked up the capsule. We were in that task force.

During the Polaris missile testing the "Jolly J" provided data from the time the missile broke the surface until it reached an altitude where air search radar could pick it up. That was the best our Fire Control Radar ever worked! We "FT's" were pretty good at shore bombardment and we did manage to shoot down a sleeve or two.

I guess the most notable thing we did was to save Kingston, Jamaica. In February of '66 the queen or some other royalty was to visit Kingston and either visit or stay at the Myrtle Bank Hotel. Well, it started on fire and threatened to burn down the whole waterfront area. The "Jolly J" and USS Suribachi AE-21 were in port and answered the call for help. We took all available firefighting equipment – including several portable pumps and went to the fire. It was a BIG one! The pool was pumped dry in a matter of minutes and water had to be pumped from the bay to fight the fire. After an all night fight, the fire was contained and all the dirty sailors – covered with soot and smoke were told to go back to their ships – Yeah, Right! We were thirsty and wanted a beer – and we got them – plenty of them from the locals whose businesses we saved. It was good liberty!

I left the ship in September of '66 as FTG3 and wanted no part of this man's Navy. In 1969 I rejoined the Naval reserves and retired as a Chief Petty Officer in 1989.

The FT gang had some characters in it – Bear, Turtle, Stein and Bobo, to name a few. There was a guy from Montana and Stan was from St. Louis.

Among the crew was a guy from a small town not 25 miles from where I grew up. He was known as "Bullsittin' Wayne".

I saw the Johnston when she was a reserve training ship in Philadelphia in 1979. She brought back memories as I toured her.

As I tour the old destroyers today, I can still pick out where my rack was, the mess decks and main battery plot as well as many other details of those days.

"PAINTING THE SKY"

By: Jesse E. (Gene) Grantham, Storekeeper (SK3)

Years on board the Johnston: 1964 to 1966

After coming on board the Johnson as an SK striker in '64 and working in the mid-ship store-room with Taffaro, Heiskenen, and "Puppy" Redmond for a while, the Ship's Serviceman that ran the ship's store left the Johnston. Our Supply Officer who knew that I had grocery store experience offered me the job. I jumped at the opportunity.........ANTHING to get me out of that hot store-room between the forward boiler and aft engine!!!

As part of running the store, one of my duties was to maintain all of the below-deck store-rooms.

On one occasion, I had to paint the small storeroom located under the ladder in the Supply Division berthing area. The rule was that no-one was supposed to paint in closed areas without a "spotter" above deck, watching you. Well, either I couldn't find one or just forgot to ask anyone and opened the hatch and took my red-lead bucket and brush and went down into the store room and started painting. Sometime during the time I was down there, someone, either as a joke or just seeing the open hatch, decided to close it. As I was so far back in the rear of the store-room, I didn't hear them close the hatch. Already slightly "high" on the fumes, even with the hatch open, the closing of the hatch just accelerated the intensification of the fumes and it wasn't long before I totally succumbed to the fumes and ended up on my back on the deck.

Even after all these years, I can still remember vividly seeing in my "mind's eye" that I was floating in air on my back….up in the sky…..painting the undersides of the clouds….

The Man upstairs (and I don't mean the crew or the ensign) decided that it wasn't my time to go and sent someone to look for me. They asked and someone told them the last time they saw me I was painting in the store room. They came to the hatch, and seeing that it had no padlock on it, opened it and there, through the fumes, they spotted me……….laying on my back…….paint brush in hand….eyes closed…….painting those clouds….

Needless to say, they dug me out and I was sick for two or three days with a mind-busting headache, before slowly recovering…..

"BATTLE STATIONS HOT POTATO"
By: Jesse E. (Gene) Grantham

During my time on the Jolly J, my battle station was in the number one twin 5-inch gun mount up forward.

Being the "new kid" on the ship, the Gunners Mate 2 in control of the mount assigned me the task of handling the powder canisters after being fired by using those bicep-length canvas gloves to handle them.

As many of you know that have been in one of the mounts, each mount has two 5-inch cannons, and each has behind it a chute that, during firing, are opened so that when the cannon fires, the rejected, empty brass powder canisters will bounce off the sloped shape of the chute and fall outside onto the main deck.

Well, since we "weren't REALLY at war", the GM2 told me that he didn't want to have the ejecting canisters hitting the back wall of the chute, chipping off "HIS" paint since that would mean that his men would then have to repaint them. Instead, he ordered me to "catch" each of the canisters as the gun fired. What this entailed was for me to stand at the rear of the port-side gun and place my right hand palm up under the trough of the gun with my left hand with palm facing the trough, right up against my right one.

When the gun fired and the breach dropped, the canister would come flying out (how fast I don't know, but it was pretty dang quick) and I had to actually catch it and drop it out the chute or, if it fell to the deck, pick it up and throw out the chute. It really surprised me the first time I did it to really see that catching the dang things was actually possible…

During one of our firing exercises during rough seas, Fire Control was locked onto the target so, each time the bow rose, the rear of the gun would rise, and vice-versa. I had to keep my hands jammed up against it……up….and down….up…and down…

The order came down........**six shot....rapid fire salvo!!**....

The shells and powder started coming up the hoists and being loaded one at a time. The first one fired, and when the canister ejected, I caught it and tossed it outside. About that time, the bow of the ship started riding up a wave so the rear of the gun started rising.....just as the gun fired. The canister came flying out and because my hands were both nearly head-high, I couldn't keep it out away from me and my hand/arm reaction brought the incredibly hot canister toward my face. I instinctively reacted by turning my head to the right and the hot canister hit me on the side of the face and ear.......burning the heck out of the side of my face and searing my left ear. I dropped the canister, picked it up and tossed out the chute.

It was happening so fast that, before I realized that I was burned and started feeling the pain, the remaining four salvos fired and I caught and ejected each of them out the chute.

Immediately thereafter, the Gun Captain and the rest of our team realized that I had been burned. He ordered me to head to the dispensary immediately. I opened the hatch on the gun mount and hit the main deck. I went down the starboard side of the ship and un-dogged the first hatch and when I opened it, there stood one of the ensigns. When he saw me coming through the hatch, he started chewing my tail about "voiding water-tight security"...........that is, until I pointed to the side of my head and ear. His eyes got as big as golf balls and his reaction and horrid facial expression scared the heck out of me since up until that time, I had no idea that I was burned as bad as I was.

I made my way to the dispensary and the doctor and corpsmen worked on me and put anti-biotic creams on the burns. They both told me that I would probably have scars. This REALLY scared me.

I asked the doc what did I have to do to keep from having scars and, believe it or not, he told me that one of the best home-remedies he knew of was to keep it coated in cooking lard. Well, being both "obedient to the doc" as well as being a Supply Division member, I had ready access to the much-needed lard. I religiously kept it basted and bandaged in it over a week and a half…..peeling the dead skin and dried "pork skins" each day…..After the week and a half, I started healing back to normal and was lucky enough to recover fully with no scars…

Thank goodness for good old hog fat!!

"LOVE THOSE NROTC CADETS!"
By: Jesse E. (Gene) Grantham

As we prepared to head to the Med for the "Kiddie Cruise", we moved up the Carolina coast and picked up the 16 foot sailboat sent to the Johnston from the Naval Academy. Each of the destroyers got one sailboat, and I believe the cruiser got three, and the Intrepid got five…all for use by the cadets. Turns out they didn't want anything to do with the sailboat…

OK, now that we've got one…………what do we do with it?

I don't remember who asked, but another sailor and I volunteered to take on the task of off-loading, rigging, and bringing the sailboat back on board when we went into each of the various Mediterranean ports we went into that summer. I don't know if there was no one else who knew how to rig it or if they just didn't want too. He and I

229

seemed to be the only ones also who knew how to actually sail a small boat.

Boy, what a cruise...liberty, liberty, liberty!!

Pappy Moore (SK1) was already disgruntled about me being in the ship's store instead of down in the SK store rooms, so when I got "assigned" to taking care of the sailboat, this just added to the steam building up under his salty old hat…especially since, when not opening the store or working on the receiving of new stock, I was supposed to be working with the other SK's.

Well, we pulled into Marseille, France and, "per duties assigned", early in the morning, my team-mate and I put the sailboat in the water and tied it off. As I was heading to the SK stores, the Supply Division Ensign caught me and said he wanted to go sailing. Orders are Orders!!! He didn't have to tell me twice!!

I immediately changed into my swim shorts, hat and shorts and he met me at the sailboat. We took off and were gone most of the day, sailing all up through the large ships in the harbor.

Now the return arrival……

As we start returning to the ship and we started getting close to the ship, there stands Pappy…..arms crossed, patting his foot, and face red as a beet. I tie the sailboat to the side of the ship and started climbing up. Once I got within "cussin'" distance, Pappy starts in on me with a tirade of phrases that turned the air blue. He was accusing me of being AWOL, being away from my duty station, and about everything else he could think of….all with added expletives….especially since (as it turns out) my Ensign had not told Pappy that he and I were going sailing.

Thank God for my Supply officer (to whom Pappy reported, thank God). He let Pappy "vent" for a short while and then calmly looked him straight in the eye and calmly told him...."Jesse was UNDER ORDERS". Pappy could have bit through a two-by-four.......but at this point he knew I was out of his reach......at least for now...

Needless to say, Pappy took pleasure for the rest of my tour on the Jolly J to give me grief any time I so much as looked sideways...........but the sailing trip was worth it all.

SHORT STORIES
By: Mark Chavez, Radarman (RD2)

Years on board the Johnston: 1966 to 1969

A SHORT STORY - I was assigned to the USS Johnston out of radar school in Great Lakes, Illinois. After some initial delay (my wife delivered our first child), I was flown to the Mediterranean to catch up with the ship. She left Naples, Italy just hours before I had arrived. The dock workers were still rolling up cables as my taxi roared up. Later in the day I reported to fleet headquarters. I then waited in Naples for a month waiting for news of the next port of call of the elusive DD-821. Also waiting in Naples was Sweazy RD3 who had left the ship for some reason, toothache maybe.

We flew to Bahrain, in the Persian Gulf, where we joined up the Johnston. Hot and dry, blazing cloudless sky, and thank God, the radar spaces were air conditioned. Many slept there rather than the confined sleeping spaces below decks, by the aft 6 inch gun mount. I believe there was some sort of air conditioning below decks as well, but not as efficient. The humidity left behind four or five inches of water in the compartment, and sloshed everyone's shoes around. I remember mopping up every morning to clear this water, left from the cooling air.

Every division had to volunteer a man for mess deck duty, and as junior man, that was me. It was supposed to be for a month, but I remember it being longer. Eventually I got to practice my rating, and stood watches with the others in C.I.C.

I remember some damage to the port side of the ship, and was told the Captain had let the executive officer bring her along pier side when docking up in Bahrain. It was mostly paint work, and he certainly needed the practice.

I remember standing in line for chow, at sea, on the port side by the potato bin. To pass the time, we threw potatoes to the sea gulls that glided beside us in the wind. There was grace in their ability to catch potato chunks in the air, and naturally, every once in a while someone would throw a piece of iron to the disaster for the seagull that caught it. Funny at the time, it makes me cringe now.

The return home had some shaky moments. We stopped at the horn of Africa, at Assab in Ethiopia. It was very primitive and had one big hotel, full of Russians running the oil refinery built by Americans. They kept to themselves. While drunk, I bought and smuggled aboard the hacked off nose of a saw-tooth shark. About four feet long with sharp fang teeth all around the edge. It was still fresh when I got it.

On the way back through the Med, we visited Beirut, Lebanon when it was prosperous and beautiful. There was a casino built half way up the snow topped mountain just behind the city. It was run by an American from Vegas. Now why doesn't that surprise me? Anyhow, he bought about ten of us big drinks so we could play the games, eat or drink more. He was a very patriotic guy. Naturally, some asshole had to screw this up. I forget his name, but he was a Sonarman. He climbed into the overhead air ducts and fell through into the ladies room. They banned us after that.

The Johnston went through the straits of Medina, a narrow passage between Sicily and the rest of Italy, then on to Malta. Valetta has a deepwater harbor, but the town is high above on the cliffs. Luckily there was an elevator. I think it cost thru-pence (3 pence). It was a very interesting city. One street was full of bars and associated businesses. There were lots of pastel yellow sandstone buildings, and there were supposed to be catacombs or so we heard. A rubble filled lot was shown to us, and the story went that a leaky gas fitting took the whole building and a few patrons as well. Not much you can do or say about that. Some of us rented bikes and pedaled over to Saint George's bay. It was supposed to be full of British nurses. There was a bar/hotel, very beautiful, right by the sea, and surprise, a scattering of nurses. They ignored us, and we left soon after.

We nearly ran out of food, and ate mostly bacon sandwiches until we got to Gibraltar. Fresh milk tasted wonderful.

I have probably forgotten lots of stuff. I hope someone else can fill in the blanks.

HALF A SEA STORY - And just what is a sea story?? They all have one significant characteristic. As a fairy tale always begins with 'Once upon a time', a sea story always begins with 'Now this ain't no shit'. That means all my stories are based on granite truth, with no names

233

changed, as they are proud of the tale. Details may be fuzzy as to the exact number of opponents or drinks consumed. The dates may not be accurate, as at sea one day runs into another and routine wears you down. However, some events are so outrageous, so superlative, that they stand alone, and cannot be shaken by facts. I present such memories for your amusement and shock of recognition.

Assab, Ethiopia was our first port of call on the homeward leg of that 66/67 Med. cruise. A grubby little town, with dirt streets, one big hotel and one bar. This local bar had four entrances, each named after a different state. I went in the one called the TEXAS Bar with about eight of my mates. Ursery, Cizio, Wilson, Brown, from the radar gang, some from Fox (the sonar gang) and some snipes. Beers were ordered, girls swept into position, and we surveyed the scene. In the light, the girls looked pretty rough. Tribal scars and tattoos, teeth filed, various blemishes and scars from infected wounds, and they smelled quite ripe. After five beers they were beautiful.

After a bit more, we decided to go up to the hotel for a look-see. When we stood up, so did everyone in the bar, and they all followed us out. Pretty strange, that. It was there I bought the saw tooth shark nose for about five dollars, I think. Some Russians were drinking there. Polite but distant. They didn't like the Ethiopians, and the followers hanging on us had to leave the bar. After a few more beers, the strangest thing happened. A bunch of us went for a walk, and then my balance suddenly went. My feet walked away underneath me and I fell backwards to the earth with a painful thump. I was O.K. but my dignity was hurt.

It was here that Speedy Martin, the storekeeper that ran the ships stores, fell ill. Nothing would shake this infection, and the ships store was off limits for fear of contamination. We couldn't buy soap, razor blades or any smokes for the last month of the cruise. When we got back to CONUS, he didn't leave the ship, until he went to hospital. Very unlucky guy. Must have been something he ate.

I remember we stopped for a swim over the side, with a gunners mate and carbine watching over us. Climbed up and down that cargo net. You try wearing frog feet. The water was great.

The red sea was beautiful at night. The bow-wake gleamed softly with phosphorescence, and the air was balmy and cool to the skin. We all heard stories of how it was impossible to drown in the Red Sea. As soon as you splashed about swimming, the sharks came and ate you.

We pulled into Jidda, Saudi Arabia, along that desolate coast. Small groups of us were invited to private homes for little parties, and we had one big bash for everyone just before we left. The big party had some flash dancers show their stuff, among them the signalmen. I remember John Wall (called Bulkhead) and Big Ski and Little Ski, brothers. Also Jake Martinez, the one who could spell. They needed him. My group was invited to the Ambassadors house (dumb luck) and he liked us so much we ended up visiting his seaside holiday house, and went snorkeling in the sea. I saw no sharks, but masses of colored coral, and thousands of tiny different colored fish that hid in the coral. There is so much color underwater, and it is so drab on the surface.

By the way, the reason for our popularity was that we brought mail sacks full of beer with us to every event. When the ex-pats working there ordered their booze, whiskey and beer weigh the same, so they only brought in hard liquor. They had no beer. We had tons of Old Milwaukee in the stores. It was rusting up anyhow.

The Suez Canal was next. A big sandy ditch, shallow and filthy. Wrecked and burned ships grounded where the Israelis had destroyed them in the six day war. We had a visit by a bum boat.

Mr. Seferd, the engineering officer didn't like their looks, and ordered the fire hoses out. Before we could wash them out of their boats, they left. Later, permission was granted for one boat to set up near the aft gun mount. Just rubbish to sell. I only bought a few things.

Beirut, Lebanon was the next port of call. Coming into the harbor was a treat. Gleaming white houses climbing up the hill sides, the bay and sky unbelievable blue, cloudless, hot sun. And behind all this, the tall mountains, snow capped and up to the edge of the sky. We arrived for New Year's Day. I wandered the city with a few mates, got cheated at a money changer, went shopping, had a few beers. It was a local holiday as well. I guess they used our calendar, a small surprise. Anyhow, we met a couple of Lebanese sailors, and they said (we thought) they would take us to a party run by their sweethearts. It looked odd that their girlfriends were so old and worn out looking, and then someone with better English explained that it was a whorehouse. Not all of us left. Somehow we scattered and found our own amusement. It was here that the SONARMAN tried to climb over to the ladies room in that terrific casino on the mountain, and got the whole ship banned. Well, we had to leave soon anyway.

Out to sea, and the weather closed down. Stormy and cold. We went up the Italian coast, I believe, and visited Bologna. Someone else please verify this.

Then it seemed we went to Barcelona, Spain. I recall visiting a grim city with Sweazy and some other guys. Not a cheerful place. After then, I believe we went to Gibraltar for supplies. I remember that big rock for sure.

We formed up with the U.S.S. Cone DD-866, and maybe some others, and crossed the Atlantic. Incredible storms for weeks. Everyone, from the chiefs groaning in the Foc'sle to the newest hand, was sick. I sat on that radar scope praying my relief would be five minutes early, as combat swayed sickeningly to and fro. We put up a swing chart, a sheet of maneuvering board paper and a hanging pencil. As you know, the ship can move in three directions at once. This only measured the roll, but it was enough. I have been sea sick only once in all those years, and this was the time.

The Charleston sea buoy was a great little sight. My first cruise was over. I was glad it was done.

SWIMMING WITH THE SHARKS

By: Bobby Love, Radarman (RD2)

Years on board the Johnston: Mid Sixties

Back in the fifties and early sixties growing up I use to watch all those WW II movies. I saw at least one where sailors who were ship wrecked were attacked by sharks. I said I will never get in that position. But I must have forgotten because after high school I joined the Navy and was later on the USS JOHNSTON DD 821. Well one time in the mid sixties we sailed across the Atlantic alone not in a task force and the Captain stopped the ship and we had swim call. We had one Jacob's ladder over the side and a whale boat with a sailor and a rifle in case of sharks. I checked the chart as a radarman and we

were in about 10,000 feet of water. Well here we were all out there splashing around and someone screamed SHARK! You immediately find out who your friends are when you get a foot in the face going up that one single ladder, ha ha ha ha. The officers took some time shooting at this big shark with several types of fire arms. The cooks as I remember got a grappling hook with meat trying to catch it but I guess they failed. Moral to this story never float around in the middle of the Atlantic unless you have to!

FROM CAPTAIN MINGO

By: John J. Mingo, Captain, USN (Ret)

Years on board the Johnston: 1965 to 1967

In the way of background, I had command of the USS Johnston DD-821 from October 1965 until March of 1967. I wished it could have been longer but I was a Captain selectee while on the Johnston and the Bureau of Naval Personnel directed me to move on. During that period the ship visited many interesting ports including Charleston

(Homeport), Norfolk, Key West, New York City, Annapolis, Guantanamo Bay (GITMO), San Juan, Kingston Jamaica, Rota Spain, Naples, Beirut, Aden, Bahrain, Jidda Saudi Arabia, Assab Ethiopia, Palma Majorca, Bandar Abbas and Kharg Island (both in the Persian Gulf).

There were numerous stories and events associated with the visits to the ports, especially those in the Persian Gulf. The Johnston was detached from the sixth fleet for a 2 to 3 month assignment to the Mideast Force in the Persian Gulf. These episodes do not necessarily reflect the opinion of the entire crew. Unfortunately, some of the most entertaining and unusual cannot be retold for various reasons. I will relate a few anecdotal events which I thought may be of some interest. Each Johnston crew member has his own unique story to tell and these are mine.

In Bahrain the dinner invitations from the American community nearly exceeded the number of sailors in the liberty party. The entire crew appeared to enjoy the visit. On Thanksgiving Day, I was in my cabin when I heard the sound of drums coming from the pier. I went to the quarter deck and observed eight British sailors in colonial uniforms marching behind a drummer, followed by a British crew member carrying a huge turkey on a tray. The turkey was delivered to the Johnston with pomp and ceremony. As you know, the British are quite good at this sort of thing.

In Abbas Ethiopia (a small village) we were hosted by the Ethiopian Navy to the extent possible. In exchange, the Johnston hosted a party ashore to reciprocate their hospitality. There was a Russian contingent ashore ostensibly doing oil exploration. I decided to invite the Russians to the party and never expected their attendance. Much to our surprise, the Russians appeared, enjoyed the food and drinks, stayed until the leader "blew" his whistle and they departed simultaneously. The Russians easily beat our crew in volleyball. We only had a pick-up team with no prior team training.

Christmas was spent in Jidda, Saudi Arabia which is located only 30 miles from the Saudi's holy city of Mecca. Many dinner invitations were extended to the crew. Surprisingly, the American Ambassador invited a number of sailors and officers to a formal dinner. Prior to arrival in Jidda, the crew formed a choir and held rehearsals in the Dash Hanger. The choir attended Christmas morning services ashore with the American community. Singing Christmas carols (in dress white uniforms) they brought tears to many attendees.

From Jidda the ship proceeded to Beirut Lebanon via the Suez Canal. The Johnston was the last military ship through the canal before the Israelis blockaded the canal in 1967. The ship celebrated New Year's Eve and New Year's Day in Beirut. Most had an enjoyable visit.

We rejoined the Sixth Fleet after departure from Beirut. Our tour was extended one month because one of the replacement destroyers was unable to meet its commitment. I assume it was a compliment to have been selected. Some family members back in homeport were not overjoyed. As a reward we were given a choice of a liberty port and we chose Palma, Majorca. The ship returned to Charleston unaccompanied.

During my tour aboard the Johnston, the ship received numerous "well dones" for operational performance, ship's appearance and military smartness. However, no event generated more "well dones" and letters of commendation than that which occurred on 27 February 1966. The Johnston was on a recreational visit to Kingston, Jamaica for its break in refresher training at Guantanamo Bay. The ship was at special sea detail ready to get underway to complete refresher training, when a serious fire broke out at the historic Myrtle Bank Hotel located at the head of the pier. The Kingston fire department requested the ship's assistance to contain the fire which threatened the hotel, adjacent buildings, lumber yards, and downtown Kingston. The fire was fed by 25 knot winds. After rigging and manning fire fighting equipment, establishing first aid, relief stations and maintaining continuous communications for eight hours, the fire was finally extinguished. Of note, hoses were rigged for over 100 feet from the hotel's swimming pool to the hotel. One hundred forty two crew members were involved in the effort. Surprisingly, many of the ship's firefighters were reluctant to be relieved by fresh replacements. Local officials and the hotel management attributed the localization of the fire to the efforts of the U.S. Navy forces. Letters of commendation and "well dones" were received from the American Ambassador, the acting Prime Minister of Jamaica, and the U.S. President, SECDEF, SECNAV and nearly all in the chain of command above the USS Johnston. I personally could not have been more proud of the crew's performance.

Another event brought pride and respect to the USS Johnston. Every ship and the commanding officer strive to win the coveted green battle efficiency award. It reflects the ship's capability in all aspects of operational expertise and teamwork. In 1966 the USS Johnston was awarded the battle efficiency award in DESRON FOUR. Another "well done" to the crew.

Myrtle Bank Hotel fire, Kingston Jamaica on 27 February 1966 From the USS Johnston Bridge

I had four important ASW assignments after my tour aboard the Johnston. However, my tour as Commanding Officer, USS Johnston DD-821, was the most rewarding and enjoyable. It was a privilege and an honor.

My deepest gratitude goes to all crew members that served aboard while I was the Commanding Officer.

U.S. NAVY HELPS KEEP FLAMES FROM SPREADING

Years on board the Johnston: 1964 to 1967

Jamaica's long-time, world famous hotel, the stately Myrtle Bank, was gutted by fire yesterday afternoon in one of the most spectacular blazes in Kingston's history.

Fanned by a brisk westerly wind, flames licked through the 92-year-old water-front hotel in Harbour Street which next Friday was to have been the scene of a gala ball to be attended by the Queen and the Duke of Edinburgh in aid of the British Empire and Commonwealth Games.

FIREMEN, SAILORS - Firemen and a large contingent of sailors from the United States destroyer Johnston and the transport vessel Suribachi berthed nearby in Kingston Harbour, clambered over roofs and walls dousing down the flaming building.

But they were beaten by the wind which drove the flames from the east wing of the main hotel building through to the west wing and at one time threatened to jump adjoining Rum Lane and set thousands of feet of lumber ablaze in the yard of Hardware and Lumber Ltd.

243

The fire started at about 2:30 p.m. — a chauffeur spotted smoke coming from the third floor in the east wing. He alerted a hotel porter.

Hotel staff rushed to the scene and turned fire extinguishers onto the smoke. Only minutes later Kingston firemen were at the scene, and then the U.S. Navymen arrived.

Hoses leading from the hotel swimming pool were turned onto the flaming third floor, and sailors and firemen with oxygen equipment raced through the hotel rooms, checking that all guests were safely out of the building.

For a time it looked as though the blaze may have been held to the east wing, but the relentless wind was too fast.

Waiters, maids — some covering their mouths with handkerchiefs like hold-up men — firemen, sailors, guests and passers-by ran through the hotel grabbing clothes, furniture, jerking telephones from the wall, throwing bamboo chairs onto the lawn.

Furniture, typewriters, clothes, telephones were piled up beneath the tall palms on the hotel's back lawn.

As firemen climbed precariously over the lower roofs jerking heavy hoses after them, guests, some in swim suits, sat calmly.

The first sign that the fire was fast-spreading came about 40 minutes after the outbreak when a group of sailors spotted flames in the banquet room.

They race in, tore down the curtains, threw furniture onto the water-soaked lawn. One sailor brought a screaming cat out and set it free a safe distance away.

Centre of building - As the blaze reached the centre of the building the flames had taken control of the third and second floors.

Through the dense grey smoke a fireman was spotted in a burning room. People below yelled to him to come out, and he quickly descended a scorching staircase.

As the flames swept into the west wing, the already gutted east wing started crumbling. Firemen and sailors were ordered onto the ground only minutes before drainpipes, air-conditioning units and wooden beams started falling from the seared shell.

On the back lawn officers with walkie-talkie equipment directed fire-fighting teams. At the hotel quay a sailor with flags semaphored across to the destroyer Johnston asking for more men, hoses and fire pumps.

Fear - A launch from the Johnston rushed them to the Myrtle Bank and they were ordered into Rum Lane...flames were dancing from the roof of the west wing and it was feared they would jump across into the lumber yard.

Said one fireman: "With this wind it will be disastrous if the lumber is set on fire. Much of Harbour street will be in danger."

But the flames didn't reach the lumber, eight hoses and a score of sailors saw to that. They watered-down the west tip of the hotel.

Water gushed from the side of the middle into Rum Lane and flowed back into the harbour. More petrol was brought in to top up the tanks of the fire-pumps.

Two men sat on the 15-foot lumber-yard wall turning water-jets onto the wing. There was one dramatic moment when part of the wing crumbled into Rum Lane just missing a group of sailors below.

Once the "battle of Rum Lane" had been won, the worst was over. As the sun set timbers still popped, smoke belched from the ruins, but the blaze was under control after more than three hours.

Relaxation - Perched on roofs, balanced on walls, the firemen could relax a little. Hotel guests and staff set up a catering service and tea and sandwiches were taken to the fire teams.

Hotel clerks were trying to organize alternative accommodations. The Myrtle Bank, with 168 beds was booked- up.

The hotel annex, to the east of the fire, was undamaged and many were crammed in there. Others were booked into boarding houses and homes throughout the Kingston area.

On the back lawn of the hotel travelers call "the crossroads of the Caribbean", a half-completed wooden platform to be used during next Friday's gala ball was piled with furniture.

The Queen's visit to the Myrtle Bank would have been one more chapter in the colourful history of a gracious resting place born before Jamaica became a tourist centre.

The Myrtle Bank has known bad times before. It started as a hotel 92 years ago in the residence of a Scottish journalist, Mr. Jones Gall. At the turn of the century, it was taken over by the United Fruit Company and run in connection with their business.

Its hey-day was in the Twenties and Thirties when it was the social centre of Kingston . . . scene of formal luncheons, sumptuous banquets and gay balls . . . events that only white colonists were invited.

In 1943 the Issa family bought the hotel and abolished the colour bar. In the Forties and Fifties it blossomed, but in 1964 the hotel was closed.

Its doors were shut only three months. In January, 1965, restyled to meet modern tourist demands, it re-opened.

End of article.

Rick was lucky enough to serve aboard the Johnston with his brother James E. Ley who served as an ASROC Technician 3rd class from 1963 to 1966. Rick has this short story to tell about his brother James.

I would watch for my brother to come through the chow line. If he didn't make it, I would make him a lunch and go looking for him. I would go up to the ASROC deck and knock on the door to the cooling tubes with a coded knock. He would then open the door about half drunk to get his food. He loved fantail shrimp.

Cinderella Liberty

By: Billy Cook, Fire Control Technician (FTG-3)

Years on board the Johnston: 1965 to 1968

Soon after joining the Johnston in May of '65, we left Charleston, South Carolina on my first cruise. The first liberty port was Kingston, Jamaica and it was my first trip outside the U.S.A. After we arrived, I was very excited but apprehensive about the possibility of going ashore. After talking with some of the old salts I decided to have sex with one of the local girls on my first liberty. I was eighteen years old and sex was one

of the biggest reasons why I had joined the Navy to begin with. Anyway, I left the ship with a third class IC Man. I can't remember his name anymore, but he was an old salt to me, because he had been in the Navy for over three years and was pretty experienced in these matters. We high-tailed it straight to one of the local strip joints. I remember that as we approached the front door of this old wooden building, some black women outside of the joint were fondling each sailor's privates as if to welcome them for what was going to happen later on the inside. It made an impression on me, because I had never seen behavior like that before, even on the strip in Charleston, SC. As we walked in I noticed that everyone in the place was black except for the sailors. We walked over to a table that was next to a stage and sat down. The stage was centered towards the back of the room next to the bar area. Immediately after we sat down, girls started coming around asking us to buy them drinks. Because I was just out of FT "A" school and a low paid seaman apprentice, I didn't have a lot of money to spend so I sat at the table drinking beer without a girl for most of the night. The other guys started buying drinks for the girls and everyone was laughing and cutting up. I noticed a doorway at the back of the stage that led into a small brightly lit room. In the room you could see an old rusty looking bed with a bare mattress. I remember thinking it was a strange place for a bed. It wasn't long after we sat down that I realized what the bed was there for. A girl soon walked up to the stage leading a sailor by the hand and went through the door into the room. Once in the room, the sailor and the girl proceeded to remove each other's clothes. As soon as they were naked, the girl jumped on the bed and the rusty old bed springs started to squeak as she rocked back and forth shaking her naked breasts from side to side inviting the sailor to join her. The sailor jumped on the bed, and they started doing it right there in front of us. Holy cow, I could not believe what I was seeing! Most every one in the place was laughing and cheering as they watched the exhibition and listened to those bed springs creak as the sailor rode that girl. I was stunned, but let me say that I was mesmerized by the show and getting excited as well. It didn't take that sailor long to climax, so the show was pretty short lived, but it sure got everyone excited. The sailor rolled to the side of the bed and the girl immediately grabbed a roll of toilet paper (TP). She pulled off several sheets of the TP, wiped herself, then threw the used TP into a waste can sitting on the other side of the bed. Then she took some more TP off the roll and wiped the sailor's penis. As they put their clothes back on and began to leave the room another girl and sailor immediately got up, walked across the stage and into the room and repeated what I had just observed all over again. For the next several hours this parade of exhibitions continued. Some of the sailors would shut the door, so you couldn't watch them, but you could hear what was going on... It was almost as if the sound of the squeaking springs were amplified, because the longer and harder the sailor labored, the louder the bed springs squeaked.

After each performance the audience would clap and hoot at the sailor as he left the room. All the time I sat there watching, listening and drinking beer. I was thinking about what I had been told in boot camp about protecting oneself from sexually transmitted diseases or STDs as they are now called. In our training we were advised to always wear a rubber or at the very least make sure you peed after intercourse. Well I didn't have a rubber, so I decided that I would not pee until after I had sex with one of those girls. Anyway, the night wore on and I was getting drunk, no I was drunk, and all of the girls but one had pretty much given up on me buying them a drink. I remember that I really needed to pee. Oh man, I had never hurt so bad! It felt like my eyeballs were floating. I began to realize that it was getting late and because we were on Cinderella liberty I would have to be back on the ship by midnight so I decided it was time. In fact, it was past time. Finally the one black girl that looked particularly fat to me sat down beside me and asked me if I would buy her a drink. In my drunken state I decided that she really didn't look that bad and I had already decided that it was better late than never. I asked her how much to go up on stage and she said five dollars. I gave her the five dollars and she took my hand and we walked. Actually I really staggered up to the stage and into the room. I shut the door because I was still modest and was way too embarrassed to let everyone watch. I still remember how drunk I was and Ohhhh how much my bladder hurt! While I was taking my uniform off, I was watching her undress and noticed that it wasn't that she was fat so much, as the woman had to be nine months pregnant. I pointed to her belly and she nodded yes, but said it was Ok, don't worry and I was like... Oh... OK. She laid down on that creaky bed and I got on top and as we started, I remembered how much pain I was in... Damn, I needed to peeeeee. We went on and on and on and I just couldn't get to a climax and all the time that bed was squeaking like crazy. She could tell I wasn't going to climax so she got on top of me and rode me furiously shaking those big breasts back and forth. But, it wasn't working. After what seemed like eternity, she got off grabbed my penis in one hand and

251

pumped me rapidly while she rubbed her vagina and shook those breasts. Bingo! That woman was experienced and knew what she was doing. And oh I was so glad that it was over. I remember watching her reaching for the roll of TP, but it was empty. To my horror she then reached over the bed, grabbed a handful of used TP out of the bucket, wiped herself and grabbed my penis in one sweeping moment with the same TP and wiped me. I was freaking out and thinking Oh shit what has she done to me! I remember putting my uniform back on and hurried in a panic making my way to the door. When she opened the door we walked out onto the stage to a standing ovation as everyone in the place whistled and yelled. We had impressed the crowd with the longevity and noises of our encounter. In my state I was not interested in taking a bow or staying around... I was hell-bent on getting to the toilet. I think that was the longest time I ever took to relieve my bladder. I think that I peed for at least ten minutes and all I could think about was that used TP and it had been lying on and along side a lot of other used TP. I just knew I was going to get the Clap and who knows what else. I remember thinking how fast could I get back to the ship so I could scrub down in a hot shower and see the Corpsman. I guess I was lucky because I didn't come down with any thing from that trip. I did visit the Corpsman later on, during a Med cruise, that included the port of Naples, and that is the beginning of another story.

"MARGINAL HURRICANE"
By: W. Frank Cobb, III, LT

Years on board the Johnston: 1966 to 1969

While crossing the Pacific Ocean, we encountered a "marginal hurricane" that lasted 3 days complete with 70 knot winds, and crashing 70 foot swells. It created severe sea sickness for at least 70 percent of the officers and sailors. Since the USS Johnston was only 300 feet long, "climbing" over the 70 foot swells was quite a task. Our Captain had us maintain bare steerage way of 3 knots. After we topped each wave, we "slid" down the far side, finally hitting/smashing into the water like a submarine, burying the first 1/3 of the ship into the water before we floated back out in preparation for the next wave. We, of course, had secured all outside hatches so we wouldn't take on any of this water we were "diving" through with each swell. Whew!

It was with real dread when I tried to sleep. My arms and legs would swing out from my rack with each wave as the Johnston was pitching 30% or more. Gravity pulled my arms and legs out of the rack with each wave, while fortunately, the trunk of my body sank deep enough in my rack to keep me in there with only my limbs swinging out. I seem to recall that I strapped myself in the rack during this storm. What a relief as the third day passed, and the storm finally let up. The storm was so powerful that the waves had bent the stanchions backward.

A Life of Service

By: Ralph A. Turner, LCDR, (Captain, USN Retired)

Years on board the Johnston: 1967 to 1968

I was born to Ralph A. and Laura B. Turner in New York City on May 11, 1931. My father's career as a Commander in the US Navy kept the family moving, but in 1951 Groton Long Point, CT became the family home.

In 1950 I graduated from Maury High School in Norfolk, VA and began attending the Naval Academy that fall. I graduated with the class of 1954.

My luck in the first duty assignment draw was very high (813). As a result, my choice of duty was reduced to aircraft carriers or troop transports. My father's last sea duty was on the carrier Midway and he informed me that Ensigns were assigned to sounding tank teams. I selected an APA homeported in San Diego and I picked a good ship. The Korean War was over and in my two year tour we were employed in the redistribution of the Marines and Army personnel. I was detached in July 1956 as the ship ended a commercial yard overhaul in Seattle.

I had applied for and was ordered to a Newport homeported destroyer via the Gunnery Officer's Course. Unfortunately the course had been moved from the Washington, DC shipyard to the Great Lakes Training Command. So much for a young man's plan for twelve weeks in the women enriched DC environment. Enroute to Newport, I spent my leave with my parents at their home in Groton, CT. My father then working for the Electric Boat Co. got me invited to a party for the current class of submarine school students. As I recall Jocko Horner and Mike Stoffel were in attendance, but dimly remembered for "across a crowded room" I was smitten by the sight of a young woman. We kept company as much as possible given the busy schedule of a destroyer. Mary June Puishys and I were married August 1958, just before my tour was over. We suffered through a longer than planned MED deployment before setting up housekeeping in Northern Virginia for my tour as an aide to the Deputy Navy Inspector General.

I had applied for PG school and was selected to attend as a Bureau of Ordnance sponsored student. The notice of selection eluded me for about five months between change of duty and IG travels. When my PG selection was made known, the Admiral as an old Ord PG was most gracious and released me to school.

In September 1959, I started in the Chemical Engineering Course at the PG school in Monterey, California. My academic section included Jack Higgins and John Reisinger plus Bill Britton '53 and John Bres '51. The years have not dulled these friendships founded in mutual academic support and enjoyable highlight for this tour of duty.

The post PG school assignment was as XO of a diesel drive LST out of Little Creek, VA. This graduate chemist could not even titrate the boiler water. The Cuban Missile Crisis provided a busy highlight for this tour of duty.

My eighteen-month LST tour ended with orders to the guided missile cruise Boston as the Fire Control Officer. Good ship Boston was a steamer. Missile shoots and MED deployments made this twenty-month tour go fast.

Shore duty in BuPers establishing the Ordnance Systems Command placement desk followed the Talos Missile Training Officer. Learning the inner workings of BuPers got me an XO tour on a Charleston, SC destroyer Johnston DD-821 headed for Vietnam. Our first day on the gun line off the DMZ in Vietnam was the day the Tet Offensive started. Our learning curve was steep but successful as we alternated between the gun line and Yankee Station plane guard. After eight months we returned to Charleston.

The Johnston went into a standby status and I received orders to the Oriskany CVA-34 as the Weapons Officer. There had been a series of ordnance related fires on carriers and ordnance PGs as Weapons Officers was the solution. Kicking and protesting were to no avail as I found myself in the aviator-dominated hierarchy of Oriskany. The saving graces of the situation rested on the facts that I had screened for destroyer command and the great pleasure in finding that Charlie Ulrick was the Chief Engineer. Department Head meetings were great fun. Despite my initial repudiation, the Oriskany tour was one of my most rewarding and educational of my professional career. Naval Officers who are carrier qualified have to be the finest aviators in the world.

Halfway into my second deployment my relief reported. In one month I went from humping ordnance on the flight deck of a Yankee Station carrier in the Tonkin Gulf to reading history in a leather easy chair in the library of the Naval War College. After spending nine months as a student in the Senior Course, I got my destroyer command.

I went to New Orleans as PCO of USS McCandless (PF 1084) and took the family. The ship was delivered to the Boston Navy Yard and placed in commission in March 1972. The outfitting workup in our homeport of Norfolk was followed by underway training at GITMO. After a stint in Norfolk we deployed to the Indian Ocean as part of the Middle East force. Regretfully, I was not allowed to complete the deployment. The change of command must have been the social highlight of Tulare, Madagascar.

Back in Washington DC area I completed the management/procurement Systems Management College, For Belvior. In June 1974, I relieved as the Director of the Ammunition Management Division, Naval Sea Systems Command. This was a challenge to rebuild the inventory and standardize the fusing function across the calibers of conventional ammunition.

My orders to be CO, Naval Station Norfolk came as a shock. Being "Mayor" of the station was a great job and a rewarding challenge to improve the service to the fleet from the pier point of view. During my tour Rod Crawford took command of the Naval Air Station Norfolk. As a team we set the standards fro shore based coordination, cooperation and management of stations for fleet support.

After Norfolk it was back to the Naval Sea Systems Command as the Director of the Ammunition Management Group. The challenge was to support the single service (Army) ammunition concept and keep the Navy's weapons stations funded.

I am most grateful that the majority of us gain our impression of New Jersey from the Turnpike. This prejudice reduced the competition and allowed me to take command of Naval Weapons Station Earle, Colts Neck, New Jersey. A flying visit introduced June to the area and she became convinced that Earle truly was in a "Garden State". The concept of AOE home porting was formulated and the idea was mine to sell at the state and local levels. Three strong Navy League Chapters were of great assistance.

257

In addition to all those duty stations already mentioned, I served aboard the USS Renville (APA 277), USS Goodrich (DDR 831) and USS Terrebonne Parish (LST 1156). My decorations include "Legion of Merit", "Meritorious Service Medal and Gold Star", "Navy Achievement Medal and Gold Star", "Combat Action Ribbon" and "Republic of Vietnam's Navy Distinguished Service Order Second Class".

In June of 1984 I retired and we moved to the family homestead in Groton, CT. I adopted John Reisinger's idea of working in education. Connecticut College in New London offered the state required education courses, review courses in chemistry and physics and accepted the GI Bill in payment. In January 1986 I accepted a teaching position on a local school system. I found teaching to be both a stimulating and an enjoyable way to spend the time in a second career. The students were knowledgeable, quick and eager to learn and in general a real pleasure to be associated with in and out of the classroom. Although my spirit remains eager and willing the body is growing older. I cut back from full time teaching for several years and stopped altogether in June 1998.

Through this life journey, I have made no better decision or been more fortunate than to have June Turner as my partner. Being a Navy wife is difficult work. June allowed me to carry on despite the moves (20 in 26 years) and separations (too many to count). She is a thoughtful and giving person who always put forth the effort to help my career all the while being a successful parent to our four children. Thanks to June we all turned out well.

A STORY FROM THE USS JOHNSTON DD-821

By: Daun "Harry" H. Harris, Radarman (RD3)

Years on board the Johnston: 1968 to 1970

After starting my tour of duty in the Navy in July 1968, I was first assigned to the USS Eugene A. Greene (DD-711) home ported out of Norfolk, VA. Although I made one short North Atlantic cruise aboard the Greene, shortly after getting aboard, we were informed that the ship would be put in reduced status and that most of the crew would be reassigned to other ships. I received orders to the USS Johnston (DD-821) in Charleston, SC, as did a number of other crew members of the Greene. When we came aboard the Johnston, the ship's captain was Commander Curran, who was soon replaced by Captain Daniel F. Anglim Jr., whom most of us called "Captain Dan" (but only behind his back, HA!). I'm sure I speak for many members of the Johnston's crew when I say that Captain Anglim was very professional, knowledgeable, competent, and both admired and respected by a vast majority of the ship's crew. This was a tough time for Navy career personnel as the Vietnam War was raging. The war was very unpopular at home and many sailors didn't really want to be in the Navy and only joined to avoid being drafted into the Army. Although my short time aboard the Johnston would be considered fairly routine, some of the people I worked with, and events that happened, made it quite memorable to me and would become a portion of my life which I will never forget.

Shortly after being assigned to the Johnston, the ship was taken to the yards and put in dry-dock where it received a major overhaul. The Johnston was an old ship then and I remember talking to one of the civilian welders who worked on the Johnston. I don't know if this welder, who later turned out to become a very good friend of mine, was trying to scare us or what, but he said he was sure glad he would never have to go to sea on the Johnston. He said that when down in the hold of the ship, one of the yard workers saw some rust, took a hammer, chipped away at the rust , and before he was done, there was a hole in the hull of the ship large enough to accommodate a regular sized automobile.

After the Johnston was taken out of dry-dock we were then sent to Guantanamo Bay, Cuba for a shake-down cruise where the ship was put through all sorts of tests. Although the hours at Gitmo were long and hard, I had to agree with the present Miss Universe (Stefania Fernandez of Venezuela) who visited there and said it was actually a very beautiful place. Although Miss Fernandez was criticized for these comments (because suspected terrorists were being held there, and this of course would make it an awful place), I had to agree that she was very much correct. Aside from our regular duties, the Johnston had to take her turn on harbor guard, which involved our steaming back and fourth in front of the entrance to Guantanamo Bay. One weekend the ship that had been assigned this task developed mechanical problems so the Johnston, to the great dismay of the crew, was assigned this task an additional time. Captain Anglim wasn't too happy about this assignment either, so shortly after putting out to sea, he ordered "swim call" and we all went for a swim in the warm waters off the coast of Cuba. Just beyond where we were swimming some of our shipmates with M-1's were on the Johnston's motor whale boat to watch for sharks. While swimming, someone yelled "Shark!!!" and I have never seen so many sailors get out of the water and back on the ship in such a short time. At first we thought the shark warning had been a hoax, but then sharks started to appear along the sides of the ship. One fellow got one of the ship's fishing rods, baited it with a piece of meat, and dangled it in front of one of the sharks. The shark took the bait but seemed to realize something was in his mouth that shouldn't be there so he jerked his head and snapped the line like it was cotton string. Someone else decided to fish using a large piece of meat attached to a large meat hook, a piece of chain attached to that as a leader, and a piece of three-quarter inch rope attached to the chain. Sharks may be lots of things, but we found out they weren't stupid as they left this bait alone. While at anchor in Guantanamo Bay, one sailor from the ship actually did catch a rather large barracuda from the fantail. Enough about Johnston fishing stories.

While at Gitmo we made one liberty call in Port Au Prince, Haiti and another to the Naval Base in Roosevelt Roads, Puerto Rico where we also did some gunnery practice at the island of Culebra. After Puerto Rico we were supposed to make a liberty call to the Virgin Islands, but we were out-voted by our married ship-mates and ended up going right back to Charleston a few days early. Captain Anglim authorized this election and our early return to Charleston.

The Johnston remained in port only a few weeks before it was assigned to duty in the Mediterranean. Shortly after leaving for the Med, our ship encountered a hurricane. The Atlantic was so rough very few of us were hungry and most of us ate nothing but a few M&M's for nourishment.

I remember walking out on the bridge on time and all I could see were giant walls of water. To even see the sky I had to press my face against one of the portholes, and look straight up. One night while steaming in these heavy seas, we were assigned to follow the USS Kennedy (an aircraft carrier), and directly behind us was an Oiler. We were all steaming into the wind and it was calculated that the Kennedy was only progressing a few knots, we were sitting dead in the water, and the Oiler behind us was actually loosing ground against the wind.

The only time we could see either of these other ships on radar was when we happened to be on the top of a swell. At one point we actually steamed into the eye of this hurricane which was quite an eerie place. There were angry clouds all around, but the sea in the eye of the hurricane was very calm and quiet. The only menacing thing in the eye that we saw was a water-spout (AKA tornado to us land-lubbers). Because it was so calm there, a few of us wondered if we could stay in the eye of the hurricane until it blew itself out, but even though he had great feelings for his crew, Captain Anglim vetoed this idea before even giving it any serious thought, HA! After passing through the hurricane and a total of 22 days at sea, we finally arrived in the English Channel. Although the Johnston never made a liberty call in Plymouth, England, our sister ship, the USS McCard (DD-822) did have to go in for repairs after its encounter with the hurricane.

A few days later we steamed through the Striates of Gibraltar and into the Mediterranean Sea. While in the Med, our duties aboard the ship were again all quite routine consisting of ASW practice, plane guarding for the Kennedy, etc. We made numerous liberty calls in Spain, France, Italy, Greece, Turkey, etc. and we were able to take part in many excellent tours provided by the USO. We spent a total of 7 months in the Mediterranean before returning to Charleston. Probably our most significant liberty ports were our visits to Turkey. At the time the Johnston was in the Mediterranean, international relations between the U.S. Government, the U.S. Navy, and the Republic of Turkey were somewhat strained. As the Republic of Turkey had been a member of the North American Treaty Organization since World War II and had continued to be a staunch ally of the United States, our government decided that something must be done to improve these strained relations. It had been several months since any U.S. Navy ships had visited ports in Turkey, so the Navy assigned the USS Johnston to be the first ship to return. Rather than steam through the Dardanelles and up to Istanbul on the Bosporus, the Johnston was sent to the eastern edge of the Mediterranean. We were briefed on the importance of these liberty calls and we were told to act as if we were ambassadors of good will. Our first liberty call was to the city of Iskenderun, near the Syrian border, which is the farthest eastern port in the Mediterranean Sea. A few days later we visited the City of Mersin which is approximately 100 miles to the west. While in these ports the Turkish government provided us with transportation and we visited numerous scenic and historic spots, one of which was the historic and religious city of Antioch. Of all of us "sailor/ambassadors" the individual who deserved credit for showing the U.S. at its very best, was a first class radarman by the name of Jesse Dawson. The people in eastern Turkey were unaccustomed to visits by tourists from foreign countries let alone sailors from a U.S. Navy war ship. The people there were friendly but they often acted in a reserved way, almost as if they were suspicious of our intentions. While browsing along the various shops, RD1 Dawson purchased a lapel pin that displayed a Turkish flag. Jesse placed this lapel pin on his uniform and he was an immediate hit among the Turkish people as wherever he was seen he was surrounded by individuals who all wanted to shake his hand. After these successful visits by the USS Johnston, the Navy continued regular liberty stops in Turkey.

Other memorable liberty ports (but considerably less historic) included our first visit to Trieste, Italy. After we first entered the Mediterranean Sea the USS Johnston (AKA the "Jolly-J") stopped at the Spanish island of Menorca. We stayed there only a short time before we continued on to Trieste. After 22 days at sea, the supplies for the mess deck were getting quite meager to say the least. Although we always had plenty to eat, at sea the Johnston's constant pitching up and down and its rolling from side to side acted like a giant butter churn which turned any fresh milk sour in just a few days. We had been using only powdered milk for most of the trip. Our supply of fresh eggs had been depleted and we were soon eating powdered eggs. The fresh meat had also been used up and according to scuttlebutt (that probably wasn't true) we were eating canned meats that had been processed back in the 1940's. Anyway, after getting to Trieste, we were all hungry for a really good meal. Several of us, including this book's editor George Sites and Johnny Jones our ship's postal clerk, went ashore to eat in an Italian restaurant. We ordered pizza thinking about American style pizza dripping in tomato sauce and melted mozzarella cheese, and heaped with sausage, pepperoni, mushrooms, etc. When our first Italian pizza arrived it turned out to be a bit of a disappointment to say the least as it was more like a dried out shingle that had once been painted with a thin coat of tomato juice. After this dinner we became considerably more appreciative of the food we were served aboard the Jolly-J and the cooks who prepared our meals. Before we lift the Mediterranean however, many of us grew to appreciate European foods a great deal more. The first time any of us ate European bread it seemed dry, hard, and was served without any butter. Very seldom could we order butter but it wasn't long before we really grew to like bread from the various European ports. Other friends of mine who were also radarmen, Don Guldenschuh and Dave Bice, often received "care packages" from home that included sausage. After receiving these packages we would often go ashore, buy some wine, cheese, and bread and have a real feast. While in Trieste we also met some tourists from the United States. They were really nice people and aside from spending a considerable amount of time with us they also drove us to the hills just outside of Trieste so we could look over into Yugoslavia. Although Yugoslavia had a communist government at the time, it was not closely allied with the Soviet Union.

When the Jolly-J visited Naples, Italy it was around Christmas time. The aircraft carrier the USS Kennedy was also in Naples where Bob Hope was scheduled to have his Christmas Show for military personnel. Many of us from the Jolly-J attended. Johnny Jones, our ship's postal clerk had been airlifted off of the Johnston and sent home to Macon, Georgia shortly after our first visit to Trieste because a close family member was having serious medical problems. Before departing the Johnston however "Jonesy" gave us a Georgia State Flag so we decided to take this flag along to the Kennedy when we saw Bob Hope's Christmas Show. Before the show started we were told by some of Bob Hope's assistants that we should cheer and laugh extra loud when Bob put on his show as portions of this program would be shown on TV back in the States and also in England. They told us that some of the jokes Bob would tell were of a dry English nature, but even if they didn't seem all that funny to us to please act as if they were hilarious. Just after the punch-line of one of Bob Hope's jokes, George Sites and I each took an end of Jonesy's Georgia Flag and held it high for Bob Hope to see. Bob saw what we had and told his cameras to be sure to take our picture. Hopefully Jonesy saw us wave his flag so he knew many of his old friends were still thinking about him and missed him on the Jolly-J.

The care packages I received from home were usually newspapers and magazines. These included copies of the "Carthage News," the "Madison Daily Journal," and "Parade Magazine." After we finished reading these publications in the radar shack I would take them down to the mess deck for everyone else where they were read by other sailors of the USS Johnston from the Captain on down. The newspapers which were from small towns in South Dakota contained articles of mostly local interest, but they did contain some news from back in the USA, something of which we received very little while we were in the Mediterranean. Anyway, before any of these papers finally ended up in the old "chit can" they were ragged, dog-eared, read, and re-read many, many times.

Probably the one thing of historical significance that took place aboard the USS Johnston while I was aboard was a relaxing of the usual Navy regulations. This order came down from Admiral Elmo R. Zumwalt Jr. who later became Chief of Naval Operations. Admiral Zumwalt, with lots of sea duty under his belt himself, realized that sea duty aboard Navy ships wasn't exactly equivalent to taking a pleasure cruise. When people presently complain about terrorist suspects being incarcerated at Guantanamo Bay, and show the cells in which they live, most destroyer sailors would look on only with envy. Although few of us would have any desire to be incarcerated on Guantanamo By with these prisoners, I doubt if anyone aboard the Johnston had as much private space as any one of these prisoners, and this included Captain Anglim. Anyway, to help improve moral, Admiral Zumwalt used the Johnston as one of his experimental ships. During this time we were allowed to grow beards, let our hair grow longer than had previously been allowed, there was no reveille, etc. To me, all of this seemed to work out OK, except at those times when we went aboard other ships that were not part of this Navy experiment. One time in the Mediterranean our ship was given some time with a Tender in Naples, Italy. While near the Tender the ship not only underwent a number of repairs, but many of us had doctor and dental appointments, etc. I was one of the first that was required to have some dental work done aboard the Tender. Several of us were in the dentist's waiting room when the Chief Master at Arms on the Tender walked in, looked at everyone in the waiting room, and one by one he told all sailors from the Johnston that we would be required to leave hip ship (with this interpretation I am using considerably milder language, HA!). When we got back to the Johnston, the Officer of the Deck asked why we were all back so soon. When we told him what had transpired on the Tender, he told us to wait at the quarter-deck, and he went immediately to Captain Anglim. The next time the motor whale boat left the Johnston it had only one man aboard, it was the Captain himself, and when he departed he didn't look at all happy. A short time later he was back on board the Johnston, and all of us were back in the dentist's waiting room on the Tender. All of this was to the great dismay of the Tender's Master at Arms. I did have to agree with the Tender's Master at Arms as with our straggly beards and long hair, we did look like a pretty scruffy lot. I also wonder at times if Captain Anglim didn't have some of the same feelings about us as the Duke of Wellington had about his army back in 1815. When reviewing his troops just before fighting Napoleon at the Battle of Waterloo, on of Wellington's aides asked him if he figured his men would scare the French. To this, Wellington replied, "I don't know, but they sure scare the Hell out of me."

Although I never met Admiral Zumwalt personally, I would have to say that he was another Navy man for whom I have a great deal of respect and admiration. I say this not only because of his efforts to make the cramped life aboard ships at sea a bit more bearable, but also because of what he did when he was Commander of Naval Forces in Vietnam. At this time many Navy men were serving aboard river patrol boats (PBR's) in the Mekong Delta. Casualties aboard these PBR's were horrendous and to improve this situation Admiral Zumwalt ordered the use of the defoliant Agent Orange along the river systems of the Mekong Delta. Although this greatly reduced casualties aboard the PBR's, it cost Admiral Zumwalt his own son. Admiral Zumwalt's son was a sailor serving on one of these PBR's and a few years later died of cancer that was believed to have been caused by Agent Orange. Although the loss of his own son broke his heart, Admiral Zumwalt never did regret his authorization of the use of Agent Orange as it saved so many lives of other military personnel who served under him. In my estimation, both Admiral Zumwalt and Captain Anglim were men who genuinely cared about the individuals serving in their commands.

When I was separated from the navy, I still had my beard and relatively long hair. As I had a small motorcycle in Charleston, I decided to ride that back home to South Dakota. I decided to visit some relatives in Michigan on my way home, and as I crossed the river from West Virginia into Ohio I was stopped by a road-block of Ohio Highway Patrolmen looking for traffic violators. The first thing they asked to see was my driver's license, which had expired while I was in the Navy. According to federal law at that time, my driver's license remained valid as long as I was in the Navy and would remain valid until I got home to have it renewed properly. My motorcycle helmet had an eye shield which caused the rushing air as I rode to blow up under my chin making my straggly beard look so wild and twisted even a hippie would have been ashamed to wear such a thing. After looking me over, with my hair and beard, the highway patrolmen didn't want to believe I had been in the Navy a few days before, but since all of my paperwork checked out, they had no other choice but to let me go on my way. For a while there however I was wondering if I wasn't going to have to call the Johnston and have Captain Dan bail me out one more time.

Fire, Fire, Fire In The After Engine Room Switchboard!

By: Tony Tomasin, Electricians Mate (EM2)

Years on board the Johnston: 1968 to 1971

Those not of an engineering rating seldom knew of the conditions faced below decks in the boiler and engine rooms of the old USS Johnston. As the Johnston was a Gearing class destroyer, she was built with most of the same antiquated power plant as her World War II predecessor the Fletcher Class Destroyers. This no luxury power plant required two boiler rooms and two engine rooms which provided steam for propulsion and electrical power for the ship. The boiler rooms had two boilers each that produced huge amounts of steam which powered the steam turbines that drove the propellers and the turbines that turned the electrical generators. Each engine room had its own propulsion turbine and turbine powered electrical generator. The steam that allowed these systems to work efficiently had to be super heated

269

to 850 degrees Fahrenheit with a working pressure of 650 pounds per square inch. Steam at those temperatures and pressures made working in the engineering spaces unbearably hot and dangerous at times. It is a fact that superheated steam is invisible to the naked eye because of its temperature. If one was to pass through a pin hole steam leak at those temperatures and pressures, it could literally cut a man in half. As hot as it normally was in these spaces, one could tell that a small superheated steam leak existed because of a rapid rise in temperature in the space. A catastrophic steam leak would almost mean certain death to those occupying these spaces.

Needless to say it was always very hot when working below decks in the engineering spaces. The only respite from the heat while working or standing watch was if you stood directly under a 16″ fan powered air duct that blew in forced air from somewhere above decks. In the engine rooms these fan power blowers or ducts were placed in front of the throttleman's station where the machinist mates stood their turbine throttle watch and one more in front of the electrical switchboards where the electricians mate stood his electrical generator and switch board watch. The comfort these ducts provided, if one could call it that, was minimal at best. If outside air temperatures were high, the air being blown below decks offered little help to those standing below them. Engineering ratings spent many hours on watch huddled under these ducts trying to draw what little comfort they could from the air being blown around them. Another factor that had a major effect on temperatures in these spaces was if the hatches that accessed the spaces were left open. All four engineering spaces had a hatch that could be accessed from the main passageway inside the ship and another hatch that could be accessed from outside the ship. As long as these hatches were left open, additional air would be drawn down into the engineering space and help dissipate some of the oppressive heat down below. When these hatches were closed for general quarters or any other reason, life was all but unbearable down there. The interior hatch was normally left open, but while underway the exterior hatch would be closed so that any waves breaking over the side of the ship wouldn't find their way down into the engineering spaces causing flooding and damage. In addition, the exterior hatches were supposed to be closed at night while underway to avoid any light that may give away the ships position.

Below the outboard after engine room hatch ran a ladder to the after engine room deck level where I stood my many electrical switchboard watches while underway. Those watches were spent in great heaping hours of monotony and sweltering heat while watching the dials, meters and lights staring back at me from the after electrical switchboard. While I had my own air duct above my head, it barely made any difference in temperature. But if I stood directly under the open outboard hatch against the ladder going up, I could occasionally feel a very small amount of cool air drifting down. The other engineering ratings sharing watch with me also knew when the exterior hatch was dogged down the temperatures increased, so it was in all our best interest to keep the exterior hatch open. Even when we weren't supposed to.

As with all good sailors, we of the after engine room found a way to bend the rules a bit regarding the closure of that exterior hatch. It was found that the hatch leading to the exterior of the ship could be closed in such a way that the handle used to secure the hatch could be positioned so the hatch would rest on the handle leaving enough space around the hatch to allow free passage of air below decks. With the hatch door only partially closed in this position, even at night underway, the light escaping around the hatch was unnoticeable. We were able to maintain our precious supply of outside air without any problems, or so we thought.

As any tin can sailor can attest, destroyers are a pretty rough riding ship. In foul weather it is not uncommon to take water over the side and awash the main deck. We were underway half way through a winter Mediterranean cruise. The seas had been rough, and the ship was pitching and rolling. At 2330 hours I had just been awakened from a restless sleep trying to hold on to my bunk for dear life. Trying not to be thrown to the deck while sleeping underway in rough weather tended to keep everyone on edge, but I knew I had to make my way forward to the after engine room to spend another dreaded mid-watch below. After several months into this cruise I was accustom to bouncing off the bulkheads in the main passage way and running up and down hill as the ship pitched and rolled. Once I made my way to the inboard hatch going down to the after engine room I could feel the rush of hot air escaping from the scuttle I would have to pass through to spend my dreaded 4 hour mid-watch. Once in front of the switch board a quick glance would verify that everything was the same as it had been the hundreds of watches that preceded this one.

This evening's watch added an additional bit of discomfort to my previous watches though. The seas had been exceptionally rough, and I could see that not only myself but the second class top watch machinist mate and his 4 assistants were all hanging on to something just to keep from sliding across the deck with each roll of the ship. I had latched an arm around the ladder going up to the outboard hatch that was supposed to be dogged down while watching the electrical switchboard in front of me. From my position I could also look at the degaussing switchboard to the right of me if that thought should ever cross my mind, but I don't believe in the 3 years I served on the Johnston it ever did.

As the monotony of the night watch progressed with the majority of the ship's crew in their bunks, things were about to get quite exciting. The first thing I noticed was that the ship seemed to make a course change and the seas seemed to become rougher. This change in course may have put the ship at an angle to the waves causing them to roll her side. I was standing under the outboard after engine room hatch when a wave broke over the deck and made its way straight down the hatch drenching me and the 480 volt electrical switchboards that controlled half of the ship. If just being drenched with cold water wasn't shocking enough for me, the sight of flames shooting out of the front of the main switchboard brought instant dread to my thoughts. The second class machinist mate top-watch rushed up to me with a look of total shock and bewilderment. I knew we were in big trouble, so I grabbed him by the arm and half shoved him up the ladder yelling at him to dog down that God damned hatch. Because he outranked me and was top dog while on his watch, he looked at me like I had gone mad but he knew enough to trust me on this one. If we took one more roll and drenching like we just had, we would be in even more trouble than we were already in. With flames, sparks and smoke shooting from around all the dials, switches and lamps on the switchboard, my next course of action was to inform the forward engine room of the emergency we were facing. The forward engine room acts as the engineering control center for all engineering spaces and the entire ship. Should any engineering emergency exist, the forward engine room would take command and determine what course of action should be taken. I rang up the forward engine room and once making contact I yelled the most dreaded words anyone could hear on an engineering watch. Fire, Fire, Fire in the after engine room switch board. Needless to say things started to get real busy from there on. Should the electrical fire in the after engine room switchboard get out of hand, power could be lost to the rear half of the ship. If damage control wasn't managed properly, and electrical power was lost to the rear generator and switchboard, it could then drag down the forward generator and a total loss of power could be experienced throughout the ship. We would in fact be dead in the water during rough seas. Then as rapidly as the switchboard started burning the flames suddenly extinguished themselves. To my and my top watch's astonishment all was back to normal except for the water that was dripping from me, the switchboards and the decks that had become awashed. We grabbed anything we could lay our hand on and started wiping down the switchboards to keep any more water from slipping inside them and mopped up as much water off the deck as we could. The next thing I knew as I looked up I could see almost every officer, chief petty officer and petty officer above the rank of second class staring down at us. Damage control parties had been rousted from their racks and were none to happy as well as rest of those assembled before us. I believe the total relief that was felt by all that no catastrophic damage had been done saved all our asses that night.

The result of the fire had a repercussion that affected every watch in every engineering space from that night on. While underway, it would always be a little hotter on watch below decks. The captain and engineering officer let it be known that at no time while underway would the exterior hatches leading to the engineering spaces remain open. So it was back to standing under the forced air ducts trying to wait out another watch and wish that we could open that outboard hatch just one more time.

My USS Johnston Story

By: John H. Jones "Johnny", "Jonesy", Postal Clerk (PC3)

Years on board the Johnston: 1968 to 1969

Although I was on the USS Johnston for a short period (October 1968 to October 1969), I got to know most of the crew. I was the Johnston's mailman!! I was assigned to the Johnston in October '68 just before she went into the Charleston Naval Shipyard for a complete overhaul. I'm sure most of you remember me in my small post office right above the first aft sleeping compartment. I bunked in that compartment on the right side as you were going down the ladder. I was also the ship's driver for the Ford pick-up we used to get the mail and other supplies.

When getting underway, I was assigned to the Special Sea and Anchor detail on the bridge as a sound powered telephone talker for CIC (Combat Information Center). I had a front row seat every time we departed or docked. While underway I was assigned to CIC where I worked with the Radarmen.

I was on the GITMO cruise, the Haiti trip, the gun practice session on the Isle of Culebra and the 1969 MED cruise, including Operation Peace keeper. I visited

Menorca and Trieste on the MED cruise. When the Johnston left for the '69 MED cruise, my wife was pregnant with our first child. In October, our baby daughter was born early and she was very ill. On 14 October I was picked up from the Johnston by a helicopter from the USS John F. Kennedy to go on emergency leave. I flew from the JFK to Athens, Greece, then to Naples, Italy and then to Rein-Main USAF base in Germany. Due to bad weather, I was delayed in Germany. While waiting to leave Germany, I was contacted by a Navy Chaplain and the Red Cross. They informed me my baby had died. I finally got home to Macon, Georgia and was re-united with my wife and family.

While on leave in Macon, I requested a transfer from the Johnston to an assignment in the states. I was assigned to the Naval Reserve Training Center in Macon (my old reserve unit). I was honorably discharged from the Navy on 12 December 1969.

I still live in Macon, Georgia where I worked for the U.S. Postal Service for 35 years. My last position with the USPS was Manager of Budget. I'm still married to the same ol' gal I was married to while on the Johnston (we've been married 42 years!!) We have one daughter, two wonderful grandchildren and a great son-in-law. I retired from the USPS in January, 2004 and I'm enjoying the retired life.

Although I was not on the Johnston for an extended period, my memories of my time on the "Jolly J" are vivid and I treasure them. (Thank you George Sites for putting together the history of the USS Johnston DD 821).

GITMO Story (SPIES??????) - Before we left for GITMO there were some container like buildings put on our helicopter deck and some extra personnel came aboard. We stopped at Key West - I got off and walked to the Post Office with the mail. Once back on the ship, we sailed west toward the Gulf of Mexico. We went the length of Cuba and then turned east toward GITMO. I guess we were doing some electronic work or spying on Cuba. We had to stand extra watches in CIC during the trip around Cuba to maintain radar and radio contacts.

We were leaving Charleston for the (1969) GITMO shakedown cruise. A 2nd class Gunner's Mate, who said he had been to GITMO before and didn't want to go back, jumped into the Cooper River as the Johnston was being pulled out into the river by the tugs. He swam away toward the pier and the waiting Shore Patrol. We never did find out his fate but he didn't go to GITMO.

THE INCIDENT - One afternoon several of us (don't remember who, but it was probably some of my Radar and Admin buddies) got permission to go "on base" at GITMO to the PX to shop. I do remember EM2 Phil Parsons bought a Pentax camera at the large PX - very busy. We decided that a cold beer would be nice so we approached an EM club. We were met at the door by a large SP who stopped us at the entrance. The SP took a good look at us and asked "Are you guys off a ship?" We replied "Yes!" He then said "Salty sailors aren't allowed in the club." I replyed, "Why - we are all in the same Navy?" The large SP took a hard look at me (5'6", 125 lbs) and said "You heard what I said. Salty sailors not allowed!" We left and went back to the ship and mentioned the incident to LCMDR Vandiver (XO). A few days later the Captain and XO had a couple of beach parties for as much of the crew as possible. We finally got our cold beer!

GITMO REMEMBRANCES - At GITMO we were docked at a service pier during our shakedown cruise. As a bridge telephone talker for CIC, I was able to actually SEE as we docked or got underway. I had a great SEAT!! I could look up in the hills around the bay and see marine gun emplacements in the hills - positioned towards Cuba. Some nights we left the pier and anchored in the bay with our 5-inch guns trained on the hills around GITMO in case the Marines needed naval gun fire support. While we were in the bay at anchor, we could see ships (some Russian) passing through the bay going to a Cuban port. GITMO was beautiful and cool at night but very hot during the day. On one particular day some of the air blowers in the engine room went out and the tech's from GITMO refused to go out for tests until the blowers were fixed (they didn't want to get too hot). I went down to the engine room with LCDR Vandiver (I was his driver and/or go-fer) to check on the repair. It was mighty hot down there, but the blowers were fixed and we got back on schedule.

I got my first sailboat ride at GITMO. On a Sunday, EM2 Phil Parsons and I were able to check out a small, two-person sailboat from the boat club on base (I'm surprised they let "salty" sailors check out a boat). We managed to sail near the Johnston anchored in the bay. It was a fun trip. Once our sea trials were over, we were glad to leave GITMO. Our trip to Cuba was my first visit to a country outside the USA.

HAITI - After GITMO, on the way back to Charleston, the Johnston stopped in Port-au-Prince, Haiti. Pulling into the port the country looked very green and beautiful. Later, we found out that the country was very poor. After we set docked, the "bum-boats" came up to the ship. They had all types of merchandise to sell us.

We were cautioned that the "bum-boat" items were of poor quality and this was true. Several of us, including an officer, Mr. Templin went on liberty. We rented a taxi and took a tour of the city hitting the high-lights. We saw the Presidential Palace, several other buildings and churches. We also went to a large shopping area where we found some nice woken masks and other items. We also went up into the mountains to a rum factory where we had samples of the local rum. We were all shocked at how poor the country was. After Port-au-Prince, the Johnston sailed to Puerto Rico (no liberty) and then back to Charleston.

One summer evening, probably after GITMO and before the MED cruise while the Johnston was in Charleston; a signalman named Saltzman had the quarter deck watch. He made the announcement over the PA system: "The Roach Coach has made its approach." Of course the "Roach Coach" was the GeDunk truck that had all kinds of goodies for us to purchase and went from ship to ship in the evening. Apparently the informal "Roach Coach" announcement made by Saltzman did not sit well with someone up the chain of command. The next evening when the "Roach Coach" pulled up to the Johnston, Saltzman, who had the duty again, made the following announcement: "The mobile canteen from the U.S. Navy commissary is now parked at the gangway." Personally I liked the first announcement better.

MED Cruise - OPERATION PEACE KEEPER & Menorca, Baleric Islands, Spain and the Port of Mahon - After the Johnston left Charleston for our MED cruise, we participated in a NATO exercise "Operation Peace Keeper" with over 40 other ships from five NATO countries. On the way to this operation we ran into some very rough weather near the country of England. I climbed up the Signal Bridge during the storm and got a couple of photos of the Johnston buried in the SEA back to the forward gun mount. I also remember being thrown out of my rack during this storm. The storm was finally over and we sailed through the Straits of Gibraltar going toward the Balearic Islands – our first liberty stop. I was on duty in CIC during the passage through the Straits.

We MED-Moored in the Port of Mahon on the island of Menorca. Several of us had liberty (me, Sites and Grew). Grew spoke Spanish, so we hired a taxi and went across the island to a resort (Ciutadella) area where there were a large number of British tourists. We were all in uniform (whites, I think) and we were a novelty to the British. We were asked many questions about the states and the Navy. We got back to the Johnston after a large supper. The next morning we had a big mail call which kept me very busy. Before we left Mahon, I remember driving a car, rented by the Johnston, to the local airport with several bags of mail from the Johnston. I got lost a couple of times in the narrow, twisty streets but I finally made it to the airport. At the airport, I parked at the curb and a ragged, one-armed man came up t me as I was getting out the mail bags and started talking loudly in Spanish and waving his one arm around. I took care of my business and left. Later I found out (from Grew) that this man was a Spanish Civil War Veteran and he expected a tip from me for his "parking spot".

We left Mahon headed for Trieste, Italy.

TRIESTE – After the Johnston left Menorca, she sailed through the MED to the city of Trieste, Italy. Here we again MED-moored and I had a front row seat on the bridge doing my CIC-sound powered telephone duty on the Special Sea and Anchor detail. I think most of the OI and OC sections had duty on the first day in port. I remember the ship hosted lunch for a number of civilians on the first day in port. I also remember our cooks going ashore and getting fresh vegetables for our mess. A lot of civies came on board for the lunch.

When we finally got liberty, Harris, Sites, myself and another sailor went to the harbor area to get some lunch and we really wanted pizza. We topped at a water front café and got a table. The waiter on duty showed his distaste for American sailors by stacking dirty dishes from a nearby table on <u>our</u> table. Suddenly an Italian woman, who was sitting with her husband and another couple, came over and really got on the waiter for his behavior. We couldn't understand what she was saying, but the waiter immediately cleared our table and took our order and he was nice about it. The pizza we ordered turned out to be a side dish and was small and not very good. Harris said it tasted like cardboard. It certainly was not like pizza in the USA. As we were eating, another waiter brought out a couple of large fish and showed them to the people at the table near us. I guess they were picking one for their meal.

After lunch we did some shopping and sight-seeing including some Roman ruins. I remember going to a small mall and buying a leather purse for my wife at a small

shop. The young lady working there left me alone in the shop while she went next door to get change for the $20 (US) I gave her.

I think that also on this liberty as we were walking around the shopping area, an older American couple, in

281

a VW Van, stopped and offered us a ride and a tour around the city. We ended up going into the mountains above the city to the border with Yugoslavia. The picture is Sites posing with the American couple and their VW Van.

I also remember going to a telephone exchange in Trieste and calling my wife in the states. It was good to talk to her as she was expecting our first child. While I was in the exchange, I was talking with an older sailor while waiting for my call to go through to the states. Turns out he was from my home town of Macon, Georgia and my Dad had taught him in high school (my Dad was a teacher and later a High School principal). What a small world and I don't recall his name anymore.

Some of our crew members that I remember are (and not in any particular order):

Mr. Rausch (Ensign)
Mr. Templin (Ensign)
Mr. Barry (Ensign)
LCMDR Vandiver (XO)
Joe Cizzio
Dave Bice (radarman)
Tom Noto (radarman)
Ken Giegling (radarman)
Daun Harris "Harry" (radarman)
Phil Parsons
Jack (John) Nix
David K. Phillips (engineman)
Louie Trapani
Melvin Kuykendall (radarman)
Al Loehr (radarman)
Bill Dallas (cook)
Saltzman (signalman)
George Sites (radarman)
Barry (tall guy, slept above me)
Thomas Grew (PN)

Roger Box (radarman)
Don Guldenschuh (radarman)
Benje Benjestorf (radarman)

Louie Trapani - I think Louie was an EM but I'm not sure. He was from New York City and proud of it. He spent most of the day avoiding the officers and chiefs because he kept his hair long. I can remember Louie stuffing his hair up under his white hat or ball cap to hide how long it was. About every two or three weeks his mother would send him a package that contained salami and a bottle of Chianti. You could tell the package was for Louie because the salami left a grease stain on the package wrapping. Louie always shared his goodies with his shipmates.

Newsletter to families back home from the MED cruise
(Newsletter provided by Jonesy)

Dear JOHNSTONIANS,

It was truly a pleasure meeting so many of you on our "Family Cruise". The weather was with us and I hope that everyone enjoyed themselves on the cruise as well as at the picnic the following day. It was certainly our pleasure to have had you aboard. To those of you who were unable to make this cruise we offer our regrets and hope you will be able to participate in the next cruise.

Upon leaving Charleston JOHNSTON, along with several other ships, sailed north-east. Each day it got a little bit cooler, especially in the evenings. About four days out of port we ran into some rough weather which gave those of us who thought we had our "sea-legs" some second thoughts. We all survived the rough weather with flying colors some a bit paler than others though, and sailed on.

On the morning of the 17th we joined up with a combined force representing various countries of the North Atlantic Treaty organization (NATO) participating in the naval exercise "Peace Keeper". This exercise, which ended the 23rd, involved over 40 ships and approximately 220 land and carrier based aircraft from five NATO nations.

Peace Keeper had two objectives. The primary one was to test the readiness and effectiveness of the NATO Striking Fleet Atlantic Community. The other purpose and the one most valuable to us on an individual ship basis, was to help perfect procedures and tactics within the Naval Forces of the North Atlantic Alliance. The exercise was a valuable experience and I believe we all learned many things from it.

With the Peace Keeper over we are going on to the MED. We are currently scheduled for port visits in Spain, France, Greece, and Italy, but with a schedule as flexible as ours there's no telling where we're liable to end up.

In case you've started wondering why you haven't received any mail from your JOHNSTON crewmember, it's because all mail sent off the ship before September 14th was lost at sea while being transferred to a carrier for delivery to the U.S. However, mail sent off after the 14th should be getting to you soon if you haven't already received it.

We have a beard and mustache contest going on that started when we sailed and will be judged the day before arrival at our first port. Prizes are in order for the "bushiest", "scraggliest", and "most handsome". About a week ago there was much face-scratching going on and some contestants just fizzled out and went for the razor. However, we have some stalwarts who persevered and the results will be known by our next newsletter.

I close with the request that you save and forward to myself any news clippings that might appear in your local newspaper concerning JOHNSTON's men and operations. JOHNSTON keeps a scrap book also and we are very interested in the successes of our crew members.

Sincerely,

A RADARMAN'S QUEST

By: George A. Sites, Radarman (RD2)

Years on board the Johnston: 1968 to 1971

Fresh out of Radarman A-School, I was told to "Report for Duty" on the William C. Lawe DD-763 stationed in Mayport, Florida. Upon arrival to the base, I quickly found out the ship had sailed for Charleston, SC. The Navy then flew me to Charleston only to find the LAWE in dry-dock. What a disappointment. I had looked forward to seeing the world and having a girl in every port just as my father did during WWII. After about a month on board, I found myself mess cooking for the next three months. Finally upon completion of repairs to the ship, we set sail to where else but GITMO. After the shakedown cruise and arrival back in Mayport, I once again found myself headed for Charleston for duty on board the USS Johnston DD-821. I was really excited; I had completed my tour of duty in the Mess Deck and was now ready to become a Radarman.

USS Johnston - I arrived on board the Johnston on December 10, 1968, got my berthing assignment and was told I had been assigned to nothing other than mess duty for the next three months. I didn't give up. I met with RDC Jackson and RD1 Dawson to start learning about being a Radarman on board a ship. This proved to be worthwhile as I advanced from RDSN to RD2 in a relatively short period of time.

In my opinion, being a Radarman was one of the best jobs in the Navy. We worked in the air conditioned CIC (Combat Information Center), rarely did any dirty work such as scraping and painting, plus we always knew what was going on because CIC was a second home to the Captain and the Executive Officer.

Admiral Elmo Zumwalt - During a couple of my years on the Johnston, Admiral Elmo Zumwalt was the Chief of Naval Operations (CNO) and he was trying different ideas to make the Navy more appealing to young men. For example, he allowed us to keep some civilian clothes on board which previously was not allowed. He also relaxed personal grooming to allow beards and longer hair. I took advantage of the longer hair. Some of the "lifer's", especially the XO didn't like this new rule. That fact was unknown to me at the time.

One time, during flight ops with the USS Kennedy CV-67, I was in CIC communicating with one of the planes from the carrier. All of a sudden someone taps me on the shoulder from behind. I turned around and the XO is motioning me with his finger to follow him. I called for Roger Box to take over and I followed the XO without any idea what was going on. We arrived at the ship's Barber Shop and the XO ordered ship's barber Vinnie Contrino to give me a "real Navy haircut". Then the XO left much to our surprise. Vinnie was a good guy and didn't scalp me. He left it as long as he thought would keep the XO off my back. It worked!

GITMO – We cruised down to GITMO for a shakedown which turned out to be not as bad as I had expected based upon my prior experience on the LAWE. I had advanced in pay grade and had a few more privileges.

One day while on the GITMO base, several of us crazy sailors decided to do some cliff diving. Looking back, that was really stupid. Anyone of us could have been seriously hurt. Thank God we all survived our cliff diving experience with only a few scratches and bruises.

On another day on the base, three of us rented or borrowed a small rowboat. There were two rules to be able to use it. First was to stay on the base side of the fence that separated the base from the other part of Cuba. The second was not to get out of the boat into the water. We thought the second one seemed really dumb. Well being the old salts we were and being tired of regulations, we not only went under the fence but one of the guys jumped into the water. He immediately started screaming and we pulled him out of the water. He had numerous stings or bites from Jelly Fish. We took him to the base hospital and told them he had lost his balance and fell out of the boat. We never did tell anyone about going under the fence.

FISHING – As the Johnston slowly patrolled the inlet to GITMO, we fished off the fantail. We caught a sand shark about three feet long. I have no idea what the cooks did with it.

SWIMMING – In addition to all the other "fun", we got to swim off the side of the ship. The Captain stopped the ship and allowed us to drift. We put a Jacobs Ladder over the side and dove in. A whaleboat manned with sailors and guns watched for sharks. Someone on board yelled "SHARK!" In a panic, we swam for the ladder. As the ship rolled, I reached for the ladder only to have my head pushed under water as the sailor behind me used my head and shoulders as a ladder. I thought I was going to drown. I never did find out if the shark call was for real. I suspect someone thought it was funny. Anyway, swim call ended.

Charleston, South Carolina – Downtown Charleston was quite nice. Good ol' southern charm. Of course we spent most of our time at South Charleston Beach, Foley Beach or Isle of Palms Beach.

Most of us had no transportation so we spent a lot of our liberty hours on the strip outside the main gate. It had every thing from lockers to hookers to bars and to delicious hot dogs. There were always people grabbing at you trying to get you to go in their bar. I'm not sure why, but I remember the "Psychedelic Pussycat" and, of course, the hot dogs.

DA' SCENE – One of the nicer places to go was "DA' SCENE" nightclub. It was clean and big with lots of girls. It had a disc jockey playing all the latest tunes plus two drummers playing live simultaneously to the music. It really gave the feeling of a real live concert. The club also had cages with beautiful girls dancing (not strippers) and psychedelic images projected on the walls. It was far out! I was a good old mid-western boy from a sheltered life in Columbus, Ohio. I had never even had an alcoholic drink. Much to my surprise, DA' SCENE had a "one-drink" minimum instead of an entrance fee. I ordered a draft beer only to find out it was either 32 or 44 ounces. I drank on it all night as my buddy QM2 Quinton Watson sucked down several of these monsters. Obviously this was not his first time drinking beer! I got back to the ship, not sure how but I'm sure I was feeling no pain.

1969–1970 MED Cruise – Like my Dad, I was finally going to see the world and hopefully have a girl in every port. For me, this was the first of two MED Cruises on the Johnston. Since I had never been out of the good ol' USA, I decided ahead of time that I would do as much sightseeing as possible before I did my partying. After all, I would probably never again in my life see these countries.

We left Charleston on September 8, 1969 and headed for the MED. The cruise was loaded with operations and lots of ports including Pollensa Bay, Menorca; Port Mahon, Menorca; Cagliari, Malta; Trieste, Italy; Navplion, France; Athens, Greece; Brindisi, Italy; D'hyres, France; Gaeta, Italy; Villefrancee, France; Naples, Italy; Iskenderun, Turkey; Mersin, Turkey and Palma, Mallorca. We were not lucky enough to get off in all of these ports. We arrived back in Charleston on March 28, 1970. Our Captain was Daniel F. Anglim, Jr. CDR and the XO was Robert B. Adgent, LCDR.

Trieste, Italy was one of our first liberties and we couldn't wait. We anchored in the port along with the John F. Kennedy CV-67. A whaleboat from the JFK finally picked us up and took us over to the pier. What excitement! As we approached the pier we could see all the beautiful women waving to us. The excitement grew – we had been at sea for what seemed forever. Finally the pier and as we climbed onto it, something seemed wrong. The women had hairy armpits. We did not know what to think. Apparently, the Italian women had not started shaving yet; although, I later found out they did in the larger cities like Rome.

Next we went on to Greece and the famous Acropolis high above the city of Athens. Athens is a beautiful city full of marvelous buildings and ruins. A lot of sightseeing took place here and, afterwards, it was great to sit in a sidewalk café have a drink and watch the people go by.

Brindisi, Italy was next and if I remember correctly, the Johnston was the first U.S. Warship to visit there. The locals were very friendly.

Palma, Mallorca was a beautiful island and a favorite of the Scandinavians for vacationing. Palma has a special meaning for me as you will read about in my adventures during the 1971 MED cruise.

We went on to Villefranche, France for some much needed R & R. It seems today that the French are not too crazy about Americans but they seemed to like the U.S. Sailors back then. Could it be because we spent so much money?

Our next liberty was in Naples, Italy which we called the "armpit of the world" probably because the harbor was so filthy. I still enjoyed walking the city, eating the pizza and drinking the sparkling wines which I hate today. Naples was the only city where I personally had any problems. I had been at the USO playing cards, talking to the girls and relaxing. I was all wrapped up talking to this one Italian girl while the other Johnston sailors headed elsewhere – probably a bar! When it came time to leave I should have called a taxi but I decided to walk back to the ship. Bad idea! It was about 2300 and dark. I chose to take a shortcut through an alley. Much to my surprise, three Italian punks tried to mug me. With a little luck, I sucker-punched one of them and ran for my life. I finally made it back to the ship on time and unharmed. Apparently, Naples hasn't changed much over the years. Nearly 35 years after my visit, my youngest son Brent while serving as an MM3 on the USS Enterprise CVN-65 had the same problem. He got mugged in Naples on his way back to his ship. His story didn't end quite like mine. He got his head split open and one of his buddies ended up with a broken leg or arm.

I took a bus tour to Rome. What a beautiful city with the Vatican, Coliseum, Catacombs, Fountain of Trevi and all the rest of the historical sites. Our tour package included a hotel room across the street from St. Peters. The tour also included an evening meal at a first class restaurant in which the food just seemed to come and come and come! Another event that made me worldly (in my own mind anyway) happened one evening walking the streets of Rome. I had to use the bathroom so I went into the public bathroom at the train station. As I walked in, a short little old Italian lady sat there with a pile of newspapers. I thought to myself how strange this seemed. I passed her and went into my stall only to discover the famous "squat and drop it". Now I realized why the lady was selling the newspapers.

292

Mersin, Turkey is the one place that I have no desire to ever return to. No particular reason, I just did not enjoy my visit there.

Europacar – This was a company that sold new cars of all brands to the various service men and women at factory cost. The sale was between the military person and the car factory. How it worked was simple. The Europacar sales rep would visit a particular ship and display sales brochures for all types of cars including Chevrolet's, Ferrari's, MG's and all the others you can think of. The military person would sign a contract for purchasing a car directly from the factory. The sales rep would then enter the order at the factory and you would then get a letter from them stating when it would be shipped and where to pick it up. I ordered an MG Midget and for $1685.00 plus $180.00 for shipping and another $35.00 for import duties it was mine. A whopping $1900.00 while they were selling for about $3500.00 (tax, title, shipping, etc.) in the states. They originally told me it would be delivered to Jacksonville, Florida and just before arriving back in the states, they switched it to Charleston. That obviously made me very happy. I loved that car. I would put the top down and put a surfboard in the back to impress the girls and cruise the beaches. I never did learn to surf.

1971 MED Cruise (SMOKE ON THE WATER) – After returning to Charleston from the 69/70 MED Cruise, Jim Wells, Paul Shane and I started jamming together with our guitars. As we practiced more, others started joining

the band. Jim Wells named the newly formed group **"SMOKE"**. The line-up now included George Sites, Lead Guitar; Jim Wells, Bass Guitar; Paul Shane, Rhythm Guitar and Trumpet; Dennis Jolin, Drums; Mike Niles, Electric Organ and Garret Hayes, Trombone. Little did we know that we were the Navy's first "Official Rock and Roll Band." Along with our new celebrity status came extra privileges such as early off, late return from liberty, no watch stations entering and leaving ports and I'm sure there were others. We would set up in the hangar facing out as if it were a stage when we practiced. When entering and/or leaving ports we moved further out on the flight deck and faced the shore.

During our "Tour", we played in a bar in Barcelona, Spain; a USO in Naples, Italy; a USAF Base in Brindisi, Italy and the most memorable was Palma, Mallorca.

When we docked in Palma, our self-appointed "manager" left the ship to drop off and pick up mail. Unknown to the band, he made a stop at Barbarella's. It was one of the largest disco's in all of Europe. He convinced the club's manager to allow "Smoke" to audition. Our manager returned to the Johnston and rounded up the band and we headed for Barbarella's. We used the amplifiers, drums, keyboard and PA system that was already set up. We started to play and we all started looking at each other thinking how great we sounded. We got the job; the manager told us what time to return that night.

We returned to the ship to clean up and get ready emotionally for our "big break". The manager and I got ready early and guitar in hand, we headed for the club. Upon arrival, the bartender fixed us drinks and the manager showed us to the dressing room – which actually had a "Star" on the door. I felt like ELVIS!

While waiting in the dressing room, our manager and I cooked up the idea that I would pretend to be drunk when the other band members showed up. Who knows why we did this.

Later on the club's manager showed the guys to the dressing room and told them he would come and get us when it was time to play. The guys opened the door and walked in. There I was stretched out on the couch acting drunk. They asked our manager, "What's wrong with Sites?" He told them the bartender kept giving us drinks and I had too many. They freaked out and started telling me to snap out of it. I continued to pretend to be drunk. Our manager did a great job of playing along with the joke.

Three knocks on the door and the club's manager yelled out, "You're on boys!" We all grabbed our instruments and headed out the door. The guys were still worried. I was trailing the others as we entered the stage through a door located in the back of the stage. As I walked to my place on the stage, I tripped on an extension cord and nearly fell. Now the guys were really nervous.

With the spotlight on us, the club's manager announced, "Please welcome SMOKE from the USS Johnston." We looked out and we were stunned at the number of people applauding and ready to watch the band perform.

Paul Shane counts down, the horns blast out and we played *Does Anyone Know What Time It Is*. We sounded great! Now the rest of the band felt good and knew I was OK to play. What a relief for them.

 After about three songs we started playing *I'm a Man*. When it came to the first instrumental guitar break, I dropped to my knees, whipped the guitar behind my head and played like there was no tomorrow. The band was shocked and so was the audience. I had never done anything like this before. We continued the song and when the second guitar break came, I flipped my guitar over and started playing with my teeth. The audience went wild and now the spotlight was focused on me. We were now officially stars, at least in our minds. It was great. The band was never told I was faking being drunk. We found out after the show that the equipment we used belonged to the "Hollies", a very famous group from the 1960's and 70's. We were told they were in the

audience watching. It's a good thing we didn't know prior to playing. We would have been even more nervous.

The next day while standing in the mess line, several sailors were giving me "high-fives" for the performance at Barbarella's. Whenever we played after that, I was expected to play with my teeth or my hands behind my head.

The rest of the '71 MED cruise was more of the same. I had seen most of the ports before so the highlight really was playing in the "SMOKE" band.

My discharge date was to be October 25, 1971 and the Johnston would still be cruising around in the MED. The XO tried to convince me to ship over but the $15,000 or $20,000 re-enlistment bonus must not have been enough to this young man to keep me. I was flown out of Barcelona, Spain up to Ireland and then to Bangor, Maine for customs and then on to Charleston, South Carolina for my last few days in the good ol' Navy. Looking back and considering my fond memories of the Navy makes me wonder why I did not ship-over for at least a few months and ride the ship back to Charleston.

IMMEDIATE REPLACEMENT ENSUED!

By: Pete Misslin, Ensign

Years on board the Johnston: 1969 to 1970

Just a quick story: When I started on the Johnston, Jack Berry (ex E-8 machinist mate) was the Chief Engineer. One day while touring with him in the after engine room, he commented to the chief in charge of the space, "You better check the clearances on the bearings on the main turbines!" He said this because they were emitting a "noise" that he didn't like. Sure enough, "leads" were taken at the next opportunity and the readings revealed that the tolerances exceeded those allowed. Immediate replacement ensued!

Pictured is Del Bartlett (left), Pete Misslin (center) and Jim Schneiders (right). The picture was taken at a restaurant in Athens in '69 or '70.

MY INTRODUCTION TO THE JOHNSTON

By: Pat Gadell, Signalman (SM3)

Years on board the Johnston: 1969 to 1971

I reported on board the Johnston late in the afternoon after having walked from the Charleston Transit Barracks where I had spent the last 3 weeks awaiting orders. My initial reaction to my orders was very positive. After all I had

298

pretty much received everything I had requested on my "dream sheet" - a DD out of Charleston (Charleston because it was close to my GA home). A DD??? Well, I don't really know how or why I came up with that.

Little did I know when reporting aboard that the ship was getting underway very early the next morning to head for Gitmo (way way before Gitmo was a household word). In the few waking hours I had spent before getting underway, I had already experienced what I felt to be a very cold welcome. To my detriment, my new shipmates quickly figured out that I was an "F'ingReserve" (one word). To this day, I do not fault my shipmates for being more than a little annoyed that I had earned my "crow"(SM3) while sitting in a classroom 300 miles away from the nearest saltwater. It was instant show-time for me as soon as we cast off lines and got underway. As we backed from the pier, another ship (The McCard DD-822 I think) sent a light signal "Delta One" It took me a bit to figure it out. Oh yeah...I think that's us. The other SM3 aboard, whose name I cannot recall told me to answer the signal. Well...I did know the Morse Code and all that stuff or I would not have passed my classroom tests, but the real deal was a whole different animal. When I failed to get the first couple of words out, I was very rudely removed from the light-stand, and it only got worse from there. To add insult to injury I was further humiliated by getting severely seasick a few hours later. I couldn't help but think of my recruiter that had been so friendly. He didn't tell me about this part!

This is not meant to be a negative story about the "Jolly J", or my shipmates. It was just a very rocky start for a 19 year old mama's boy that was going to grow up fast, ready or not. In the coming weeks at Gitmo, I pretty much went from a scared kid with no self confidence to a cocky little S.O.B.! It was a life long lesson that I still treasure. I am grateful for the Navy and the Johnston for teaching me to reach deep into my soul to find courage and confidence that only the military can instill in a young man.

As I have made my way through my career and adult life, that experience reminds me that sometimes all you can do is put one foot in front of the other, even if you don't know where you are going.

THE JOHNSTON VERSION OF A SNIPE HUNT

Being an experienced Boy Scout, I was quite familiar with veteran campers taking advantage of the young and naive newbies. I was a prime candidate to provide entertainment as they sent me on the obligatory, yet fictitious, "Snipe Hunt."

I should have known that I was a prime candidate to fall prey to old salt veteran sailors as soon as they discovered that they had a young, naive newbie aboard.

In my eagerness to please, I willingly did as I was told. My first assignment was to go down to the Bosuns' locker and tell them that I needed about 6 feet of "white nylon waterline." I came back empty handed and red faced as I quickly discovered that I had been had.

Not to be deterred, my next assignment a few days later was to go take this coffee can and go down to the Bosuns' locker and tell them that I need them to fill up my can with "Relative Bearing Grease." Ha! Had again!

A short few days later, with red faced memories still very fresh, I received my next assignment. Take this coffee can down to the Bosuns' locker and tell them to fill it up with "Monkey Shit." THIS time I was ready! I told my leading petty officer that I wouldn't do it. I initially stood firm while he threatened to write me up. Luckily, another young sailor took pity on me, and took me aside, and advised me that there really was such a thing as "Monkey Shit." He told me it's the black caulking compound used for caulking around plexiglas on the signal shack, and the bridge. This time I ventured down to the Bosuns' locker and returned with my mission complete.

I guess at the time, I never thought that these would be good memories. But 40 years later, in my mind it is priceless.

Chapter 6

THE VIETNAM WAR

FROM THE CHAPLAIN

By: Eli Takesian, Chaplain

Years on board the Johnston: 1964 to 1967

I was DESDIV 42's chaplain, which included the CONE, JC OWENS and JOHNSTON. I rode JOHNSTON 90% of the time.

I have one story from the TET Offensive of 1968. Here are two excerpts of an interview I gave in 2002 to the University of North Carolina:

"The Navy recalled me to active duty. From December 1964 to March 1967, I circuit-rode destroyers in the Atlantic, with two deployments to the Mediterranean, and one to the Persian Gulf. Having served aboard four fine destroyers, perhaps I shouldn't tell which one was my favorite; however, since it happened so long ago, I confess that it was USS JOHNSTON (DD-821). Terrific crew! I'll return to JOHNSTON later in the interview."

"In Hue' we were completely outnumbered by North Vietnamese forces (approximately 2400 infantry Marines attacking 10,000 to 15,000 entrenched NVA troops). Marines hadn't engaged in street fighting since the battle for Seoul, Korea (1950). We were not trained for it, as most of our time had been spent in the boondocks. NVA soldiers were occupying buildings and working out of spider holes. The configuration of streets was such that one could easily get lost.

I was in the Citadel, with the 1st Battalion 5th Marines.

"On February 17, 1968, at about 1600, Major Thompson (the battalion commander) announced, suddenly, that the entire battalion would be moving forward in 30 minutes, just before dark. We saddled up. At the designated moment, the entire battalion pressed forward. The CP (command post) and BAS settled inside a ravaged Roman Catholic parochial school.

That night the situation became worse. Our own casualty figures had caught up with us. An ARVN (South Vietnamese Army) unit was supposed to cover our left flank … but never showed up. Because of attrition, we the pursuers were becoming the pursued, as fresh NVA troops, attempting to enter the fray, were climbing over the Citadel walls, to trap us. Our artillery support was insufficient. So we radioed US Navy ships, requesting H&I (Harassment and Interdiction) fire support to prevent the enemy from breaking through. Two ships assisted - a cruiser and the destroyer USS JOHNSTON (DD-821). I detached from JOHNSTON a year earlier, almost to the day. I had once been present for her crew when they needed me … now they were present in Hue' for my Marines and me when we needed them. The entire night was boom-boom-boom, all around us, rounds accurately placed, providing needed protection, thanks to superb firing from the cruiser and the USS JOHNSTON DD-821. What a small world!"

NAVY, THEN AND NOW:

Provided by: Ernest B. "Buck" Snyder, Radarman (RD2)

Years on board the Johnston: 1964 to 1967

Then - If you smoked, you had an ashtray on your desk.
Now - If you smoke, you get sent outside and treated like a leper, if you're lucky.

Then - Mail took weeks to come to the ship.
Now - Every time you get near land, there's a mob topside to see if their cell phones work.

Then - If you left the ship it was in Blues or Whites, even in home port.
Now - The only time you wear Blues or Whites is for ceremonies.

Then - You wore bellbottoms everywhere on the ship.
Now - Bellbottoms are gone and 14 year-old girls wear them everywhere.

Then - You wore a Dixie cup all day, with every uniform.
Now - It's not required and you have a choice of different hats.

Then - If you said "damn," people knew you were annoyed and avoided you.
Now - If you say "damn" you'd better be talking about a hydroelectric plant.

Then -The Ships Office yeoman had a typewriter on his desk for doing daily reports.
Now - Everyone has a computer with Internet access and they wonder why no work is getting done.

Then - We painted pictures of pretty girls on airplanes to remind us of home.
Now - We put the real thing in the cockpit.

Then - Your girlfriend was at home, praying you would return alive.
Now - She is on the same ship, praying your condom worked.

Then - If you got drunk off duty, your buddies would take you back to the ship so you could sleep it off.
Now - If you get drunk off duty, they slap you in rehab and ruin your career.

Then - Canteens were made out of steel and you could heat coffee or hot chocolate in them.
Now - Canteens are made of plastic, you can't heat them because they'll melt, and anything inside always tastes like plastic.

Then - Our top officers were professional sailors first. They commanded respect.
Now - Our top officers are politicians first. They beg not to be given a wedgie.

Then - They collected enemy intelligence and analyzed it.
Now - They collect our pee and analyze it.

Then - If you didn't act right, they'd put you on extra duty until you straightened up.
Now - If you don't act right, they start a paper trail that follows you forever.

Then - Medals were awarded to heroes who saved lives at the risk of their own.
Now - Medals are awarded to people who show up for work most of the time.

Then - You slept in a barracks, like a soldier.
Now - You sleep in a dormitory, like a college kid.

Then - You ate in a Mess Hall or Galley. It was free and you could have all the food you wanted.
Now - You eat in a Dining Facility. Every slice of bread or pat of butter costs, and you can only have one.

Then - If you wanted to relax, you went to the Rec Center, played pool, smoked and drank beer.
Now -You go to the Community Center and can still play pool, maybe.

Then - If you wanted a quarter beer and conversation, you could go to the Chief's or Officers' Club.
Now - The beer will cost you three dollars and someone is watching to see how much you drink.

Then - The Exchange had bargains for sailors who didn't make much money.
Now - You can get better merchandise and cheaper at Wal-Mart.

Then - If an Admiral wanted to make a presentation, he scribbled down some notes and a YN spent an hour preparing a bunch of charts.
Now - The Admiral has his entire staff spending days preparing a Power Point presentation.

Then - We called the enemy things like "Commie Bastards" and "Reds" because we didn't like them.

Now - We call the enemy things like "Opposing Forces" and
"Aggressors or Insurgents" so we won't offend them.

Then - We declared victory when the enemy was dead and
all his things were broken.
Now - We declare victory when the enemy says he is sorry
and won't do it again.

Then - A commander would put his butt on the line to
protect his people.
Now - A commander will put his people on the line to
protect his butt.

DAMAGE CONTROL

By: John Gilbert, LTJG

Years on board the Johnston:
1965 to 1968

        I was sent to Damage
Control School in Philadelphia.
On my dream sheet (requested
assignment), I asked for a ship
in the Pacific. There was a
War over there and I was a
patriot. Instead I was
assigned to the USS Johnston
DD-821, a Gearing class (WWII)
FRAM 1 (Fleet Rehabilitation
and Modernization - completely
rebuilt late 50's/early 60's)
tin can (destroyer) home ported
in Charleston, S.C.

        Damage Control school at

the Philadelphia Naval Yard was a few months and very pleasant. I lived in the BOQ (Bachelor Officers Quarters). Meals and accommodations were great. The only problem was at the conclusion I knew I would have to go aboard the ship and join the real world.

I made my way to Charleston. I remember standing on the pier and looking at the Johnston for the longest time. I remember thinking – I'm not ready for this. I took a deep breath and walked up the gang plank – the newest crew member. When I was high lined off the ship in Vietnam some 34 months later, I had the distinction of having been aboard longer than anyone save one of my boys, Hardman, a first class electrician. I was on my third Captain, third Executive Officer and right on down the line with everyone in the Wardroom (officers).

The Johnston had a full complement of 14 officers and over 300 enlisted men on a hull some 400 feet long. It was crowded. I was DCA (Damage Control Assistant) and R Division Officer. I was in charge of the approximate 30 enlisted personnel in R Division. I don't think I ever got completely comfortable with being in charge. I guess I got better at it but never comfortable. I worked for the Chief Engineer – initially, later and forever. In addition to me, he had B Division (Boilers – we had four in two boiler rooms) and M Division (Machinists – the two steam engines in two engine rooms). It is interesting that now (1998), there are no active US Navy ships with steam boilers. I wouldn't recognize the Engineering Department of a modern Destroyer. I didn't so much mind being R Division Officer. Me and my boys were responsible for all the engineering equipment outside the main propulsion spaces – the boilers and engine rooms. It was considerable – from the anchor windlass on the bow to the steering gear at the stern and a whole bunch in between. I hated being DCA. I could not stand all the Mickey Mouse damage drills that I was expected to run – constantly. GQ (General Quarters) at sea was awful and the drills alongside the pier just as bad. I never did grow to like them.

But I did like my gang of enlisted sailors. My biggest group was electricians. At one time I had two EMCs (chief electricians) – quite an honor for a DD (Destroyer). Chief Butts made Chief on board and got his initiation underway. The other EMC, Chief Roberts, had a perpetual stooge going. Once we were standing on the pier examining a faulty shore power connection – a piece of cable 4" in diameter. It exploded. I was wearing a short sleeved shirt. I jumped back, knocked down the Chief, and burned my arm on his cigar. Had the scar for years. As an aside, we used our own generators for electric power when we had steam up. Alongside the pier, we used shore power – a big mother cable. In addition to Electricians, R Division had Damage Control men/welders, machinery Repairmen, Machinist Mates, Engine Men and ICmen (Internal Communications men worked on all interior phone links (lots) and the gyrocompass). R Division went from stem to stern and top to bottom. The ICmen maintained the anemometer, the wind gauge on the very top of the mast to the pit sword, a device on the keel that measured speed thru the water.

I joined the ship just after a major Med (Mediterranean – 6th Fleet) deployment. We operated out of Charleston for a while and then went into an extended yard period – like four months. After this inactivity, we were sent to Gitmo (Guantanamo Bay, Cuba) for refresher training. On the way, Carole and I got married in Key West. I could go on but this is a Navy story.

There are a number of "events" from my Navy days that I can still remember. I'll try to fill them in chronological order. After getting kicked into shape in Gitmo we were allowed to go to Kingston, Jamaica for liberty. We needed it. While there a "damage control" moment occurred. Not far from where we were tied up was the Myrtle Bank Hotel, a big old landmark building. It caught fire. I was sent over with my Damage Control party to offer assistance. We done good – although my whites never recovered. I didn't have time to change uniforms. We put our portable pumps at the pool and were getting water on the fire long before the Kingston fire brigade got going. We got everyone out and at a critical point, moved our hoses to the downwind buildings to keep the fire from spreading. We kept at it all night. When the danger was past, I lay down on a lawn chair and fell asleep. The poor XO lost me and I never told him where I had been. We were heroes, got congratulation letters from the Prime Minister, Secretary of Defense and I think, the President. The Johnston got the "E" – the outstanding ship in the squadron.

After refresher training, we operated with the 2nd fleet – made some Caribbean cruises and then back across the Atlantic to the Med and the Middle East. On they way, we had an incident that took the bloom of the rose so to speak. We had a collision with a fleet oiler. We were refueling in the mid Atlantic. We were steaming 100 feet off the oiler's starboard side with fuel lines over fore and aft. My station was aft with the "Oil King", a Second Class Boilerman responsible for maintaining our oil inventory – what tanks we drew from, keeping an even keel, ballasting and so forth. A big job. Three tin cans went down during a WWII typhoon due to not ballasting.

We got too close to the oiler. The Captain ordered an emergency breakaway. Break the lines and get away! Back aft we did fine. Cut loose the hose. It was a pigtail stuck into a trunk. Let it loose while black oil was coming over hundreds of gallons a minute. You can imagine the mess. Up forward they were having a hard time. There the oil line came over on riding pulleys attached to a cable. The cable was attached to the Johnston with a pelican hook. They got the oil hose free but not the cable - they couldn't break the pelican hook open.

This is where I picked up the action. I was at the fuel tank sounding tube in after officer's quarters. I was up the ladder to the Dash helicopter deck in a flash. What a sight. We were tethered to the oiler (a big ship) by the forward cable and I swear I could hear the Chief Boats beating on the hook with a sledge hammer trying to break its hold. We had right rudder on trying to pull away. Since the bow couldn't move away (the cable prevented it), the stern was swinging in dangerously close to the oiler - like real close. The bridge saw it too and switched the rudder. As the stern swung away, the bow turned also and we headed toward the oiler's starboard side. This time the correction wasn't in time. I could see we were going to hit. I headed down the ladder and raced to Damage Control Central. It looked like that was where I should be. While racing down the passageway, I felt the ship hit.

The damage was not severe. We were on the same course. It was like a terrier bouncing off a Saint Bernard. The anchor absorbed most of the energy. One fluke punched a hole thru our hull and the other a hole in the oiler. The anchor itself broke loose and disappeared into the Atlantic along with all 120 fathoms of anchor chain. The last 20 fathoms are painted yellow and the next to last section red. This is to let you know how much chain is left when using the anchor. The First Lieutenant watched it all go over the side.

It was a bad show but we got over it. We took an anchor off a DD going home. There was a hearing but we survived.

We operated in the Med for awhile. Spent some time in Naples. Then we took the Suez Canal to the Red Sea and the Persian Gulf. We operated there including exercises with the Auzzie navy. The officer5s had a cocktail party in Aden – the tip of the Arabian Peninsula. While we were on shore, the crew enjoyed a movie on the Dash Helicopter deck. While watching the movie, some 50 caliber machine gun rounds came in overhead. The movie was moved to the mess deck. There was a lot of unrest in Aden at that time. The British were moving out. The Johnston had to wait for Vietnam for the next incoming fire.

Maybe I should explain a little about Aden. It is part of South Yemen. Anyhow, the British were leaving and it was an armed camp. We had a beer party for the crew (we carried beer but did not drink on board). We were transported in buses with chicken wire over the windows. This is to keep grenades from coming in. The military compound we mustered in had a grenade come over the wall just before we got there. It was a dud.

We spent a memorable Christmas in Jidda (better than the Charleston Naval Shipyard – the previous year), traversed the canal back and spent New Year's in Beirut. Had a really good time. This was before Beirut was destroyed in a civil war. We refueled in Suda Bay, Crete. What a place! We tied up at a stone quay where the water was so clear it looked like the ship was suspended in air. Never seen anything like it. Some day I would like to go back. Frank Powell, my English Uniroyal engineering buddy, said it was amazing we could get in. Apparently the Royal Navy lost a considerable number of destroyers there trying to take off the British garrison when German paratroopers overran the island. Mountbatten had to keep switching his flag as the destroyer he was on went down. No sign of any of that when we were there.

While underway from Crete, we ran into another "damage control" moment. A mistral, a Mediterranean storm, blew up. The Med is shallow. Maybe that is why this storm was so choppy. I have never seen waves come at us with such regularity and precision. The looked sculpted. Now bear with me on this. I was an Engineer not a Boatswain's mate. I think this is what happened. The hawse pipe cover to one of the anchors carried away. The hawse pipe carries the chain from the chain locker up two decks to the anchor. The cover keeps the sea water from going down the hawse pipe every time the bow dips into a wave. Well with this storm, the bow was flinging green water over the bridge with every wave. And with every wave, the chain locker was filling up.

Normally this is not a problem. An R Division Damage Control man monitors the water level with a sounding tube. When the water level got high, the water is pumped out via an in-line submersible pump. Well the pump shorted out. Tough service – sea water. Chief Roberts and his crew replaced the pump. That one shorted out also. And so on and so on. I don't know how many pumps failed, but we were getting short when we finally go one working. The pump emptied the locker no problem. But just above the chain locker was a Bosun's storage locker. The hatch gasket leaked and with all the pressure of the green water we were under and all the time needed to find an operating pump, the locker had two feet of water sloshing around. Lots of weight. I was on the bridge and came down to assess the situation. Let me be up front and say I was not a happy camper. I was wading around in two feet of water with my brown shoes while my white shoes had never recovered from the soaking and the mud at the Myrtle Bank Hotel.

313

I told the poor damage control man on watch, to loosen the dogs on the hatch going down to the chain locker. He did so reaching down through all that water. Well getting the hatch open with all that water on top was no cake walk. The hatch was two feet square. With both of us lifting, we got it open. It was obvious he had no idea of the mechanics of what we were doing. The minute the hatch was open, the air in the chain locker came up with a great WHOOSH. He turned white as he thought the ocean was coming up to get him. The poor guy was terrified.

The water drained into the now dry chain locker where the newly installed pump took it over the side. The ship was saved (joke). The hatch gasket was replaced. Great moments of Damage Control. My shoes were never the same.

After a four and a half month deployment, we were set to come home. There was little drama at first. The ship to relieve us was late. As a consolation prize, we got liberty in Majorca. Good time. And then because we were late, the Captain ordered a high speed run to the Azores where we would refuel for the trip home. Well we burned black oil big time. And when we got to the Azores, there was no fuel to be had. Bad news! We headed for Bermuda with very low fuel reserves. At high speed, a destroyer can burn fuel at a prodigious rate and we had used up a great deal of our inventory. So we headed across the big water on one boiler (out of four) cross connected to both turbines. Not good. No reserves. No allowances for bad weather. As I remember, minimum fresh water (made by evaporating sea water). No showers. Fuel conservation. Finally a oiler was sent out to refuel us. I always felt we cudda' made it. The oiler was out of Newport and some pissed off I can assure you.

We operated out of Charleston for a considerable time. We went to San Juan, Puerto Rico for some artillery shell trials. We shot at drone jet planes and actually hit one. It crashed into the sea - very spectacular I was told and I am sure, very expensive. Then we raced to Southport (?) N.C. for the Forth of July. We anchored in the Cape Fear River. The town really rolled out the red carpet for us.

The ship had a nasty incident while leaving San Juan, Puerto Rico. To get underway, the Sea Detail is set. Since this is a vulnerable time, extra hands are stationed at various points to head off problems. A detail is stationed on the bow to handle lines, the anchor windless, etc. We cleared the sea wall and immediately hit some rough waves. One way washed over the bow (no major obstacle there) and sent some of the crew on the bow flying. One poor seaman was knocked down and sent crashing into the gun mount. The mount stop (a barrier that stops the gun from training on the ship itself - a no no) opened up his thigh. Our Corpsman, who I maintain could do open heart surgery in an emergency, recommended he be airlifted off and put in the hospital. Done, and all very exciting, in a choppy sea too.

In November 1967, the whole squadron was ordered to Vietnam - all seven ships. This was to be a seven month deployment. Since I had only four months left in the Navy, all I could do was stay with the ship.

The night before we left, I guess I had the duty (1/3 always on board). All of a sudden there was a bump - not too bad. One of the Navy harbor tugs had backed into us midships. The collision cracked a rib and dented the hull - after all they aren't called tin cans for nothing. The tender sent over a crew and made emergency repairs. The next morning the Johnston and the rest of DesRon 6 (Destroyer Squadron 6) headed down the Cooper

315

River on the start of a journey half way around the world and to the Vietnam War.

We in R Division had already been introduced to the hard reality of the War. Earlier R Division had received a EN2 (2nd Class Engine man). He had spent most of his 18 year career in the Gator Navy – the Amphibians – shore assault units. They have lots of boats and accordingly lots of engine men to maintain them. He was a great guy. He threw himself into overhauling our whale boat engine and a high pressure compressor that was the bain of my existence. He called me "Hoss" which I don't think you will find in Navy Regs. He was a wonderful addition to our group.

He wasn't on board all that long when he got orders to Vietnam. The fresh water navy – the river boats – needed engine men and he went. He didn't want to go. He was planning on finishing his naval career on the Johnston. He was almost there. He headed West and made arrangements for the Navy to ship his mobile home and family to the Pacific.

You know how the story ends. Some all too short period of time later, Chief Roberts came back to my stateroom saying he had bad news. A friend of his was in the same trailer park. The trailer had barely been put down when, one night, it was pulled back out and left. Roberts' friend asked around and found out that our engine man's wife was taking her family home – her husband had been killed in action. He thought Roberts would want to know.

Back to the past. Amid big time hoopla, the squadron headed down the river. I remember our Chief Sonarman sliding up to me on deck and whispering to me "I'd love to be a submariner tonight". They had the town to themselves.

The first day out we "wiped" one of the shaft main bearings. The Forward Engine room powered one shaft and screw while the After Engine room handled the other. We had twin screws on the Johnston. The forward shaft ran haft the length of the ship - a considerable distance. It was supported by shaft bearings. We burned up one of these bearings. We dropped out of formation on one screw while the bearing was replaced. The new bearing lasted no longer than the original one. The problem - the harbor tug that backed into us had managed to tweak the keel. The ship was not bent - ever so slightly. We would have to go into a shipyard where all the shaft support blocks could be trued up and the shaft realigned. So we parted from DesRon 6 and steamed on one screw to Mayport, Florida and an emergency yard stay. The shipyard set us straight and in a few days we were on our way. The good side to all this. We found our way to Vietnam by ourselves. No squadron exercises, no fleet drills. Solo steaming. Vastly preferable. The bump from heaven.

We ran down the Atlantic to the Panama Canal. We ran up the Pacific. Into San Diego and Pearl Harbor just as the rest of the squadron was leaving. Like Walter the Mouse. From Pearl we went to Wake Island to refuel. Outside of Wake, we ran into a typhoon or the significant edge of one. We actually had a Damage Control Moment. The ship was in a following sea. The ship would drop her stern into a wave and it would wash up and over the stern. There was enough water coming over that one of the deck stanchions was bent forward. As it bent it peeled back a portion of the deck - just like a tin can. The last compartment just below the deck is after steering. It started shipping water. This was a little more serious than the flooding in the Med. There was a lot less water but the steering gear is nothing to take lightly. Without a functioning rudder, the Johnston would become something closer to a barge than a "greyhound of the sea". Again one of the Damage Control men tracked me down. The hole was in a hard to reach place and no one had been able to seal it. I checked it out. These things have to be taken care of with the materials on hand. I went forward to our machine shop operated by one of my boys. He had a big thick foam rubber seat on his chair. I told him "For the good of the ship", we were going to surrender his cushion. Folded twice and jammed against the hole with a 2x4, the cushion was the perfect damage control device. I assume that he got his damp cushion back when we finally tied up at Wake and welded the deck back together.

It was during this typhoon that the rudder started acting up. As the ship rolled, there was enough play in the rudder housing that the rudder would occasionally "clunk" as the rudder post slammed back and forth in its housing. This was very serious indeed. I decided to tackle this as an engineering problem (which it was). I had one my men mount what I remember as a dial gauge on the rudder post housing with the dial gauge actuator up against the rudder post itself. There were two rudders – one behind each screw but only one acting up. The rudder post actually stuck up above the housing which was a hollow tube. The dial gauge measured the play of the rudder post in thousandths of an inch. Every time it "clunked" we recorded the lateral distance it actually moved. Then, using the ship's drawings, we determined the maximum amount the post should move if the top and bottom bearings were fully operational. Each of these bearings had specified clearances. Well what we measured was like 3 or 4 times the play specified. I drew all this up and presented it to the Captain. Using this information, we requested a dry docking to rebuild the rudder bearings. We didn't get it. The Navy sent some divers down who "fixed" the problem. It continued to "clunk". After I left the ship, the Johnston was put in drydock and the rudder was repaired. Great moments in marine engineering!

From Wake we went to the Philippines, Subic Bay, as a kind of staging area before Vietnam.

As I have mentioned, we carried a unmanned drone helicopter DASH (Drone Anti-Submarine Helicopter). It required JP5 fuel. The JP5 tank and pumping system were my responsibility. The JP5 tank was a small tank that had been carved out of an existing black oil tank. Previous to this deployment, the bulkhead between the JP5 and the black oil tank developed a crack with black oil contaminating the JP5. We were underway so I was told to try to weld it on the fly. We dumped the JP5 into the black oil and cleaned up the JP5 tank to the best of our ability. The oil tank was topped off. We figured it would be safest that way. R Division had a E8 (Super Chief) Ship Fitter who was our most experienced welder. Someone had to go into the tank with him as a fire watch. Considering the nature of the operation, I figured it better be me. So we crawl in - very little head room. As soon as the Chief put the welding rod on the crack, the heat would open the crack, black oil would leak out and catch on fire. We tried three times with no success. Another job for the tender. They put a plate over the whole crack. Why didn't we do that?

Back to the Phillipines. One of the missions in the war zone was to refuel any stray manned helicopters that flew into our operation area. At Subic we were to be supplied with a special fitting that the helicopter's fuel hose could mate too. Subic had none on hand. We really needed it. The Captain in his direct way, told me to get one, period. I thought that even though Subic was out, maybe Clark Air Force Base (now buried under volcanic ash) might have one. I hitched a ride over there with my requisition. No joy. I mentioned my plight to a mechanic who said that the helicopters had a similar fitting inside the cockpit where the fuel hose connected on their end. Sitting out on the edge of the air strip were some shot-up helicopters going back to the US for complete renovation. They were boarded up with plywood. I asked the mechanic if he had a pry bar and a 2 ft pipe wrench. He looked at me sideways and gave me the tools. I mean what could he do? I pried open a man sized crack in the plywood of one of the birds and crawled inside. My introduction to the war. Inside you could see daylight through the bullet holes. And on the forward bulkhead was a fueling connection topped with my sought after fitting. I removed it with the pipe wrench and carried it back to the ship. Let the record show that during my brief stay in the war zone, a battle weary marine helicopter low on fuel buzzed the Johnston looking for JP5 and we supplied it – via my "hot" fuel fitting. I know. I was there – down in the hold next to the JP5 pump and praying "don't fail me now".

While in the war zone, the Johnston would have two missions. One was plane guarding – following 1000 yards behind the carrier during flight ops. We were a beacon for the incoming planes and right there if a pilot had to ditch and be picked up. But our big role was gunfire support for the troops on land. Our 5" guns were going all the time.

To get our guns ready, the Gunners Mates did a lot of maintenance work on our way from Subic to Vietnam. In the middle of the night, the 2nd Division Officer and in charge of the guns, woke me up. The after mount was apart and his boys couldn't put it together again. Well nothing like a crisis. I got up and dressed and joined him in the gun mount. There were parts hither and yon. His gang showed me this humongous bolt like two feet long that, I guess, held the breech assembly to the barrel. They showed me how they could thread it half way home and then, no matter how much muscle they used it would go no further. It is not what you know but who. I knew the R Division Machinery Repairman who gave up his seat cushion outside of Wake Island, could handle this. I found my way to his rack in the R Division berthing area and got him up. Like me, he was needing a challenge.

He immediately knew the problem. The bolt was machined to a very tight tolerance. It had been burred very slightly. We couldn't see it but it was there. We all trudged down to his tiny machine shop. The bolt went into his vise. He covered it with a grinding compound and we all took turns running a nut up and down the shaft. I remember all of us, two officers, and the gunners mates – a band of brothers – working on this in the middle of the night. When the nut spun free, we took it back to the gun mount and watched the gunners mates thread it home – a job well done.

While on the gun line in Vietnam, the ship went on two watches. For six hours we manned the forward 5" mount and half the crew manned the rest of the ship. Then we switched to the after mount for 6 hours. We called this "port and starboard". In *Kidnapped*, Robert Louis Stevenson calls this "turn and turnabout". I like that better. In the book, the 1st and 2nd mate used the same bunk. One on watch while one slept. We called this "hot bunking" but we never had to do it. Just a little historical note.

In didn't have a position of any importance. The Communications Officer and myself were the only short timers. Our enlistments expired real early in the deployment. We couldn't do anything critical because we would have left a hole when we departed. The Communications Officer was real short. I think he left from Subic. So while we were on the gun line my position was in Damage Control Central waiting for the hit that never came. From here I wrote the letters that follow this article. I was very much on the periphery of what was happening around me. My mind was on home, finding a job and Getting On With My Life. We were in the war zone with lives in the balance but I wasn't there – what Hemingway called a "separate peace". Yet there were several things that happened t me that are burned into my mind.

When I was on watch, we manned the forward mount. Instead of staying in Damage Control Central, I tended to wander about the ship. One fine morning we were on gunfire support in the Northern sector. Things were quiet while I walked the port side just forward of the after mount, now unmanned. On the near horizon was a piece of Vietnam. What I didn't know was that this was North Vietnam. I was talking to one of the sailors from First Division (if it moves, salute it – if it doesn't, paint it) when we both heard something strange. We both looked up and saw a geyser rising a short distance from the ship. It appeared about 6" in diameter and maybe 20 feet high. The North Vietnamese shore batteries had taken us under fire. What we were looking at was a miss. Just like the movies from WWII. Wow! What a rush! We both dived into the open door of the gun mount, the nearest sanctuary.

Up on the Bridge, the Captain said to head for the splash. I could hear the engines winding up to flank-speed. The shore batteries would try to bracket us – put a round over us followed by a round under. Then a closer round over and a closer round under. In short order they would find us at the center. By steering into each splash you hope the gunners will be forever alternating between too long and too short. The Captain must have been doing something right because we weren't hit as we zigzagged out of there at flank speed. This was all very real.

As soon as we were out of range, the PA system came on. The Captain's voice came on "the XO observed the fall of shot and wants all hands to know we qualify for combat pay." Combat pay or hazardous pay is earned by everyone spending so much time in the war zone (a matter of some days) or by anyone receiving enemy fire. We had just qualified.

It seems every war has its turning point. I have read that the turning point for Vietnam was the 1968 Tet offensive. The biggest battle was at the ancient city of Hue on the Perfume River some 8 miles in from the coast. The Johnston and Lt(jg) Gilbert were there.

We had new barrels on our guns. The marines were pinned down in the Citadel. Some heavy ordnance was needed to reduce the very heavy walls. It was thought that we could do this. The problem was that 8 miles is a long shot for a 5" fun from a relatively unstable platform. To try to stabilize the platform, we anchored ½ mile off the beach - a sitting duck. It looked like I could reach out and touch some land - at least a short swim. This turned out to be the closest I got to the actual land mass of Vietnam.

When we were in the Red Sea, the Division chaplain rode with us. When we got back to Charleston, he left with orders to Vietnam. He ended up assigned to the Marine Battalion that was in the thick of it a Hue. So much so that he saw the NVA massing for the attack. That must have been pretty close. He heard "Tampico" which was our radio call sign come over the air. He knew his old shipmates were there and he said it felt real good. He had thought his goose was cooked. The next thing he knew shells started landing all around his position and the attack was broken up. In his mind, he was saved by the Johnston.

Before I left the ship, I had one more searing experience. An experience that shows deep down we are all tribal animals and, with a minimum amount of provocation, will pick up a club and beat the hell out of any other tribe. While I was waiting for orders to come home, the North Koreans seized the US Navy ship Pueblo in international waters.

The Pueblo was an electronics spy ship. This was an accepted form of surveillance. The Russians had their trawlers. We had ship like the Pueblo. It was to sail around North Korea beyond the 3 mile limit and gather information. The Koreans got upset and decided to take it. We had our hands full in Vietnam. They sent out a couple of armed boats and boarded her and towed her back to a North Korean port – essentially an act of war (or piracy). There was some gunfire. One sailor was severely wounded as I remember.

So there I was – overdue for discharge stateside. The previous day, I went to my rack thinking I would be going home any moment now. I woke up to flank speed (all out) and "What the Hell is this?" I scurried up to the bridge where I saw a carrier ahead of us in the distance. The Captain told me about the Pueblo. Then he told the crew via the PA system. We were being detached with a carrier group to take on North Korea. My God, the ship was alive. We were going to kick some butt! I even got caught up in myself. One minute I'm going home and the next I'm wrapped up in the next war. I tell you it is all right there – just below the surface.

It didn't last long. The Captain of the Pueblo was coerced into confessing to trespassing in North Korean water. The crew was returned although the Koreans did keep the ship. Our task force was sent back to Yankee Station and the war in Vietnam continued.

The Pueblo captain was a tragic story. He was an orphan from Boy's Town who had elevated himself to a command position in the Navy. Now he was done. He was cleared in a court martial but his Navy career was over. He would be denied promotion and take an early retirement.

As for me, this was pretty much it. We left Yankee Station, the carrier ops position, and went back on the gun line. At the next refueling, rearming operation, I was high lined off to the oiler. The oiler took me to Subic where I hopped a ride to Clark, Honolulu and Treasure Island (San Francisco). It was a week of physicals, paper work and then home to Charleston.

While at Treasure Island, I inherited another mission. Until now, this has been all but forgotten. At the BOQ, I met a navy flyer and we went out drinking every night. This was every night, all night. To the point that at one time I overslept and missed one of my separation appointments. This pilot was on an assignment that he was trying to resolve with the help of the bottle. He had been very close to a fellow student during flight training. At graduation each had signed a statement that should one be killed, the other would accompany the body home. His buddy was at Khe Sahn, the American equivalent to Dien Bien Phu. While lifting off, his chopper took a direct hit. He was waiting at Treasure Island for his buddy's body. Then he was taking his buddy home to his buddy's parents and four sisters. Every evening he came and got me. I just couldn't say no. He was still waiting when I left.

This is my story. In all honesty, I never was much of a naval officer. My oppositional disorder got in the way of my fitting smoothly into the ship's company. In my defense I loved my boys in R Division and I think they felt the same way about me. The Johnston was a good ship, and I was very much a part of it. Years later I ran into a fellow officer who had made a career in the Navy after starting out on the Johnston with us. His biggest regret was that he had never again found another "band of brothers" like we had been on the old Johnston.

MY MOST MEMORABLE DAY ABOARD THE USS JOHNSTON

By: John Argonti, Fire Control Technician (FTG2)

Years on board the Johnston: 1966 to 1968

After boot camp in San Diego, and "FTG A" school in Bainbridge Maryland (dead of winter, lots of snow!), I reported aboard the Johnston in Late spring or early summer of 1966. I was assigned to the ship until late summer 1968; just prior to the ship going into dry-dock. I sailed on 2 major cruises and several short ones.

The most memorable cruise I made was the cruise to WESTPAC and Viet Nam. We journeyed through the Panama Canal, to Hawaii, rode out a typhoon, visited many ports in the Far East, and then returned home to Charlestown. And, by the way, we got shot at while supporting the Marines at the DMZ during the TET Offensive.

My duty station, while we were on the gun-line, off of the Viet Nam coast, was in the Fire Control Director, above the bridge. The Director was manned by 3 enlisted personnel and 1 officer. My watch was with LTJG Nelson, BM Treibel, and FTG Mike Lawson. Mike Lawson and I used to rotate duties between operating the Fire Control Radar (back end of the director) and being the pointer in the front. For 99% of the time, duty in the Director was pretty boring since shore bombardment is controlled by CIC and the Plotting Room (the room next to the scullery). We passed the time watching the mounts fire, telling sea stories, etc. By the way, my Doctors attribute my deafness to the time I spent in the Director!

The job of the pointer was to keep the crosshairs on the selected target using a hand control to control the elevation, up and down, and also operate the firing trigger. The trainer does the same but for right and left. The radar operator's job was to lock onto the target, if able, or to determine the approximate range to the target. All the way across the Pacific, we practiced a  drill called counter-battery. That is the term used if you are taken under fire. When a counter-battery is called, the FT's in the plotting room throw the proper switches and give the Director control of the guns.

I'll never forget that day in early February 1968! I was manning the pointer station when I heard a whine and an explosion close by. Then the words "Counter-Battery, Counter-Battery" came over the sound powered headphones. Mr. Nelson used his hand controller to slew the Director toward the location of the shore battery. BM Treibel and I found the flashes of the gun firing at us and locked it into our crosshairs; Mike Lawson was calling out the range to the beach. The commence fire was given and I squeezed the trigger. Every time we saw a flash, a few seconds later we heard the projectile pass close to the ship. The Johnston started maneuvering to get out of harm's way. We could see our shells exploding and Mr. Nelson was giving the plotting room the corrections that were needed. The Mount 51 gun crews were really pumping out the shells, faster than any of us had ever witnessed before. Mount 52 was out of commission with a problem. With me holding down the trigger, as soon as a gun was loaded and the breach was closed, the gun fired. Then we saw a large explosion where the flashes used to be and the shore battery went silent. When the cease fire was given, I released the trigger, I think my fingerprints are still engraved into that handle and trigger because I was holding on so tight. It happened really fast and we did exactly as we were trained to do. I didn't think about it until it was all over and then I really needed a smoke bad!!

That was my most memorable day aboard the Johnston! There were some memorable liberties too, but I can't talk about them here!!

"SMITTY" SAVED MY TAIL!

By: Jonathan "Toby" Mack, (LTJG)

Years on board the Johnston: 1966 to 1968

Art Smith saved my tail one night and possibly a lot of other peoples' too. On the 0400 - 0800 watch the morning of June 6, 1968, we were coming into San Diego on our return from WESTPAC. I had the OOD watch, and "Smitty", as all knew him, was the Boatswain's Mate of the Watch. It was about 0430 and the XO has just come up to the bridge to shoot stars. We were steaming in formation with DESDIV 42 – second ship in a column of four at 17 knots and we're at radio silence. The guide was the lead ship in the column (can't remember which one) with the Commodore aboard. The Commodore's night orders were to split plants at 0430 because we were coming into restricted waters.

Our station was 1000 yards behind the guide and the other ships were spaced 1000 and 2000 yards astern of us. The JOOD (ENS Randy Mills) was watching the SPS-10 repeater and giving periodic ranges to the guide to make sure we stayed on station. After a few range marks of 1000 yards, he gives me one of 850. I wonder what gives with the guide, and knock off ten turns and call for another range – 800 yards. I knock off some more turns and we're down to 750 yards, and now the ship astern is starting to close. I keep knocking off turns to no avail and now we're 500 yards from the guide and the following ship is 500 yards astern. XO is out on the bridge wing shooting stars.

Smitty is watching all this and we look at each other and decide it's time to get the hell out of the formation in a big hurry. So Smitty grabs the wheel from the helmsman and I give him a left full rudder all ahead full and he instantly cranks it around for all he's worth and we clear the stern of the guide ship by about 150 yards. Turns out the guide ship, sleeping Commodore and all, went dead in the water – completely unannounced. They had dropped the load while splitting plant. Since we heeled over about 30 degrees on the left full rudder, I think we rolled Captain Curran out of his bunk and by the time he got to the bridge we were clear of everybody. The Skipper broke radio silence and called the guide to ask if they had in fact gone DIW, and the response was "Wait One!" A little later the Commodore flashes us a message to the effect that they had in fact gone DIW and conveyed his thanks and compliments to a heads-up Tampico bridge watch which had narrowly averted a disaster.

Editor's Note: The following Deck Log Chronology was supplied by Toby Mack. It covers the time period of January 1, 1967 to June 22, 1968, the day the USS Johnston returned to Charleston from WESTPAC. He went to the National Archives facility in College Park, Maryland, and requested the Johnston's deck logs covering the span of time from our return from the Middle East through our Vietnam deployment.

Basically, He copied all entries that indicated where the Johnston was, and with whom, throughout the period as well as any other significant happenings.

USS JOHNSTON (DD-821) Deck Log Chronology 1 JAN 67 – 22 JUN 68

1 JAN	In port Beirut, Lebanon
4 JAN	0952 Underway for Naples, Italy
9 JAN	1600 Joined DESRON 4 and TF61- USS JC OWENS (DD827), MCCARD (DD822), CONE (DD776), BORDELON (DD881), Columbus (CG12), BELKNAP (DLG26), FREEMONT (APA44), INDEPENDENCE (CVA62)
14 JAN	Med moored to USS CASCADE (AD16) Naples, Italy
18 JAN	Underway for Gibraltar
21 JAN	Moored Gibraltar
21 JAN	Underway for ops in Western Med
26 JAN	In port, Palma Mallorca
30 JAN	Underway for Rota, Spain
31 JAN	In port Rota for fuel
31 JAN	Underway for Charleston
9 FEB	Arrived Charleston Pier Papa, moored port side to USS EVERGLADES (AD24)
9 MAR	1400 - CDR Robert W. Curran relieved CDR John J. Mingo as CO
10 MAR	Underway for St. Thomas with USS CONE
13 MAR	Anchored Charlotte Amalie, St. Thomas USVI
13 MAR	Underway for exercises
14 MAR	Moored Charlotte Amalie, St. Thomas USVI
15 MAR	Underway for exercises
18 MAR	Moored San Juan, PR
21 MAR	Underway for Charleston
22 MAR	Fired exercise torpedo from Mk. 32 tubes – lost it. Fired ASROC torpedo – recovered it.
27 MAR	Arrived Charleston
14 APR	Underway for exercises – Caribbean/Puerto Rico operating area
1 MAY	In Charleston
6 JUN	Family/guest cruise Charleston harbor
8 JUN	Underway for Norfolk
9 JUN	Import Norfolk
12 JUN	Underway for San Juan – exercises
24 JUN	In port San Juan
26 JUN	Underway for Mobile, AL
3 JUL	In port Mobile, AL

5 JUL	Underway for Charleston
9 JUL	Arrive Charleston
20 JUL	Underway for Norfolk
21 JUL	In port Norfolk
24 JUL	Underway for exercises Virginia Capes/Jacksonville operating areas
5 AUG	In port Charleston
28 AUG	Underway Charleston operating area – exercises
31 AUG	In port Charleston Pier Quebec
25 SEP	Underway for Jacksonville operating areas
30 SEP	In port Charleston
15 NOV	Underway for WESTPAC and Vietnam via Panama Canal
19 NOV	In port Mayport, FL
24 NOV	Underway for Panama Canal
28 NOV	Transit Canal - Underway for Pearl Harbor
10 DEC	In port Pearl Harbor
12 DEC	Underway for Midway
14-16 DEC	Encountered and rode out Typhoon
17 DEC	In Midway for fuel
18 DEC	Depart Midway for Guam
23 DEC	In Guam for fuel
23 DEC	Underway for Subic Bay, Philippine Islands
26 DEC	0100 - Off Samar Island – Northeast corner of island bears 230°, 44 miles. Rendered honors to USS JOHNSTON (DD-557) at site of sinking
26 DEC	0800 - 12° 32.5'N, 123° 53.5'E – Transiting San Bernardino Strait
27 DEC	Arrived Subic Bay Naval Base, moored starboard side to USS ORLECK (DD886)
5 JAN 68	Underway for Gulf of Tonkin. Screen/plane guard RANGER (CVA61) until 31 Jan
31 JAN	In Subic – dry dock – inspection reveals damage to rudders
2 FEB	Out of dry dock
6 FEB	Underway for gunline
7 FEB	1617 - Entered combat zone 111E, 17° 27'N
8 FEB	Set condition II, firing on targets ashore (Hue – Tet Offensive)
9 FEB	1647 - Received five rounds counter-battery fire

12 FEB	1226 - Received two rounds counter-battery fire, 62 yards off port bow
27 FEB	Gunfire support off Hue City
29 FEB	From deck log: "1740 - Observed strange bird of unknown species perched on one leg atop a common box adrift, bearing 015." – W.A. Efird
8 MAR	Rearmed – sank pallet of 8-inch powder casings with 50 cal. fire as directed by CO NEWPORT NEWS (CA148)
10 MAR	Left Gunline for Kaohsiung, Formosa
12 MAR	In port Kaohsiung, Formsoa
21 MAR	Underway from Kaohsiung for Tonkin Gulf
26 MAR	Joined USS RANGER (CVA61) screen
28 MAR	Arrived Gunline for gunfire support ops
3 APR	Screen/plane guard RANGER
13 APR	Inport Subic Bay
14 APR	Underway for Hong Kong – R&R
15 APR	Moored Hong Kong
20 APR	Underway for Tonkin Gulf with RANGER
7 MAY	In port Subic
9 MAY	Underway from Subic to Buckner Bay, Okinawa
11 MAY	Anchored Buckner Bay, fueled, then underway for Yokosuka, Japan
13 MAY	Moored Yokosuka
16 MAY	Drydock Yokosuka for rudder repairs
23 MAY	Out of drydock, underway for Midway then Pearl Harbor
31 MAY	Refueled Pearl, underway for San Diego
6 JUN	Arrive San Diego
10 JUN	Underway for Rodman, Canal Zone
18 JUN	At Rodman, transited canal
22 JUN	Arrived Charleston

NAVY MEMORIAL - WASHINGTON DC

By: Jonathan "Toby" Mack

Back in 2003, the wardroom members that did Johnston's Vietnam cruise got together at the Navy

Memorial in Washington for a small reunion and to dedicate a plaque honoring the previous USS Johnston (DD-557) which our ship was named for. The plaque commemorates the earlier Johnston and the honors ceremony we conducted while en route to Vietnam when we steamed right through the waters where the first Johnston was sunk.

I wrote the dedication ceremony as follows:

U.S. NAVY MEMORIAL FOUNDATION
PLAQUE DEDICATION - 27 SEPTEMBER 2003
USS JOHNSTON

In the photo were (left to right - ranks and positions at the time of the Vietnam cruise) Johnston plaque on wall top right:

CDR John J. Mingo, Commanding Officer (until March 9, 1967)
LTJG Jim Meyer, Electronic Materiel Officer
LTJG Toby Mack, ASW Officer
ADM William J. Crowe, Jr., Chairman, Joint Chiefs of Staff
LTJG John Major, Gunnery Officer
LCDR Eli Takesian, DESDIV 42 Chaplain
Bill Mercer, Survivor, USS Johnston (DD-557)
LT Chuck Mullins, Weapons Officer
LTJG John Gilbert, Damage Control Assistant
CDR Bob Curran, Commanding Officer

4:00 PM - MACK:

Admiral Crowe, ladies and gentlemen. Good afternoon, and welcome to this special Navy Memorial plaque dedication ceremony honoring the USS JOHNSTON. Would you please rise for the playing of the national anthem, and remain standing for the invocation, offered by our shipmate Captain Eli Takesian, Chaplain Corps, US Navy, Retired.

ANTHEM AND INVOCATION

4:05 PM - MACK

Admiral Crowe, thank you very much for being with us this afternoon. The mission of the U.S. Navy Memorial Foundation, which you so ably lead, is to honor, preserve and celebrate America's naval heritage and core values. We have come here with that purpose, and you do us a great honor, sir, by joining with us and participating in our ceremony.

I'm sure we've all done our homework and refreshed our memory of the Admiral's exceptional record of service to our country as military leader and statesman. Beginning with graduation from the Naval Academy in 1946, Admiral

335

Crowe's active duty Navy career culminated with his appointment by President Reagan to serve as Chairman of the Joint Chiefs of Staff from 1985 to 1989. His service continued as an advisor to Presidents, and as a statesman in the capacity of Ambassador to the United Kingdom from 1993 to 1997. Admiral Crowe has served the U.S. Navy Memorial Foundation as Chairman Since 2000. Please welcome Admiral William J. Crowe, Jr. to the podium.

4:10 PM - ADMIRAL CROWE

REMARKS

4:18 PM - MACK

Thank you, Admiral. Whenever sailors go to sea together, strong bonds develop. We once crewed a fine ship with a proud tradition and name, USS JOHNSTON. We worked hard as a team to keep that name's honor - to do our jobs and to serve our country and to see that JOHNSTON's mission and assignments were accomplished in the finest U.S. Navy tradition. And now more than thirty-five years later here we are again visiting and celebrating the memories and dear friendships we share from many years ago.

In thinking about how we might spend this short time together, I saw an opportunity to do something important that relates directly to the reason we are here. So as your self-appointed organizer, I have taken the privilege to add historical context to our gathering.

As a Foundation Trustee, I come here fairly often, and as I walk through these rooms, I am always drawn to the special place next door where Navy people have placed tributes to their ships and comrades. From my first visit, I was inspired by that wall of plaques, and believed that the name JOHNSTON belonged there. So I considered what kind of tribute such a plaque might make.

I checked the web and found a site for USS JOHNSTON (DD557). Like many of the rest of you, during my JOHNSTON years I knew that we were named after an earlier JOHNSTON sunk during World War II in an historic battle, but I had never gone deeply into the details. Now in front of me on my computer screen was a pair of official, detailed reports of the action in which she fought and was sunk, and the incredible damage she sustained before going down. Together they made a powerful, transfixing drama of courage and sacrifice. So I sent a note off to Bob Curran with copies: "Hey Skipper, you've got to read these reports." Bob responded: "I hope you remember that we passed right through the site of that battle and rendered honors, on our way over to Vietnam in 1967." Thinking back, I remembered, and then knew what the plaque should commemorate.

How our onetime gray steel home came to be called JOHNSTON is a story of one of the most heroic stands in the history of naval warfare. Most Naval historians agree that save only for the incredible courage and sacrifice of the men of the first USS JOHNSTON and a small number of her sisters, the nature, if not the final outcome, of the last stages of the war in the Pacific could have been very different. At minimum, the massive Allied invasion force at Leyte might easily have been decimated, and the retaking of the Philippines delayed, with huge cost of American lives and material.

Here, then, is the historical context of our presence in this theater – appropriately named in honor of the pre-eminent destroyerman Admiral Arleigh Burke - the capsule story of how USS JOHNSTON gave everything and saved the day. I've borrowed heavily from Naval historian Thomas J.

Cutler's excellent book, "The Battle of Leyte Gulf", published in 1994. Cutler's account includes the experiences and observations of our friend Bill Mercer, who fought his ship that day and saw most of the action from his topside battle station on a twin 40MM antiaircraft gun mount.

In late October 1944, American plans for the retaking of the Philippines culminated with MacArthur's landing at Leyte on October 20. For several days, a massive armada of amphibious assault ships lay anchored in Leyte Gulf unloading, while the bulk of the huge U.S. Pacific fleet of carriers, battleships, cruisers and destroyers patrolled surrounding waters ready to repel the expected Japanese counterattack.

And indeed the Japanese were coming in force, committing most of what remained of their Navy – a still very formidable force of battleships, cruisers and destroyers, plus their few remaining carriers.

Thus the stage was set for the Battle of Leyte Gulf, called by Cutler "the biggest and most multifaceted naval battle in all of history" – involving 282 American, Japanese and Australian ships with over 200,000 men. Dozens of ships were sunk, and thousands of men went to the bottom of the sea with them.

To drive the Americans from their objective, the Japanese planned a giant seaborne pincer movement, with three powerful task forces led by battleships converging on the Leyte landing beaches. A fourth force, including their four remaining carriers, was positioned well north of the island as a decoy. One of the most powerful of these forces, the Center Force under command of Japanese Admiral Kurita, was to steam eastward through the San Bernardino Strait, turn south down the east coast of the island of Samar, and converge on the Leyte beaches from the north. The other two groups were to come up from the south after transiting Surigao Strait.

During the 23rd and 24th, all three Japanese attack forces were detected well west and south of their objective. The two southern forces were virtually annihilated by surface forces of Admiral Kinkaid's 7th Fleet. The third force, Admiral Kurita's Center Force, was attacked on the afternoon of the 24th by carrier air strikes from Halsey's 3rd fleet, while approaching the western entrance to San Bernardino Strait. With several of his ships sunk or badly damaged, Kurita was observed at dusk to reverse course and retire to the west. Satisfied that he had been both heavily damaged and sent packing, our commanders thought that this force, too, was now out of action.

In fact, while taking some losses, Kurita's fleet still packed a powerful punch, now consisting of four battleships, eight cruisers and seven destroyers. After dark, he again reversed course to the east, and transited San Bernardino Strait undetected during the night of the 24th and 25th.

In the meantime, during the day of October 24th, most of the 7th Fleet, including all of its heavies, were still far to the south cleaning up the remains of the other two Japanese forces. At about the same time, the Japanese decoy force was detected well to the north. The ever-aggressive Halsey swallowed the bait and took off in hot pursuit with the entire 3rd Fleet. Through a tragic series of failures of communication, both Halsey and Kinkaid thought the other had left sufficient firepower to cover the eastern end of the strait in the event any Japanese units came through from the west. In fact, it was left entirely unguarded.

Just to the south, down the east coast of Samar, were stationed three 7th Fleet task units, each consisting of six small CVE escort carriers, or "baby flattops", which were essentially small, thin-skinned merchant ships fitted with flight decks, capable of making no more than 17 knots, and each carrying a detachment of about 25 planes. Designated Task Units 77.4.1, 77.4.2, and 77.4.3, and known by their call signs, Taffy 1, Taffy 2 and Taffy 3, each CVE group also included a screen of a few destroyers and destroyer escorts.

Their assigned mission was air support for the landing force ashore on Leyte, as well as antisubmarine patrol to keep Japanese subs from attacking the transports. Thus their aircraft were armed with a combination of depth charges and anti-personnel weapons, without either torpedoes or armor-piercing bombs that would be effective against heavy combatant ships. They were positioned on a north-south axis along the Samar coast, with Taffy 3 farthest north, Taffy 2 in the middle, and Taffy 1 farthest south and closest to Leyte.

Taffy 3 was comprised of the CVE's Fanshaw Bay, Kalinin Bay, White Plains, St. Lo, Kitkun Bay, and Gambier Bay. The escorts were three Fletcher-class DD's: Johnston, Hoel, and Heerman, and four DE's: Samuel B. Roberts, Dennis, Raymond and John C. Butler.

At dawn on 25 October, Kurita burst out of the eastern end of San Bernardino Strait and, turning south toward Leyte, ran smack into Taffy 3, each group completely surprised by the presence of the other. Kurita opened fire at 36,000 yards and immediately 18 and 16-inch rounds started falling among the carriers and escorts. The slow, defenseless carriers' fate seemed certain. Johnston was the closest U.S. ship to the Japanese fleet, so many rounds started falling in her vicinity. Johnston's skipper, Commander Ernest Evans, immediately ordered flank speed and turned directly for the oncoming Japanese.

Bill Mercer sat at his battle station as trainer for one of the twin 40MM gun mounts, on the port side just below the bridge. So he could hear the captain's orders, and when he heard "Left full rudder!" he started strapping on his life jacket. Johnston began laying a thick smoke screen between the Japanese and the US carriers, and when within range, opened up on the closest Japanese cruiser with her five-inch guns. With most Japanese guns now trained on Johnston and near misses splashing all around, Evans figured his time was nearly up, and told his OOD, "We can't go down with our fish still aboard. Stand by for a torpedo attack!" Turning directly for the Japanese armada, Johnston, still miraculously unhurt, closed to within ten thousand yards, firing furiously, and launched all ten torpedoes. Some found their mark. Ducking back into her own smoke screen to retire, Johnston emerged to see a Japanese heavy cruiser burning brightly.

But at that moment, Johnston's luck ran out. Three 14-inch shells slammed into her after engine and fire rooms, followed by a 6-inch salvo that struck her port bridge wing and penetrated her 40MM magazine. Several were killed or badly wounded, and Commander Evans sustained serious wounds but kept fighting his ship.

Meanwhile, the Japanese force was bearing down on the fleeing CVE's at 30 knots. It seemed that nothing could save the ships of Taffy 3 from complete destruction in short order. The heavily damaged Johnston was down to one engine and half speed and had expended her torpedoes. Taffy 3 commander Admiral Clifton Sprague, in desperation, ordered the remaining escorts to commence a torpedo attack. With Johnston steering from emergency steering aft, Evans ordered her in astern of the other DD's and DE's, firing her remaining guns in support of her comrades. Johnston continued to absorb a ferocious pounding from heavy-caliber Japanese rounds.

With limited steering ability but still firing, Johnston continued to close the Japanese battleship KONGO, coming within five thousand yards, firing furiously, and eventually approached the battleship so close that its giant guns could not depress far enough to fire back at Johnston.

And so the battle went, and of course the mortally wounded Johnston, along with her sisters USS Hoel and USS Samuel B. Roberts, soon succumbed to an avalanche of large-caliber shells. As Johnston slipped beneath the sea, a Japanese destroyer approached, adding new terror to her survivors now clinging to rafts and nets. Instead of receiving the expected strafing, the sailors watched as some of the Japanese crew threw them cans of food, and then watched as a Japanese officer stood stiffly on the bridge in a motionless salute, as Johnston disappeared.

Of course the saga doesn't end there. The battle raged on for a while longer, and eventually the CVE Gambier Bay was sunk by gunfire. The Japanese continued to close and pound the remaining carriers, whose only response could be from a single five-inch gun each carried. But just when all seemed lost, the Japanese fleet inexplicably ceased firing and turned away. A memorable comment came from a young signalman on Admiral Sprague's flagship, who was heard to exclaim, "Dammit, they're getting away!"

But for Johnston's survivors, and those of Hoel, Roberts, Gambier Bay, and St. Lo (which was sunk by a Kamikaze shortly after the battle), a very new ordeal was beginning. Over the next 48 hours the survivors battled thirst, their own wounds, and frequent shark attacks that took the lives of many more. In all, over one thousand men were finally rescued, but not until the 27th. — two full days and nights later.

Of JOHNSTON's crew of 320, 278 survived the action to abandon ship. Of these men, 45 were known to have died in the water of their wounds, and another 92, including the skipper and XO, were never found and reported missing in action. 141 of Johnston's crew were finally rescued. CDR Evans was awarded the Congressional Medal of Honor posthumously, and the keel was laid for DD821 on 26 March 1945, to be named JOHNSTON in their honor.

Cutler concludes his story of the Battle of Leyte Gulf with the following paragraph, which I quote verbatim:

"One is reluctant to begin singling out individual ships and their commanders, because all played important roles and because there are many examples of outstanding performance that deserve recognition. But in the case of the Taffy 3 escorts, an exception would be in order. What the men in those ships did on that October morning off Samar deserves to be a focal point of the nation's naval heritage, ranking with John Paul Jones' epic "I have not yet begun to fight" battle. Commander Ernest E. Evans received the Congressional Medal of Honor posthumously for his incredible courage in taking JOHNSTON "in harm's way". One of the buildings at the Navy's Surface Warfare Officers' School in Newport, Rhode Island, rightfully bears his name. But there should be more tributes. A statue commemorating the deeds of those ships and the men who crewed them in the Battle of Leyte Gulf should be erected in the nation's capital so that all Americans will be reminded of the kind of courage and sacrifice this nation can produce when circumstances require."

And so our tribute today and the small metal plaque next door, while not the statue Cutler urges, is nevertheless a gesture which is our privilege to make. Many years ago we were invested with, and today we still hold, the legacy bought so dearly by Bill Mercer and his shipmates. Bill, we've heard the history-book version. Now please come up and tell us what it was like on board USS JOHNSTON on the morning of October 25, 1944, and the couple of days afterward.

4:40 PM - BILL MERCER

REMARKS

4: 55 PM - TAPS

Now it is appropriate to close this part of the ceremony with a moment in memory of those who served aboard USS JOHNSTON (DD557) and died on those days and later, as well as those of our own shipmates of USS JOHNSTON (DD821) who are no longer with us. Please rise for the playing of taps.

TAPS

Now please let's gather outside the Theater at the Navy Memorial Commemorative Wall to view our commemorative plaque. Immediately following, refreshments and dinner will be served here in the Heritage Center.

USS JOHNSTON DD557 - DD821
The Officers and Men of USS Johnston (DD821)
Salute the Crew of USS Johnston (DD557)

Sunk during their heroic defense of TU 77.4.3 (Taffy 3)
Battle of Leyte Gulf - Battle off Samar - 25 October 1944

Honors Ceremony At the Site: 11° 50'N - 126° 10'E
While enroute to Vietnam - 26 December 1967

MY SHORT HISTORY WITH THE "JOLLY J"

By: Raymond "Harold" Ponsell, Signalman (SM3)

Years on board the Johnston: 1967 to 1968

I was assigned to the Johnston in about Aug 1967. Shortly thereafter I was a striker for Signalman and was moved to the signal bridge. I remember a few of the names but unfortunately not all. There was the First Class Mike Shibariski who was naturally called "Ski." There was E-5 Cline, what an ol' salt as my memory tells me. He introduced me to "Salty Dogs" at the Hong Kong Hilton as I remember. There was Gordon Schrader E-4 from Murfeesboro, Tennessee. He turned out to be my running buddy. There was a Larry Smith, a Mike Dees who had just gotten married and Jacobo Martinez "Jake" I hope some or all of these guys get this message as I would love to talk to them after all these years.

Sometime around Nov. we sailed for Vietnam. Somewhere around Cuba we lost a shaft bearing, if my memory is correct, and we alone went back to Mayport for repairs.

Mayport sits next to Jacksonville Florida which is my home town. I visited with family and friends while the ship was in Mayport. Finally the ol' girl was ready for a sea trial and I borrowed my dad's car to drive to Mayport for the sea trails. Well as Navy luck goes she passed the sea trial and we went straight on south headed for the Far East. Now there were no cell phones etc in the sixties so around, as I later learned, 10pm my Dad called the base to learn why I and his car weren't home.

Dad told me later he had a heck of a time getting on the base and retrieving his car.

A few of the shipmates visited some local drinking joints while the ship was in Mayport and a few of them brought along a lil' present with them, nothing the needle couldn't cure :)

I was REALLY impressed with the Panama Canal, some kind of technology and this 19 year old (at that time) thought it was something.

The single ship convoy over was pretty cool in my opinion as I was born in Jacksonville and had hardly left the area before joining the Navy. San Diego was short and quick and I don't remember much about it.

Guam was cool as I got a "care package" from home and the guys on the signal bridge really enjoyed sharing the homemade Pecan Logs my mom had sent.

Our arrival in Subic Bay was REAL CULTURAL shock to this young southern boy. I had never heard of much less seen that kind of poverty. The Philippines turned out to be interesting, Olangapo City, was really weird. Yea I got a lot of shoe shines on the bridge leaving and entering the base, beat the alternative black shoe polish on the whites. Any one remember the base club "Sampitago" $.25 call brand drinks and then to Olangapo City for warm San Miguel beer.

The Gulf Of Tonkin and the firing line was something else. I actually enjoyed all the activity while we were shooting. The plane guard duty was interesting to say the least. Yep I got my "Gulf of Tonkin Yacht Club" patch and the "Stompin' in the Tonkin patch".

Hong Kong was great, enjoyed the sites, food and all. Got my "crow" there on the fantail from Cmdr Curran. Kaoshong Taiwan, WHAT A PLACE. I tried to ship over for permanent shore duty there, THANK GOD THE NAVY SAID NO!

I remember the BIG STORM we went through on the way over, that was something else. I remember something about a galley fire somewhere in the cruise and all we had to eat that night was "battered, fried Egg Plant" I have loved it ever since. Anyone remember Cook Friley, the big guy?

How about all the pirated records we had to throw overboard on the way back? I hated that!

I am sure there are many; many things I am forgetting and may never remember or might if someone else's memories jog mine.

347

I got out of the Navy in Dec 68 and piddled around on several jobs until April 75' when joined the Jacksonville Sheriffs Office in Jacksonville Fla. I retired from there in December 2001.

Tish and I moved into our motorhome and will travel the USA for a few years to find the PLACE we want to live. Hopefully this posting could lead to a chance to meet some of the former shipmates sometime in the future.

ANTIQUE MEMORIES - 1968

By: Mark Chavez, Radarman (RD2)

Years on board the Johnston: 1966 to 1969

Antique memories are not so reliable. Any who wants to correct this may do so. The Johnston was in Nam during the Tet offensive, and I watched the city of Hue disappear from the surface radar scope.

It was 1968, and we had gone through an interesting passage to get there. From Charleston, our home port, we visited Mayport, Florida. The Johnston then continued to the Panama Canal. U.S. military ships had priority, but we had to wait for a day. Surprisingly narrow, concrete structure set in the jungle. Some lakes part way through. It was a fairly boring passage. The Pacific had more to offer, up the coast and over to Hawaii. We had one guy, a surfer type, go AWOL for the whole time we stayed. Wartes was his name - Very laid back. He just wanted to experience the place with no distractions. Everybody else behaved themselves. Next stop was Okinawa, the legendary home of Karate. A sand dune from where I stood.

Out from Wake was when, I believe, we hit some huge tropical storm that blew us way off course. Safety rigging was torn away, and overhead plating peeled back like the proverbial sardine can. It was then that our steering problem developed, as well as a ballast difficulty. It was months before any of this was sorted. I remember an incident about the ballast where we nearly lost Don Phillips. A day or two after the storm, Moltz and I were cleaning the aft shower space, a radarman responsibility (I don't know why). The side door was open for ventilation and dogged back. We had just finished the usual scrub with a toothbrush (I am not joking) when Shorty Phillips walked by the open hatch. He stopped to chat, as sailors sometimes do. Just then we made a course correction to Port. The ballast was not corrected properly, and this buried the Starboard side deep into the oncoming swell. Philips suddenly dropped what he was carrying and grabbed the coaming about chest high. Moltz and I watched a wall of green water sweep by the open hatch, completely blocking the door. We stood there stunned and all we could see of Shorty was both his hands locked to the open hatchway as that rush of water tried to carry him away. Not a drop came through the door, it was moving so fast. He hung there in that cold green current for what seemed almost a minute before the ship righted itself and that water fell away. He was shocked, but alright. And he never again went outside the skin of the ship when it was underway. I don't blame him.

We finally tie up alongside another tin can in Subic. This ship had just come off the gun line and looked a mess. Rust everywhere, rigging in tatters and salt encrusted. She looked shocking. The Johnston always shone with polished brass and whitened rigging. What tremendous contrast. Here I witnessed something really dumb. A piece of cargo had been chasing us from port to port, always arriving just a bit too late. It was some sort of key for the forward gun mount. It was solid steel in a box a foot long. It slotted into a ratchet affair fixed to the deck, and locked the gun mount in place when firing. It finally caught up to us, and one of our guys was handing it to a gunners mate colleague in the motor launch, when it slipped from his hands and fell straight to the bottom. Finding it in that century old harbor ooze and muck wasn't possible, and there it lays today. I don't know how he explained that one to Captain Curren.

Eventually we entered the war zone. We saw Subic Bay, Hong Kong, Yokuska, Japan, Kau Shung, Taiwan, and a certain six thousand yard chunk of beach over and over again as we held station on the gun line. We were given I corp, just south of the DMZ. We had to be careful as the enemy had a big gun on a flatbed railcar that they could run into position and get us, if we were not alert. We earned the combat action ribbon there. But it wasn't that big artillery gun, just some crazy guy pinged us a few times with his rifle, a slight risk to the lookouts. The captain was keen to add to his chest display, (first tour and no medals as yet) so he put the ship in for a ribbon for being under fire. You see, for the captain to get his medal, we all had to get it. I always wondered where the admirals got all those ribbons and awards. Not quite cereal box issue, but close.

The war was hard work. When we weren't firing H & I we replenished our stores, got more ammo (USS Vulcan) or loaded across something vital. When we left Nam our guns were all worn out, and had to be replaced. On that Harassment and Interdiction fire, all I can say is that it kept us awake and nervous, if not the enemy. Every time the gun mount approached perpendicular to the side, and blasted away, bits and pieces fell from the overhead onto your chest. The first time that happened, I recall Joe Cizio leaping from his bunk in alarm, thinking he'd been shot. He was the toughest guy on the ship and very macho. It couldn't have happened to a better chump. That colored his shorts a bit. Remember that Joe ???

That's where we were when we had the emergency call to get down to Hue. The city was under attack. When we got there we found that Hue was just out of range of our six inch guns. The Manley, a cruiser, was more useful having eight inch guns. Talk about power. We stood off a few miles away and watched as she pounded the beach. Her guns were deafening, and the pressure wave slapped you in the face with each shot. As for the city, she slowly crumbled away. From a very sharp square paint, Hue became a very broken outline, then almost nothing. Obliterated in a few days.

We had R & R in Japan and everyone bought pearls for the girl back home, or their mum. Mikimoto pearls, next to the seaman's club were very popular. Sixth floor, I think, was the restaurant. It had great service and fair chow as well. We usually began as a group of six to eight guys, but split off as the urge to wander hit us.

In Subic Bay, the authorities wanted everyone to avoid the town, and set up some entertainment on Grande Island. They brought in girls to dance with; had live bands and the drinks were cheap - so cheap we ordered five at a time. I have dim memories of being fifteen or so drinks behind and trying manfully to keep up. Dempsey, the postal clerk was our champion. What a soak he was, and never looked too bad. Funny metabolism. Since the postal clerk had to do something while at sea, he worked in combat with us radar guys. He became quite good at it, as well. Thinking back on all this, it's no wonder my recollections are a bit piecemeal. They led me astray. Or I lead them astray. Mums and girlfriends would not have approved.

Back to the gun line again. Worse this time as we knew what to expect. Call for fire every day from some crazy marine running through the jungle. He had a radio, Comanche board, and guided our fire onto the target. Left 100, up fifty and fire for effect. I manned surface radar for approximate navigation. From my memory of that shallow coast, I would guide the ship onto target until acquired by fire control. Then they would shoot until target was destroyed. Could be a machine gun nest, troop concentration or recoilless rifle detachment. We had a reputation of being very accurate, but this meant we were popular. Actually not so good for us poor squids re-arming every other day.

Subic Bay was dangerous. Violence was everywhere. All the bars had armed guards. The bar girls had knives. The taxi drivers might kidnap you and gang assault you sexually, the shoeshine boys put razors to your Achilles tendons for a ransom, and our boys, the jungle marines and army, used Subic as a halfway house to learn manners before returning to the States. They didn't like sailors. And another thing,... the city smelled funny. You could smell Subic Bay miles at sea. There was a bridge over the river going into the harbor that had a crowd of divers on it. Throw a coin and they dove into that filthy river. I was shocked. First time third world poverty stared me in the face. Well, the second, if you count the paint crews in Hong Kong that painted your ship for the privilege of all your garbage for a week. No joke. No exaggeration. The Far East opened your eyes.

While on the gun line, we had a priority message to detach and proceed north to Korea. Seems one of our spy boats had been captured. The U.S.S. Pueblo hit the news. All our tactical publications were compromised, and new ones were to be issued. Chaos for a day. The captain reminded the admiral that our steering was faulty. We could hold true at six knots when firing at shore targets, but active cut and thrust was beyond us.

352

So we were detached yet again, to go to Subic for repairs. Up onto one of those dry dock ships, and while the rudder was being fixed, they sand blasted below the water line to get the barnacles off. That was a mistake. Most of the hull was old. The midsection, was recent. Had been added later by (FRAM, fleet repair and maintenance). They just cut the ship in half and added this section. But the rest of the hull was paper thin. The sand blasting stripped away large sections of that single hull. In the end, they welded huge patches onto the side. It worked, for I am here to tell you about it. Back to the gun line and we found the rudder was still not fixed. We were sent to Japan for another refit. Yokuska had never been bombed during WW11, because our navy wanted those dry docks. Multiple ship repairs, professional treatment. It was there that the steering was finally fixed. I can report that Japan has tiny little earthquakes all the time. Our ship sat on concrete, shored up with big wooden beams. Very solid. Can't move. So Gary Benjesdorf and I were assigned to paint the top of the mast black. A radarman responsibility, as our antennas were up there. So we clambered up to this teeny tiny platform just big enough for two cans of paint, safety roped our selves in place, and began to slop on that paint. For about a half hour, we made progress. Then the quake hit. Probably unnoticeable at ground level, the tall mast and whip antenna magnified that movement to a very rapid back and forth shake. I dropped my brush and hung on to save my life. Benjy also wrapped his arms instantly around the mast, and while the ship moved like a dog shaking a rat, he painted the side of his face with that brush. This was no joke. Scared doesn't cover it. It lasted seconds, but it seemed forever. Time slowed down and I can remember his bulging eyes and terrified face. I must have looked pretty grim myself. When our knees got under control, we abandoned the job.

It is flowing back to me now. The guys in the radar gang; Plummer, Moltz, Phillips, Benjesdorf, Cizio, Watson, and some of the officers...Howard Seeley, Blankenship, Mack, Capper, Captain Curren...and the many faces with no names, like forgotten brothers, united by common experience. I hope more guys write in about their experiences.

TO CLOSE FOR COMFORT

By: Richard Street, Storekeeper (SK2)

Years on board the Johnston: 1967 to 1969

It was March 1968, and the TET offensive was in full swing. The Johnston was on the gun line off the coast of Hue, South Vietnam. The VC had taken Hue and we were shelling day and night to keep them off our guys who were dug in around the city. Both fore and aft mounts would fire pretty much around the clock until we ran out of ammo. We would then head out to sea and hook up with a supply ship (I think it was the Ticonderoga) to replenish and re-arm. The incident that I remember so well was transferring crates of white phosphorous (willy peters) from the supply boat to our helo deck.

My replenishing station was aft phone to phone with the supply ship. The seas were fairly rough and we had a little trouble hooking up, but we eventually starting pulling crates of powder cases and projectiles on board. As one crate of willy peters was just about to clear the bulkhead supporting the 2nd deck, both ships rolled toward each other lowering the line and crate. The crate brushed the edge of the bulkhead and flipped upside down. Suddenly the deck was being hammered by projectiles falling out of the crate. It's amazing what goes thru your mind when this kind of thing happens. I

354

had a flashback to high school days when our chemistry teacher took a small piece of white phosphorous out of a jar of water to let us observe what happens when it came in contact with air. It created a pretty hot fire immediately. That was maybe a quarter of an ounce, and these shells weigh 56 pounds apiece.

The chief boats called for an emergency breakaway and we turned away from the supply ship. I've never seen guys moving as fast as they picked up the projectiles and tossed them over the side. I don't think anybody breathed until the last one had been thrown over. After things calmed down you could hear the nervous laughs, but that one I'll never forget.

The Shoot at Vieques

By: John Rausch, LTjg

Years on board the Johnston: 1969 to 1970

One of my memorable experiences aboard JOHNSTON was being made an instant expert on 5"/38 caliber projectiles. Following our spring/summer 1969 REFTRA at (the now more famous) GITMO, JOHNSTON was scheduled to do gunfire support at the Atlantic weapons range at Culebra Island. Because of an earlier in-bore explosion of a 5"/38 projectile at Culebra and the subsequent search for the barrel pieces, the ship was redirected to Vieques Island to shoot. As I recall, there was additional recent evidence of problems with the old 5"/38 projectiles. Just before the shooting began,

355

the ship was directed to "inspect" the base fuses on all projectiles fired. Being a new JO, I was given a couple of minutes of instruction of what to look for - an uneven feel around the fuse as I recall. I was assigned to the forward magazine where I felt the base of every projectile that went up to the mount during my watches there. I remember being quite happy to do so as it beat being in the mount as a check-site officer. We shot for what seemed like 24 hours - a lot of rounds. The ship's store was in shambles and other minor damage occurred because of the shocks. We were rewarded by a couple of days in Puerto Rico where we present during the first moon landing. The ship then headed for Charleston. As I recall, our navigation was off and we overshot the port traveling a good distance beyond "Buoy 2 Charlie" before reversing course.

L-R, Del & Linda Bartlett, Garda & John Rausch
& Andy Zander

"REPORTING ABOARD SIR!"

By: Robert Stepien, Seaman (SN)

Years on board the Johnston: 1969 to 1971

    Well, I remember taking a plane out of McQuire Air
Force Base to pick up my ship the USS Johnston DD-821.
By the way, I came from upstate New York and could have
gone to WOODSTOCK, but I chose the Navy instead. I think
it was late June or early July 1969. The Johnston was in
port in GITMO, Cuba. It was my first time on a ship and
everyone knew that I had just got out of boot camp at
Great Lakes. As the day went by, everyone accepted me and
I started to fit in. I was assigned to First Division.
I was going to be a "Deck Ape". I was only 18 years old,
I had just got married, and my wife was due in July with
our child and I was going to be a "Deck Ape". What the
hell is a "Deck Ape"????? I am being told that I am one
by BMC Marshall Mean. Navy lifer and a man I will never
ever forget. My duties were to swab the deck, paint,
remove flying fish every morning when at sea from the
deck and a whole bunch of other deck ape duties. It
seemed like everything was our duty. This was the Navy?
Again, this was my first time on such a large "boat" so I
thought it was going to be a cake walk. Well, we left
GITMO, I am at sea now and I thought I was going to
DIEEEEEEE puke. Puke, Puke, Puke! Did I mention three
solid days of Puke, Puke, Puke! And as I laid on the
deck, (Half Dead) and being yelled at for what reason I
did not know. I quickly learned to puke over the Fantail
not over the Bow. So after a few prayers and thinking I
was going to die as a Navy man during the war, I finally
pulled out of it and got my "Sea Legs". "What a Life!" I
said to myself. Anyway as I mentioned my wife was due
with our child. I got called to the XO's room and he
handed me a note which read "Wife and child are doing
good, 7 Lb. 5 Oz. boy and he was named Shane Robert
Stepien. That was July 15th, 1969. Today my son Shane is
40 years old and has a growing business in New York, is
married, and has three beautiful children - my grand

kids; Spencer, Addison and Jameson. I also have a 37 year old Daughter Shelby who came after the Navy. I am remarried to my beautiful wife Tracy. When I was married and on the Johnston, my current wife was only four years old.

These are just a couple of my stories I have to share. There are many more including Captain's Mast, sneaking onboard the ship late and being "Over the Hill" for five hours while being caught in Spain. There are probably more, but that will have to do for now.

Chapter 7

YEARS 1970 THROUGH 1979

The Chief Hates Hammers......

By: Tim O'Brien, Machinist Mate (MM2)

Years on board the Johnston: 1970 to 1971

I was fortunate enough to serve on the Johnston from 1970 to 1972. Like most of us who crewed the "Jolly J", I have many great memories. I was a Machinist Mate in the forward engine room, and one of the funniest things I remember involved our Chief... John Cates. Over the years, I've noticed that there are usually two kinds of mechanics: those whose abilities are "okay" or "average", and those who are very good at what they do. But every once in a while, you run across someone who just plain has a gift as far as the ability to fix things. Cates was that kind of guy... and he _hated_ hammers! I don't mean he just didn't like them. He detested 'em! The last thing you wanted was to have Cates see a hammer in your hand in "his" engine room.

He'd always make a point of asking what you were going to do with it. When you told him what you were working on, he'd always tell you to go put the hammer down and get a wrench… that you didn't "fix" things with a hammer! And usually, he was right…

There was, however, this stubborn bilge pump on the lower level of the forward engine room. All of us knew that to light it off (start it), you needed a hammer. We even kept a 3-pound hammer hidden near the pump for just that reason. It was an old steam-driven reciprocating ram (think steam locomotive) pump. When you first started it, until it warmed up, it would make exactly 3 strokes and stop. At which point you would use the hammer to give the valve body two good raps. The pump would make 3 more strokes and stop again, whereupon you repeated the process, after which the pump would run great with no further attention needed. We had all unsuccessfully taken our turn trying to adjust the valve linkage to avoid having to use the hammer. Like I said, all of us knew this… all of us that is except Chief Cates. Sometime around halfway through the 70-71 Med cruse, I went down to pump the bilges and had just drawn the hammer back to administer the second "whack" to the valve body when Guess Who grabbed my wrist from behind! What he said next probably couldn't be printed here, but it was along the lines of "Tell me exactly why you were getting ready to hit my pump with a hammer…" When I told him that's how we had been doing it since I had reported aboard, I actually thought he was going to have a coronary.

Cates then proceeded to try to show me the "right" way to start this pump. After the 4th time it stopped on him, I made the mistake of offering him the hammer. Now he has to prove his point, so rather than get the pump running to pump the bilges (which are getting pretty full) off comes his khaki shirt and he tells me to go get

360

tools so we can fix the pump the right way, and that we wouldn't be needing a *%#*&!# hammer to do it! By the time we had taken the valve body apart, cleaned everything up with emery cloth, reassembled and adjusted it three times, the pump still wouldn't run, we had missed chow, and the water in the bilges was literally up to the deck plates. Cates looked at me… I looked at Cates… we both looked at the hammer lying alongside the pump. Then Cates said "Hand me the damn hammer"… which he used to start the bilge pump. He handed me back the hammer and said "Keep the hammer down here… and we never talk about this again…" Knowing how Cates was, I never brought it up…

U.S.S. JOHNSTON (DD821) – A PROUD HERITAGE

By: Burnham C. "Mike" McCaffree, Commander (Rear Admiral, USN Retired)

Years on board the Johnston: 1970 to 1972

Our U.S.S. JOHNSTON was one of 98 ships in the final World War II class of destroyers – the Gearing class. JOHNSTON was named after a destroyer that was sunk after surface action against a vastly superior Japanese force during the Battle of Leyte Gulf, to commemorate that ship and her heroic Captain, Commander Ernest E. Evans, who was awarded the Medal of Honor posthumously, and to carry on the name of our namesake who served gallantly during the Civil War. Whether we knew it or not, that was the heritage that greeted each of us when we reported aboard JOHNSTON for duty.

How did our JOHNSTON fare as successor to the DD 557? Whereas the DD 557 had a life of only one year, the DD 821 was in commission from 1946 to 1980. Those were "Cold War" years, and most of DD 821's service was in the Atlantic Ocean and the Mediterranean Sea, to which she deployed about 15 times to show the flag and conduct peacekeeping operations with other NATO naval forces. In 1968 JOHNSTON deployed to the Western Pacific, where she conducted shore bombardment missions in support of U.S. ground forces in northern South Vietnam.

The DD 557 had a very short life, and almost all of her commissioning crew of 273 men was still with her when she was sunk in October 1944. The DD 821, on the other hand, had thousands of crewmembers during her long active service. One thing they had in common is that these destroyermen represented the best, the fighting qualities of the American sailor, as epitomized by Commander Evans, that have served our nation so well in war and in peace since its beginning.

MEMORIES - During the summer of 1971 Destroyer Squadron TWO was deployed to the U.S. Sixth Fleet in the Mediterranean. JOHNSTON was equipped with a van full of communications and electronic emission intercept equipment, with a detachment of specially trained technicians who would copy electronic transmissions of Soviet Navy warships. The van was stored in our helicopter hangar. In June JOHNSTON was sent to the eastern Med to shadow ships of the Soviet Mediterranean Squadron in order for our "techies" to tape their voice and radio communications.

One day July day we were in the midst of about five Soviet anchored warships, which included the LENINGRAD (an ASW carrier), a KRESTA II heavy cruiser, a couple of destroyers, and an oiler. We went to General Quarters for routine training, doing engineering and damage control drills and other types of training. Our Gunnery Officer, LT Cannon, told Mounts 51 and 52 to conduct local exercises to give their pointers and trainers experience in aiming the guns locally rather than in the usual automatic radar-controlled mode. Well, that sounds like a good training idea, but guess what Mt. 51's pointer and trainer aimed at? Yep, they were aiming at the biggest target they could find – the LENINGRAD!

All of a sudden, CIC called on the squawk box that our electronic warfare equipment was detecting a lot of Soviet fire control radars being aimed at us. And then our OOD and his lookouts reported that several of the Soviet warships had aimed their gun mounts at JOHNSTON. Next, the techies sent word from the van that they were getting an awful lot of electronic activity and radio transmissions from the Soviets. And very soon thereafter, the LENINGRAD started sending us a flashing light message from their Admiral. It said, in so many words, that we had committed a hostile act by pointing our gun mount at their ship, and they would interpret this as an ACT OF WAR if we did not immediately cease and desist. [By then LT Cannon had realized the cause of all the commotion – I suspect I "helped him" understand the problem – and Mt. 52 had been trained to centerline.)

Well, I figured that a) we were very badly outgunned by the several larger, newer Soviet warships; b) I better send a FAST apology to the Soviet Admiral as well as secure the ship from GQ; and c) hopefully the Soviets weren't interested in starting World War III by shooting at JOHNSTON. [I also thought that JOHNSTON would be getting a new Commanding Officer pretty darned quick as soon as our Admiral got my report of what had happened!] Fortunately, things calmed down – although the KRESTA cruiser chased us out of the anchorage – and our Admiral stuck up for us when the Soviet Union sent a report to Washington, but that was sure an exciting day for JOHNSTON.

COMMANDER ERNEST E. I, U.S. NAVY (DECEASED) WINNER OF MEDAL OF HONOR – During the summer of 1950, my first summer as a Midshipman at the U.S. Naval Academy, I attended the dedication of a room in Bancroft Hall, the Academy's dormitory. The room was dedicated to Commander Ernest E. I, U. S. Navy, who was a graduate of the Naval Academy class of 1931 and had won the Medal of Honor posthumously for exceptional heroism as commanding officer of USS Johnston (DD-557) off Samar on 25 October 1944 during the Battle of Leyte Gulf. One of the honored guests at the room dedication was Commander I' son, Ernest E. I, Jr., who was a classmate of mine.

Ernest and I were assigned to different parts of the Brigade of Midshipmen, so we did not become friends during our four years at the Naval Academy. Upon graduation in 1954, Ernest received a commission in the United States Marine Corps. In the ensuing 30 years, he had a very successful career commanding Marine infantry battalions and in other key operational billets, and in demanding staff assignments in the Washington area. He retired as a Colonel, USMC, and resides in Vienna, VA.

My career as a surface naval officer took me a very different route. In September 1970, 20 years after I attended the Bancroft Hall room dedication, I had the good fortune to take command of USS Johnston (DD 821), the successor to the ship which had become a legend in the Navy's destroyer force because of the heroic actions of her captain and crew. While the men who served in our Johnston were never tested in the crucible of combat at sea, we knew of the legacy of the DD 557 and I believe we would have acquitted ourselves honorably if confronted with the challenge our predecessors had met so valiantly.

"SMOKE" GETS IN YOUR EYES - JOHNSTON had a hard-rock combo called "SMOKE" in the early 1970s that performed for our crew and sometimes for wider audiences. I remember a couple of performances by our combo that attracted some international attention.

During our Med deployment in the spring and summer of 1971, "SMOKE" had developed a good repertoire of music. One "rope yarn Sunday" we were anchored in the East of Crete anchorage area in close proximity to ships of the Soviet Mediterranean squadron. SMOKE set up on the ASROC deck and began to perform. Most JOHNSTON men who were not on duty came up to the 01 level to enjoy the music and take a semi-holiday break. All of a sudden we realized that more and more sailors were coming topside aboard the ASW carrier LENINGRAD to listen to our rock band's melodious strains as they skipped across the water. Then we saw some Soviet sailors - probably the ship's masters- at-arms - running around on deck waving their hands and presumably "encouraging" their shipmates to get below, and we heard announcements over their topside 1MC speakers that we assumed were telling them to do so. Once LENINGRAD's topside was empty, over their 1MC speakers we began to hear Russian folk music and classical music, with the volume set on LOUD. SMOKE continued to play and entertain our crew, and we noticed a few brave Soviet sailors stick their heads out of watertight doors and hatches. Score one for the Americans!

On a July Saturday afternoon in Brindisi, Italy, our ship was moored pierside in the downtown portion of the waterfront. SMOKE was playing on the ASROC deck and the XO and I were sitting at the outside hotel café across the street. Pedestrians who were walking along the waterfront stopped to listen. Then traffic began to back up outside the hotel because drivers were stopping to listen also. Next, I saw two Guardia policemen start walking towards the quarterdeck. I thought, "Oh, boy, we've in trouble." The ship's Command Duty Officer met them on the Q'deck and I could see a discussion, and they disappeared for a few moments. Then they appeared on the ASROC deck, and what did they do? The Guardia walked over to the lifelines and loitered there for the next 15 minutes, enjoying the beat of SMOKE's music just as much as our crew and the passers-by were doing!

"SMOKE" performs at Officers' Dance in Charleston - During JOHNSTON's deployment to the Mediterranean Sea in 1971, the ship's combo "Smoke" performed frequently on board ship for the crew, and occasionally in ports the ship visited. As a result of very favorable reviews that resulted from SMOKE's performances in those port visits, SMOKE received an unexpected invitation to perform upon the ship's return to its home port of Charleston, SC.

By way of explanation, JOHNSTON was assigned to Destroyer Squadron FOUR in Cruiser Destroyer Flotilla SIX. Each year the Flotilla had a formal dinner dance at the Charleston Naval Base Officers' Club in honor of the Cruiser Destroyer Force, U. S. Atlantic Fleet. CRUDESFLOT SIX was commanded by a Rear Admiral.

Shortly after JOHNSTON's return to Charleston's return from our Med deployment, I received an "invitation" to call on the Admiral. He informed me that the Flotilla Dance Committee had selected SMOKE as the band they wanted to invite to play at the gala CRUDESLANT dinner dance, and he asked my opinion of the selection. I explained that I had never heard our combo perform any dance music, but the Admiral responded that SMOKE had been exceptionally popular everywhere they performed overseas. It was clear he thought SMOKE was an excellent selection to play at the formal dance for which he was to be the host, and the "deal was done." The Flotilla Dance Committee invited SMOKE to perform, and they accepted.

Several weeks later, a hundred or so officers in their mess dress uniforms and their wives or dates in their beautiful gowns gathered in the at the Officers' Club for the annual CRUDESLANT dinner dance, which featured SMOKE as the dance combo for the evening. I should not have had any reservations. SMOKE "smoked" the whole crowd from the Admiral down to the junior-most officer and all of the ladies. I don't recall the combo performing any waltzes or even many foxtrots, but they played the current rock favorites so well that they got great applause for every number – and they got us all out on the dance floor dancing around with great abandon! It was the most successful Flotilla dance any of us could remember, and certainly the loudest!

CPO Standards

Submitted by: Rear Admiral Mike McCaffrey

Never forget this, a Chief can become an Officer, but an Officer can never become a Chief. After all, Chiefs have their standards!

Recollections of a WHITEHAT.

"One thing we weren't aware of at the time, but became evident as life wore on, was that we learned true leadership from the finest examples any lad was ever given, Chief Petty Officers. They were crusty old bastards who had done it all and had been forged into men who had been time tested over more years than a lot of us had time on the planet. The ones I remember wore hydraulic oil stained hats with scratched and=2 0dinged-up insignia, faded shirts, some with a Bull Durham tag dangling out of their right-hand pocket or a pipe and tobacco reloads in a worn leather pouch in their hip pockets, and a Zippo that had been everywhere. Some of them came with tattoos on their forearms that would force them to keep their cuffs buttoned at a Methodist picnic.

Most of them were as tough as a boarding house steak. A quality required to survive the life they lived. They were, and always will be, a breed apart from all other residents of Mother Earth. They took eighteen year old idiots and hammered the stupid bastards into sailors.

You knew instinctively it had to be hell on earth to have been born a Chief's kid. God should have given all sons born to Chiefs a return option.

A Chief didn't have to command respect. He got it because there was nothing else you could give them. They were God's designated hitters on earth.

We had Chiefs with fully loaded Submarine Combat Patrol Pins, and combat air crew wings in my day...hard-core bastards who remembered lost mates, and still cursed the cause of their loss...and they were expert at choosing descriptive adjectives and nouns, none of which their mothers would have endorsed.

At the rare times you saw a Chief topside in dress canvas, you saw rows of hard-earned, worn and faded ribbons over his pocket. "Hey Chief, what's that one and that one?" "Oh hell kid, I can't remember. There was a war on. They gave them to us to keep track of the campaigns." "We didn't get a lot of news out where we were. To be honest, we just took their word for it. Hell son, you couldn't pronounce most of the names of the places we went. They're all depth charge survival geedunk." "Listen kid, ribbons don't make you a Sailor." We knew who the heroes were, and in the final analysis that's all that matters.

Many nights, we sat in the after mess deck wrapping ourselves around cups of coffee and listening to their stories. They were light-hearted stories about warm beer shared with their running mates in corrugated metal sheds at resupply depots where the only furniture was a few packing crates and a couple of Coleman lamps. Standing in line at a Honolulu cathouse or spending three hours soaking in a tub in Freemantle, smoking cigars, and getting loaded. It was our history. And we dreamed of being just like them because they were our heroes. When they accepted you as their shipmate, it was the highest honor you would ever receive in your life. At least it was clearly that for me. They were not men given to the prerogatives of their position.

You would find them with their sleeves rolled up, shoulder-to-shoulder with you in a stores loading party. "Hey Chief, no need for you to be out here tossin' crates in the rain, we can get all this crap aboard."

"Son, the term 'All hands' means all hands."

"Yeah Chief, but you're no damn kid anymore, you old coot."

"Horsefly, when I'm eighty-five parked in the stove up old bastards' home, I'll still be able to kick your worthless butt from here to fifty feet past the screw guards along with six of your closest friends." And he probably wasn't bullshitting.

They trained us. Not only us, but hundreds more just like us. If it wasn't for Chief Petty Officers, there wouldn't be any U.S. Navy. There wasn't any fairy godmother who lived in a hollow tree in the enchanted forest who could wave her magic wand and create a Chief Petty Officer.

They were born as hot-sacking seamen, and matured like good whiskey in steel hulls over many years. Nothing a nineteen year-old jay-bird could cook up was original to these old saltwater owls. They had seen E-3 jerks come and go for so many years; they could read you like a book. "Son, I know what you are thinking. Just one word of advice. DON'T. It won't be worth it."

"Aye, Chief."

Chiefs aren't the kind of guys you thank. Monkeys at the zoo don't spend a lot of time thanking the guy who makes them do tricks for peanuts.

Appreciation of what they did, and who they were, comes with long distance retrospect. No young lad takes time to recognize the worth of his leadership. That comes later when you have experienced poor leadership or let's say, when you have the maturity to recognize what leaders should be, you find that Chiefs are the standard by which you measure all others.

They had no Academy rings to get scratched up. They butchered the King's English. They had become educated at the other end of an anchor chain from Copenhagen to Singapore. They had given their entire lives to the U.S. Navy. In the progression of the nobility of employment, Chief Petty Officer heads the list. So, when we ultimately get our final duty station assignments and we get to wherever the big Chief of Naval Operations in the sky assigns us, if we are lucky, Marines will be guarding the streets. I don't know about that Marine propaganda bullshit, but there will be an old Chief in an oil-stained hat and a cigar stub clenched in his teeth standing at the brow to assign us our bunks and tell us where to stow our gear... and we will all be young again, and the damn coffee will float a rock.

Life fixes it so that by the time a stupid kid grows old enough and smart enough to recognize who he should have thanked along the way, he no longer can. If I could, I would thank my old Chiefs. If you only knew what you succeeded in pounding in this thick skull, you would be amazed. So, thanks you old casehardened unsalvageable son-of-a-bitches. Save me a rack in the berthing compartment."

Life isn't about waiting for the storm to pass. It's about learning to dance in the rain.

JOHNSTON CAN BE UNDERWAY IN 48 HOURS!

By: Ernest "Ernie" Joy II, (LT)

Years on board the Johnston: 1970 to 1972

I served as the Engineering Officer on board the Johnston and retired from the US Navy as a Captain.

In 1971, shortly after returning to her homeport at Charleston following extended at-sea operations, JOHNSTON was dispatched on short notice for an undisclosed assignment. The crew responded magnificently. Here's how the events unfolded.

371

One evening, with most of the crew on leave or liberty, the CDO took a call from the CINCLANTFLT duty officer who asked: "How soon can you be ready to get underway?" Without hesitation, the CDO responded: "JOHNSTON can be underway in 48 hours." The fleet duty officer then said: "Very well, make it so." As soon as the CDO notified the skipper, the duty section was mustered and immediately began preparations for getting underway. The ship's recall bill was activated, and within 48 hours most of the crew was back onboard. By then, stores had been loaded; fuel and water topped off; and the engineers had steam up to the main stop valves ready to test engines. The ship was ready to get underway. The only thing missing was a mission: CINCLANTFLT said that would come once the ship was at sea.

At quarters the day we got underway, the XO brought with him the morning newspaper to try to find out where we might be headed. No help! Scuttlebutt was rampant as to where we might be going. Once at sea, the skipper learned the ship was to proceed at flank speed to Naval Station Key West and await further instructions. Suspense mounted. The ship moored at Key West in less than 48 hours, and remained in port for about a week. During this time, the crew rotated ashore for some well deserved but unexpected liberty. Several families of crewmembers drove to Key West to spend what little time they could with their Sailor. Finally, the long awaited tasking arrived: JOHNSTON was to proceed to sea and conduct surveillance operations as directed by the National Command Authority. The crew responded with skill and professionalism, resulting in kudos from the Fleet Commander for a job well done.

ERNIE'S IN THE RACK AND HE WON'T BE BACK!

By: Ernie Joy, LTjg

The CICWO story goes something like this: During my tour as Engineer Officer I had developed a reputation for getting seasick in rough weather, especially when having to work or stand watch above the main deck. It all began while at sea one day I called for a relief while standing watch on the bridge. In no time at all, a story began to circulate throughout after officer's quarters that the Captain had inquired as to my whereabouts. The OOD who relieved me, LTjg Steve Baer told the Skipper, "Ernie's in the rack and he won't be back". Quickly the word spread throughout the ship.

Some time later, while deployed in 1971, the ship encountered some heavy weather one night and I had the mid watch as CIC Watch Officer. LTjg Clint Adams who I had trained to stand bridge watches was the OOD. Unbeknown to me, he had arranged for the rest of the watch-standers in CIC to have cigars with them, and to secure the hatch leading out of CIC once they lit up. In no time at all, the space was filled with cigar smoke and it had the desired effect. Once again I had to call for a relief, and when properly relieved, I returned to my rack from which all hands knew I would not be back.

"Italian Ship Drivers Can Be Exciting!"

By: Albert C. Myers, LTjg (Captain, USN retired)

Years on board the Johnston: 1970 to 1973

It was a beautiful morning in the Mediterranean Sea in the middle of the spring of 1971, and USS Johnston (DD-821) was hard at work participating in a major NATO exercise called "Dawn Patrol". It is hard to imagine how many ships participated in that exercise from virtually all the navies of NATO – most navies back then had many more ships than they do today, and certainly that was the case for the U.S. Navy. There were ships from the British, US, Italian, Turkish, and other navies involved, and ships back then maneuvered at much closer quarters than they do today.

As a young Ensign on his first navy deployment, I was gradually getting adjusted to the routine of a 1 in 3 watch rotation on the bridge as Junior Officer of the Deck (JOOD) and Conning Officer, with occasional stints as the CIC Watch Officer (CICWO). My duties as Communications Officer kept me quite busy between and during my assigned watches, and it seemed like every few hours or so, we had to adjust to a new communications plan because of all the NATO requirements and due to the unique communications needs of individual exercises (or "serials" in NATO parlance) that the ship was assigned to. And of course our UHF radios would often either not work when required, or, as I like to think, we could not communicate because of radio problems on other ships. In any event, "Exercise Dawn Patrol 71" for me was a sleepless marathon punctuated by some very exciting times. Of course we would also go to General Quarters (GQ) for hours at a time, particularly for our frequent gunnery exercises. So I could not wait to get to port for a break (or so I thought, but our Executive Officer saw to it that we stayed pretty busy in port as well).

That brisk May morning promised to be very interesting to me and my Officer of the Deck (OOD) as we

374

prepared for our forenoon (0800 to 1200) bridge watch by first passing through CIC. We could tell from the ship's movements that there was a lot of maneuvering going on with a lot of bell changes. In CIC we learned that the Johnston was assigned to protect a U.S. aircraft carrier (it might have been the USS Forrestal (CVA-59)) from simulated incursions by NATO ships that were playing the role of Soviet Navy ships. Those aggressor ships were supposed to get close to the carrier and our job was to "shoulder" them, or block them away so that they could not impede the carrier.

When we got to the bridge, I could tell we would NOT be relieving the watch for while.

As I went to the starboard bridge wing to track down the off-going JOOD, I noticed a large and sleek Italian destroyer bearing down on us - it looked close, way too close for comfort. It turned out to be the Italian ship "Impetuoso", and she was trying to get between us and the carrier we were protecting. As the Italian ship came up on our starboard side, I saw our Captain (Commander *Burnham C. ("Mike") McCaffree, Jr.)* also out on the starboard bridge wing with the OOD, the JOOD, and several other officers. The "Impetuoso" was cranked up faster than we were at that time - she was probably doing about 25 knots, and I think we had about 23 knots rung up.

Then the Captain said "This is the Captain, I have the Conn". He was very matter of fact about it, but we could tell this was serious stuff. I thought the Italian ship was going to strike our starboard side between the starboard bow and amidships, but the Captain increased our speed to probably 27 knots and put a little left rudder on, so that the ships were now parallel, but still very, very close. The Captain was determined that we would not let the "Impetuoso" get between us and the carrier. When ships gets as close as we were - probably less than 60 to 80 feet, there is a tendency for the ships to be drawn together by the Bernoulli Effect, but we managed to stay apart. The Italian then veered off and slowed down and tried to cut under our stern, but the Captain anticipated that, and turned left to block him. This intense maneuvering continued for another 30 minutes or so, with the Italian coming dangerously close to us on several occasions. We could tell he was frustrated by not being able to get between us and the carrier, something the Captain was bound and determined he would not let happen.

When the Italian finally broke away, all on the bridge breathed a collective sigh of relief. My OOD and I exchanged glances which basically said, "Wow, I am glad that did not happen on our watch, and thank god for the Skipper."

We later learned the CO of the "Impetuoso" was admonished for coming so close to us and for putting both ships at risk – and I totally agree with that. But seeing our Captain carry out such a splendid example of ship-handling was very impressive and instructive, and it was a positive lesson learned for me during my future shipboard assignments. When I myself later became the CO of a Guided Missile Destroyer, I recalled Captain McCaffree's great example of taking ownership, and his determined, highly proficient, and calm manner when under pressure.

USS Johnston – the beginning!

By: Pascual Goicoechea "Cubes", Ships Serviceman (SH3)

Years on board the Johnston: 1970 to 1973

Shipmates: It is with memorable and melancholic irony that I write these lines.

Earlier today I was afforded the last of several 'retirement ceremonies', this last one being the official luncheon and final farewell. I remain on terminal leave until 29 April, at which time I will be transferred to the 'retired list'. Two weeks ago I sent former shipmate and upcoming author of our ships' history, George Sites, the retirement words to my Staff and Soldiers at the time. He may/may not publish same, although he has my permission to do so. In the content of that farewell, I noted to the Joint Command audience where my military career was formed and how it culminated at today's luncheon 41 years later.

The memories of our ship, **_USS Johnston DD-821_**, for me began when I arrived aboard her in Charleston, South Carolina as a Ship Serviceman (seaman). Our Division Chief was SKC Tom Vassey who later retired and was succeeded by SKC Fred Helms before changing home ports to Philadelphia. As a 'seaman striker', I trained under SH3 Vinnie Contrino and SH3 Vinnie Mazzeo, as ships' barber. Both these fellows were the barbers, but who soon would be retiring. Under them I learned to cut hair 'fairly well' although at the time I sensed an apprehension by some officers to come and visit 'my quarters'. When both Vinnies finished their naval obligation, they went on to cut hair on 'the outside'. Vinnie Mazzeo opened his own shop in Sag Harbor, Long Island.

My duties as ships' barber made me the de-facto priest, counselor, consort and advisor for many of the crew. I enjoyed the friendships and all the memorable moments shared in that small space. To this day I remember the names and nick-names we called one another as well as where we hailed from. In the cook section was Bob (Big Bob) Stokes from St Paul, Herb Dula, John

Foster, and Johnnie Parker from Pine Bluff, Arkansas; Gunners' Mates (Guns) Robert (Big Abe) Aber whose photo is enclosed 'drinking' from a spiked watermelon at Packer Bar in Philadelphia; Signalmen Rolando (Rolo) Gonzales from New Orleans (Metarie), who followed his dad into the optometry business, and Richard (Sammy Seaweed) Lokken….who hailed from everywhere; Sonar Technician Howard (Howie) Rodden who hailed from El Dorado, Texas; Steward, Baltazar (Shorty) Custodio from Manila, PI; Ships' Serviceman Alphonse (Stubby) Stubblefield from Nebraska, and in whose laundry everyone converged during cold North Atlantic deployments; Storekeeper Chief Alfred (Fred ain't dead) Helms, who hailed from Philadelphia; and lastly from the deck division, Chief Mongan whom everyone was terrified to run afoul of, and who retired in Baltimore….likely to run the waterfront there, and John (Jed Clampett) Konrady.

These memories and more, some perhaps too 'colorful' to print here laid my career foundation for the next 37 years that followed. When I joined the Navy I had no aspirations to make it, or the service, my career. We came to America as Cuban refugees in 1960. For I to serve in the Navy of the Nation that had been so generous and gracious to my family, was the least I could do; the pride I had of such duty remains difficult to put into words even today.

Our Nation to this day, remains the noblest in the history of mankind, though there are many in the citizenry that think otherwise.

When I was 'rung' out on my final day aboard **_Johnston_**, (4 bells actually) aside from sending Chief Mongan into a cardiac, I became emotional at what I was leaving behind on that quarterdeck.

I returned to finish my formal schooling at the University of Miami but within two months of having left the ship, began to miss the Navy, more importantly, the camaraderie not found anywhere but in the profession of arms. I remained in the Naval Reserves in Miami, where the CO of the reserve center was none other than Commander Boyd, the executive officer under Commander (Admiral) McCaffree! When I finished college in 1976, I queried Commander Boyd about going through OCS and returning to the Navy. The Viet Nam war was over by then and the Navy was downsizing; the only officers being sought after were those with a nuclear engineering degree to drive subs, or fighter pilots, for what I did not possess the eyesight for. I looked into the Army, and the rest is a history that ended this afternoon.

Gentlemen, if my farewell words of two weeks ago are printed, you will note that I closed with the analogy, '….to have served with you has been as unique as a fingerprint.' Well, it holds true, and for me began with those of you I had the honor and pleasure to serve with on that fine greyhound of the seas, **_our Johnston_**. Our collective memories are ours alone, no one else's, certainly no one that has not served our Nation. Our chests are filled with the pride that will fill us to our last breath, to the memories, to a ship, the smell of sea spray, the sweet smell of hemp/manila rope, the aroma of diesel, the hissing of steam lines, of 'red lead' paint, bunker C oil, and……camaraderie.

It would be an indescribable delight for me to link up with many/all the names I mention herein; let me hear from you! God Bless each and all of you.

Respectfully submitted,

Pascual (Cubes) Goicoechea
United States Army, (Ret)

Retirement Ceremony & Speech to the Troops

General; Distinguished guests; Ladies and Gentlemen; thank you!

I am moved by the tribute that you render me today.

It is an honor to receive this medal, the Legion of Merit (LOM), a symbol of distinctive achievement in our chosen profession. It is a medal whose heraldry was conceived in the dark days following Pearl Harbor, and whose establishment by Congress coincided with our first victories in that conflict at Midway and Guadacanal.

It is just as touching to feel the spirit of camaraderie that fills this assembly today. It is an affirmation of a mutual affection and a love affair that for me began 41 years ago, and that in fact was a continuance of a love for life itself instilled unto me by loving parents some 20 years before that.

I am humbled to stand before you to express my appreciation. I will attempt to articulate with a wide brush some of the memories that span four decades of service to our Nation. Memories firmly held together by the two eternal bookends of those years, and aptly called 'enlistment' and 'retirement'.

We came to America from Cuba in May of 1960. My mother died from cancer years earlier, and my father who had been a staunch anti-communist, would not have been allowed the luxury of a natural death had he been nabbed. We settled in a small rural community in Texas and quickly assimilated into America. Although citizenship was still then five years away, we took great pride in calling ourselves….. 'Americans'. Some Texans took exception to this however, stating that _they_ would be proud if we just called ourselves…. 'Texans'. Monetary assistance to arriving refugees did not exist, nor was any expected. We were delighted to receive the monthly allowance of Civil Defense rations which consisted of powdered milk, sugar, salted codfish, dried beef, cheese in small wooden crates, John Wayne crackers and hard candy. My dad, who had been a banker, took on a day job as a bricklayer and at night pumped gas at the local ESSO station. To supplement our meat allowance he purchased a .22 rifle from Western Auto and on the evenings he did not work, we would hunt rabbits. Extra money was made by selling pop bottles found by the roadways, a paper route, paper drives, painting homes, mowing lawns, washing windows and selling car batteries at the local lead smelter.

America……..what a great country!

Dad often said that nothing came easy in America, however, unlike any other nation on the planet, it afforded unlimited opportunities to individuals who possessed motivation, self reliance, a desire for hard work and a spirit of rugged individualism. The catalyst for making all this possible was defined in the meaning of the word, 'freedom'.

Prosperity and success both came in the years that followed and culminated in the attainment of American citizenship.

In the summer of 1969 several of my friends and I left for college intending attendance at the University of Texas in Austin. In the short span between June and August of that year we canoed the 120 miles of the Guadalupe River to the Gulf of Mexico, camped on desolate Padre Island, drove to Ft. Davis in West Texas to marvel at the beauty of the land, traveled to the Superstition

Mountains of Arizona in search of the Lost Dutchman Mine, met and got to know members of the Mescalero Apache Nation in New Mexico, searched for UFO's in Roswell, cruised 6th street in Austin and got a back-full of salt-shot for stealing, and eating, a ranchers' goat. For us then, academia could never deliver the marvels that life so readily afforded.

America……..what a great country!

That fall, the 'boys of summer' joined the Navy as a direct result of 'esteemed academic standing' and a Navy recruiting campaign that promised a job, an adventure, and an opportunity to see the world.

At the time of enlistment I held no aspirations for a military career but did have a sense of duty to the Nation that had been so generous to my family.

I spent the next four years aboard a Gearing Class destroyer, the USS Johnston (DD-821), whose keel was laid in Orange, Texas during WW II. That destroyer sailed the Caribbean and Mediterranean Seas and Atlantic Ocean in the time I was aboard. Those became the happiest years of my career and formative laid the foundation for the next 36 that followed.

I left active duty to finish my formal studies, yet remained in the active Naval Reserve while I did so. By that time, the Viet Nam war was over and the Navy was not accepting anyone without a nuclear engineering degree. I accepted an Army commission in the Infantry and in that capacity served in numerous positions of increased responsibility to include four company commands, both in the active and reserve forces, in geographic locations as disparate as the oceans I had sailed years earlier. Those years as well were filled with countless memories, honorable accomplishments and forged friendships. Much of this has been detailed in the narrative (you) afforded me earlier.

In 1999, and exactly thirty years after my enlistment, I reported to this command (SOCOM). Now, years later, and as I attain the second bookend of my career called 'retirement', I attest that no man could ask for a more fitting tribute than to retire in the company of so many professionals as assembled here, whose history and lineage is enriched by unparalleled duty and honor in service to our Nation.

Though military history has well recorded the accomplishments of past leaders, there is no shortage of present day American heroes as evidenced by the actions of SGM Michael Stack; SFC Paul Smith, SPC Pat Tillman, Major Mark Mitchell and the mass reenlistments of Soldiers, Sailors, Airmen and Marines serving in Iraq with the 1st Armored, 1st Cavalry, 1st ID, 2nd Indianhead, 3rd Armored, 4th ID, 10th Mountain, 82nd Airborne, 101st Airmobile and the 1st, 2nd and 3rd Marine Divisions…..to name a few of the nearly dozens of other distinguished units and sister services.

I am humbled to have arrived here and be departing now. The journey here was not easy but was well worth it. In large measure I made it due to the perseverance earned and learned from my dad, who taught me early on who I was and instilled in me a sense of duty and pride; my own learned 'situational awareness' taught by life's hard knocks; friends who stuck by me when there was little else to hold unto; God, who does run the place down here and with Whom oftentimes I seek an audience with, and lastly my drill instructor, Navy Senior Master Chief John Paskowski, who passed his lessons of perseverance where he had learned them in far off islands with names like Saipan, Tarawa, Iwo Jima and Okinawa.

Ladies and Gentlemen; to have served with you has been as unique as a fingerprint.

I would be remiss if I did not mention....

➢ SFC Ramon Fuentes: (Qui Non/ Phu Kat, Republic of Viet Nam) (Coin) Kept me in the straight and narrows; Argentina, Panama, Peru, Uruguay

➢ Col Margaret Myers: Whose professional SOCOM medical staff, in the performance of their duty..........saved my life

➢ Andy Anderson: (Sverdrup) Whom I share a common denominator with and who gave new meaning to the phrase, 'because I can'

➢ Maurice 'Mo' Pickett and Ed Webb: My priests in absentia; for all the sounding board discussions held in confidence

➢ Dave Holdsworth: For your mathematical guidance

➢ Bill Jeannes: The Texas flag I bestowed onto you flew over my base camp in Iraq during the 1st war

➢ Rick Kinsey: My motivational and mental counselor/consort

➢ Mike Zujovich: For the countless times you picked me up at the airport after midnights due to I getting kicked out of domestic airlines for...............fitting a terrorist profile (!)

- FO/ Chris Drewello: Shipmate, thank you for your friendship!

- To all you wondering for whom I root for during the Army/Navy game……..I still root for Navy

- Sharon Bacheler: (flowers) (Secretary extraordinaire). Form flow/ SOCOM forms 14/16 and copier malfunctions.

- Mention kids: (Carolina, Veronica, Erica, Michael)

- Sharon: (flowers) Key to my stability today; best friend, advocate and wife!

General;

In the spirit of our joint command;

This former Sailor turned Soldier;

And from this stage that today serves as a naval quarterdeck;

I request permission to go ashore for the last time.

"ALL THIS FOR $90 A MONTH"

By: Dana Beyerle, Quartermaster (QMSN)

Years on board the Johnston: 1971 to 1972

The Atlantic is like a glassy lake in April 1971 when the USS Johnston passes Fort Sumter and leaves behind Buoy 2 Charlie out of Charleston. We depart the New World under steam power heading east through the Sargasso Sea, hugging the curvature, the horizon always

ahead, our wake a jagged, boiling trace, on to old
civilizations in Europe and north Africa. Weeks later
phosphorescence in the sea tips us off to impending
landfall. Billions of stars start where night meets sea.
Jupiter's moons visible in the dark. We smell what
becomes Spain, ancient, moldy, different, weird. After
Rota, we transit the Strait of Gibraltar, Europe to port,
Africa to starboard. We are to cruise independently while
shadowing Soviet ships. This is the height of the Cold
War in the eastern Med. Soviets are still welcome in
Egypt until next year when Anwar Sadat kicks them out.
Israel is our ally and was just two years off a war
opposing Arab states backed by Soviets. Another war is
just two years in their future, not mine. Our cruise is
filler between two of the most momentous Mideast events
since the foundation of the Jewish state in 1948.

Imagine a cruise in azure seas even though it is a
working cruise, a military cruise with potential dangers.
A man overboard from an aircraft carrier sidelines us for
a day or two while we search, unsuccessfully. Soviet Bear
aircraft over-fly our search box, one or more propellers
feathered to conserve fuel. Shadowing Bears are our PC-3
Orion sub hunter airplanes. We pull into some great
ports, the French Riviera, an eye-opener for young men
many unmarried and away from home for the first time. I
don't have to tell anyone what liberty is like. Golfe
Juan near Cannes. Athens in Greece. Threading our way
into downtown Brindisi on Italy's heel. Smelly and dirty
Napoli, 625 lire to the dollar. Beautiful, beautiful
Barcelona, Palma on the resort island of Majorca. Palma
with its European discothèques and our ship's rock 'n'
roll band, "Smoke," playing at Sergeant Pepper's or
Barbarella's, I think it is the latter, is the height of
the cruise. It wasn't today's European technobeat but
real rock 'n' roll by accomplished musicians. Palma is
Scandinavia's summer playground. Oh, the cultural
encounters. In Barcelona after rambling up flower-lined

Las Ramblas, that beautiful boulevard from the Christopher Colon waterfront statue to the Plaza de la Cataluyna, I take a bus with some young Spanish students, to an old monastery in the foothills to the north. Saint Miguel del Fai is a beautiful box canyon with a waterfall at the end. This is in the former French part of Spain, a more liberal part of an otherwise extremely conservative country where less than 40 years before in the Civil War dictator Francisco Franco massacred his countrymen, even in the Plaza de Catalunya. Franco is still dictator in 1971 and Spain as it is today is ashamed of the massacres. Franco likes to see us in uniform so we wear them ashore and get hotel rooms to change into civvies. Thank you Elmo Zumwalt.

Athens, a beautiful place where the sun and sky are different, if that's possible. The Dafni Wine Festival. Ouzo, banned in the United States for its narcotic effect. Still light at 10 p.m. walking back from the Acropolis, the center of the beginning of Western civilization. Crete, a World War II battleground stepping point for North Africa. Knossos. King Midas. A quick jaunt by Malta to Tunis, in Africa, and a bus ride to the embassy and dancing under the watchful eye of Marine guards. We transit the Strait of Messina at night, our lights attempting to disguise us as a merchant ship to anyone who cares. There is Sicily's active Mount Etna glowing eerily red. Another volcano is on Isla Stromboli. In France, it's a train ride to Nice, past Nice, to Villefranche, a cliff-top view of the harbor where millionaire yachts anchored. A terrible storm gets us, the aclinometer registering 55 degree rolls. Swimming in the Med. We lose a shipmate during this cruise, a self-inflicted knife wound, according to the deck log.

And then there is the event. One day south of Greece near Antikythera where seamounts reach to within 50 fathoms of the surface, a Soviet helicopter carrier anchors so it can refuel from a tanker brought up astern. We are at general quarters. As a quartermaster, my duty station is on the Johnston's helm and I am there that day, the captain in his starboard bridge-wing chair. This is the Cold War in earnest. The Soviet helicopter carrier has a bevy of protection, at least one Kashin-class guided missile destroyer. (It might have been a Kresta II cruiser. Whatever the ship is it has surface-to-surface missiles forward, big scary things.) At general quarters, the canvas covers to our 5-inch guns are off, if my memory is correct. Fire control asks the bridge what to focus on: "Put it on the nearest object." Fire control (and we're talking GUN fire control radar) focuses on a Soviet ship, a thousand yards or so off our starboard side. Their radar guys pick up our radar emission frequency, recognize it as fire control. Their forward

front 5-inch gun mount swings over. I'm sure a Soviet sailor says "Oh, Samovar!" In slow motion that lasts forever, to starboard one of the Soviet ships bucks at the bow, churns at the stern. Suddenly some of its anchor chain flies on deck, broken. Missiles come out of the silos as the ship heads our way. They're parallel to us on our port side, close. I say, "Captain, look." Cdr. B.C. McCaffree, the Johnston's captain, sees the Soviet ship putting its hull between us and their capital ship, missiles menacing. Their port bridge wing is lined with crew with binoculars. The pucker factor is high. Captain McCaffree yells for fire control to swing the radar off the ships. I think I escape death, our ship sunk. But we live to hit the beach again.

Heading back eventually to Charleston and reality in October. We soon steam to Philadelphia - a 90-mile sea and anchor detail in the dead of winter down the Delaware River is no picnic. We steam to the James River where Washington won our war of independence, because of rumors that anti-war demonstrators in canoes will assault a weapons depot. The good guys win. As a quartermaster I am proud we never ran aground on my watch, or anytime. For a quartermaster it doesn't get any better than that. I get out in October 1972 nearly four years to the day after President Lyndon Johnson says in a letter, "Greetings." The Army's loss is the Navy's gain. The Cold War is over. There's a new type of war. I'm steaming into early geezerness as we all are, my memories mostly intact, my stories bigger each year, my pride in serving always growing. May the sun be at your back, red sky at night, the water deep but calm under your keel, the elusive green flash awaiting off your bow. QMSN Dana Beyerle, August 2009.

YANKS CHASE RUSSIAN SHIPS IN FRENZIED OPERATION TATTLE-TALE

Navies Play Hide-and-Seek Games in Mediterranean

By: Hugh A. Mulligan

Article appeared in the Columbus Dispatch on Sunday, July 25, 1971 (article provided by George A. Sites)

Columbus Dispatch Editor's Note – Who's watching the Russians while the Russians are watching the West in the Mediterranean? U.S., British and other NATO ships and submarines are chasing the Russians in a hide-and-seek game in international waters. Veteran AP war reporter Hugh A. Mulligan became the first correspondent ever to go along on Operation Tattle-Tale and tells what it's like to go Soviet-chasing on a U.S. Destroyer.

ABOARD THE USS CONE IN THE MEDITERRANEAN – Wednesday, 6 a.m. – four bells chime down the steel gangways. The bosun pipes a shrill note and growls into the intercom: "Station the special sea and anchor detail." Like the song says, we sail at the break of day.

The USS Cone, a 26-year-old destroyer rejuvenated with anti submarine rockets, lowers and folds her stern ensign, raises the American flag on her mast, drops the Italian pilot into his bobbing "pilata" boat and slips past the seawall of Catania, Sicily.

WE ARE BOUND for the Sicilian Channel, off Tunisia, to intercept two new Soviet warships, which have just come into the Mediterranean from the Baltic. One is the Krivak 500, a guided missile destroyer that navigator LTJG Ted Strickland, who also serves as Intelligence officer, calls "the hottest thing in the Soviet fleet."

The other is the Boris Chilikin, a tanker-supply ship reputed to give the Russians a capability of alongside, underway refueling for the first time. Both are prototypes of a class, floating proof of the spectacular growth of Soviet sea power.

The number of Soviet naval ships in the Mediterranean has increased greatly in recent years, the fleet growing from modest trawlers to "the most modern warships that money can buy." The United States and its allies have responded by shadowing the Russians all over the ancient landlocked sea to see what's what with the new Russian armada.

THAT IS WHAT the Cone is doing, a seagoing gumshoe in a game of mutual spying from Haifa to Gibraltar.

The Cone's cruise begins with a sailor's benediction: fair skies and following seas. By mid-morning, the Cone turns into Augusta Bay, a NATO fuel depot.

Down in the wardroom, over the omnipresent coffee cups, there is excited speculation over where the Russians are going. Lt. Bob Hunsinger, from Spartanburg, S.C., known below decks as "The Gunslinger," because he is the Cone's weapons officer, thinks they may be headed up to the Black Sea to join the Soviets' largest surface fleet.

LTJG Rick Buttina, the operations officer, from Garden City, L.I., votes for Alexandria, Egypt, where a number of Russian warships have been "hanging loose" since President Sadat came to power.

EXECUTIVE Officer Lt. Cmdr. George Jenkins of Charleston, S.C. mentions two other possibilities. "The Guys," as they are now called, could be on the way to the large international anchorages of Crete, where Soviet ships operating in the Med often drop the hook to save fuel, or else they could be en route to join the new helicopter carrier Leningrad, which two days ago came down from the Black Sea.

NATO surveillance planes and ships, keeping a close eye on Gibraltar and the Bosporus, the two natural choke points for traffic in and out of the Mediterranean, always know when there is a new girl in town.

Along about noon, Combat Information Center, the radar, radio and sonar brains of the ship located just aft of the bridge, passes the word on yellow teletype paper that there is no chance of the Russians going around the north side of Sicily through the Straits of Messina.

THE STRAITS have been closed to all navigation to repair high tension wires stretched from the pylons on opposite banks.

"Never mind the Russians. Where are the wives?" asks LTJG Earl Rumble, the damage control officer from Eureka, California.

Rumble's wife and several other wives have flown over from the Cone's home port of Charleston, S.C., hoping to join their husbands in Barcelona, the Sixth Fleet's favorite liberty port. But now the Cone is deployed on Operation Tattle-Tale, tailing the Russians who knows where, and in days to come the whereabouts of the wives will constitute as baffling a mystery as the activities of the Soviets.

SKIMMING THROUGH sparkling seas at 22 knots off Malta, the Cone prepares a little surprise to worry Russian Intelligence officers. "The Gunslinger" goes aloft with two seamen to rig a cargo net, minus its rope webbing, on the starboard kingpost in a vertical position like a weird radio apparatus. Like sending out phony radio and blinker signals, rigging outrageous gear is one of the little games rival navies play at sea.

The sun goes down in a fiery flash of green refracted light on the empty horizon, a nightly phenomenon. Still no Russians. There is a scramble for places at "Paint Your Wagon," tonight's movie. It is blackout time aboard the Cone: all gangways lit with red lamps, the bridge a ghostly glow of green dials.

The captain, Cmdr. Harold Hinkley of Denver, is in his black leather barber chair on the starboard side of the bridge scanning a moonlit expense of silent sea.

THURSDAY: Radarman George Taylor of Columbus Ohio, standing the 6-to-12 watch, reports the first contact just after breakfast. West, 264 degrees.

The contact, still several hours away, is bearing down on us at 24 knots. "All engines ahead full," order LTJG Al Offner of New Orleans, the officer of the deck. The ping jockeys in the sonar room lean into their headsets, but LTJG Paul Kindim, the anti-submarine warfare officer from Wauwatosa, Wis., complains: "The Mediterranean, with 2400 ship contacts on any given day is noisier than New York harbor."

By noon, three ships have come over the horizon. The "Big Eye" telescope on the signal deck identifies them as the Boris Chilikin, the Krivak 500 and an Italian destroyer named "Impetuoso." The captain breaks out a grog ration: Cokes for everyone on the bridge.

THE WIND HAS come up, furrowing the green sea in white caps. As the Cone closes in, boilerman Gregg Ligett comes topside and sets up a 500-mm lens camera. He is followed by Boilerman Jeff Sommerville of Yakima, Wash., with a tripod camera and a 1,000-mm lens.

"Don't fire until you smell the vodka on their breath." Ligett tells Sommerville.

The Russians, now staring back at us through telescopes and binoculars, probably will never believe that the best cameras on board belong to the enlisted men, bought in the duty free ports and ships stores. The man with the battered Yashika is the intelligence officer. That is the American way.

"Range, combat?" the captain asks.

"1200 YARDS," comes the answer. The crew of the Cone views the two newcomers the way the blind men saw the elephant. "The Gunslinger" admire the Kirvak's depth charge mortars.

The executive officer likes her sleek lines and raked masts. The radar boys wonder about the four canvas-shrouded antennas aft of her big air search radar.

Engineer Kelly Spears of Maryvile, Tenn., would like the Boris to blow her tubes so he could determine whether she's got steam boilers or gas turbines.

OUR NEXT announcement, if the Russians can hear it, must come as a jolt: "Bible study class will meet on the fantail. . ."

The ship's doctor, Lt. John A. Gastright of Dayton, Ky., snubs the Soviets and sticks to his cabin, working on his model kit of the whaleship Charles W. Morgan.

The two Russians and their Italian shadow continue on an easterly course toward Greece. We tag along at a discreet distance.

FRIDAY: A shimmering, bright windless morning finds the Boris riding lower in the water after fueling from a Soviet merchant tanker. Out of deference to her bulk, the Krivak knifes along at 16 knots, followed by the Italian destroyer and the Cone.

An RAF Shackleton recon plane makes a low pass over the Boris, causing her to rotate her huge air search radar antenna; then a U.S. Vigilante jet, skimming over the water like a silver swordfish, whines by.

Toward noon, Navy Corsairs from the Carrier Forrestal swoop down for a look. The Russian guided missile destroyer exercises her three-inch gun mounts, but there is nothing menacing in the gesture.

"LIKE JOHN Wayne somersaulting his six guns." explains the chief engineer, who then goes back down his hole to listen to country music cassettes. Late in the afternoon we close to within 1,000 yards to count the Krivak's portholes and get a better look at her weaponry, but the aptly named Impetuoso comes in almost beside her, like a Neapolitan waiter peering over the customer's shoulder at the menu.

The Krivak pulls away, but the Italian circles her. For nearly an hour, the two execute a pas de deux in the gathering twilight. Then the Italian blinks out "arriverderci" on her signal lights and drops over the horizon for home.

SATURDAY: "All hands on deck for the international boat show." We are awakened by the friendly voice of the captain, welcoming us to the busy international anchorage of Kithira, northwest of Crete, where during the night the Krivac and the Boris have dropped the hook.

At least eight Soviet ships are gently bobbing in the morning haze. The deck officers have "Weyer's Warships of the World" open on the bridge and already have identified two Zulu class Soviet submarines, two light cargo ships nuzzled beside the Boris and a Sverdlov class cruiser.

"She's old by their standards, but new by ours." The captain comments, pointing out that the average age of U.S. 6th Fleet ships are 18 1/2 years; the average age of Soviet ships, just over eight.

EARLY IN THE afternoon, the Boris and the Krivak suddenly up anchor, head north, turn sharply to the east, then swing south and west in an almost complete circle.

If the Russians are listening in, what can they make of our next loudspeaker announcement, "All personnel from the 2nd Division not on watch muster on the mess deck for venereal disease training."

Toward sunset the Krivak has pulled in close to the Boris and is about to refuel. This is what we have come to see, and the Cone is the first NATO ship ever to witness this new Soviet capability.

"It makes their Mediterranean operations far less dependent on liberty ports like Alexandria and Port Said," points out Bob Hunsinger.

SUNDAY: We are under way, bound for Souda Bay on the north side of Crete to top off our own fuel at the Royal Hellenic navy docks. The USS Lester, a destroyer escort, is pacing our old post back at the anchorage.

The Cone's motto is "Wherever Duty Calls." Late in the day we get the word to head east, toward Turkey, to intercept the Soviet helicopter carrier Leningrad and a new guided missile cruiser coming our way.

"**THERE GOES** Barcelona," moans Ens. Chris Troy of Alexandria, Va., whose wife is waiting for him on the dock somewhere.

"The Gunslinger" goes aloft to prepare another FOL antenna, this time a real Rube Goldberg job security-wrapped in acres of canvas, but the wind comes up and blows it away before the Soviet intelligence officers can reach for their headache pills.

The communications shack makes up for the loss by sending out a cryptic message: "Due to power economy measures, the sun will not set until midnight. Execute operation John Paul Jones."

MONDAY: The Russians are everywhere. There is the Leningrad, new and powerful, looking like a battleship up front and an aircraft carrier behind. The captain, who never seems to leave the bridge, describes her as "the most powerful antisubmarine weapon in the world."

There is a Kynda class light cruiser bearing the name Groznly and the number 842, and next to it what the exec officer calls a "brand new, hot stuff" Kresta II Class guided missile destroyer with no name and the number 585. There is a tank-landing ship with a dozen trucks and some Soviet marines in blue berets out on deck.

There is a submarine tender, a diving tender, another guided missile destroyer, three small swift patrol boats, a naval oiler, a pair of merchant tankers and, from the pings echoing in the sonar room, a number of submerged submarines.

CIC REPORTS that as of today there are 64 Soviet warships in the Mediterranean compared with the 6th Fleet's current total of 49. "She could blast us out of the water with no trouble at all." says "The Gunslinger," with an admiring glance at the Kresta II.

Moving in for a closer look, we also note, from the poor paint job, that the diving ship's number, 953, recently was 825. Swapping ship's numbers is a favorite Soviet game. "Sometimes," says Paul Kindem, "the subs will have one number on the port side and a different one on the starboard." NATO intelligence helps keep track of Soviet ships by counting the dents and rust spots in their hull plates.

At dusk, we steam 20 miles out to sea so the engineer can "dump, pump and blow," dump garbage, pump bilges, blow tubes. Like the Russians, we weight our refuse and puncture our empty cans, so neither side learns anything from the other's leavings. "Bet you didn't know peanut butter was a top secret!" says a sailor.

TUESDAY: There are so many Soviet ships now at anchor off Crete, "Weyer's Warships of the World," has replaced a blue book called "The Greedy Gynecologist" as the most popular book aboard.

WEDNESDAY: Still walking the line east of Crete, in company with the Leningrad, the Groznly and the Kresta II, which has returned during the night. The sight of so many Russians has even prompted the Doc to come on deck and leave the Charles W. Morgan unfinished on his desk.

With the aid of a Russian dictionary, one of the lookouts is translating the writing on the helicopter hangar of the Kresta cruiser: "Our Motto: Outstanding Service, Highest Battle Readiness in the Year of the 24th Congress of the Soviet Communist Party."

"Ask them if they want to swap movies," suggests the Doc. "Maybe we can unload "Hello Dolly" for a couple reels of "Ivan the Terrible."

THURSDAY: The Cone is east of Crete, watching the Leningrad and the Groznly and a newcomer, a tanker. The USS Johnston DD-821 is west of Crete keeping an eye on Boris Chilikin, Krivak 500 and half a dozen other Soviet ships.

Vice Admiral, Isaac Kidd Jr., commander of the 6th Fleet is aboard his flagship, the cruiser Springfield, in Gaeta harbor, north of Naples, holding forth on the growth of Russian sea power.

When he took over the fleet three years ago, the Soviets averaged only a few hundred ship-days a year, which is the number of days a single ship spends in the Mediterranean. Now they are averaging "many thousands of ship-days."

"TO WHAT purpose, I wish I knew," Comments the admiral, "but they are spending a considerable fortune to acquire a navy of considerable consequence at a spectacular rate of growth."

At the end of World War II, a destroyer cost about $2.7 million; today's price tag is $40 million for a non-nuclear guided missile model. The admiral dates the rapid growth of Soviet naval power from the Cuban missile crisis: "Evidently they are determined never to be embarrassed that way again."

From his vantage point as a veteran Soviet watcher, Admiral Kidd sums up the Russians as "able navigators, smart seamen, competent professionals who, from what we have seen, hit what they are shooting at."

AS FOR BEING a navigation hazard, of which we, the British and the French accuse the Russians, and they in turn accuse us, the admiral thinks that "good manners at sea are fundamentally good navigation. You don't cut across each other's bow."

"We're not looking for trouble; we're looking for information. We watch them and they watch us. We learn from each other . . . and respond with alacrity."

Visiting Ship Treats NCO Club Members; Presents Plaque, "Smoke"

By: Giovanni Argentina

Article appeared in the APULIA SCENE - Brindisi, Italy in September, 1971 (article provided by George A. Sites)

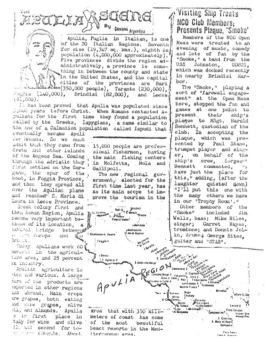

Members of the NCO Open Mess were treated to an evening of music, comedy and lots of fun by the "SMOKE", a band from the USS Johnston DD-821, which was docked recently in nearby Brindisi Harbor.

The "SMOKE", playing a sort of "farewell engagement" at the Open Mess here, stopped the fun and games at one point to present their ship's plaque to MSgt. Harold Bennett, custodian of the club. In accepting the plaque, which was presented by Paul Shane, trumpet player and singer, on behalf of the ship's crew, Sergeant Bennett commented, "I have just the place for this," adding, (after the laughter quieted down) "I'll put this one with the many others we have in our 'Trophy Room'."

Other members of the "SMOKE" include Jim Wells, bass; Mike Niles, singer; Garret Hayes, trombone; Dennis Jolin, drums; George Sites, guitar and "STAR".

THEY DON'T COME ANY GREENER THAN THIS!

By: Robert J. Stokes, (CS3)

Years on board the Johnston: 1970 to 1974

When I first came on board the USS Johnston, I was seventeen years old, from Minnesota, never been on an airplane before and had never seen the ocean. Can you get any greener than that?

Two days after reporting aboard, we were underway and heading for the Mediterranean Sea for a six-month cruise. About five days into the cruise, I was told to report to the hole for a bucket of steam for the Captain. I fell for it hook, line and sinker! I carried an empty bucket up and down four levels before safely reporting to the Captain's Quarters and feeling like an idiot. Needless to say, I fell for the Sea-Bat thing also.

After all of that, I met some of the greatest guys in the world and the experience made a man out of me. If I could do it all over again, I wouldn't change a thing.

YOU'RE NEVER TOO "SALTY" TO LEARN!

By: Price D. Acord, (PNCM USN Retired)

Years on board the Johnston: 1971 to 1972

I served aboard Johnston from Mar 71 thru May 72. I was a PNC at the time. I don't have any real exciting stories to tell, but I must say that it was the best tour of duty in my entire 23 year naval career. I was honored to have served with such great sailors while aboard the Johnston. Whenever conversations start about my Naval career, the USS Johnston and the men thereof are foremost in my memory. Thanks to you all.

One of the things that comes to mind while serving aboard the Johnston happened while standing the 4-8 watch while in the MED. It was just after daylight the OOD called and asked me to put the big spy glass on two Russian ships to see if they were refueling (now you have to keep in mind that I was a west coast sailor, I had made Chief and had a little bit of salt in my veins but I had little experience with Soviet ships). I looked, seeing that they were one behind the other, I reported that were not refueling. A few minutes later the OOD called again with the same request and again I replied no. Again the OOD called to ascertain it they were refueling. For the third time I replied no. The OOD then asked if they were bow to stearn, and of course they were, at which time I was informed that was the Russian way of refueling. So I learned something that morning.

"PORT HOLE PEEP SHOW"

By: Brion W. Crum (BTFN)

Years on board the Johnston: 1971 to 1974

I don't remember the date or year to be exact but it was on board the "Jolly J" when it happened. We were in dry dock in the Philly ship yard in the mid 70's, George Doroshenko and I were both confined to the ship (restricted) and the USO was giving the crew a show which was being held on the flight deck (helo). It was dark and we had been watching the show for some time and then decided to go to the mess deck for coffee. Along with us was a young fireman named Gower. He was tagging along with us, so down the inside ladder we went which took us out at the officers Wardroom. Now as soon as we hit the bottom of the ladder, we saw the Wardroom's door was in the wide open position and inside were all the show-girls changing their costumes. They saw us, we saw them, they screamed and then proceeded to close the door. What they didn't know was eagle eye Crum saw the port-hole was in the open position. As the door slammed shut, I said to George, "Hey, the port-hole is open, lets check it out!", so the three of us headed to the other side and had a look. At this spot on the ship they kept the empty fuel cans and they were right under the port-hole. This brings me to the climax of the adventure. As

403

we were watching the girls change their costumes and come right up to the port-hole unaware of us outside, Gower said to George, "Damn, I must be dreaming. Pinch me to wake me up!", as George pinched him, he let out a scream and kicked the fuel cans. The noise made the girls aware that we were there. This forced us to run to keep from being caught and as we left I heard the port-hole cover slam. That was the end of the "Port-Hole Peep Show" from the USO. To this day I think of this and laugh wondering what ever happened to those beautiful girls of the USO.

DREAM SHIP STORIES

By: Larry Dencer, Electronics Technician (ETC USN Retired)

Years on board the Johnston: 1971 to 1975

DREAM SHIP - The Johnston was on a Med cruise when I reported onboard, and after the Med cruise it went back to its homeport in Charleston, South Carolina. After the Med cruise stand down it was ordered to Philadelphia, PA, to train reserves.

I was only supposed to be onboard for 3 years, but in 1974 the Bureau ran short of money to transfer people, so I was extended for 3 months. After the 3 months I was extended another 3 months for the same reason. Finally, they extended me an additional 6 months, thus giving me 4 years onboard.

When I graduated from ET School in 1960 I had submitted my "dream sheet" for a destroyer of any kind, but instead I was sent to the amphibious navy for my first 3 ships. At last, in 1971 I finally got my destroyer, the ship that I had been looking for my whole career.

The job of training reserves was not the most glamorous job in the world, but it was necessary work. We would take our reserves out to sea for training with a liberty call in the glamorous port of Mayport, FL, for several days, then more steaming and training and finally bring them back to Philadelphia and send them home to their families.

The Johnston was the only ship in the squadron who would always get underway, so as a result we would have to take the other ships training commitments when they could not. Sometimes that meant we were gone from our homeport for extended periods of time. I loved sea duty, and this didn't bother me at all, but it did get to the younger members of the crew. This was not a happy time for the members of the crew with young families, and some of the senior members also didn't appreciate it. As I have already stated, I enjoyed sea duty and these extended periods of time away from our homeport was just part of the job and it didn't bother me.

One of my most memorable times onboard occurred when the Johnston was steaming around Cape Hatteras in really nasty weather, and we ended up cracking the torpedo deck and having 8-10 feet of water in the chain locker. I thought she was riding low by the bow, and sure enough, we were. We got it repaired in the Philadelphia Naval Shipyard, and things went back to normal after that.

Two of my most memorable division officers were LTJG E.A. Murphy, and Ensign Stephenson (later LTJG). Mr. Murphy was one of the most capable and caring division officers that it has been my pleasure to have served with. Mr. Stephenson was right out of college when he came onboard, so we had our moments, but he was a capable and efficient division officer when I left. Mr. Stephenson, if you are reading this, I want to apologize for some of the stuff I put you through. My most memorable moment with Mr. Stephenson was a shouting contest over something that I can't remember now. We were both a little headstrong, and the shouting contest was just our way of trying to express our opinion about the correct way to do something. I can't even remember who won, if anybody did.

My time onboard the Johnston was filled with both good and bad memories, but mostly I choose to remember the good. It was my "dream ship", and I am proud to have served onboard her.

BURIAL AT SEA - One of the Johnston's jobs was to perform a burial at sea for those who wanted it. One day we got underway with the cremated remains of a deceased sailor, and we steamed to the appropriate location to dispose of the remains. I was one of the burial-party on the fantail, dressed out in whites, as we all were. The XO opened the container to spread the ashes into the ocean, and at the same time the OOD turned the ship so that the wind was coming over the fantail towards the burial party. The XO poured out the ashes, and the ashes thoroughly engulfed the burial party. I got a large mouthful of the cremated sailor's ashes, and ever since then I have actively avoided eating cremated remains.

USS Johnston DD-821 circa 1974. .From Left to Right: BTCS Logan (Senior Enlisted Advisor), RMC Voisen, OSC Booth, ETC Dencer, OSC Bennett, Ensign Stephenson (OE Division Officer)

"MAN OVERBOARD!"

By: Bruce Sauerwine, Quartermaster (QM2)

Years on board the Johnston: 1971-1975

An incident took place during the Mediterranean cruise in 1971 that will forever remain in my memory. The ship was attached to the 6th fleet and on this particular date was performing exercises with the carrier USS America CVA-66, although most of our exercises that summer were with the carrier USS Saratoga CVA-60.

USS Johnston DD-821 circa 1974 — Top to bottom, Left to right - Bruce A. Sauerwine, Paul LaPointe, Chief Shalek, Terry Cassidy, Hank Riley, Craig Curry, Ken Stroud, Fred Baish

We were assigned to plane guard for the carrier and to follow the carrier as it launched planes in the early morning. We received a radio call that a flight officer on the America had been blown over the side as he apparently got too close to a plane's exhaust. No one on the Johnston had seen it happen but we had approximate coordinates to use. We were detailed to search for the officer and rescue, if possible, or if not to retrieve the officer's body. The carrier continued on with its mission, as did the other ships in the task force.

We began running the designated search pattern (as I recall, a series of increasingly smaller boxes). After some time we were joined by a British destroyer which had heard the radio transmissions and offered to help. The British searched for about an hour but ultimately had to depart as we carried on.

After a few more hours, a Soviet destroyer (which no doubt also heard the radio calls) arrived and began cutting in front of us, disrupting our search pattern. Naturally, each time they cut in, we had to change course. We called them and requested that they not interfere, but it was to no avail. I assume they did this not only to harass us but also with the hope that they might retrieve the officer and his equipment (for their own use).

This action continued for some time. After having spent considerable time in our effort, we were growing tired and frustrated. All day long, all of our "off-duty" sailors were assigned to the open decks to keep watch. At this time (late afternoon) I was standing my watch on the bridge. The Johnston was alone to deal with the threat as the task force was now many miles away. Our captain, on the bridge of course, in frustration and very seriously, suddenly shouted to us on the bridge, "If that son of a bitch does that again, I'm shooting!" In reply, both the Officer of the Deck and I said to the Captain words such as "Sir, you might want to re-think that" and "That might not be a good idea."

The Captain said nothing to us but took a minute or two to compose himself. This was a man who I greatly admired and who was otherwise always calm and collected. As if the Soviets had heard him, they left us as suddenly as they had arrived. Would we have fired even warning shots if they had not left? We'll never know.

The Captain said nothing more to me or the OOD and the search effort continued. I, at least, was way out of line to speak up. At the time I was relatively new to the ship and a lowly QMSN. I had reacted to his words as a person, but not as a sailor. My words were never mentioned to me, however. What is far more important is that such action as firing at the Soviet ship, even in warning, could have become an international incident, or even worse. On such small things the world turns.

Nonetheless, our search continued with the sea now fairly rough and daylight ending. Finally a lookout spotted the body of the flight officer. He was 4-5 feet under the surface, with all of the gear he wore holding him down just below the surface. We put out some men with grappling hooks in a small boat, but despite repeated tries in the rough seas, we could not retrieve him. A totally frustrating and sad day ended with us having to report that we achieved our mission only partially. We found the body but could not retrieve it. Ultimately, we had to leave the area so I don't know if his body was ever retrieved.

Reserve Ship Johnston DD-821
By: Terry Zieba (FTG2)

Years on board the Johnston: 1973 to 1976

The USS Johnston was a reserve ship while I was on board. We would typically sail for one week out of the month for reserve training and stay in the homeport the remainder of the month. Once a year, we would make a cruise typically to the MED.

I thought the following two articles would be of interest to my fellow Johnston shipmates.

Liquid Coal

Article appeared in the "All Hands" magazine, March 1974
Provided by Terry Zieba

There was an experimental mood concerning fuel within the Navy long before the energy crunch hit the headlines. Few were surprised, therefore, when the Naval Reserve Force destroyer USS Johnston (DD821) was, last November, used to test a liquid fuel derived from coal.

The test was a part of Project Seacoal – a series of experiments with liquid coal products to find substitutes for energy sources now employed by naval ships and planes. The fuel used was called Seacoal I, to distinguish it from other fuels still to be tested, and was processed from a synthetic crude developed by the Office of Coal Research (OCR), Department of Interior. The experiment was conducted to demonstrate the compatibility of the fuel with shipboard power plants and to provide information to industry for production purposes.

Project Seacoal is an extensive program to evaluate and use synthetic fuels in Navy boilers, gas turbines and pumps over the next three years. The *Johnston* test evaluated the synthetic obtained by OCR in its Project COED (for Char Oil Energy Development process). It is one of four processes being studied by OCR and the Bureau of Mines which can produce liquid fuels from coal. The products of the processes have many of the properties of crude oil.

The Navy plans to evaluate each product once it is developed to the point that it is usable in Navy propulsion systems. Project Seacoal II will designate the next phase of navy testing of coal-derived liquid fuels. Additional possibilities for Navy use are synthetic fuels derived from oil shale and tar sands which also are being studied by the Department of Interior.

The concept for Project Seacoal I originated with the Combat Systems Advisory Group of the Naval Material Command. The group, having kept itself informed concerning OCR progress in fuel studies, recommended Navy testing of OCR's COED fuel.

COED fuel is obtained through a process called *Pyrolysis*. The basic fuel (coal) is crushed and then decomposed by using heat, pressure and catalysts. Pyrolysis is then followed by a hydrogen treatment which produces the synthetic oil-like fuel. The Pyrolysis also produces a number of by-products.

The cost of producing COED synthetic oil can be reduced by selling the Pyrolysis by-products for commercial use. Predicated on this, the ultimate cost of production is estimated at around $5 per barrel (42 gallons). In September 1973 (before the general price rise in petroleum products) a barrel of navy distillate, which is now being used by the Navy, cost around $5.25.

As with most new products, everything does not come up roses the first time around. Initial testing of COED proved the fuel to be unsafe for Navy shipboard use because of it low flashpoint. The fuel had to be distilled to remove the light fractions which were responsible for the low flash point.

COAL POWER—TV newsmen film the Philadelphia-based Reserve Force destroyer *USS Johnston* (DD 821) during an underway test of Project SEACOAL I. Powered by liquid coal fuel, *Johnston* became the first U. S. Navy combat ship to be powered by coal since the 1920s. (Photo by LCDR G. A. Phillips, USNR.)

A Navy contract was then let to eliminate this deficiency and the final processed fuel, Seacoal I, is considered to be as safe as navy distillate fuel. It is about the same consistency as cough syrup and its sulphur content is low thus making it environmentally acceptable.

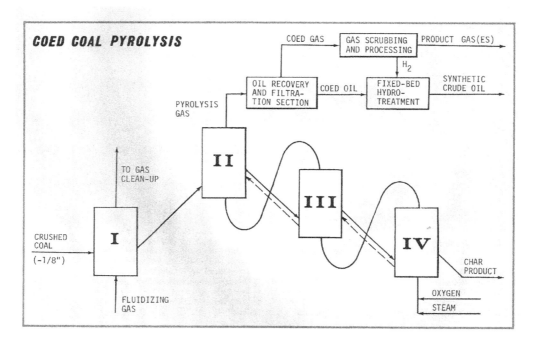

Also, the fuel is thicker than some others used by the Navy. It can't be poured unless its temperature is at least 60 degrees F or higher. The Navy prefers a 10 to 20 degree pour point. This difficulty, however, could be overcome by using a fuel preheater in the ship; also, it may be possible to improve the pour point.

A considerable amount of work is still to be done, of course, before the most efficient new fuel is found although encouraging strides already have been made. If progress continues, it may not be too much longer before the Navy will again be steaming through the world's oceans powered by coal albeit in a liquid form.

For an example of what's involved in the process of converting coal into synthetic crude oil - it's called

414

COED Coal Pyrolysis – see the chart accompanying this article.

U.S. Gobs Declare Halifax 'Friendly'

By: Hattie Densmore, Staff Reporter
Article appeared in "THE MAIL-STAR" newspaper, Halifax, Canada on Saturday, June 19, 1976

Commodore Arnold Evans, USN, Emerson, Ohio, says his Reserve Squadron #30 came to Halifax "because it is a port naval people like to visit.". . .

The commodore, who is traveling on USS Johnston, one of three U.S. Reserve destroyers which arrived in Halifax Friday, said several of the men on the ships have been in Halifax before and wanted to return. "They have always found Halifax people friendly and hospitable."

Commodore Evans, who is paying the port city his first visit, said his ships, which are home-ported at Philadelphia, are manned about 35 per cent by reserves and 65 per cent active duty force.

The U.S. Reserves have six destroyers on which the forces train. Four of these destroyers are based at Philadelphia; one at Bayonne, New Jersey; and one at Baltimore, Maryland.

USS Johnston is captained by Commander Vibert Davis, USS Corry by Commander Guy Achambault and USS Rich by Commander George Stefencavage.

Commodore Evans was surprised when he entered the harbor late because of thick fog offshore, to see two American gun boats, USS Tacoma, PG 92, and USS Welch, PG 93, also in port along with two ocean minesweepers, USS

Alacrity MSO 520, and USS Assurance MSO 521. He did not know the other ships were also coming to Halifax.

All will stay at the dockyard for Armed Forces Day today, with the USS Johnston, berthed at jetty 5, open to the public.

Commodore Evans says his reservists drill one weekend each month and does a two week period of active duty each year. On this period now under way they left Philadelphia on Saturday, June 12 and exercised at sea, then came to Halifax for their port visit following which they will start for home port Monday June 21. He said the visit to Halifax is the highlight of their course.

He said the reservists ranging in age from 17 to 58 when they join, come from all fields of endeavor in the U.S. community. They are trained to assist in civil emergency or to be called to active duty in time of war. Many of them are retired naval personnel from the regular force. They are trained to do escort work, gun fire support, and anti air warfare training. They do not do fisheries patrol.

The destroyers used by the squadron are World War 2 ships refitted for reserve training. Although they are 30 years old, he said they are in good condition and they continually update the equipment on board.

Commodore Evans said he wholeheartedly agrees with a recent statement by U.S. Ambassador Thomas Enders that there is outstanding co-operation between the Canadian and the U.S. military. He said, "We train together and exercise side by side." Americans come to Canada on exchange trips and Canadians go to the U.S. for the same reason. "We use each others services and support at the bases."

Also traveling with the squadron is Commander Charles Shoemaker, Allentown, Pennsylvania, head of the fleet training Unit 406, and Commander William Spane, Philadelphia, head of the support training unit.

SEA FEVER

By: John Masefield
From the "Change of Command Ceremony
U.S.S. Johnston (DD-821)" program dated 12
October 1973
Provided by Terry Zieba

I must go down to the seas again, to the
lonely sea and the sky,

And all I ask is a tall ship and a star to
steer her by;

And the wheel's kick and the wind's song
and the white sail's shaking,

And a grey mist on the sea's face, and a
grey dawn breaking.

I must go down to the seas again, for the
call of the running tide

Is a wild call and a clear call that may
not be denied;

And all I ask is a windy day with the
white clouds flying,

And the flung spray and the blown spume,
and the sea gulls crying.

I must go down to the seas again, to the
vagrant gypsy life,

To the gull's way and the whale's way
where the wind's like a whetted knife;

And all I ask is a merry yarn from a
laughing fellow-rover,

And quiet sleep and a sweet dream when the
long trick's over.

Find a Band

By: George K. Rozinak, (Ensign)

Years on served on the Johnston: 1974 to 1977

It was May 1975. I was the First Lieutenant and
Captain Dugan decided he wanted a band for his change of
command ceremony. I was given the order to find a band. I
had three days to find one. Where was I going to find a
band in three days? I guess the task was given to me
since I had unorthodox methods for getting things done.

So, my first thought was to get on the phone and
start calling every station on the east coast to find a
band that had no commitment in the next three days. I
spent hours on the autovon line in the chief engineer's
stateroom with no success. Then, I realized that no one
wants to talk to a mere Ensign. At the same time, they
were not going to follow my requests. I also realized the
Captain never said it had to be a Navy Band. So what was
my next step?

I had to promote myself to Rear Admiral P. J. Smith. I also had to forget talking to Navy Commands. I started to think what bases were around the Philadelphia Navy Shipyard who would have a band that I could transport here without too much difficulty? My two choices were McGuire Air Force Base and Fort Dix. The Air Force guys were no help at all.

So, my last shot was Fort Dix. I got the official band leader of the Fort Dix Army Band. We will call him Chief Warrant Officer Brown. I identified myself as Admiral Smith and explained that I had a good friend of mine that was having his change of command on the USS Johnston DD-821 at the Naval Shipyard Philadelphia. I told CWO Brown that I owed this Commander a favor and he wanted a band for his ceremony. I said I would be deeply grateful if he could help me out on this matter. CWO Brown said he would be deeply honored to help out the Navy. He had a 15 piece band that could meet our needs. I said that was great and I would have my aide, Ensign Rozinak escort you from Fort Dix.

I informed the Captain, I found a band. I also told him that his friend, Admiral Smith got the band for you. Captain Dugan asked who was Admiral Smith. I explained that the less you know the better it would be for him. I think they called it plausible deniability. He laughed and said well done. I also told him that Admiral Smith's aide, Ensign Rozinak was going to escort the band to the change of command from Fort Dix. He basically said do what you got to do. I also pointed out that we need a letter and certificate of appreciation from the admiral. That was also dropped in my lap.

So, the big day arrived and I had the duty driver take me to Fort Dix band center. I sent the duty driver back to Philly. Big mistake! I asked CWO Brown how he was going to get the band to the shipyard. His reply was that he thought the Navy was going to provide transportation. Where am I going to get a bus for a 15 piece band right now? I saw these buses going around the base. I stopped one of them and said I need your bus. The bus driver said that he could help me out and would have to talk with his dispatcher. Luckily, the Army folks had no idea of what I was or what my rank was. The bus driver asked where we need to go on the base. I said we need to go to the Philadelphia Naval Shipyard. His reply was that he could not leave the base. I said don't worry about it, Admiral Smith will take care of everything. I signed a piece of paper to that affect and off we go to Philly.

We are now crossing the Walt Whitman Bridge. I am changing into my choker white uniform. As we are crossing the bridge, I thought to ask, you guys do know the Navy Hymn, don't you? The response was, we are an Army Band. It just seems that this assignment has all kinds of pitfalls. So, I started to hum the Navy Hymn to this Army band crossing the bridge while I am changing into my choker whites. The band was trying to play along while I was humming this to them.

As we arrived to the site of the change of command, I made it into my uniform; the band got off the bus and assembled inside the hall. The change of command started. The band played on when it needed to play. I have to say the Army Band did a fair job playing the Navy Hymn. There were a few squeaks from the clarinets, but they got through it. I gave CWO Brown a letter and certificate of appreciation from Admiral Smith and managed to arrange the transportation back on the bus I commandeered off of Fort Dix.

Commander (Doc) Dugan moved on and he was grateful to have an Army Band play at his change of command. CWO Brown has a Certificate of Appreciation and Letter of Appreciation hanging on his wall in his office from a fictitious admiral signed by a real Navy Ensign. I hope he never finds out.

Bicentennial at Penn's Landing
July 1976
By: George K. Rozinak, Ensign

What timing to be in Philadelphia for the Nation's Bicentennial. It wasn't all that easy. I was tasked a few weeks ahead of time to take the motor whale boat up the Delaware River to Penn's Landing to measure soundings to see if we can get the Johnston up there without getting stuck in the mud. I almost felt like Mark Twain measuring the river 150 years ago. Actually it was going to be a fun day as long as the motor whale boat didn't break down. We also had to make sure that we were taking the soundings at low tide so that we had the worse case scenario since we were going to be there for couple of days.

The trip was uneventful and we did the soundings as we were supposed to do. I gave all the readings to the quartermasters and the judgment was that we should be able to sit up there without getting stuck.

There was a buzz of activity all over Philadelphia that summer for the big celebration. On the shipyard, the U.S.S. Intrepid was being outfitted to be a floating museum in the back basin. This was long before it ever was even thought of as a floating museum. The Intrepid now sits on the Hudson River in New York. The Base was getting a huge manicure to make sure we looked good for the public. I was responsible to make sure the Johnston sparkled. The entire ship was given a fresh coat of paint. The main deck was treated with new nonskid paint. All the fire stations were properly outfitted and dressed up. We looked like a brand new ship instead of a leftover WWII Gearing Class Destroyer. We were the flagship for DESRON 30. We had to shine and we did.

The day came for us to head up to Penn's Landing. It was a spectacular day to make the move. The whole area was all dressed up with tall ships, the U.S.S. Olympia, and the U.S.S. Johnston. There were fire boats shooting sprays of water in the air and we were rigged for dress ship.

During the time at the landing, we conducted tours of the ship. There were people from all over the country during the celebration. This was during the time the Navy changed the uniform for the enlisted. It was referred to as the "salt and pepper" uniform. I do not know what the reason was for the change. It made the enlisted uniform look somewhat like the officer uniform. Not one of the brightest moves of the Navy.

The reason I brought up that factoid was that during the time we were down there, a demonstration ensued. It was the "Students against the Vietnam War". The funny part was the war was over for two years. The reason for these folks to be around was that President Ford was in the vicinity giving a speech. When the speech was over, he actually flew over our ship. Then the demonstrators came down along side the ship and started chanting "Bring them out of the holds!". We couldn't figure out why they were saying that. Then, we figured they thought the enlisted were also officers and we were keeping the enlisted away from the demonstrators. The Captain ordered fire hoses to be rigged to repel boarders. A few of the master at arms team were caring M-14 rifles to show force. The demonstrators grew tired of chanting and they finally dissipated and dispersed.

It was one of those defining moments to be proud to be an American. It was a transition time for all of us, both civilian and military. We were healing our wounds from an unpopular war. Once again, we were learning to be Americans. It was a time for the whole country to get back to our roots and understand our freedom, greatness, and why we stand apart from the rest of the world. It is also understanding our obligations to maintain our freedoms and appreciate where we came from as a nation.

I recently had the honor to attend my Son's graduation from basic training in the Army. He graduates in a couple of weeks from Officer training. It did me proud to see all the young men and women wearing their uniforms with pride in self and in their nation. My mind is at ease knowing we have passed that spirit off to the next generation.

God bless our Service men and women who have served and who are serving, now.

"No Problems . . . Just Challenges"
By: Sam Ramirez, Yeoman (YN3)

Years on board the Johnston: 1973 to 1976

I'm the good looking one on the left!

1974 - Rockland, Maine Seafood Festival. Most of what follows is true to the best of my knowledge. In the late spring of 1974, the crew of the USS Johnston learned that we had been selected for a week-long liberty cruise to be taken in August of that year. Apparently, the Commandant of DESRONTHIRTY was from Maine and he was sending the Johnston to represent the U.S. Navy at

Rockland, Maine's annual Seafood Festival, which is now called Lobster Festival and is in its 63rd or 64th year.

Preparations for our appearance included the creation of a drill team that had the precision of a poorly-made time piece. Since I was on a drill team in boot camp, I was somehow selected to be on the ship's drill team. I remember practicing on the pier over the summer in the Back Basin and we got to the point where if we didn't do any fancy moves, at least we would not embarrass ourselves.

But what I really wanted to be was one of the dozen or so sailors who were selected to be escorts for the Sea Princesses in the parade. I could see myself getting into a port-of-call romance with whatever Sea Princess I was asked to escort and having a great time. I think the Captain understood this because he selected only married sailors to escort the lovelies.

We got underway in early August and headed down the Delaware River for the 72 mile sea and anchor detail that got us to the Delaware Bay. I'm not sure if this is true, but I remember someone saying that ships in the Philadelphia Naval Shipyard had the longest sea and anchor detail of any US Navy port in the world. Once at the mouth of the Delaware Bay, we made a hard left and started steaming north.

Before we got to Rockland, I remember that the ship stopped in Portland, Maine for a few days. I remember going to a bar in my whites and someone called out my first name as if I were a regular at the bar. This took me by surprise because I had never been in Portland, and had certainly never been in this bar. Apparently, there was a sailor stationed in Portland who had an uncanny resemblance to me and his name was also Sam. The other Sam came in later and while we would not pass for identical twins, I could certainly see the resemblance.

A bunch of us decided to hitchhike down to Old Orchard Beach which was a few miles south of Portland. It was unseasonably hot and we wanted to cool off in the Atlantic Ocean. I remember buying a leather pouch at old Orchard; it was one of the few things I had long after I was discharged from the Navy, the pouch was perfect for storing contraband. I remember seeing all these people in the water and after changing into our swim wear, my shipmates and I all ran to get in the water only to stop shortly after getting our feet wet. The water was as frigid as any I had ever been in and I used to swim in quarries in the spring when I was kid in NW Ohio. I later learned that most of the swimmers were Canadians and to them, the Maine waters were warm.

I was on watch as we pulled into Rockland, Maine. I remember because as we were pulling into the bay, there was a heavy fog. As the local pilot guided us in, all of a sudden the fog broke and the rocky shoreline and town made its appearance, it was a postcard perfect image I'll never forget. We had to anchor out in the bay so the only way to get into town was via the ship's motor whaleboat. In addition, some of the locals would come out with their boats and they would give us rides to and from the ship.

Well, the parade was uneventful and the festivities throughout the week consisted primarily of drinking and eating more fresh seafood than you would ever want to eat.

As I mentioned, it was an unseasonably hot that August, which became more apparent as none of the bars had air conditioning which made it uncomfortable when we hit the beach to drink. Apparently, it never got hot enough for them to invest in air conditioning. However, we did discover the bar in the Thorndike Hotel which was in the basement, and which was air conditioned. The bartender there also made the best Bloody Mary that I ever had before or since. I remember our last night in Rockland as I was heading back to the ship after one too many Bloody Mary's that I ran into our Weapons Officer Lt. S.T.W. (Stormy Thomas Williams) Hicks, who was on Shore Patrol duty that night. When he told me the last boat to the ship was leaving before we got underway the next day I started to run away. Suffice it to say I was caught and made the last boat.

On the morning that we left, the townsfolk came out and delivered two 55 gallon barrels of live lobsters that we enjoyed on our trip home.

I happened to be the Captain's bridge talker on the sea and anchor detail. The day we were getting underway to leave Rockland I was still drunk from the Bloody Marys so I could hardly speak, so the Captain sent me back to switch with the after lookout, for which I was grateful. When I got back there, the Ship's Store clerk was smoking a joint and I said the Captain sent me back because I was too drunk to talk. I wonder if the Captain ever new that he replaced a drunk with a stoner!

That week in Rockland was the second best week I spent in the Navy. The best week was the week before I got discharged in Boston a year and a half later. With one week to go I was a one digit midget and also "next"! Next to get discharged! I remember writing the following graffiti in a bathroom stall when I took my last dump aboard the Johnston, "I'm so short, I left yesterday!"

To all the sailors who I had the privilege of serving with during boot camp and my tour on the Johnston, thanks for providing memories that will be with me until I'm deep-sixed!

----

150 BROTHERS

By: Michael Maggio "Magg", Operations Specialist (OS3)

Years on board the Johnston: 1974 to 1976

That's me in the middle.

I joined the Johnston in 1974. It was a very old ship at the time – 29 years old to be exact. The ship was built in my father's navy during World War II. The ship I joined had a very proud crew even though the ship was in its retiring years. We were an active crew on a reserve destroyer. A reserve destroyer had a reserve detachment that would report one weekend per month. What that meant, was the rest of the crew had to perform double duty on a decaying ship. We had less than half the crew that normally supported the ship. This was even more taxing when we went to sea without the "reserve detachment".

With that said, we would much rather do the double-duty with our "brothers" than have the assistance of the reserves. Interesting program they had back in the "cold war". The reservist worked 2 days a month and knew enough to come in and then direct a team who lived and worked the ship every day. I really never understood the concept and I believe it eventually got scrapped. To me, these were guys getting retirement pay or getting away from something else on a weekend. They all looked very sharp and I remember not looking forward to a reserve weekend. They weren't doing their time.

The normal ship's crew was like 150 brothers. That is how I remember it. I did not have any dislike for any active shipmates on the Johnston. Actually, I did not dislike any of the reserves either; I just did not like the concept. We stood together as one and I am very proud to be associated with each and every member of the crew. We would have never expected to go to General Quarters on a reserve destroyer in an era when Vietnam was being evacuated by the United States! All we did was chase Polish fishing vessels and Russian submarines and we could not keep up with the submarines. The worst that happened to us was getting spit upon in airports by anti-war protestors and Hare Krishna's. At least a good friend of mine claims a Hare Krishna spit at him in an airport. He wasn't a very peaceful fellow and who knows, it may have been provoked.

I remember how we use to drill for "General Quarters", "Collision" and "Fire". I used to think it was ridiculous. Then one night we were at sea with the core crew and attached to ships from Norfolk. As always, we were hunting for Russian submarines but only finding whales. I am guessing about 600 miles off the coast of the United States on our way to Nova Scotia. I personally was not a witness to the call, but from a Quartermaster the following message was sent to the bridge.

"Bridge - Main Control - fire - fire in Bravo 4"

Now since I was a seaman, who spent most of his time in the upper infrastructure, I cannot remember what Bravo 4 was. After all, this was well over 30 years ago. All I can remember is it was below decks and below the water line and it was tight, dirty, greasy and hot down there. That is all I needed to know to keep me away from being down there underway. However, my bunk was also below the waterline. I thought about that often.

That night I remember hearing;

"General Quarters, General Quarters all hands man your battle stations. This is NOT a drill".

We had an explosion in the engine room in one of our electrical boards (Bravo 4). That night is etched in my mind for eternity. I learned something that night as I finally understood what all the drilling was for. I was extremely impressed with the crews' execution and professionalism of an actual GQ call.

As it turned out, the crew extinguished the fire and we limped back to Philadelphia. We eventually ended up in the East Boston Navy Yard where I was discharged.

The picture is of two of my Johnston brothers and me. They are YM3 Sam Rameriz, OS3 Michael R. Maggio and Seaman Scott McCall (also known as fire truck). This picture was taken in the back basin of the Philadelphia Navy Yard in 1975 on the fantail of the Johnston. I had

just completed my watch on deck. The plan of the day is
in my top pocket.

SUCH ARE MY RECOLLECTIONS

By: Mike Gilmartin, Electricians Mate (EM3)

Years on board the Johnston: 1975 to 1976

I served aboard the Johnston (DD-821) from May 1975
to July 1976. I reported as an Electricians Mate -
Fireman. During my tenure aboard, I was promoted to EM3.
I picked the ship up in Norfolk, where it was preparing
for a yard period back in Philadelphia, then its home
port. Shortly thereafter the ship participated in a
gunnery exercise at Bloodsworth Island in the Chesapeake,
which was followed by an ammunition "offload" at Leonardo
(Colts Neck), New Jersey. From approximately June 1975
through late winter 1976, the ship underwent overhaul
alternating between Philadelphia NSY and a private
shipyard, Bromfield, in East Boston. The overhaul
winter---75/76---will be remembered as a cold and
uncomfortable one by the crew. Among the sources of
discomfiture was a lack of heating due to overhaul during
a record cold snap.

The ship conducted a shakedown cruise out of Boston
in the late winter (March 1976), during which she was
took on minor water, as I recall, through a split seam in
the aft deck---such was the sea state.

During the Bicentennial celebration the Johnston was
pier side near the foot of Chestnut Street in
Philadelphia and very near the spot where then President
Gerald Ford landed. I will recall the day first because
the crew was restricted to the ship on what appeared to
be one of the great party days of American history and,

second, because I had to stand deck watch with an M14 rifle---which I thought a little curious given our stateside locale.

I transferred to the Richard L. Page (FFG-5) home ported in Norfolk, where I served out the remaining two years of my hitch participating in Med deployments.

The Johnston's crew during the time that I was aboard her will be remembered as capable in that they held together a ship that was in an advanced state of aging, and for being quite spirited. I've always imagined them as being a little like a capable, yet defiant U Boat crew. They certainly looked the part. For sure, the "snipes" were convinced that the plant was one "light off" away from blowing up. The other big memory was six hour "Sea & Anchors" down the Delaware all the way to Cape May. That's a long time in the rather remote forward diesel compartment. I took the opportunity to begin a short history of Vietnam (then an intellectual passion), which was subsequently foisted upon the officers in the Ward Room---it having been discovered by the XO on his rounds. I was good naturedly chastised by the Engineering Officer, Lt Dennis F. Daley---a history buff himself.

Anyway, such are my recollections. Mike Gilmartin.

MESS DUTY

By: Mike Sheda, Seaman (SN)

Years on the Johnston: 1975 to 1977

My name is Mike Sheda 'Yul' and I was a deck ape from 1975 to 1977. I can't remember if it was just the new deck apes that boarded the ship that served on mess duty or if all newbies got stuck with this wonderful duty. Maybe one of you can answer that question and also who I had mess duty with? I will say this much, we had a good Captain but the one right under him, the XO I think, was really tough. I was always told; "You better get his food to him and it better be perfect. If it ain't, you will catch hell up one side and down the other!" I'll say this for his sake and any others who want to listen. When strangers are in charge of giving you your food, it is always best for you be polite and on your best behavior. Enough said!

Popcorn Eating Contest
By: Steve Zenes, Radioman (RM1)

Years on board the Johnston: 1975 to 1977

I remember the good times we had during our MED cruises. While I was on the Johnston, it was a Reserve Destroyer and we deployed each month for a weekend. We also did two weeks in the Med during the summer.

The USS Johnston was homeported at the Philadelphia Naval Base while I was onboard.

I remember the pop corn eating contest we had on the stern of the ship. Each department had two representatives. The winner was a Boiler Technician who consumed 8 bags of popcorn in ten minutes. All of us had a great time rooting for our own guys. I believe this happened in 1973.

Three Musketeers

By: Michael L. Graziano, Lieutenant

Years on board the Johnston: 1979 to 1980

They say that everyone has a twin somewhere in the world, but three look-a-likes? In the USS Johnston Wardroom (picture circa 1980) are pictured Lt. Lawrence Desmond (left) and Lt. Michael L. Graziano (right). The two Lieutenants were often mistaken as twins. Missing from the photo is Lt. Lauriston S. Taylor, a dead ringer for both Desmond and Graziano. The trio was referred to (affectionately) as the "Three Musketeers".

Chapter 8

THE FINAL 5 DAYS
By: Ed Zaikowski, Historian

Tuesday, 7 April 1981--A Gearing class destroyer is seen coming up the Delaware River in Philadelphia. Downriver of the Navy Yard this is quite a common sight. However, a mile upstream of the yard it's a rare event. The ship was being towed and was berthed two piers from where I was. Being an amateur naval historian and enthusiast of anything "destroyer", I was more than curious. Also, I had just spent a working weekend aboard the USS J.P. KENNEDY and was more destroyer minded than usual. Tin cans just don't tie up in this area of Philly. Her hull numbers were painted out so I didn't know who she was. My first thought was that she was headed for scrap. That afternoon I went to the pier watchman and asked questions. He said the ship was manned by four men from Taiwan and was awaiting an ocean tow in three of four days. I did not attempt to board the ship at this time.

Wednesday, 8 April 1981--I approached the ship with a floodlight, camera and companion. As we walked by, she appeared in good shape. Three Oriental men were sitting on the pier near the fantail. I introduced myself and said that I heard the ship was headed to Taiwan for scrap. A very concerned look came over at least one face along with a denial. It was then that I learned that the ship was the ex-USS JOHNSTON (DD-821). One man in particular was friendly and spoke decent English. He eventually told us the ship would be commissioned in the Taiwan Navy, but since the U.S. no longer recognized Taiwan, it could not receive direct military aid. After friendly discussion, my friend and I were permitted to go through the ship with the man. We entered the ship through the door at the "break" which leads to the wardroom on the port side. We went aft through the inboard passage. There seemed to be many extras stashed everywhere, such as submersible pumps lashed to the ladder leading to the steam tables, an extra welder by the forward fire room hatch, etc. We toured the forward engine room and discovered it was in excellent condition. The bilges were dry and gleamed with fresh primer paint. The storeroom was full. My mind envisioned all the parts necessary to rebuild the KENNEDY's air compressors. After getting to the after tan room, we decided to look at the machine shop and after diesel. The berthing compartment leading to these spaces was literally filled with hundreds of extra mattresses, bunk frames and canvas. The Machine shop was fully operational, including a drill bit in the drill press. Looking down into the shaft alley, the fresh primer was again in evidence. Our last trip was to the bridge. The only thing missing there was the ships wheel. We walked back across the 01 level. On deck, the ASROC launcher was missing and its foundation plated over. We were told it was being repaired and would be shipped over. A shore power cable was lying on deck still connected inside, with bare leads outside. Just as we stepped off the ship, a car pulled up with two men inside. Both seemed concerned at our presence. One said he was the ship's "captain", the other an agent for

Taiwan. He was not Oriental, but spoke with a European accent. While on board I took photos in various locations. Our host would not allow himself to be in any.

Thursday, 9 April 1981--The ocean tug "FRIESLAND" has arrived sometime during the night and tied up alongside the JOHNSTON. There is much activity aboard. A crane is on the pier and pulls up the ship's anchor chain in preparation for towing. Some small items are hoisted on and lashed down.

Friday, 10 April 1981--Upon arrival this morning I am quite surprised to see a fuel barge alongside with a hose hooked up to the forward fueling trunk. Not being able to contain my curiosity any longer, I visited the ship again. I looked for the man who took us through the ship on Wednesday, but did not find him. I started a conversation with the somewhat nervous agent for Taiwan who was friendly and informative. He has lived in this country for 20 years and is a ship broker. He obtained the JOHNSTON and was preparing it for Taiwan, thus the ship did not go directly from US Navy to Taiwan hands. This explained why the ship came to a remote municipal pier. He was very worried because a valve on one of the fuel tanks was leaking due to a split weld. They had hopes of fueling and also loading distilled water and getting underway on the afternoon tide. Problems with fueling are compounded by no lights on board ship. I offered to attempt to start one of the emergency diesels for lights, but am told there are switchboard problems. The tug captain invited the broker and crew to lunch on the tug. I talked to him and he said he hoped to make Taiwan in 73 days. I jokingly said if we had 100 good men, we could steam the ship to Taiwan. It brought a nervous laugh. Before leaving, I found the man who gave us the tour and gave him a large photo of the JOHNSTON from 1976. He said he was very happy to have it, as he expected to be an officer on her after commissioning.

<u>Saturday, 11 April 1981</u>--I stopped by and saw the oil barge still there, but no water barge in sight. Things were quiet and activity was restricted to fueling.

<u>Sunday, 12 April 1981</u>--I learned from a reliable source that they departed sometime in the early morning. Now I have time to reflect on the events of the past four days. My suspicions (and a wild imagination) after seeing the ship's interior plus the fuel oil and water delivery were that the ship would be met somewhere in international waters, a crew put aboard and she would steam for points unknown. In reality I suppose Taiwan took advantage of a situation and loaded up on spare parts for her aging fleet of Gearing class DD's and the fuel and water being sensible ballast for her tow. I am quite content in knowing I was one of the last Americans to walk the JOHNSTON's decks before she truly became a "showboat to China".

The following is an email to Duane Mallast regarding DD-821's final disposition, dated April 14, 2004.

Dear Mr. Mallast:

Reference is made to your e-mail dated March 23, 2004. Thanks for your concern to the national defense affairs and support to the navy. Regarding the questions that you mentioned in your e-mail, our explanation is as follows:

1. The Ex-USS Johnston, DD-821, was delivered to the ROC Navy on February 27, 1981 in U.S. On April 12 of the same year, this ship was tugged from U.S and arrived at Tsoying Naval Harbor, Kaohsiung, Taiwan on July 9. Admiral Chien CHOU, the CINC of ROC Navy at this period,

presided over the commission ceremony for this ship and christened her as ROCS Cheng-Yang, DD-928. In 1987, this ship was conducted the overhaul and weaponry system modernization so as to meet the requirements of battlefield environment around the Taiwan Strait.

2. With efforts of all hands, this ship carried out missions successfully. Owing to the aging propulsion system, this ship was decommissioned on December 16, 2003. At present, this ship is in port at Kaohsiung Harbor and will be the target ship for fleet in the future.

3. The further information about the ROC Navy ships will be provided by the Chinese web site "Chinese Ships Museum".

"http://vm.rdb.nthu.edu.tw/cwm/"

We do hope that above-mentioned explanation will meet your requirements. Your continued comments and support to our navy will always be appreciated. Best wishes to the health and happiness of you.

ROC Navy General Head Quarters 2004.4.14

The following is an e-mail received April 22, 2009 from the ROC Navy to Tony Tomasin, President USS Johnston DD-821 Association.

Dear Mr. Tomasin,

I regret to inform you that the ex-ROCS Chen-Yang DDG-928 was sunk as a target during the Hang-Kuang 22nd Exercise on 20 July, 2006 off the coast of Yilan County, northeast of Taiwan (N24-42'30", E122-02'00"(WGS-84), N24-42'36.6", E122-01'30.5"(GRS - 67)). She has completed her last contribution to the ROCN in a way as described by 2 Timothy 4:7 "I have fought the good fight, have finished the course. I have kept the faith." She will live eternally in the hearts of everyone who has served on her regardless of their nationalities. I sincerely hope that we will continue to work hard to bring the fellowship of our Associations and our Navies closer in the near future. On behalf of the Chen-Yang Association, I would

like to send our warmest regard to your members
and wish you all a successful reunion.

Sincerely,

RADM Cheng-Yi Chang, ROCN(Ret.)

President

ROCS Cheng-Yang DDG928 Association

Chapter 9

OLD SAILORS AND VETERANS

DEFINITION OF "A VETERAN"

A Veteran - whether active duty, retired, National Guard or reserve - is someone who, at one point in their life, wrote a check made payable to "The United States of America", for an amount of "up to and including my life". "That is Honor and there are way too many people in this country who no longer understand it".

Author Unknown

From The United States Navy Memorial

A SAILOR'S PRAYER

Now I lay me down to sleep

441

I pray the Lord my soul to keep,

Grant no other sailor take

My shoes and socks before I wake,

Lord guard me in my slumber

And keep my Hammock on its number,

May no clues nor lashings break

And let me down before I wake,

Keep me safely in thy sight

and grant no fire drill tonight,

And in the morning let me wake

Breathing scents of sirloin steak,

God protect me in my dreams

And make this better than it seems,

Grant the time may swiftly fly

When myself shall rest on high,

In a snowy feather bed

Where I long to rest my head,

Far away from all these scenes

And the smell of half-done beans,

Take me back into the land

Where they don't scrub down with sand,

Where no demon typhoon blows

Where the women wash there cloths,

God thou knowest all my woes-

Feed me in my dying throes,

Take me back I'll promise then

Never to leave home again. . . . .

FOUR YEARS LATER

Our father who art in Washington

Please, Dear Father, let me stay

Do not drive me now away,

Wipe away my scalding tears

And let me stay for thirty years,

Please forgive me all my past

And things that happened at the mast,

Do not my request refuse

And let me stay another cruise.

WHEN A VETERAN LEAVES THE 'JOB'

When a Veteran leaves the 'job' and retires to a better life, many are jealous, some are pleased, and others, who may have already retired, wonder if he knows what he is leaving behind, because we already know.

1. We know, for example, that after a lifetime of camaraderie that few experience, it will remain as a longing for those past times.

2. We know in the Military life there is a fellowship which lasts long after the uniforms are hung up in the back of the closet.

3. We know even if he throws them away, they will be on him with every step and breath that remains in his life. We also know how the very bearing of the man speaks of what he was and in his heart still is.

These are the burdens of the job. You will still look at people suspiciously, still see what others do not see or choose to ignore and always will look at the rest of the Military world with a respect for what they do; only grown in a lifetime of knowing.

Never think for one moment you are escaping from that life. You are only escaping the 'job' and merely being allowed to leave 'active' duty.

So what I wish for you is that whenever you ease into retirement, in your heart you never forget for one moment that you are still a member of the greatest fraternity the world has ever known.

Civilian Friends vs. Veteran Friends Comparisons

CIVILIAN FRIENDS: Get upset if you're too busy to talk to them for a week.

VETERAN FRIENDS: Are glad to see you after years, and will happily carry on the same conversation you were having the last time you met.

CIVILIAN FRIENDS: Have never seen you cry.

VETERAN FRIENDS: Have cried with you.

CIVILIAN FRIENDS: Keep your stuff so long they forget it's yours.

VETERAN FRIENDS: Borrow your stuff for a few days then give it back.

CIVILIAN FRIENDS: Know a few things about you.

VETERAN FRIENDS: Could write a book with direct quotes from you.

CIVILIAN FRIENDS: Will leave you behind if that's what the crowd is doing.

VETERAN FRIENDS: Will kick the crowd's ass that left you behind.

CIVILIAN FRIENDS: Are for a while.

VETERAN FRIENDS: Are for life.

CIVILIAN FRIENDS: Have shared a few experiences...

VETERAN FRIENDS: Have shared a lifetime of experiences no citizen could ever dream of...

CIVILIAN FRIENDS: Will take your drink away when they think you've had enough.

VETERAN FRI ENDS: Will look at you stumbling all over the place and say, 'You better drink the rest of that before you spill it!' Then carry you home safely and put you to bed...

CIVILIAN FRIENDS: Will talk crap to the person who talks crap about you.

VETERAN FRIENDS: Will knock them the hell out OF THEM....for using your name in vain.

CIVILIAN FRIENDS: Will ignore this.

VETERAN FRIENDS: Will forward this.

Old Sailors

Old Sailors sit and chew the fat 'bout how things use to be, of the things they've seen and places they've been, when they ventured out to sea.

They remember friends from long ago and the times they had back then, of money spent, beer swilled & spilled in their days as sailing men.
Their lives are lived in days gone by, with thoughts that forever last, of Dixie cup hats and bell bottom blues, and the good times in their past.

They recall long nights with a moon so bright far out on a lonely sea, and thoughts as youthful lads, when their lives were unbridled and free.

They know so well how their hearts would swell when the flag fluttered proud and free, and the stars and stripes made such beautiful sights as they plowed through an angry sea.

They talk of the bread Ole Cookie would bake and the shrill of the Bo'sun's pipe, and how the salt spray fell like sparks out of hell when a storm struck in the night.

They remember mates already gone who forever hold a spot in the stories of old, when sailors were bold and lubbers a pitiful lot.

They rode their ships through many a storm when the sea was showing its might, and the mighty waves might be digging their graves as they sailed on through the night.

They speak of nights in a bawdy house somewhere on a foreign shore, and the beer they'd downed, as they gathered around cracking jokes.

Their sailing days are gone away, never more will they cross the brow, but they have no regrets, for they know now, they've been blessed 'cause they honored their sacred vow.

Their numbers grow less with each passing day as their chits in this life are called, but they've nothing to lose, for they've paid their dues, and they'll sail with their shipmates again.

I've heard them say before getting underway that there is still some sailing to do, and they'll exclaim with a grin that their ship has come in, and the Lord is commanding the crew.

For you crusty old salts
written by a Korean War Sailor

Come gather round me lads and I'll tell you a thing or two,
about the way we ran the Navy in nineteen fifty two.

When wooden ships and iron men were barely out of sight,

I am going to give you some facts just to set the record right.

We wore the ole bell bottoms, with a flat hat on our head,

and we always hit the sack at night. We never "went to bed."

Our uniforms were worn ashore, and we were mighty proud.

Never thought of wearing civvies, in fact they weren't allowed.

Now when a ship puts out to sea, I'll tell you son - it hurts

when you suddenly notice that half the crew is wearing skirts!

And it's hard for me to imagine, a female boatswain's mate,

stopping on the Quarter deck, making sure her stockings are straight.

What happened to the KiYi brush, and the old salt-water bath?

Holy stoning decks at night - cause you stirred old Bosn's wrath!

We always had our gedunk stand and lots of pogey bait.

And it always took a hitch or two, just to make a rate.

In your seabag all your skivvies, were neatly stopped and rolled.

And the blankets on your sack had better have a three-inch fold.

Your little ditty bag ..it's hard to believe just how much it held,

and you wouldn't go ashore with pants that hadn't been spiked and belled.

We had scullery maids and succotash and good old S.O.S.

And when you felt like topping off - you headed for the mess.

Oh we had our belly robbers - but there weren't too many gripes.

For the deck apes were never hungry and there were no starving snipes.

Now you never hear of Davey Jones, Shellbacks Or Polliwogs,

and you never splice the mainbrace to receive your daily grog.

Now you never have to dog a watch or stand the main event.

You even tie your lines today - - back in my time they were bent.

We were all two-fisted drinkers and no one thought you sinned,

if you staggered back aboard your ship, three sheets to the wind.

And with just a couple hours of sleep you regained your usual luster.

bright eyed and bushy tailed - you still made morning muster.

Rocks and shoals have long since gone, and now it's U.C.M.J.

THEN the old man handled everything if you should go astray.

Now they steer the ships with dials, and I wouldn't be surprised,

if some day they sailed the damned things - from the beach....computerized.

So when my earthly hitch is over, and the good Lord picks the best,

I'll walk right up to HIM and say, "Sir, I have but one request

Let me sail the seas of Heaven in a coat of Navy blue.

Like I did so long ago on earth - way back in 1952.

Chapter 10

ON THE LIGHTER SIDE

I hope we can all laugh as we look back over the years and think about all the issues each of us had as individuals in the Navy – the good, the bad and the funny. Please take no offense to the following jokes - they are only intended to remind us of our time in the U.S. Navy.

Having just moved into his new office, a pompous new Captain was sitting at his desk when a seaman knocked on the door. The Captain quickly picked up the phone, told the seaman to enter, then said into the phone, "Yes, Admiral, I'll be seeing him this afternoon and I'll pass along your message. In the meantime, thank you for your good wishes, sir." Feeling he had sufficiently impressed the young enlisted man, he asked, "What do you want?"

"Nothing important, sir," the seaman replied, "I'm just here to hook up your telephone."

Officer: "Sailor, do you have change for a dollar?"

Sailor: "Sure, buddy."

Officer: "That's no way to address an officer! Now let's try it again!" "Sailor, do you have change for a dollar?"

Sailor: "No, SIR!

Q: How do you know if there is a Navy fighter pilot at your party?
A: He'll tell you.

Q: What's the difference between God and Navy fighter pilots?
A: God doesn't think he's a fighter pilot.

Q: What's the difference between a Navy fighter pilot and a jet engine?
A: A jet engine stops whining when the plane shuts down.

A Navy Master Chief and an Admiral were sitting in the barbershop. They were both just getting finished with their shaves when the barbers reached for some after-shave to slap on their faces.

The Admiral shouted, "Hey, don't put that stuff on me! My wife will think I've been in a whorehouse!"

The Chief turned to his barber and said, "Go ahead and put it on me. My wife doesn't know what a whorehouse smells like."

"Well," snarled the tough old Navy Chief to the bewildered Seaman, "I suppose after you get discharged from the Navy, you'll just be waiting for me to die so you can come and piss on my grave."

"Not me, Chief!" the Seaman replied. "Once I get out of the Navy, I'm never going to stand in line again."

A young ensign had nearly completed his first overseas tour of sea duty when he was given an opportunity to display his ability at getting his Destroyer under way. With a stream of crisp commands, he had the decks bussing with men and soon, the ship had left port and was streaming out of the channel.

The ensign's efficiency had been remarkable. In fact, the deck was abuzz with talk that he had set a new record for getting a destroyer under way. The ensign glowed at his accomplishment and was not at all surprised when another seaman approached him with a message from the captain.

He was, however, a bit surprised to find that it was a radio message, and he was even more surprised when he read, "My personal congratulations upon completing your underway preparation exercise according to the book and with amazing speed. In your haste, however, you have overlooked one of the unwritten rules -- make sure the captain is aboard before getting under way."

A navy man walks into a bar. Sitting himself down, he tells the bartender, "Quick, pour me a drink, before the trouble starts!"

The bartender pours a drink and watches as the man quickly downs it.

Putting the glass on the bar, the sailor says, "Give me another drink before the trouble starts!"

The bartender pours another glass and the sailor drinks it as quickly as he had the first, before asking for another, again adding, "- - - - before the trouble starts!"

After several more rounds of this the bartender says, "Look sailor, you've been in here ten minutes and you keep talking about trouble starting. Just when is this "trouble" going to start?"

The sailor looks at the bartender and says, "The trouble starts just as soon as you find out that I ain't got any money!"

NAVY VACATION

A full months pay,
A three day pass,
A fifth of Four Roses,
A winsome Lass,
A hectic night,
Of wild whoopee,
A.W.O.L.
Then a weeks Mess.

A SAILOR'S LIFE

I'm sitting here and thinking of days I left behind,
And I think I'll put on paper what's running through my
mind.

The people on the outside think a sailor's life is swell,
But I'll let you in on something Mate, a sailor's life is
Hell.

A sailor has one consoling thought so gather close and I
will tell,
When I die I will go to Heaven cause I've served my life
in Hell.

I've scrubbed a million bulkheads and I've chipped ten
miles of paint,
For meaner places this side of Hell I swear to you there
ain't.

I've stood a million hours just waiting for my mail,
And I've stood a million watches on every special detail.

I've shined a million miles of brass and I've scrubbed my
dirty duds,
I've slung a million hammocks and I've peeled a million
spuds.

I've cruised a million miles and I've made a million
ports,
I've spent the night in dirty jails for trying to be a
sport.

But when those final taps are sounded and I lay aside
life's cares,
I'll take my final shore leave right up those golden
stairs.

Tis then Saint Peter will greet me and loudly he will yell,
Take your front seat in Heaven Sailor, cause you've done your hitch in Hell.

(MORE TRUTH THAN POETRY)

A young Ensign approaches the crusty old Master Chief and asked about the origin of the commissioned officer insignias.

"Well," replied the Master Chief, "the insignias for the Navy are steeped in history and tradition. First, we give you a gold bar representing that you are very valuable but also malleable. The silver bar also represents significant value, but is less malleable. Now, when you make Lieutenant, your value doubles, hence the two silver bars. As a Captain, you soar over the military masses, hence the eagle. As an Admiral, you are, obviously, a star. Does that answer your question?"

"Yes Master Chief" replied the young Ensign. "But what about Lieutenant Commander and Commander?"

"That, sir, goes waaaay back in history - back to the Garden of Eden. You see, we've always covered our pricks with leaves."

A Petty Officer Second Class, a First Class and a Chief are off the ship together for lunch. While crossing a park they come upon an antique oil lamp. They rub it and a Genie comes out in a puff of smoke. The Genie says, "I usually only grant three wishes, so I'll give each of you just one."

"Me first!" says the Petty Officer Second Class. "I want to be in the Bahamas, driving a speedboat, a beautiful woman at my side and not a care in the world." Poof! He's gone.

"Me next!" says the First Class. "I want to be in Hawaii, relaxing on the beach with my personal masseuse, an endless supply of pina coladas and a beautiful woman." Poof! He's gone.

"You're next," the Genie says to the Chief. The Chief says, "I want those two back on the ship right after lunch."

An old Chief and an old Gunny were sitting at the VFW arguing about who'd had the tougher career. "I did 30 years in the Corps," the Gunny declared proudly, "and fought in three of my country's wars. Fresh out of boot camp I hit the beach at Okinawa, clawed my way up the blood soaked sand, and eventually took out an entire enemy machine gun nest with a single grenade. "As a Sergeant, I fought in Korea alongside General MacArthur. We pushed back the enemy inch by bloody inch all the way up to the Chinese border, always under a barrage of artillery and small arms fire. "Finally, as a Gunny Sergeant, I did three consecutive combat tours in Vietnam. We humped through the mud and razor grass for 14 hours a day, plagued by rain and mosquitoes, ducking under sniper fire all day and mortar fire all night. In a fire fight, we'd fire until our arms ached and our guns were empty, then we'd charge the enemy with bayonets!"

"Ah," said the Chief with a dismissive wave of his hand, "all shore duty, huh?"

A Captain retired after 35 years and realized a lifelong dream of buying a bird-hunting estate in Alaska. He invited an old Admiral friend to visit for a week of pheasant shooting. The friend was in awe of the Captain's new bird dog, "Chief". The dog could point, flush and retrieve with the very best. The Admiral offered to buy the dog at any price. The Captain declined, saying that Chief was the very best bird dog he had ever owned and that he couldn't part with him. Six months later the same Admiral returned for another week of hunting and was surprised to find the Captain breaking in a new dog.

"What happened to Chief?" he asked.

"Had to shoot him," the Captain replied. "Another old shipmate came to hunt with me and couldn't remember the dog's name. He kept calling him 'Master Chief.' After that, all the dog would do was sit on his butt and bark."

The Five Most Dangerous Things in the US Navy"

1. A Seaman saying, "I learned this in Boot Camp..."
2. A Petty Officer saying, "Trust me, sir..."
3. A Lieutenant JG saying, "Based on my experience..."
4. A Lieutenant saying, "I was just thinking..."
5   A Chief chuckling and saying, "Watch this shit..."

Is sex work?

A U.S. Navy captain was about to start the morning briefing to his staff. While waiting for the coffee machine to finish its brewing, the captain decided to pose a question to all assembled.

He explained that his wife had been a bit frisky the night before and he failed to get his usual amount of sound sleep.

He posed the question of just how much of sex was "work" and how much of it was "pleasure?"

A commander chimed in with 75-25% in favor of work.

A lieutenant said it was 50-50%.

An ensign responded with 25-75% in favor of pleasure, depending upon his state of inebriation at the time.

There being no consensus, the captain turned to the seaman who was in charge of making the coffee. What was HIS opinion?

Without any hesitation, the young seaman responded, "Sir, it has to be 100% pleasure."

The captain was surprised and, as you might guess, asked why?

"Well, sir, if there was any work involved, the officers would have me doing it for them."

The room fell silent.

God bless the enlisted man.

Appendix A
COMMANDING OFFICERS
Thanks to Wolfgang Hechler & Ron Reeves

CDR	Elmer C. Long	Aug 23 1946	Jul 24 1948
CDR	Forrest R. (Tex) Biard	Jul 24 1948	May 21 1949
CDR	William C. Howes	May 21 1949	Aug 04 1951
CDR	John B. Dudley	Aug 04 1951	Aug 28 1952
CDR	Wayne W. Watkins	Aug 28 1952	Sep 30 1954
CDR	Paul T. Roy	Sep 30 1954	Oct 19 1956
CDR	J. C. Rock	Oct 19 1956	Jul 01 1958
LCDR	William H. Glye	Jul 01 1958	Aug 08 1958
CDR	M. B. Davis	Aug 08 1958	Aug 15 1959
LCDR	William H. Glye	Aug 15 1959	Nov 04 1959
CDR	Emory P. Smith	Nov 04 1959	Apr 25 1961
CDR	William H. Morgan	Apr 25 1961	Jan 10 1962
LCDR	Howard N. Kay	Jan 10 1962	Sep 07 1962
CDR	Robert J. Fay	Sep 07 1962	Jun 10 1965
CDR	Robert C. Pringle	Jun 10 1964	Oct 30 1965
CDR	John J. Mingo	Oct 30 1965	Mar 09 1967
CDR	Robert W. Curran	Mar 09 1967	Mar 09 1969
CDR	Daniel F. Anglim, Jr.	Mar 09 1969	Sep 04 1970
CDR	Burnham C. McCaffree, Jr.	Sep 04 1970	Jun 23 1972
CDR	George I. Knowles	Jun 23 1972	Oct 12 1973
CDR	Ferdinand C. Dugan, III	Oct 12 1973	Aug 14 1975
CDR	Vilbert H. Davis	Aug 14 1975	Aug 16 1976
CDR	Delma C. Robison, Jr.	Aug 16 1976	Aug 17 1977
CDR	James C. Kronz	Aug 17 1977	Jun 16 1979
LCDR	Robert J. Maloit, Jr.	Jun 16 1979	Apr 18 1980
CDR	Henry F. Dalton	Apr 18 1980	May 23 1980
CDR	William F. Mellin, Jr.	May 23 1980	Feb 27 1981

Note: Commander Burnham "Mike" C. McCaffree, Jr. later advanced to Rear Admiral

Appendix B
USN SHIPS WE OPERATED WITH
(In no particular order)

USS New Jersey BB-62
USS Saratoga CVA-60
USS Enterprise CVN-65
USS Essex CVS-9
USS Intrepid CVS-11
USS Ticonderoga CVA-14
USS Kearsarge CV-33
USS Lake Champlain CVS-39
USS Torsk SS-423
USS Thomas Jefferson SSBN-618
USS Nautilus SSN-571
USS Newport News CA-148
USS Long Beach CGN-9
USS Manley DD-940
USS John Paul Jones DD-932
USS Forest Sherman DD-931
USS Newman K. Perry DD-844
USS Cone DD-866
USS Charles R. Ware DD-865
USS Joseph P. Kennedy Jr. DD-850
USS Perry DD-844
USS James C. Owens DD-776
USS Laffey DD-724
USS Compton DD-705
USS The Sullivans DD-573
USS Conway DD-507
USS Mitscher DL-2
USS Bainbridge DLGN-25

USS Yosemite AD-19
USS Yellowstone AD-27
USS Mississinewa AO-144
USS Pawcatuck AO-108
USS Allagash AO-97
USS Kankakee AO-39
USS Sabine AO-25
USS Alstede AF-48
USS John F. Kennedy CV-67
USS Forrest B. Royal DD-872
USS America CVA-66
USS Constellation CVA-64
USS William R. Rush DD-714
USS Fresno CL-121
USS Fiske DD-842
USS Roosevelt CV-42
USS Bristol DD-857
USS Black DD-666
USS Midway CV-41
USS Cascade AD-16
USS McCard DD-822
USS Forrestal CVA-59
USS Robley D. Evans DD-552
USS Valley Forge CV-45
USS Des Moines CA-134
USS Blue DD-744
USS Nashville LPD-13
USS Missouri BB-63
USS Neosho AO-143
USS Sampson DDG-10
USS Semmes DDG-18
USS Stickell DD-888
USS Waldron DD-699

USS Brownson DD-868
USS S.B. Roberts DD-823
USS C.H. Roan DD-853
USS W.R. Rush DD-714
USS Alacrity MSO-520
USS Assurance MSO-521
USS Rich DD-820
USS Corry DD-817
USS Tacoma PG-92
USS Welch PG-93
USS Juneau CL-19
USS Valley Forge CV-45
USS Suribachi AE-21
USS Neches AO-47
USS Orleck DD-886
USS Ranger CVA-61
USS Everglades AD-24
USS JC Owens DD-827
USS Bordelon DD-881
USS Columbus CG-12
USS Belknap DLG-26
USS Independence CVA-62
USS Freemont APA-44
USS Keppler DD-765
USS Manley DD-940

AUTOGRAPHS

AUTOGRAPHS

AUTOGRAPHS

AUTOGRAPHS

AUTOGRAPHS

Made in the USA
Middletown, DE
12 April 2021